1828 ★ 1848

THE JACKSONIAN ERA

THE NEW AMERICAN NATION SERIES

Edited by HENRY STEELE COMMAGER *and* RICHARD B. MORRIS

David B. Quinn	DISCOVERY AND EXPLORATION.*
Wallace Notestein	THE ENGLISH PEOPLE ON THE EVE OF COLONIZATION, 1603-1630. TB/3006.
Charles Gibson	SPAIN IN AMERICA. TB/3077
Mason Wade	FRANCE IN AMERICA.*
Wilcomb E. Washburn	THE INDIANS IN AMERICA*
John E. Pomfret	FOUNDING THE ENGLISH COLONIES.*
Wesley Frank Craven	GROWTH OF THE ENGLISH COLONIES, 1660-1710.*
Jack P. Greene	THE ENGLISH COLONIES IN THE EIGHTEENTH CENTURY.*
Louis B. Wright	THE CULTURAL LIFE OF THE AMERICAN COLONIES, 1607-1763. TB/3005.
Lawrence Henry Gipson	THE COMING OF THE REVOLUTION, 1763-1775. TB/3007.
John Richard Alden	THE AMERICAN REVOLUTION, 1775-1783. TB/3011.
Richard B. Morris	CONFEDERATION AND CONSTITUTION.*
Henry S. Commager	CONSTITUTIONAL DEVELOPMENT, 1789-1835.*
John C. Miller	THE FEDERALIST ERA, 1789-1801. TB/3027.
Marshall Smelser	THE JEFFERSONIAN ERA.*
George Dangerfield	THE AWAKENING OF AMERICAN NATIONALISM, 1815-1828. TB/3061.
Francis S. Philbrick	THE RISE OF THE WEST, 1754-1830. TB/3067.
Glydon G. Van Deusen	THE JACKSONIAN ERA, 1828-1848. TB/3028.
Clement Eaton	THE GROWTH OF SOUTHERN CIVILIZATION, 1790-1860. TB/3040.
Louis Filler	THE CRUSADE AGAINST SLAVERY, 1830-1860. TB/3029.
Russel B. Nye	THE CULTURAL LIFE OF THE NEW NATION, 1776-1830. TB/3026.
Frederick Rudolph	CULTURAL DEVELOPMENT, 1830-1860.*
Bernard Schwartz	AMERICAN CONSTITUTIONAL HISTORY, 1835-1877*
Ray A. Billington	THE FAR WESTERN FRONTIER, 1830-1860. TB/3012.
David M. Potter	THE COMING OF THE CIVIL WAR.*
Richard Current	THE CIVIL WAR, 1860-1865.*
Frank E. Vandiver	THE CONFEDERACY.*
David Donald	RECONSTRUCTION.*
John A. Garraty	HAYES TO HARRISON, 1877-1890.*
Harold U. Faulkner	POLITICS, REFORM AND EXPANSION, 1890-1900. TB/3020.
Foster Rhea Dulles	AMERICA'S RISE TO WORLD POWER, 1898-1954. TB/3021.
John W. Ward	CULTURAL HISTORY, 1860-1900.*
Rodman Paul	THE FAR WEST AND THE GREAT PLAINS.*
George E. Mowry	THE ERA OF THEODORE ROOSEVELT, 1900-1912. TB/3022.
Arthur S. Link	WOODROW WILSON AND THE PROGRESSIVE ERA, 1910-1917. TB/3023.
Arthur S. Link	WORLD WAR I.*
Loren P. Beth	CONSTITUTIONAL HISTORY, 1877-1917.*
Max Lerner	AMERICAN CULTURE IN THE TWENTIETH CENTURY.*
Paul Murphy	THE CONSTITUTION IN CRISIS TIMES, 1918-1965*
John D. Hicks	REPUBLICAN ASCENDANCY, 1921-1933. TB/3041.
William E. Leuchtenburg	FRANKLIN D. ROOSEVELT AND THE NEW DEAL, 1932-1940. TB/3025.
John Hope Franklin	THE NEW SOUTH *
A. Russell Buchanan	THE UNITED STATES AND WORLD WAR II, Volume I. TB/3044.
A. Russell Buchanan	THE UNITED STATES AND WORLD WAR II, Volume II. TB/3045
Alfred B. Rollins, Jr.	POST WORLD WAR II—Domestic Affairs.
Kenneth W. Thompson	AMERICAN FOREIGN POLICY SINCE 1945*
Clifford Lord	STATISTICAL VOLUME.*

** In preparation*

1828 ★ 1848 THE JACKSONIAN ERA

BY GLYNDON G. VAN DEUSEN

HARPER & ROW, PUBLISHERS

NEW YORK, HAGERSTOWN, SAN FRANCISCO, LONDON

To EMMA LITTEER

who gave more to the preparation of this book than she could ever know

THE JACKSONIAN ERA: 1828-1848

Printed in the United States of America

This book was originally published in 1959 by Harper & Brothers in The New American Nation Series, edited by Henry Steele Commager and Richard B. Morris.

First HARPER TORCHBOOK edition published 1963 by
Harper & Row, Publishers, Incorporated
New York, Hagerstown, San Francisco, London

Library of Congress catalog card number: 58-13810

ISBN: 0-06-133028-0

83 84 30 29 28 27 26 25 24 23 22 21

Contents

Illustrations

These photographs, grouped in a separate section, will be found following page 110

Maps

Editors' Introduction

OVER THE past fifty years much historical writing on the Jacksonian Era has been based upon Populist postulates. Andrew Jackson himself has been portrayed as the heir of Thomas Jefferson and the forerunner of Franklin Delano Roosevelt, and as the friend of labor, the common man, and the debtor. He has been credited with reformist impulses which in fact he never understood and for which he had little sympathy. Contrariwise, his opponents, the Whigs, have been depicted as Hamiltonians and their party that of big business and the large landed interests. Recent years—as the present perceptive study attests—have witnessed substantial revisions of these historical judgments. It has been demonstrated that Jackson's support came in large measure from entrepreneurs and small farmers, and to a much less degree from labor, and that he himself had no understanding of the special problems confronting the new industrial labor or any sense of identity with the workingman. His assault on the Second Bank of the United States, indubitably an adroit political move, was hardly in the interest of debt-ridden farmers, but found its chief support from new business groups and rival bankers. The destruction of the Bank, often applauded as a deathblow to financial monopoly, had questionable results. It ended federal regulation of bank credit, but shifted the money center of the country from Chestnut Street to Wall Street.

In short, while few strong Presidents could boast so little constructive legislation to their credit, Jackson had a sound instinct for public opinion, and was a consummate politician. His most permanent influence was his conception of the President's office and his enlargement of executive authority.

As Mr. Van Deusen demonstrates with impressive authority, the political issues between the major parties in the Age of Jackson cannot be neatly polarized. The major parties differed on many matters, but not on fundamentals. This should come as no surprise to those who are aware that European and American political parties in the first half of the nineteenth century pursued divergent paths. In Europe conservatives repudiated the French Revolution and the things for which it stood, while in America all responsible statesmen claimed to be heirs of the American Revolutionary tradition, albeit that tradition was interpreted in diverse ways. While European parties were divided along class lines and advocated diametrically opposed solutions of the problems of government, party divisions in America transcended class and caste and were founded on personal rivalries, sectional differences, and on transient economic issues, such as the tariff, the bank, and internal improvements. The Jeffersonians when in office borrowed much of the Hamiltonian program, and the Federalists after their leisurely liquidation split off into the opposing National Republican and Democratic parties. Differences in the interpretation of the Constitution existed between the two major parties. Yet the Democrats under Jackson repudiated interposition and nullification, aligning themselves with the Hamiltonians in the Whig party and repudiating the sectionalism of Calhoun.

These revisionist views, and many more facets of a vigorous and flamboyant era are reviewed by Mr. Van Deusen in his lucid and judicious book. Without overlooking the intellectual and constitutional issues of that day, subjects which are reserved for special volumes in this series, the author properly focuses on the fascinating political struggle and provides a sinuous unity by a Presidential synthesis of the period. Basing his study upon a firsthand knowledge of major unpublished collections for the era, Mr. Van Deusen gives us fresh insights into the personalities and intra-party struggles that divided both the Democrats and the Whigs and into the factors explaining the rise of nativist and antislavery political organizations. These raucous political battles occurred at a time when business was expanding, technology was rapidly improving, transportation was undergoing a revolution, mixed state and private enterprise was flourishing, and a new entrepreneurial class wedded to the philosophy of laissez faire shared in a business boom and was smitten by the first major business depression in American history. Through this exciting time of nationalist fervor and gaudy expansionism Mr. Van Deusen guides us with a steady hand and offers us fresh portraits of American political leaders from Andrew Jackson to Zachary Taylor.

This volume is one of The New American Nation Series, a comprehensive, co-operative survey of the history of the era now embraced in the United States from the days of discovery to the second half of the twentieth century. Since the publication by the House of Harper of the American Nation series, over a half century ago, the scope of history has been immensely broadened, new approaches explored and developed. The time has come for a judicious reappraisal of the new history, a cautious application of the new techniques of investigation and presentation, and a large-scale effort to achieve a synthesis of new findings with the familiar facts, and to present the whole in attractive literary form.

To this task The New American Nation Series is dedicated. Each volume is part of a carefully planned whole, and fitted as well as is possible to the other volumes in the series; at the same time each volume is designed to be complete in itself. From time to time the same series of events will be presented from different points of view: thus the volumes on constitutional history and intellectual history will in some ways retrace ground covered in this volume. That all this may result in some overlapping is inevitable, but it has seemed to the editors that repetition is less regrettable than omission, and that something is to be gained by looking at the same period and the same material from different and independent points of view.

HENRY STEELE COMMAGER

RICHARD BRANDON MORRIS

Preface

MY PURPOSE in writing this book has been to present, fairly and impartially, the history of the twenty years, 1828–48, in American life. They were years full of color and movement, years full of significance for the American future.

The Jacksonian era has been the subject of a great deal of historical writing, the volume of which has increased, rather than diminished, with the passage of time. Much of this writing has been the product of patient and understanding scholarship. Some of it has been prejudiced against Jackson and Jacksonians. Most of what has been written in recent years has been sympathetic to Jackson and his supporters and critical of the Whigs. I hope that the present volume holds an even balance in its treatment of the two great parties, and accurately portrays their strengths and weaknesses.

The political parties in the Jacksonian period, like those of today, were made up of congeries of conflicting interests. These interests were sometimes conceived in national terms. They were often regional, or narrowly local, in character. National parties are always subject to the play of centrifugal forces, and the great responsibility of statesmen is to keep these forces under control so that the parties may function effectively on the national stage. I have tried to show the party structures of the Jacksonian period, and to describe the ways in which the leaders strove to keep them organized and operating as effective units of action.

Jacksonian Democracy, viewed in the large, had both strengths and weaknesses. It joined an appreciation of the common man, and a desire to serve his needs and aspirations, with an inadequate concept of the economic methods by which liberty and equality might be achieved and maintained on behalf of the masses of mankind. The Whigs, on the other hand, although they had a more realistic appreciation than had the Democrats of the needs of a dynamic economy, were handicapped, as Professor Hartz has pointed out, by the lack of either a feudal aristocracy or a significant canaille with which to contend, and also by their unwillingness, or their inability, to understand and share some of the most fundamental aspirations of the ordinary American citizen. Each party had its strong points and its defects, and in the national elections each appealed to approximately half of the country's voting population. I have sought to show why the tide of political battle moved now this way and now that. I have also tried to indicate where pettiness of spirit predominated, and where statesmanlike concepts and noble aims held the center of the stage.

The research necessary for this book has been done chiefly in the Library of Congress and in the New York Public Library. I owe a large debt of gratitude to the librarians and the heads of the manuscript divisions in those institutions. I am also deeply grateful to Mr. John R. Russell, Director of Libraries and Librarian of Rush Rhees Library at the University of Rochester, and to the assistant librarians of Rush Rhees Library for the patient and unflagging courtesy with which they met my requests for assistance when I was in the process of writing this book. A semester's leave of absence, granted by the University of Rochester, was vital to completion of the work, and is much appreciated.

Professor Charles Vevier read the second and third chapters of the manuscript and provided some interesting suggestions. I wish to express my appreciation to Professor Henry Steele Commager and Professor Richard B. Morris for their constructive criticisms; to Dr. Henry Blumenthal for lending me a paper written by him on "The Foreign Policy of the Jackson Administration"; and to Mrs. Beatrice Burch and Mrs. Charles T. Willis for typing and proofreading the final manuscript. Finally, as so often in the past, I again express my appreciation to my wife, Ruth Litteer Van Deusen, who understands and forgives the efforts of her husband to get back into the nineteenth century.

G. V. D.

CHAPTER 1

A People in Motion

THE AMERICANS of the Jacksonian era were a self-reliant, versatile, ingenious people. They were the product of a mixture of nationalities, English, Scottish, German, Irish, Dutch, French, and others as well. Blessed now for some generations by distance from the cockpit of Europe and by possession of a rich and theretofore unexploited country, they were engaged in manufacturing a nationality of their own. They were an industrious people with neither time for nor interest in the development of a leisure class. They were an optimistic people and, being optimistic, they were profit-minded and risk-minded, rather than security- and thrift-minded. They admired boldness and respected material success.

These Americans of the Jacksonian generation were both a naïve and a complex people. They had a firm faith in democracy and freedom. The Declaration of Independence with which their ancestors had begun the American Revolution had asserted that all men are created equal and that they have a right to life, liberty, and the pursuit of happiness. The Revolution had been fought, in part, to make good these assertions of principle. Many, if not most, Americans in Jackson's day were fully aware of the beliefs to which their forebears had pledged their lives, their fortunes, and their sacred honor, and they were as determined as their ancestors had been to uphold and develop these beliefs. In their eyes, the United States was a great evangelist, sounding the trumpet of freedom, leading the way along a path that Old Europe, sooner or later, would have to follow.

Exhilarated by the conviction that America was the pioneer in forging a new era for mankind, Americans in the Jacksonian period undertook a variety of experiments that were designed to broaden the area of freedom. They tested new religious faiths and philosophies that ranged from spiritualism and Mormonism to transcendentalism and Unitarianism. Some tried to establish religious or quasi-religious Utopias. Others undertook socialistic and communistic experiments that were supposed to bring in their train freedom from want and from social maladjustment. Devoted humanitarians ministered to the deaf, the blind, and the insane; penal reforms were instituted; secular education was widened and its quality improved; a temperance movement gathered headway. There were crusades for peace, for women's rights, and for the abolition of slavery. America was offering a challenge to the rest of the world, the challenge of a free society seeking a better way of life.[1]

Along with their search for freedom, Americans found some time for cultivation of the more aesthetic side of life. They supported a Greek revival that, together with ridiculous tiny temple-fronted houses, produced banks and churches in the classical mode and such noble architectural monuments as Monticello and the buildings at the University of Virginia. A nationalistic school of nature painters flourished, the Hudson River school. American society furnished opportunity and stimulus for a literary movement headed by Washington Irving, Ralph Waldo Emerson, Henry Thoreau, Herman Melville, Nathaniel Hawthorne, Edgar Allan Poe, and Margaret Fuller. Americans developed the lyceum and the public lecture, subscribed to bigger and better newspapers, and supported literary magazines that maintained a high level of excellence. Here was the beginning of a noble cultural tradition.

By and large, however, this Jacksonian era had little time for the cultural side of life. It was mainly absorbed in the strenuous pursuit of material gain. In that pursuit it often wasted the substance of the land by farming with no thought of soil conservation, or, in the business world, by the most venturesome kind of enterprise. Cruelty also reared its head, sometimes largely unthinking, as in the tolerance of slum conditions in the cities; sometimes deliberate, as in the treatment of the Indians and the gouging and knifing combats that took place on

[1] The best treatment of America's leadership in the search for this better way is Alice F. Tyler, *Freedom's Ferment* (Minneapolis, 1944).

the frontier. Whether in the city or in the country, the Americans of this early day sometimes exhibited a greediness that was typified by the remark of the old frontier farmer: "I ain't greedy for land," said he. "All I want is jist what jines mine."

The mixture of restless vigor, urge for quick material achievement and idealistic fervor that characterized these early Americans was peculiarly fitted to make expansion a keynote of the Jacksonian period. Many felt that it was the right, the duty, and the opportunity of Americans to expand the area of freedom and to enrich it, whether by the development of domestic resources, by continental conquest, or by the extension of American influence and American ideals to more distant quarters of the globe. Expansionism in this period pushed the American nation to the Pacific and to the Rio Grande, and sent clipper ships into the seven seas. It fostered dreams of great trade development in the Orient. "Our population," wrote William Henry Seward in 1846, "is destined to roll its resistless waves to the icy barriers of the north, and to encounter Oriental civilization on the shores of the Pacific."[2] In a humbler and more practical sense, expansionist fervor set Americans to conquering the problems of transportation and business development within their own borders.

Americans whose lives spanned the era from 1800 to 1850 must have been amazed at the changes in transportation that took place before their eyes. They saw the oxcart, the stage coach, the clumsy flatboat, ark, and scow, give way to the steamboat and to railroads run by steam power. They saw the channels of many rivers widened and deepened, thousands of miles of canals built in the North and West, and thousands of miles of railroad lines threading their way across the country from the Atlantic coast toward the Mississippi River. They witnessed a transportation revolution.

The consequence of this drastic change in the means and methods of transport was a well-nigh miraculous change in the cost, the speed, and the volume of transportation. Within one generation of thirty years, from 1825 to 1855, the cost of the land transport of bulky products fell some 95 per cent. Freight rates on the Mississippi-Ohio system fell about 75 per cent for downstream and 90 per cent for upstream traffic, and between Buffalo and New York they fell from one hundred dollars to less than eight dollars per ton. At the same time the speed of freightage quintupled. Where loaded wagons on turn-

[2] William H. Seward, *An Autobiography* (New York, 1891), p. 791.

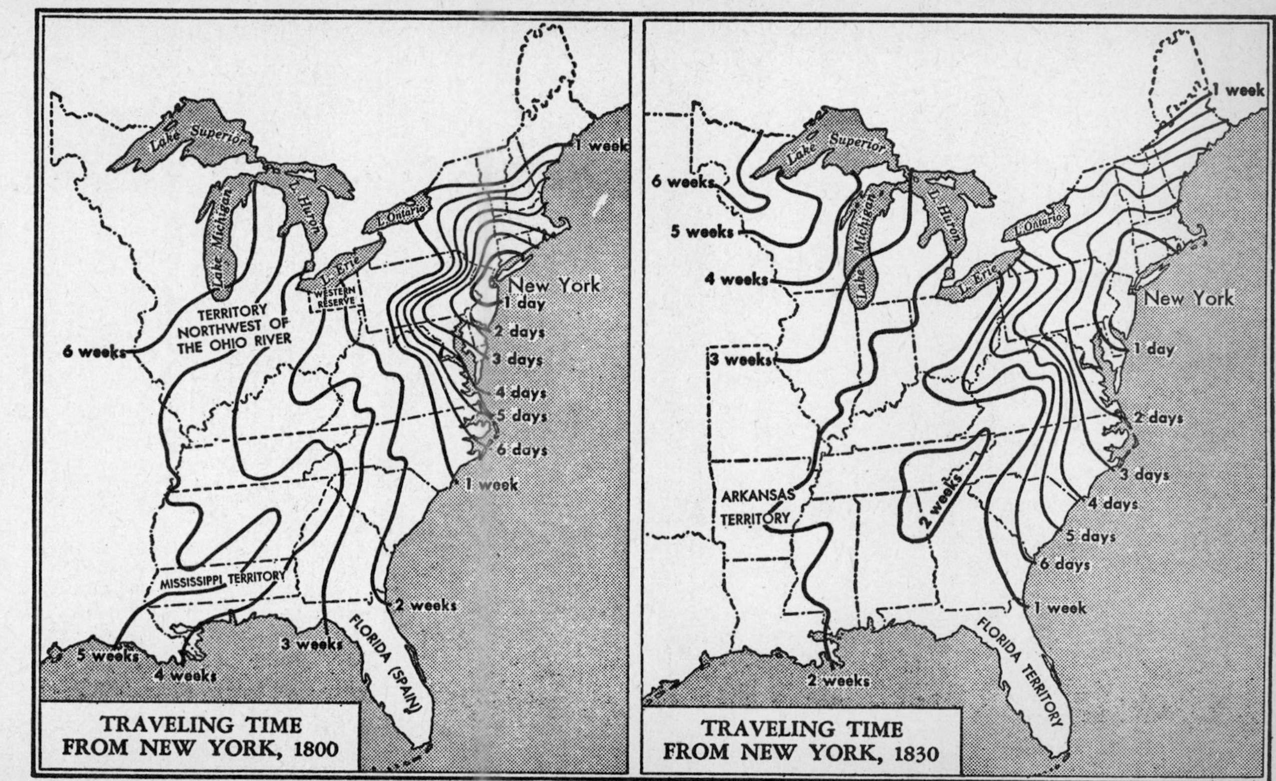
Lake Superior
Lake Michigan
L. Huron
L. Erie
L. Ontario
WESTERN RESERVE
TERRITORY NORTHWEST OF THE OHIO RIVER
MISSISSIPPI TERRITORY
FLORIDA (SPAIN)
New York
1 day
2 days
3 days
4 days
5 days
6 days
1 week
2 weeks
3 weeks
4 weeks
5 weeks
6 weeks
1 week
TRAVELING TIME FROM NEW YORK, 1800
Lake Superior
Lake Michigan
L. Huron
L. Erie
L. Ontario
ARKANSAS TERRITORY
FLORIDA TERRITORY
New York
1 day
2 days
3 days
4 days
5 days
6 days
1 week
2 weeks
3 weeks
4 weeks
5 weeks
6 weeks
1 week
2 weeks
TRAVELING TIME FROM NEW YORK, 1830

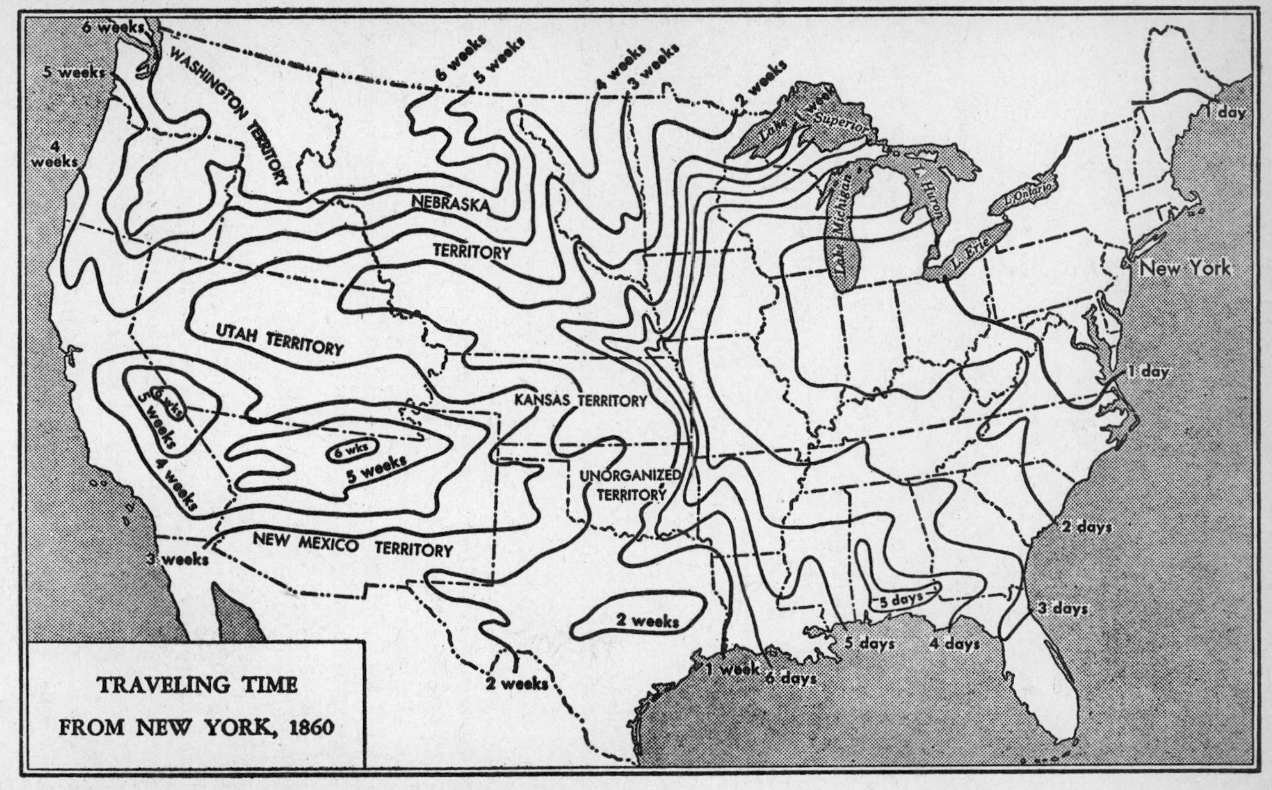

TRAVELING TIME FROM NEW YORK, 1860

pikes had moved at the rate of two miles an hour, railroad freight cars now traveled at from ten to twelve. Similar changes took place in the speed of river traffic.[3] In the Mississippi Valley region, after 1820, the total value of commerce floated down to New Orleans doubled each decade, and there was an even greater expansion of trade between the East and the West. Calhoun's dream of binding the country together by means of its roads and canals was in a fair way of being realized before his death in 1850.

The development of transportation facilities was one of the factors that made possible the amazing speed with which the West was populated in Jackson's day. As though driven by some mystic force, fur traders, missionaries, speculators, ne'er-do-wells, lawyers, farmers, merchants, millers, blacksmiths, boatmen, journeymen printers, card sharps, and desperadoes moved toward the setting sun. Between 1810 and 1830 the West took over two million people out of the eastern states, and this exodus did not abate in the succeeding years. Indiana's population doubled between 1830 and 1840. The population of Illinois tripled during the same decade, moving from 157,445 to 476,183. Kentucky and Tennessee had each around 800,000 in 1840, and their population was still rapidly increasing. In 1840, 6,376,972 people, more than one out of three in the total population of the country, lived in the trans-Appalachian West.[4]

The rapidity with which the West was being settled meant that American life felt, in marked fashion, the influence of the frontier. And according to the thesis of Frederick Jackson Turner and his disciples, the frontier has always been the great source of nationalism, democracy, and individualism in the United States, as well as a "safety valve" for social discontent. Historians differ as to the validity of the Turnerian hypothesis. There is much to be said for the point of view of Turner's critics that the American character and the American way of life owed at least as much to European thought and traditions as they did to the impact of life on the frontier. Urban development, too, even at this early period, was having a distinct effect upon American institutions. Indeed, it is possible to sustain the argument that American individualism and initiative owed more to the stimulus of an ex-

[3] George B. Taylor, *The Transportation Revolution, 1815–1860* (New York, 1951), pp. 132–139, 173–175.

[4] Fred J. Guetter and Albert E. McKinley, *Statistical Tables Relating to the Economic Growth of the United States* (Philadelphia, 1924), p. 5; Charles H. Ambler, *Transportation in the Ohio Valley* (Glendale, Calif., 1932), p. 60.

panding economy, in all its various forms, than they did to the specific influence of the frontier. Even the most fervent advocates of the frontier hypothesis must admit that much that was wasteful, reckless, and cruel stemmed from the frontier environment.

Despite the limitations of the frontier thesis, however, the fact remains that the frontier was a leveling influence, and that it was an incentive to ingenuity and self-reliance. Equally beyond dispute is the fact that it had a profound influence upon fundamental national policies concerning tariffs, internal improvements, and public lands. And it may reasonably be maintained that it acted as a psychological safety valve, affording a compensating image of what the urban laborer might do if he had the gumption to go West and do it.[5]

The mass migration of population into the frontier regions of the West meant that the American economy was remaining predominantly agrarian in character. By 1850, all the wooded region and prairie lands east of the Mississippi which were of good quality and were not in the hands of speculators had been occupied by settlers, and the same could be said of the better farming areas in the southern states. America's production of agricultural goods was growing by leaps and bounds, and American surpluses of wheat, cotton, tobacco, and naval stores were pouring into the European markets.

America was still a land of farmers but, even so, the picture was beginning to change. Willy-nilly, the United States economy was becoming increasingly diversified, one in which the city and city influences were playing a more and more important role.

Steadily, year by year, the great disparity in numbers between urbanites and ruralites melted away. In 1800 the farmers had outnumbered the town and city dwellers of the United States by a ratio of fifteen to one; in 1830 the ratio was a trifle less than ten and one-half to one; in 1850 it was only five and one-half to one.[6]

[5] Frederick J. Turner, *The Frontier in American History* (New York, 1948), pp. 1–38 and *passim;* Helene S. Zahler, *Eastern Workingmen and National Land Policy, 1829–1862* (New York, 1941), pp. 3–146, 177–201; George R. Taylor (ed.), *The Turner Thesis: Concerning the Role of the Frontier in American History* (Boston, 1949), *passim;* Richard Hofstadter, "Turner and the Frontier Myth," *The American Scholar,* XVIII (fall, 1949), 433–443; Murray Kane, "Some Considerations on the Frontier Concept of Frederick Jackson Turner," *Mississippi Valley Historical Review,* XXVII (1940–41), 379–400.

[6] *Historical Statistics of the United States, 1789–1845* (Washington, 1945),

Significant in connection with this growth of urban communities was the development of cities, both in the East and in the West, with 8,000 or more population. These cities quadrupled in number between 1820 and 1850, and even more rapid was their growth in size. Pittsburgh's population increased from 7,000 to 46,000, that of Cincinnati from 9,000 to 115,000, Boston from 42,000 to 137,000, New York from 123,000 to 515,000.[7] America was obviously not going to remain the land of Jefferson's dream, a land of virtuous farmers. The growth of the cities meant the development of great centers of business and industrial power that would have gladdened the heart of Alexander Hamilton. America's wealth, America's power, and the rise of complex social and economic problems were going hand in hand.

Labor became a social problem during the first half of the nineteenth century. Urban growth meant an increasing labor element in the towns and cities where industry was located. Philadelphia, which was a great textile center, was a good example. There, as early as 1820, the manufacturing suburbs, such as Northern Liberties, Kensington, and Southwark, had a combined population of some 45,000. Twenty years later this had risen to just over 200,000. Similar concentrations took place in other industrial centers. These labor class groupings furnished a growing market for the products of the farms. They were also centers of discontent and aspiration. And by the eighteen-thirties the laboring class had become possessed of a voting strength that had to be reckoned with by the politicians of the Jacksonian period.[8]

The labor discontent of the Jacksonian period had been long a-borning. Manifestations of it had appeared with the birth of the new nation, for the wages of skilled labor had started to decline and "sun to sun" labor hours, traditional in farming communities, were still the rule in the urban areas. Shoemakers, printers, and tailors had established a number of local unions and had begun to strike for better hours and wages, and to seek restraint on the employment of "inferior workers." There had been a few efforts at collective bargaining.

---

p. 25. Urban statistics are figured on the basis of incorporated places of 2,500 or more population.

[7] *Census for 1820* (Washington, 1821), population statistics; J. D. B. DeBow, *Statistical View of the United States* (Washington, 1854), pp. 342, 372, 375. The figures given in the text are, of course, in round numbers.

[8] John R. Commons *et al.*, *History of Labour in the United States* (4 vols., New York, 1918–35), I, 176; Arthur M. Schlesinger, Jr., *The Age of Jackson* (Boston, 1945), pp. 8–9.

These early efforts at improvement of labor conditions had met with scant success. The hostility of employers, the influx of unskilled labor, lack of leadership, and the attitude of courts that were quick to dub unions and strikes "criminal conspiracies" had combined to prevent the development of any significant labor organization. Many laborers, too, believed that America was a land of opportunity, where failure was the result of the shortcomings of the individual. Down to the Jacksonian era there was nothing that could be called a labor philosophy, whether of co-operation or of class struggle.

By 1828, however, the picture was beginning to change. Grievances over hours and wages continued, and to these had been added complaints about lack of educational opportunity, compulsory state militia service, and other inequities in the social structure. There was, too, a scarcity of skilled and semiskilled workers and a growing consciousness of the fact that a considerable number of artisans and mechanics now enjoyed "the God-given privilege of the franchise." This state of affairs produced a spread of trade unionism in the principal urban centers, a demand for better wages and a ten-hour day, and a number of workingmen's political parties, especially in Massachusetts, New York, and Pennsylvania. These parties demanded more and better public schools, abolition of imprisonment for debt and of compulsory militia systems, and the establishment of mechanic's lien laws as a guarantee that the laborer would receive at least some portion of his hire.

Thanks in part to these efforts of the artisans and mechanics, educational opportunity was improved in the eighteen-thirties, imprisonment for debt and the cumbersome state militia systems were largely abolished, and, by 1840, federal employees had been put on a ten-hour day. These gains, however, were more than counterbalanced by severe losses.

For one thing, labor's organized activities in the field of politics had proved to be short-lived. The workingmen's parties lasted only a few years. Their vitality was sapped by lack of money and leadership, and by the skill with which the major parties stole planks out of the "Workie" platforms. Worse still, from the point of view of the labor movement, was the fate of the trade unions, which had spread with some rapidity during the early part of the decade. When the panic of 1837 brought widespread unemployment and a collapse of wages, the trade union movement speedily dissolved into nothingness. So far as a labor movement was concerned, everything had to begin again.

During the eighteen-forties, labor turned to general panaceas, rather than to political action or unionization. Those who might have led a rejuvenated labor movement apparently did not understand the social significance of the industrialization that was making headway before their eyes. The history of the preceding ten years, coupled with the influx of cheap labor, made difficult the utilization of the old methods of labor organization. Under these circumstances, the laborers turned for relief from a falling standard of living to experiments with producers' co-operatives, to Associationism (an American brand of utopian socialism adapted from the teachings of the Frenchman, Charles Fourier), and to agitation for free land and unalienable homesteads. Disunited and following wandering fires, labor was scarcely a formidable political force in the decade of the eighteen-forties. The one really bright spot in the labor picture of this period was the decision of the Massachusetts Supreme Court in *Commonwealth* v. *Hunt* (1842) which upheld the legality of labor unions.[9]

The possibility of labor's emergence as a political force, a possibility that appeared to be a probability in the early Jacksonian period, was due in large part to the nation's steady advance toward universal manhood suffrage. Whether universal suffrage came as a result of the political idealism bred by the Revolution, or the conviction of Jefferson and the Jeffersonian Republicans that government should be based on wide popular support, or the relative decline of freeholders, or the influence of the frontier, or the more practical consideration that a politician's advocacy of wider suffrage was bound to ensure him the support of those enfranchised as the result of his efforts, the fact was that suffrage qualifications had been steadily lowering since the founding of the Republic.

By 1820 there was a general tendency to substitute the payment of taxes for the holding of property as a basis for the right to vote. Massachusetts and Pennsylvania permitted all who paid either state or county taxes to vote. New York, after its constitutional revision of 1821, had only a trifling tax qualification for the voting privilege and this was eliminated by referendum in 1826. Not a few states had uni-

[9] Richard B. Morris, Introduction to John R. Commons *et al.*, *Documentary History of American Industrial Society* (new ed., New York, 1948), Vol. III; Norman Ware, *The Industrial Worker, 1840–1860* (Boston and New York, 1924), pp. 1–152, 198–226; Foster R. Dulles, *Labor in America* (New York, 1950), pp. 20–88; Philip S. Foner, *History of the Labor Movement in the United States* (New York, 1947), pp. 48–53, 97–213.

versal white manhood suffrage, Vermont and New Hampshire having led the way in the seventeen-nineties, to be followed before 1820 by such western states as Indiana, Illinois, and Missouri.

Limitations on the suffrage continued to decrease during the ensuing decades. By 1850 all the states save North Carolina had abandoned property qualifications, while low tax restrictions were to be found in only six states.[10]

The lowering of suffrage qualifications did not mean that pure democracy had triumphed. The ballot was still an open one, and any watcher at the polls could tell how votes were being cast. Negroes and women were still considered unfit for the franchise. But by Jackson's time most adult white males in the United States had the right to vote on election day. So shrewd an observer as Alexis de Tocqueville, writing in the eighteen-thirties, declared that "the principle of the sovereignty of the people has acquired in the United States all the practical development that the imagination can conceive."[11]

But if the political rights of the common man were expanding in the day of Andrew Jackson, so also were the power and significance of the business community. This community was made up of two major groups. The first, which may be called the elite group, consisted of those who had already achieved a prominent place in the economy—the guides and guardians of such organizations as the Second Bank of the United States, the immensely profitable textile concern known as the Boston Manufacturing Company of Massachusetts, the Appleton Company (a textile business chartered in 1828 with a capitalization of $1 million), or the Boston and Sandwich Glass Company, which yearly manufactured $250,000 worth of glass. These were concerns that had arrived in every sense of the word. They and their owners had position and power in the business and the political communities.

The second group of business concerns was much larger than the elite group. It was made up of what may be called the self-employed entrepreneurs—the bankers, insurance men, merchants, and manufacturers, generally capitalized at less than $100,000 and doing business on a correspondingly small scale. Some of them were making comfortable profits, others no profits at all. Many of these smaller busi-

[10] Kirk H. Porter, *A History of Suffrage in the United States* (Chicago, 1918), pp. 20–36, 47–50, 72, 77–107.

[11] Alexis de Tocqueville, *Democracy in America* (2 vols., New York, 1945), I, 57.

nesses were of a highly speculative nature, especially in the western part of the country. All were pushing, eagerly competitive, anxious for a more important and more profitable place in the economy.

Business entrepreneurs were rapidly increasing in number during the Jacksonian era. Banking is an illustration of this. Banking had begun in the United States in 1782 with the establishment of the Bank of North America in Philadelphia. At the beginning of the Jacksonian period there were 329 banks in the United States, and by 1837 there were 788. In each decade there also appeared thousands of new business firms: manufacturers and distributors of textiles, boots and shoes, leather goods, glass, iron; exporters of products that ranged from wheat and cotton to American locomotives; importers of products that ranged from fine cutlery to champagne. Some of these business ventures were carefully managed; others did business on a shoestring and took long chances. American business, save when depression clamped down on it, was growing at a rapid, almost a feverish, pace.[12]

A central feature of this business growth was the development of the corporate form of business organization. American banks, from their beginning, were established by acts of incorporation. They were, by and large, extremely profitable undertakings, profits of 10 per cent and more on bank stock being by no means uncommon, and their success enhanced the popularity of incorporation for other forms of business activity. In an era when great central pools of capital were nonexistent, incorporation was a most effective means of acquiring the financial sinews necessary for the exploitation of business opportunities. Road companies, canal companies, and insurance and manufacturing concerns found it much to their liking, especially after the Supreme Court's decision in the Dartmouth College Case (1819) protected corporation charters from the assaults of state legislatures. During the eighteen-twenties, there was a great development of large and small incorporated businesses, and this continued during the ensuing decades. Whether for good or for ill, the corporation had arrived on the American scene.

Business expansion in the Jacksonian era, facilitated though it was

[12] McLane's *Report,* 22nd Congress, 1st session, 1831–32 (2 vols., Report No. 308); Bray Hammond, *Banks and Politics in America* (Princeton, 1957), pp. 48–62, 144–172; Schlesinger, *Age of Jackson,* pp. 8–9, 334–341; Glyndon G. Van Deusen, "Some Aspects of Whig Thought and Theory," *American Historical Review,* LXIII, No. 2 (Jan., 1958), 305–322.

by the practice of incorporation, was by no means free from difficulties and dangers. The American entrepreneur often had to contend with stiff foreign competition, bad communications that made uncertain the receipt of raw materials and the delivery of finished goods, currency confusion, and the ups and downs of a series of business fluctuations that varied from wild inflation to the severe depression of the latter eighteen-thirties. There was also conflict between the rising entrepreneurial class and the elite group, the former being anxious for bank credits and resentful of the superior privileges of the wealthier bankers and businessmen. These latter had the means to expand already established enterprises, and the money and influence to push favorable charters of incorporation through the various state legislatures. They were mainly conservative in politics, generally preferring the Whig to the Democratic party, and their aspiring and resentful rivals often challenged them or their representatives in the political arena, as well as in the marts of trade.[13]

To dwell too much on the vicissitudes of the business world in the first half of the nineteenth century would be to distort the picture. With all its toil and trouble, this was the heyday of the entrepreneur. It might almost be said that the world climate of opinion had shifted to meet his needs. Gone was the era of rigorous, authoritarian control, whether by church or feudal lord or state, over the economic life of the community. In its place had come the day of Adam Smith, of Thomas Robert Malthus and David Ricardo, of Jeremy Bentham and Jean Baptiste Say. Authoritarian power had come into disrepute, and the thinkers on social and economic problems now bowed before the controls exerted by a semimystical force which they called "natural law"—the counterpart in the social order of scientific law in the physical order. Man was told that he was, by nature, good, and that self-help was the great thing in his improvement of his station; that the sum total of the efforts of individuals in their own interest would be the maximum social good; that that government governed best which governed least. Even pessimists about the future like Malthus and Ricardo regarded government intervention as ineffectual in the alleviation of social distress, as something worse than the disease.[14]

[13] Richard Hofstadter, *The American Political Tradition and the Men Who Made It* (New York, 1948), pp. 55–58; Bray Hammond, "Public Policy and National Banks," *Journal of Economic History,* VI (May, 1946), 79–84.

[14] Charles Gide and Charles Rist, *A History of Economic Doctrines from the*

It would have been difficult to find a climate of opinion more congenial to the spirit of American enterprise than that engendered by the laissez-faire social and economic philosophers. The American businessman, living in the midst of an expanding economy, saw opportunities for money-making on every hand. Untrammeled by any feudal heritage, stimulated by the conditions of his environment, blessed by the social philosophers, he was in a singularly fortunate position to lay the foundations for economic developments that were to make the American economy one of the wonders of the modern world.

A basic factor in the booming business development of the Jacksonian period was the rise of industrial technology. American industry had been primarily of the home manufacturing variety until after the War of 1812. Then the growth of population, the development of transportation, the increase of both foreign and domestic markets, and a characteristically American interest in physical comfort (Europeans were soon to marvel at our elevators, furnaces, and hot and cold water systems) created demands which put inventive genius at a premium. There was an immediate response by American inventors.

Patents, which in the first decade of the nineteenth century averaged some seventy-seven a year, rose by 1850 to nearly a thousand per year. During the period from 1790 to 1860, the United States granted more patents than England and France combined. "I apprehend," said a witness before an English parliamentary committee in 1841, "that the chief part . . . [of the] new inventions . . . have originated abroad, especially in America." And patents were only one aspect of the increase.[15]

A leading spirit in the development of a textile industry that proliferated a series of new inventions and improvements was Samuel Slater, who had come to America in 1789 with the plans of the English textile machinery so clearly fixed in his mind that he could build water frames and power looms on this side of the Atlantic without the aid of blueprints. Such developments as the carding machine invented by John Goulding and the new power loom invented by a Harvard graduate, Francis Cabot Lowell, kept the textile industry in a state of constant change and development. This was paralleled in other indus-

---

Time of the Physiocrats to the Present Day (2nd. Eng. ed., Boston, 1948), gives an excellent treatment of early nineteenth-century economic thought.

[15] Victor S. Clark, *History of Manufacturers in the United States, 1607–1928* (3 vols., New York, 1929), I, 402–437.

tries. Between 1830 and 1840, the United States took and maintained the lead in printing-press invention, largely due to the efforts of Robert Hoe (1784–1833) and his son Richard (1812–86). Samuel F. B. Morse patented the telegraph in 1837 and completed the first telegraph line, from Baltimore to Washington, in 1844. New and improved forms of pin machinery, new methods of rolling copper and brass and of manufacturing iron tubing, appeared. America became a leading center of machine tool manufacture and design. New forms of lathes and planes, new forms of drills, gear cutters, and dies, crowded upon the market. A wide variety of mechanisms for turning out finished iron products was invented, and nails, tacks, bolts, files, spikes, wire screws and chains, all formerly produced by hand, were now produced by machines. By the decade of the eighteen-thirties, American machine tools were challenging those of Europe in variety and efficiency.[16]

Technology meant a vast increase in productivity, but technology alone could not supply the goods America needed. Just as important was a labor supply. This was furnished, in part, by the sons and daughters of New England farmers, and by other local sources. It was furnished more significantly by the increasing flow of immigration.

Between 1828 and 1844, half a million immigrants arrived in the United States, and in the later eighteen-forties the number of arrivals swelled into a flood of over 200,000 each year. Even cholera epidemics and tales of great economic depression in America acted only as momentary deterrents of this exodus of Europe toward the New World. Harassed by oppression, revolution, high taxes, bitter winters, and recurrent food shortages, their imaginations fed by the glowing tales of contractors' agents and ship captains about the paradise beyond the sea, Germans, Irish, English, Scottish, and Welsh—Pietists, Lutherans, Catholics, and Jews—felt the call of strange horizons. "*Amerika, du hast es besser,*" wrote Goethe in 1831, an opinion echoed by multitudes of men.[17]

This influx of foreigners stirred a variety of feelings, most of them unfriendly, in the hearts of America's native population, which had a

[16] Joseph W. Roe, *English and American Tool Builders* (New York, 1926), pp. 119–123, 128, 217–247; Waldemar Kaempffert (ed.), *A Popular History of American Inventions* (2 vols., New York, 1924), I, 226, 247–252, 294; II, 322–337.

[17] Marcus L. Hansen, *The Atlantic Migration, 1607–1860* (Cambridge, 1940), pp. 120–122, 123–171.

predominantly English and Protestant heritage. The prospect of invasion by masses of outlanders with strange ways, many of them Catholics, some radicals and atheists, was portrayed by fanatical propagandists as an alarming menace. The Irish newcomers showed a tendency to settle in the eastern cities, while the Germans who did not go out on the land favored the growing urban centers of the West. Both Irish and Germans, being poor, often congregated in slum sections, there to be viewed askance by the surrounding natives, whose alarm and disgust increased with the menace of job competition. Anti-Catholic and antiforeign riots repeatedly disgraced such northern metropolitan centers as Boston, New York, and Philadelphia. As time went on, too, the preference of the immigrants for the northern and western sections of the country kindled the resentment of white Southerners. It was only natural that the invaders should go into those areas of the economy where they felt most at home, but the people south of Mason and Dixon's line viewed this movement as one which was building up the political power of states that were becoming increasingly hostile to slavery. The alien "menace" thereupon became the subject of excited comment in various parts of the South. As early as 1839, a New York handbill exhorting Irishmen to vote right, lest they lose America, was being circulated in New Orleans as proof of the dangers of foreign immigration.[18]

The fears and alarms of the native American population, north and south, soon found political expression. The immigrants early showed a tendency to join the Democratic party, some because of their belief that Jefferson and Jackson were the great symbols of freedom and the exponents of the rights of the common man, others because Democratic party organizations early grasped the potential that lay in the foreign-born vote and outdid themselves to curry favor with the newcomers. It was then only natural for the Whigs to seek what capital they could by marshaling under the Whig banner those alarmed by the foreign influx.

When, as in New York City, the Democratic love of the immigrant manifested itself by wholesale fraudulent registration of alien voters just before election day, the political reaction was sharp and bitter. In 1835 a Native American party was organized in New York City. The following year it ran a candidate for mayor and in 1837, by fusion

[18] W. Darrell Overdyke, *The Know-Nothing Party in the South* (Baton Rouge, 1950), p. 6.

with the Whigs, it carried the city election. A few years later, nativism, as the antiforeign movement was called, was embittering municipal contests in New Orleans. The movement sought political expression in other areas of the country, and in July, 1845, delegates from thirteen states met in Philadelphia in an attempt to form a national political organization. All that resulted from this meeting was a declaration of principles, but the signs of the times were portentous. The heyday of nativism was not to come until the great foreign tide created by famine and revolution swept into the country at the end of the eighteen-forties, but the groundwork for a nativist movement of major proportions was clearly laid during the preceding period.[19]

The dynamic America of the Jacksonian period produced in kaleidoscopic succession a host of problems, political and economic, and about these theorists argued at length. The Jeffersonian concept of a simple government, narrowly restricted by frugality and by strict construction of the Constitution, was generally accepted as the ideal political system. The revolt against a tyrannical central government was still fresh in the minds of this generation, and the states' rights theory of the Virginia and Kentucky resolutions was a handy weapon to wield against the threat of a Leviathan state at Washington. But the growing need for the maintenance of national unity by means of a strong hand at the helm of the national government, and what seemed an equally apparent need of vigorous governmental action if equality of opportunity was to be maintained on the American scene, made inexorably for an increase of power at the nation's capital. Followers of Old Hickory had to accept the facts of life as they found them expressed in his vigorous words and deeds, the while they shrank from such further expansion of governmental action as was prescribed by the Whigs. Extreme opponents of the national government's power oscillated uneasily between the Whig and Democratic positions.

There was division of thought along economic as well as political lines. The Jeffersonian ideal of an agrarian economy was still a powerful influence. On the other hand, the advocates of a balanced economy, one in which industrialism would play an important role, found many supporters among the business and political leaders of the period, and

[19] *Ibid.*, pp. 1–15; Ray Billington, *The Protestant Crusade, 1800–1860* (New York, 1938), Chaps. I–X; Louis D. Scisco, *Political Nativism in New York State* (New York, 1901), pp. 16–77; Carroll John Noonan, *Nativism in Connecticut, 1829–1860* (Washington, 1938), Chaps. I–VI.

not a few among the rank and file. An inevitable corollary of the struggle between agrarianism and industrialism was the division of opinion over the tariff. Should it be kept low, in the interests of the farming regions with their great export of staples, or should it protect national industry against foreign competition? The tariff was a vital issue, albeit often a local one.

Other problems provoked division of opinion along different social and economic lines. The currency of the country was often inadequate and disordered. Men differed widely over the ways and means of its improvement. The rise of business corporations excited many to enthusiasm, others to distrust and alarm. Should corporations be checked and destroyed, or should they be encouraged to develop? On this question men differed with vigor and acerbity.

Such were the great political and economic questions of the Jacksonian era. The writings of the protagonists on both sides made a literature of considerable volume. Among the writers, a few stand out as of more than ordinary importance.

There were no more influential exponents of the point of view generally adopted by the industrialists of the Jacksonian age than Mathew Carey (1760–1839) and his son Henry Charles Carey (1793–1879). The former, born in Dublin, Ireland, had emigrated to America in 1784 under threat of prosecution in the old country for libel of the English government. He settled in Philadelphia, where he became an affluent printer and publisher and a stout Jeffersonian Republican. As the years went by, however, Mathew Carey deserted Jeffersonian agrarianism. His Anglophobia, the evidence he saw of the pernicious effects of British dumping on the American market, and a grudging but real admiration for English industry and enterprise combined to make him a most ardent advocate of the development of American manufactures and of a protective tariff. From 1819 to 1833 (when he turned from pamphleteering to charitable activities), he flooded the country with pamphlets, newspaper essays, circulars addressed to manufacturers, and memorials to Congress.

Carey's influence was enormous. He played a major role in organizing the Philadelphia Society for the Promotion of National Industry, and the Society for the Promotion of Internal Improvements, both effective propaganda agencies. His advice on bank-note issues was listened to with respect by his friend Nicholas Biddle. He was a stanch and effective supporter of Henry Clay and the American system, so stanch, in fact, that he was hanged in effigy at Columbia, South Carolina, along with the famous Kentuckian whom he so much admired.

He was a defender, par excellence, of the manufacturing interest. He saw the lack of balance in the American economy of his day and, in season and out, preached, as an answer to that imbalance, the development of industry. A balanced economy, he asserted, would mean general prosperity, class harmony, and a salutary increase in the nation's population and power. It would also mean lower prices for and improved quality in American manufactured goods. He used the argument, if not the words, so often heard in this period, "far-fetched is dearly bought." The rising industrialists of the time owed much, whether for good or ill, to this immigrant publicist.

Mathew Carey had views on matters other than industry and its protection. He believed that banks were essential to the nation's economic welfare and that they should be banks of issue, with a paper currency backed by specie. He was an enthusiastic advocate of internal improvements at national expense. He believed that government should be "allowed to interfere, to organize, and to direct whenever its activities" would promote the national good. Like Clay, he had a vision of an American system of economic development fostered by the national government, developing the nation's wealth and power until it could stand alone, independent of Europe. Carey claimed Alexander Hamilton as his spiritual father and was wont to refer to his own system of thought as the Hamiltonian school of political economy.[20]

Henry Charles Carey followed in his father's footsteps as an influential publicist. A man of wealth, whose business affairs always seemed to prosper, he enjoyed high standing in Philadelphia society. He was an indefatigable writer, though prolix and often tiresome, and during the eighteen-forties was America's foremost advocate of a protective tariff.

Like his father before him, Henry Carey urged the importance of a balanced economy, one in which industrial activity would play an important part. The means to this happy state of affairs was protection, the blessings of which would be manifold. A protective tariff would

[20] Mathew Carey's philosophy is developed in Kenneth W. Rowe, *Mathew Carey, A Study in American Economic Development* (Baltimore, 1933), and in Earl L. Bradsher, *Mathew Carey, Editor, Author, Publisher* (New York, 1912). For Carey's influence, see Rowe, Mathew Carey, pp. 527–533.

increase wages, lower the cost of living, and make money more plentiful by keeping in the country specie which would otherwise be siphoned out by an unfavorable balance of trade. By means of the tariff, agriculture would be provided with a dependable home market in the nation's growing industrial centers. A flourishing home economy would mean that the nation would have no disposition for adventures abroad; therefore a high-tariff policy would promote peace. It would bring high wages and general prosperity, thus elevating woman's position in society. In short, the tariff would bring the whole country to a level of gracious living, high thinking, and sound morality.

Henry Carey never tired of emphasizing the need for American self-sufficiency. America's "mission," he declared, was not to open up trade with distant parts of the world. "The cost of a mission to Japan would build half a dozen furnaces that would add more to the wealth of the nation in five years than the commerce of that country would do in half a century." The true American mission was to set an example to the rest of the world by developing an internal empire where self-government and a high standard of living would create a perfect harmony of interest.

Optimism was a fundamental part of Carey's philosophy. He took to his bosom J. B. Say's law of markets—the dictum that the production of goods and services automatically provides an equivalent in consuming power—but he blithely rejected the grim Malthusian law of population and Ricardo's equally gloomy iron law of wages. Unlike these pessimistic free-trade theorists of the laissez-faire school, Carey preached that economic nationalism was a sure way of promoting international peace and good will.

Carey exerted a significant influence upon American thought in the Jacksonian era. Business interests subsidized reprints of his various writings. Horace Greeley spread his teachings through the columns of the New York *Tribune*. New York University gave him an honorary degree. President Thomas Hill of Harvard later called him one of the greatest philosophers of the times. His was the voice of hope, constantly proclaiming that protection and the development of industry would mean peace and happiness for all good Americans.[21]

[21] The best example of Carey's thinking is to be found in his *The Harmony of Interests* (New York, 1852). His remarks on the American "mission" are to be found on pp. 227–229. See also Joseph Dorfman, *The Economic Mind in American Civilization, 1606–1918* (3 vols., New York, 1946–49), II, 789–809.

If protection had its exponents among the intellectuals of the Jacksonian era, so did the doctrine of free trade. William Cullen Bryant (1794–1878) devoted the influential New York *Evening Post* to expounding the virtues of a tariff for revenue and to denunciations of what he termed the manufacturers' "exorbitant demands" for protection. Such demands were sectional, and therefore promoted national discord. They were also inevitably productive of increased taxation. Bryant believed in laissez faire, and in holding government to a minimum of activity.[22] He was a thoroughgoing Jacksonian Democrat.

Another outstanding free-trade theorist was Francis Wayland (1796–1865), the Baptist president of Brown University from 1827 to 1855. Wayland was a conservative who believed that the real basis of a sound economy was popular morality. His social ideals centered around personal liberty and the sanctity of private contracts. The making of profits, he declared, was a basic human right. Banks and corporations were useful institutions whose faults, where there were faults, lay not in the concerns themselves but in the legislation that had brought them into being. Labor unions were unnecessary and unjust, wages being properly determined by competition. Protection of business interests by the tariff was equally a menace to a sound social order.

Protective tariffs, said Wayland, were subsidies paid to the industrialists by the rest of the community. They resulted in a vicious spiral wherein tariffs and prices rose while production declined. They distorted the economy by the special favors they conferred, by making it a prey and sport of lobbies and special interests, and by nourishing weak industries that had no right to existence in a healthy economy. They represented an illegitimate extension of the power of government, for "the interference of society with the concerns of the individual, even when arising from the most innocent motives, will always tend to crush the spirit of enterprise, and cripple the productive energies of a country."[23]

Wayland's influence was considerable. His *Elements of Political Economy* went into numerous editions and its views were spread abroad in popular abridgments. A school of imitators sprang up in the

[22] Parke Godwin, *A Biography of William Cullen Bryant* (2 vols., New York, 1883), I, 253–260, 325–326; Allan Nevins, *The Evening Post* (New York, 1922), pp. 350–351, 356, 361.

[23] Francis Wayland, *Elements of Political Economy* (Boston, 1837), p. 152.

textbook field. He had a significant impact upon the thought of his generation.[24]

Another social and political philosopher of the early nineteenth century who had a marked influence upon the thought of the Jacksonian era was John Taylor of Caroline (1753–1824). Taylor was a Virginia planter, lawyer, and Revolutionary War veteran with a taste for politics. A stout Jeffersonian, he was an opponent of "consolidation" of power in the national government, and of the broad construction of the Constitution so dear to the hearts of the Hamiltonian school of thought. He could be counted upon to come to the defense of states' rights when these were challenged by the federal government.

Taylor's economic thinking was hostile to the development of the business community. In his view, it was the farmer who produced the wealth of the country, and the farmer was a "blood brother" of the town mechanic in his economic interest. Farmers were men of easy conscience, for they were men of virtue. It was not without significance, in Taylor's view, that Paradise was generally conceived of as an agricultural society.

Farming was the nation's true foundation. The capitalists of the towns and cities, on the other hand, produced little save economic burdens for the virtuous agrarians. Protective tariffs and other unjust bounties showered upon industry were in reality loads upon the rest of the population. The tariff especially was "a tax upon the rich and poor of the whole community, all being consumers, for the exclusive benefit of the rich of one occupation. This is aristocracy in its worst character." Indeed, the wealth acquired by manufacturing and industry in general was chiefly acquired, Taylor held, at the expense of the agrarian class. The business class was a parasite class which used banks, funding systems, paper money, and corporations to build up an aristocracy more powerful than those of priestcraft or feudalism.

The role of government, Taylor held, should be minimal. It might assist society in such matters as furnishing aid in soil conservation and disseminating information about useful tools of production, but, like any dangerous instrument, it should be used with the greatest caution. The utmost favor it could render farmers and mechanics was neither to help nor to hurt them.

Taylor's fundamental theme was that the virtuous political and economic principles of the Revolutionary era were being supplanted

[24] Dorfman, *The Economic Mind,* II, 758–770.

by the shibboleths of a foreign, nonproductive, monopolistic business system. This was sapping the foundations of the country and destroying the security and freedom of the one productive class—the agriculturists. His goal was the maintenance of a vigorous agrarian society, a goal that seemed to him all the more realistic since he believed that the United States would remain predominantly agrarian for at least two hundred years.

The thinking of John Taylor of Caroline was immensely influential in the Jacksonian era. It was basic to the thought of Calhoun, McDuffie, and other southern leaders of the planter class. It was one factor in the reluctance, and often the downright aversion, with which powerful elements in the Jacksonian Democracy greeted the rise of the business community. It was, still later, a factor in the South-North struggle that precipitated the Civil War, and traces of it may even be discerned in the Populist and Progressive movements at the end of the nineteenth century.[25]

Rivaling the ideas of Taylor in influence were the views of William M. Gouge (1796–1863). This Philadelphian was at various times a newspaper editor and a free-lance writer on economic subjects. He was also a Treasury clerk under Levi Woodbury from 1834 to 1841. Gouge's most influential work, published in 1833, was *A Short History of Paper Money and Banking in the United States, Including an Account of Provincial and Continental Paper Money to which is Prefixed an Inquiry into the Principles of the System, with Consideration of Its Effects on Morals and Happiness.* His writings, says a competent critic, were "shallow, flashy, and journalistic,"[26] but in his day he was regarded by many as a great authority. He was certainly the principal economic theorist of Jacksonian Democracy.

Gouge held very positive views about the nature of money. Real money, he declared, was wealth, just like flour, iron, or any other commodity. Its value was a compound of its utility and its scarcity. Gold and silver made the best money, for they were durable and their

[25] Taylor's philosophy is best studied in his *An Inquiry Into the Principles and Policy of the Government of the United States* (new ed., New Haven, 1950), which contains an excellent introduction by Roy F. Nichols; and in Eugene T. Mudge, *The Social Philosophy of John Taylor of Caroline* (New York, 1939). There is a brief but perceptive sketch, "John Taylor," in the *Dictionary of American Biography* (21 vols., New York, 1928–44), XVIII, 331–333.

[26] Hammond, *Banks and Politics*, p. 298.

values were easily ascertainable. No nation had ever arrived at great wealth without the use of gold and silver money, and there had never been any instance of "a nation's endeavouring to supplant this *natural* money, by the use of paper money, without involving itself in distress and embarrassment."

Bank notes, said Gouge, constituted an artificial and dangerous inflation of the currency. Their emission led to booms and panics and gave the bankers who issued them an unfair advantage in what should be equally open to everyone—the making of profits. The ordinary citizen had a better chance of winning in a fairly conducted lottery than he did in a paper-money system. Gouge disliked all paper-money issues, but grudgingly admitted that it might be necessary to have some large paper bills. Twenty-dollar bills, however, should be the minimum.

Since paper money was so suspect, it naturally followed that banks of issue were dangerous institutions. They substituted inflationary paper for metallic money and thereby fostered unsound systems of credit. They were also dangerous because of their form. They were corporations.

Banking corporations, like corporations in general, said Gouge, were incompatible with equality of rights. "Corporations are unfavorable to the progress of national wealth. As the Argus eyes of private interest do not watch over their concerns, their affairs are much more carelessly and much more expensively conducted than those of individuals." They could succeed, Gouge asserted, only if they achieved monopolies, or the advantages of monopolies. They were also suspect because they never died, and because they had a complete want of moral feeling. Gouge quoted with approval an English writer who had said that "Corporations have neither bodies to be kicked, nor souls to be damned."

Gouge's ideal was a free society in which opportunity should remain substantially equal for all. This opportunity would be used by the individual to achieve that affluence which was a natural and just reward of industry in the United States. Inequality of condition would be one of the characteristics of this society, but only the inequality that springs from natural conditions such as skill, prudence, industry, economy, and enterprise. All institutions, all laws, that gave some members of the community advantage over the rest should be destroyed or most obstinately resisted.

Gouge wanted a minimum of rules and regulations in his social order, for he felt that legislation often fostered privilege. The best social system, in his opinion, was one "in which there should be no laws or institutions of any kind except such as are absolutely necessary. . . ."

Obviously, the ideal government for such a society would be one that kept its activities at a minimum. Its financial operations, for instance, should be limited to collecting, safekeeping, and disbursing the public moneys. "Further than this, Government should have no more concern with Banking and brokerage than it has with baking and tailoring."

How should such a government be established? Gouge answered that it should be done through the efforts of the farmers and mechanics. They should control the government, and they should see to it that society was safeguarded from the dangers inherent in banks, corporations, and other institutions of privilege. Political leadership, Gouge felt, should come from the rural regions. The farmers of the country were least subject to corrupt financial pressures, and they had the strongest of motives for establishing a society that would be good because it would be free.[27]

Such was the trend of Gouge's thought. He was alarmed by the inequities he saw developing in American society. He sought to eliminate these inequities by destroying the practices and institutions which had given them birth. His fear of paper money, his dislike of banks and other corporations, his emphasis on small government and on a free society, were all reflected, as was his tendency to confuse freedom and equality, in the thought and the policies of the Jacksonians.

[27] William M. Gouge, *A Short History of Paper Money and Banking in the United States* (Philadelphia, 1833). The above paragraphs are based on a careful study of the book. See especially pp. 7 ff., 41, 44, 51, 52, 78 f., 91, 97–98, 118–122, 124, 133, 140, 230, 235.

CHAPTER 2

Launching the Jacksonian Ship of State

THE OFTEN conflicting interest and prejudices of the farmers and of the growing business class, the aspirations of the urban laborers, the ambitions of political leaders, all served as background for the political activity of the Jacksonian period. It was inevitable that political parties should be wary in their choice of issues, and that they should plot their programs of action with the utmost care. Only by so doing could they hope to establish voting strength and maintain an organization that would give them victories in the national elections.

This wariness of real issues led the politicians in the campaign of 1828 to rely chiefly upon misrepresentation and personal abuse. That canvass was a bitter one, and the National Republican supporters of John Quincy Adams contributed their share of the bitterness. They denounced Andrew Jackson as ignorant and hot-tempered, an irresponsible butcher of men, a liar and a blasphemer, a coconspirator with Aaron Burr. They asserted, with smirks and sneers, that he had lived in sin with his Rachel before they had been legally married. They cited Jefferson as declaring that this wild Tennesseean was unfit for the Presidency, and that his election would be dangerous to the public safety.[1]

The supporters of Andrew Jackson were not to be outdone by the National Republicans in the field of scurrility. Posing as crusaders for

[1] *National Intelligencer,* Sept. 4, 29, Oct. 6, 1828; Clay Papers, XII, Porter to Clay, Mar. 26, 1828; Porter Papers, Clay to Porter, Apr. 2, 1828; *View of General Jackson's Domestic Relations,* American Antiquarian Society, pp. 8–9.

retrenchment and reform, they denounced Adams and his party in unmeasured terms. "Look! Look! Look!" shrieked Isaac Hill's *New Hampshire Patriot,* which then went on to spread the news that every Federalist was for Adams, including all the living members of the Hartford Convention. As for "King John the second," he was portrayed as an unprincipled hypocrite whose mania for office had brought him money from the public treasury equal to sixteen dollars a day from the date of his birth. Corrupted by long residence in European courts, especially the Russian court, where he had prostituted a beautiful American girl to the carnal desires of Czar Alexander I, he had come back to his country a menace to its most sacred institutions. He hated popular government, and inwardly detested the heroes of the American Revolution. A Sabbath breaker, he had ridden "like mad" through New England on Sundays, arrayed in a jockey's costume and creating a general disturbance on the Lord's day. He had wormed his way into the Presidency by a corrupt bargain with that Judas of the West, Henry Clay, and there he had lived extravagantly, wasting the people's money on such fripperies as silk inexpressibles, a billiard table, and a blue portfolio embroidered with chenille and decorated with gold tassels, costing one hundred dollars. He was the fit representative of a party which consisted of those who despised democracy and battened on the sufferings of the poor.[2]

The election of 1828 was not fought over great issues. Few elections are. Questions important to the nation, it is true, were before the public eye—the tariff, land policy, internal improvements—but on these questions there were no clear-cut party stands. It was, rather, chicanery, slippery tactics, and downright falsehoods upon which the politicians relied to win the contest.[3]

It was, nevertheless, a significant election. The voters swept the Military Chieftain into office by a decisive victory. The West, the South, and New York and Pennsylvania gave Jackson 178 votes in the Electoral College to 83 for Adams. This was due to a variety of causes. It may possibly be attributed to a desire on the part of the plain people

[2] Richmond *Semi-Weekly Inquirer,* Sept. 23, Oct. 3, 7, 10, 1828; *National Intelligencer,* Oct. 27, 1828; *New Hampshire Patriot,* Jan. 7, Feb. 4, Mar. 10, 11, May 12, June 2, July 28, Sept. 22, 29, 1828; John B. McMaster, *A History of the People of the United States* (8 vols., New York, 1883–1914), V, 510–515.

[3] Professor Channing observes that "possibly it was more honorable to have been defeated in 1828 than to have been elected." Edward Channing, *A History of the United States* (6 vols., New York, 1912–25), V, 376.

for a government that would be more responsive to their needs and interests. It may be that slavery was a hidden issue, for Jackson was a slaveholder and Adams was an opponent of slavery.[4] But it was chiefly the result of adroit leadership on the part of the Jacksonians and of Jackson's reputation, both as a hero and as a plain, simple, virtuous man of the people.[5]

Whatever the complex of factors responsible for the result, it certainly represented a swing from control by the National Republicans, a party dominated by wealth and conservatism, to the Jacksonion Democracy, a party which, though not led by the plain people, was to prove itself aware of their problems and of their voting potential.

"The Aristocracy and the Democracy of the country are arrayed against each other," exultantly wrote New York Democratic leader Michael Hoffman to his friend Azariah Flagg.[6] This, Hoffman felt, would make future electioneering easy. The matter, however, was not quite as simple as that.

The National Republican party, headed by Adams, Clay, and Daniel Webster, had its center of gravity in New England and elements of very considerable strength in New York, Pennsylvania, New Jersey, Maryland, and Kentucky. Local issues and the personalities of its leaders had played a considerable part in its formation. Its adherents constituted a mixture of industrialists, business leaders, farmers, laborers, and mechanics who believed that high tariffs and internal improvements at national expense would be beneficial to themselves and to the country. Those who accepted the idea of a strong central government with widening administrative powers—a Hamiltonian viewpoint that was dear to the heart of John Quincy Adams—naturally gravitated into the party of which Old Man Eloquent was the leader. People who saw the value of the Second Bank of the United States as a bulwark of sound currency and credit, who

[4] Arthur M. Schlesinger, Jr., *The Age of Jackson* (Boston, 1945), pp. 15–42; Samuel F. Bemis, *John Quincy Adams and the Union* (New York, 1956), p. 149. Bemis says that slavery was "the most significant issue" of the election. But see Frederick J. Turner, *The United States, 1830–1850* (New York, 1935), p. 36. Turner indicates that, in the South, Adams showed his greatest strength where slaves were most abundant.

[5] What, said the Albany *Signs of the Times,* if Jackson does make errors in spelling? So did Washington and George Clinton. It isn't necessary to be a college teacher to be President of the United States. *New Hampshire Patriot,* Apr. 21, May 5, 1828.

[6] Flagg Papers, Hoffman to Flagg, Nov. 8, 1828.

glimpsed a future of material progress directly fostered by the policies of the national government, and who were by nature conservative in their social outlook were likely to find themselves in the ranks of the National Republicans—cheek by jowl with speculators and gamblers in the country's future who desired a currency and credit more ample than safe. National Republicanism was a loosely organized, volatile political entity, if entity it could be called. Its outstanding characteristics were its nationalism, its confidence in the business class, and its optimism about the nation's future.

The Jacksonian Democrats of 1828 were still wont to refer to themselves as "Republicans," thus paying tribute to their Jeffersonian heritage. Their centers of strength lay in the West and the South, although they were also powerful in the poorer farming districts of Pennsylvania, New York, and Massachusetts. The development of the early Jackson party in Ohio and, to some extent, in Tennessee indicates that in those states there was very little difference in the social and economic status of the Jacksonians and the opposition. This was probably the case throughout the West.[7]

The Democracy's rise to power in the West was largely due to the fame of the Hero of New Orleans, and to the skillful use of local issues, a combination of factors which played an important part in other sections of the nation as well. There was also a tendency in all parts of the country for debtors desirous of cheap money, and therefore hostile to the Bank of the United States and to a Supreme Court that had declared bankruptcy and relief laws invalid,[8] to gravitate into the Democratic ranks. There, too, were to be found local bankers who disliked Nicholas Biddle's big bank in Philadelphia, and southern planters who were coming to hate protective tariffs and to look with suspicion upon national support to internal improvements for which the South had little use. Workers who were envious of the rich, and fearful of exploitation by the business class, were apt to vote Democratic. Idealists, alarmed by concentrations of power and anxious to preserve both liberty and equality, were attracted to the Democracy. And, to

[7] Harry R. Stevens, *The Early Jackson Party in Ohio* (Durham, N.C., 1957), pp. 147–64 and *passim;* Charles G. Sellers, Jr., "Jackson Men with Feet of Clay," *American Historical Review,* LXII (Apr., 1957), 537–551; Thomas P. Abernethy, *From Frontier to Plantation in Tennessee* (Chapel Hill, 1932), pp. 239–49, 262–76; Marvin Meyers, *The Jacksonian Persuasion* (Stanford, 1957), p. 5.

[8] Sturgis *v.* Crowninshield, 1819.

compound the mixture further, a considerable sprinkling of old Federalists, men like Roger B. Taney of Maryland, James Buchanan of Pennsylvania, and William Drayton of South Carolina, anxious for political preferment and sensitive to the handicap of their Federalist background in this day of rapidly growing manhood suffrage, moved into the Democracy as a means of removing the stigma of their aristocratic past.

At the head of this motley host of the Democracy, with all of its conflicting interests and aims, strode the Old Hero of the Hermitage, now the people's choice. He was a man who lacked formal education, and who always found it difficult to learn of others, though he could, on occasion, take advice. He was a man of violent and sometimes ignorant prejudices. But he also had great courage and strength of will, together with a driving force seldom equaled in the annals of the Presidency. Flanking him on either side and casting suspicious glances toward one another (for both desired to succeed him in the Presidency) were the suave and astute Martin Van Buren of New York, known as the "Red Fox of Kinderhook," and the humorless, intense logician of the South, John Caldwell Calhoun. Bluff Senator Thomas Hart Benton of Missouri strode pompously in the front ranks, although a little behind Van Buren and Calhoun.

Since both the National Republicans and the Jacksonian Democrats represented uneasy congeries of interests, it was the duty of their leaders to mold programs of action that would not only keep each party intact but also draw to it support from the ranks of the opposition. Adams no longer attempted to do this, for with defeat he had abandoned the responsibilities of leadership. But Clay, Webster, Jackson, Van Buren, and Calhoun had this obligation very much on their minds as the day approached for the Old Hero to take over the reins of government.

Inauguration day, 1829, marked the close of a Washington winter so severe that some of the poor froze to death in the nation's capital.[9] But now the bitter cold had given way to balmy weather, and for days, on horse and on foot, thousands of sightseers and well-wishers converged upon Washington, intent upon witnessing the inauguration. They swamped the inns and other lodging places. They crowded the streets. And on the great day itself they packed the area in front of the

[9] Margaret Bayard Smith, *The First Forty Years of Washington Society* (New York, 1908), p. 283.

Capitol where Jackson, dressed all in black out of reverence for the memory of his beloved wife, Rachel, delivered his inaugural address.

The Hero's first message to the people was scarcely impressive. Reading in a voice so low that only those in his immediate vicinity heard a word of it, he promised to perform the duties of the executive branch without transcending them; straddled, not very gracefully, on the tariff and internal improvements; pledged economy and the extinguishment of the national debt—"the unnecessary duration of which is incompatible with real independence"; promised reform to all.[10]

The inaugural over, Jackson went down Pennsylvania Avenue to the President's House, and the crowd followed hard on his heels. A reception had been prepared at the presidential mansion. The people, "from the highest and most polished down to the most vulgar and gross in the nation," wrote eyewitness Justice Joseph Story, pushed into the grounds and into the house itself. All order dissolved. There was a mad rush to congratulate the Hero and to get a share of the punch, ice cream, cake, and lemonade. Cut glass and china were smashed in the ensuing melee, ladies fainted, men's noses were bloodied. The President, saved by a cordon of his friends from being pressed against the wall, or even trampled, had to make his escape by a back door to his rooms at Gadsby's Tavern. The mansion was only saved from further damage by taking the bowls of punch out on the lawn, the crowd following the refreshment.

Thus the democracy demonstrated its devotion and its caprice. And thus the people's leader was started upon his presidential career. To fastidious Justice Story "the reign of King 'Mob'" seemed triumphant.[11]

The Cabinet had been in the making long before the inaugural ceremonies took place. It reflected, to some extent, the uneasy coalition of sectional interests that went to make up Jacksonian Democracy. Van Buren, Secretary of State, was from New York; Samuel D. Ingham of Pennsylvania was at the Treasury; John Branch of North Carolina at the Navy, and John M. Berrien of Georgia was made the

[10] James D. Richardson, *Messages and Papers of the Presidents* (11 vols., New York, 1910), II, 999–1001.

[11] Van Buren Papers, Jas. A. Hamilton to Van Buren, Mar. 5, 1829; Smith, *Washington Society*, pp. 283, 284, 290–296; William W. Story (ed.), *Life and Letters of Joseph Story* (2 vols., Boston, 1851), I, 563; Washington *City Chronicle*, Mar. 7, 1829.

Attorney General. The Postmaster General, "General" William T. Barry, was from Kentucky, and John H. Eaton, Secretary of War, came from Jackson's own state of Tennessee.

Neither Van Buren nor Calhoun had much to say about the composition of the Cabinet, although, as events were to prove, Calhoun had more supporters there than had the Red Fox of Kinderhook. Jackson had made the decisions, and he was proud of his handiwork. It was, he boasted, "one of the strongest . . . that have ever been in the United States." Actually, save for Van Buren, it was composed of mediocrities, or worse, and was destined to be of little use to its chief.[12]

More important than the Cabinet itself was a shifting group of men about the President who gradually came to be known as the "Kitchen Cabinet." The most influential member of this coterie was undoubtedly Secretary of State Martin Van Buren, a skillful, intelligent leader, seasoned by years of struggle in the turmoil of New York State politics.

Next in importance in the Kitchen Cabinet was the Fourth Auditor of the Treasury, Amos Kendall. This son of New England had migrated to Kentucky and for a time had been in the pay of Henry Clay. Later, as editor of the Frankfort (Kentucky) *Argus,* Kendall had championed relief laws for debtors. Clay, an opponent of these laws, had offered Kendall a government job in Washington, early in Adams' administration. Kendall had been willing enough to take this position. He then had no preference between Adams and Jackson and he declared that he would take "some pride in vindicating you [Clay] from the aspersions with which your enemies would overwhelm you." But the post offered was refused, since it paid only $1,000 and Kendall wanted $1,500. A year later, probably because the Kentucky Jacksonians threatened to publish a rival newspaper, Kendall came out for Jackson. Clay thereupon took the federal government's printing away from the *Argus.* From that time on, Kendall was a vitriolic opponent of both Clay and Adams, and a most fiery supporter of the Hero. Brought to Washington on the Jacksonian payroll, he wrote, or at least

[12] Van Buren Papers, Cambreleng to Van Buren, Mar. 1, 1829, Louis McLane to Van Buren, Feb. 19, 1829, Jas A. Hamilton to Van Buren, Feb. 12, 13, 16, 18, Mar. 25, 1829, Thomas Ritchie to Van Buren, Mar. 27, 1829; Jackson Papers (second series), Jackson to J. C. McLemore, Apr. 1, 1829; James A. Hamilton, *Reminiscences of James A. Hamilton* (New York, 1869), pp. 87–103, 215–16; John S. Bassett, *The Life of Andrew Jackson* (2 vols., New York, 1911), II, 409–420.

drafted, many of Jackson's state papers. He was a skillful intriguer, and a vindictive partisan.[13]

A third member of this group was Isaac Hill, Second Comptroller of the Treasury until the Senate refused his confirmation. Hill had been editor of the *New Hampshire Patriot* and was a party man through and through. He was also a cripple and inclined to be bitter in spirit. Always ready to raise the cry of the poor against the rich, he was yet conservative by nature, had supported the conservative William Harris Crawford and the caucus system of presidential nomination in 1824, had championed a protective tariff, and in later years became a successful businessman. His ethics may be judged by his circulation of the story that Adams had acted as procurer for the Czar, and by his advertising in the *Patriot* a quack medicine for which he was acting as agent. Hill's influence was considerable during Jackson's first term.[14]

Francis Preston Blair, who came from Kentucky, where he had succeeded Kendall as editor of the Frankfort *Argus,* was a fourth member of the Kitchen Cabinet. A frail man, sharp-faced, but insignificant in general appearance (he weighed only a little over one hundred pounds), Blair was summoned to Washington by Kendall in the name of Jackson's friends. His task was to edit the Washington *Globe,* a paper which took for its motto "The world is governed too much," and which was created to extol the administration's virtues and to defend it against its critics. The *Globe* performed its duties to perfection, for Blair was a skillful publicist and a master of political invective. A political realist of the first order, he contributed a good deal to the stability of the party, while he exasperated Jackson's opponents. Some years later, David Campbell, governor of Virginia, wrote to William C. Rives: "I know the editor of the *Globe well* altho I never saw him since he was a small boy. He was born in Abingdon. I have a perfect knowledge of the character of his family and himself—and that knowledge would induce me to have very little confidence in him."[15]

Another of these intimates of Jackson was Major William B. Lewis

[13] Henry Clay Papers, Kendall to Clay, Apr. 28, Oct. 4, 1825; Joseph Desha Papers (Library of Congress), Desha to Kendall, May 6, 1831, Kendall to Desha, June 2, 1831; Glyndon G. Van Deusen, *The Life of Henry Clay* (Boston, 1937), pp. 217–218; Schlesinger, *Age of Jackson,* pp. 68–69.

[14] Bemis, *Adams,* p. 147; *New Hampshire Patriot,* Nov. 8, 1824, January 21, 1828, and *passim.*

[15] William C. Rives Papers, Campbell to Rives, June 15, 1837.

of Tennessee. For years Lewis had worked to make Jackson President, and when the great day came he had been summoned to accompany the Hero to Washington. There he lived in the White House, his expenses being met by his salary as Second Auditor of the Treasury. He was a shrewd, farsighted, subtle politician. Too conservative for some of Jackson's friends, he sometimes found himself in disagreement with White House policy on important issues, but the old General stubbornly kept him in his confidence.

From time to time, other men were high in Jackson's favor and might even be called members of this inner circle. Such were Roger Brooks Taney of Maryland, later Secretary of the Treasury and Chief Justice of the Supreme Court; or Edward Livingston, United States senator from Louisiana, later Secretary of State and Minister to France; or even Jackson's old friend and future enemy, Senator Hugh Lawson White of Tennessee.

Individual members of the Kitchen Cabinet had considerable influence with Jackson, especially in matters of press and patronage. Much of the administration's policy—just how much we shall never know—was distilled from the minds of these men. But it was in essence an ever-changing body of informal advisers, rather than an organized, behind-the-scenes power that dictated the policies of the Old Chief's administrations.

The new administration was no sooner installed than it set about fulfilling its promise of retrenchment and reform. Efforts were made to cut down the cost of government. Kendall estimated that over $50,000 was saved in the Treasury Department within a year, and that at least $280,000 in savings resulted from uncovering peculations in the customhouses and among other receivers of public money. There was some reduction in the numbers and therefore in the amount of salaries paid to customs inspectors, and the consular service was shaken up. Such steps were in accord with campaign promises and they resulted in some temporary savings.

Over-all Treasury expenditures, which in 1828 were $16,394,843, fell to a little over 15 million a year in 1829 and again in 1830. The civil, miscellaneous, and diplomatic expenses were reduced from $3,676,052.64 in 1828 to $3,237,416.04 in 1830. The cost of the naval establishment was reduced almost $700,000, from $3,925,867.13 to $3,239,428.63, in 1830.

The retrenchment effort, however, was spotty and scarcely spectacular. Postal deficits increased, jumping from $30,030 in 1828 to $82,125 in 1830. The cost of the military establishment, which in 1828 was $5,719,956.06, rose in 1830 to $6,752,688.66. By 1833 the cost of the Navy was back where it had been in Adams' last year of office. Expenditures in the executive departments, which had been just over $500,000 in 1828, rose to $542,000 in 1830 and to $658,608.41 in 1833. Treasury expenditure, which had started bravely downward in 1829 and 1830, had risen to some $23 million in 1833. Jacksonian retrenchment was not general and it was mostly temporary.[16]

Reform went further than the removal of a few clerks and customs inspectors in the interest of honesty and economy. The President regarded rotation in office as "a leading principle in the republican creed,"[17] and during his administrations it was established as a practice in the federal government.

Jackson was not simply a spoilsman. He wanted to remove inefficient officeholders and punish corrupt ones, such as the embezzler Tobias Watkins, Kendall's predecessor in the Treasury. The President held correctly that the idea of property right in office is un-American, and that rotation in office gives the people a sense of sharing in their own government. And it is only fair to add that the removals under Jackson were not nearly so sweeping as his excited opponents tried to make out. During the first year and a half of his Presidency, only 919 officeholders out of 10,093 were removed. During his eight years in office, something less than one-fifth (probably nearer one-tenth) of all federal officeholders were turned out. This was scarcely wholesale proscription.[18]

But "turning the rascals out" went further than removal for just cause. There can be no doubt that Jackson thought of removals and appointments as being conditioned, at least in part, by loyalty or lack of loyalty to him. It was also easy to importune him into very improper appointments, and he seems to have done little to restrain such politicians as Isaac Hill and Postmaster General Barry from using the patronage with more emphasis on partisanship than on efficiency. It

[16] Senate Documents, 21st Congress, first session, Document No. 3, pp. 26–30; Executive Documents, 22nd Cong., first sess., Doc. No. 3, pp. 35–41; Senate Documents, 23rd Cong., second sess., Doc. No. 2, pp. 22–33; *Historical Statistics of the United States, 1789–1945* (Washington, 1949), p. 301.

[17] Richardson, *Messages and Papers,* II, 1012.

[18] Erik McK. Eriksson, "The Federal Civil Service under President Jackson," *Mississippi Valley Historical Review,* XIII (Mar., 1927), 527–529.

is small wonder that as shrewd a Democratic observer as Gideon Welles of Connecticut, looking back in 1838 at the Jacksonian regime, should have deplored the Hero's laxity in the use of the appointive power. Welles noted that as a result of Jackson's policy, "office-seeking and office-getting was becoming a regular business, where impudence triumphed over worth."[19] Thus used, rotation in office lowered the prestige and the standards of public service.

The spoils system was to prove a creeping blight through the years. It threatened paralysis of the national party organization because it inevitably increased the power of local political machines. It fostered the appointment of party hacks and the consequent degradation of the administration of government. The Hero from the Hermitage must bear a heavy load of responsibility for the development of these evils in the national government, although it is doubtful that he perceived them. He saw administration in terms of individual officeholders, rather than as a process of government.[20]

"Retrenchment and reform" had come in with a blare of trumpets, but its promise had been scarcely fulfilled. Inefficiency in the public service not only persisted but was in fact augmented. In place of Tobias Watkins, embezzler under John Quincy Adams, there appeared under the Jacksonians one Samuel Swartwout, an embezzler on a much grander scale. In the perspective of history, the administration of Old Man Eloquent compares very favorably for honesty and efficiency with that of Andrew Jackson.

There is little to indicate that Old Hickory had a well-thought-out philosophy of party or of government. There is more evidence that the Jacksonian policies derived from belief in the worth (and the voting strength) of the common man, the importance of equality of opportunity for all, and the necessity of national unity. As the years went by, the leadership of the party became more and more intent upon basing political democracy squarely upon economic democracy. Thus it remained faithful to the Jeffersonian idealism that was its heritage.

[19] Van Buren Papers, Welles to Silas Wright, Apr. 27, 1838.

[20] Leonard D. White, *The Jacksonians: A Study in Administrative History, 1829–61* (New York, 1954), pp. 5, 33, 300–303, 318–320, 326–346; Carl R. Fish, *The Civil Service and the Patronage* (New York, 1905), pp. 105–133. See also Jackson Papers (second series), Kendall to Jackson, Nov. 19, 1828, Jackson to J. C. McLemore, Apr., 1829; Welles Papers, J. M. Niles to Welles, Feb. 19, 1829, Amos Kendall to Welles, Sept. 13, 1830; Van Buren Papers, Thomas Ritchie to Van Buren, Mar. 27, 1829.

At the same time, the Jacksonians were to find very difficult indeed the problem of reconciling their ideas of "little government," and their suspicions of industrialism, with the facts of the economic order that was rapidly developing around them. Their problem, and it was one which they fumbled badly, was how to maintain an equality of economic opportunity in the midst of a generation that was both profit-minded and risk-minded.

A second problem, and one that was immediately pressing in 1829, was the maintenance of party solidarity. For, almost at once, sectional interests and personal ambitions threatened to tear the party asunder.

Signs of dissension within the Democracy had begun to appear before Jackson's inauguration. Disappointed office seekers were many, and some of them had powerful friends. Jealousies sprouted right and left. The suave Van Buren, exerting to the utmost his skill in political management, helped Jackson to assuage the heartburnings of those who felt themselves slighted, and speedily found himself a secure place in the General's esteem. This was noted by the Calhoun faction, and jealousy of Van Buren began to grow. It was a delicate situation, made all the more so by the Eaton scandal.

The Secretary of War, at thirty-eight a wealthy widower, had married for the second time on New Year's Day, 1829. His bride, six years his junior, was the beautiful and vivacious Margaret (Peggy) O'Neale Timberlake, daughter of a Washington tavern keeper, and herself the widow of a navy purser.

Eaton had stayed at various times at the O'Neale tavern, and rumor had linked his name with Peggy's even before the death of her husband. Timberlake had committed suicide, and the story spread that he had cut his throat because of his wife's entanglement with Eaton. The infatuated Tennesseean had consulted Jackson about the situation and Old Hickory, who knew Peggy and liked her, had approved matrimony as a means of stopping the gossip. But the marriage had occurred only four months after Timberlake's death, and the tongues had wagged more furiously than ever. The character of the gossip was typified by Churchill Cambreleng's comment to Van Buren that the wedding reminded him of Swift's remark on such unions ". . . about using a certain household . . . and then putting it on one's head."[21]

Now Eaton was in the Cabinet, and everyone was asking how his

[21] Van Buren Papers, Cambreleng to Van Buren, Jan. 1, 1829.

wife would be received by Washington society. The question was soon answered. Floride Calhoun, wife of the Vice-President, refused to have anything to do with Peggy, and the ladies of the Cabinet followed the example thus set.

Jackson was furious. "I did not come here," he declared, "to make a Cabinet for the Ladies of this place, but for the Nation. . . ."[22] Peggy was "chaste as a virgin," in the General's eyes, and he tried to convince everyone of the truth of this assertion.

The husbands of the Cabinet ladies now found themselves in an embarrassing situation. Not so Van Buren, who was a widower. He took pains to be courteous to Peggy, arranging dinner parties in her honor, and his stock with the General rose accordingly. The latter, at first convinced that Clay was at the bottom of Peggy's difficulties, finally laid the blame squarely on the shoulders of the Calhouns; and as Van Buren's prestige rose, that of his rival went down.[23]

"The Eaton Malaria," as Van Buren dubbed it, showed that Jackson was a man of strong prejudices. There was plenty of other evidence to the same effect. The General showed small respect for Cabinet opinion as such, treating his Cabinet not as a council of state, but as so many individual officers bound to do his bidding or resign. His Cabinet met only sporadically, and then more for the purpose of enabling him to hear opinions on matters that he deemed important than as a meeting of equals gathered together to determine policy.[24] Jackson usually made his own decisions, and before his first year in office had ended he had arrived at some specific ideas regarding public policy.

Old Hickory's first communication to Congress, December 8, 1829, manifested his determination to maintain America's rights abroad. It also made it clear that he stood only for the most cautious steps toward tariff reduction, that he believed in distribution of the surplus revenue (once the national debt had been extinguished), and that he was

22 Jackson Papers (second series), Jackson to J. C. McLemore, Apr. 1, 1829.

23 *Ibid.*, also a Jackson memorandum [1831?]; Peggy Eaton, *Autobiography* (New York, 1932), *passim;* Queena Pollack, *Peggy Eaton, Democracy's Mistress* (New York, 1931), p. 81; Ben: Perley Poore, *Reminiscences* (2 vols., Philadelphia, 1886), I, 122–125.

24 Richard P. Longaker, "Was Jackson's Kitchen Cabinet a Cabinet?" *Mississippi Valley Historical Review,* XLIV (June, 1957), 94–108; Albert Somit, "New Papers: Some Sidelights upon Jacksonian Administration," *ibid.*, XXXV (June, 1948), 91–98; William MacDonald, *Jacksonian Democracy* (New York, 1906), pp. 226–228.

definitely suspicious of the Bank of the United States. Here was no pussyfooter, a fact that was made all the more evident as the "interposition" of state sovereignty between the people and the national government came to hang like a black cloud over the land.

During the eighteen-twenties, as the business interests of the North had pushed the tariff higher and higher, the South had become increasingly restive. That agricultural region had finally been stung to fury by the 1828 "Tariff of Abominations." There resulted a crescendo of protest, led by South Carolina, and the development of opposition based on a combination of history and political philosophy. Its theory was that the Union had been established by the state governments, that the powers of the Union were distinctly limited, and that any of its acts which exceeded those powers could quite properly be nullified by state action.

Calhoun had given force and logic to this line of thought by his South Carolina Exposition (1828). The United States government, declared the Exposition, is specifically granted the taxing power only for the purpose of raising revenue. Any protection resulting from such a tariff must be purely incidental. The tariff of 1828, and the protective system in general, were, therefore, "unconstitutional, unequal, and oppressive, and calculated to corrupt the public virtue and destroy the liberty of the country." They made Southerners "the serfs of the system,—out of whose labor is raised, not only the money paid into the Treasury, but the funds out of which are drawn the rich rewards of the manufacturer and his associates in interest. Their encouragement is our discouragement."

The existing protective system, said Calhoun, had the effect of a tax of 45 per cent levied upon southern exports for the benefit of a moneyed aristocracy. It enshrined exploitation and privilege, and its inevitable tendency was to make the rich richer and the poor poorer.

Calhoun recognized that the North outnumbered the South two to one in population, and that it might, therefore, invoke the principle of majority rule in regard to tariff legislation. He found a constitutional remedy for this in the right of interposition by a state against "the despotism of the many." Authority for interposition by a state against the "unconstitutional" acts of the national government, he declared, is authorized in the writings of Hamilton, Madison, and Jefferson, and by the very nature of the Union as laid down in the Constitution.

Interposition, in Calhoun's eyes, was one of the powers reserved to the states, and "the omission to enumerate the power of the States to interpose in order to protect their rights,—being strictly in accord with the principles on which its framers formed the Constitution, raises not the slightest presumption against its existence." A state could, then, through the instrumentality of a state convention, declare null and void an act of the national government. And if the national government that was coming into office on March 4, 1829, did not effect a return to first principles, especially in the matter of the tariff, the right of nullification could and would be exercised by South Carolina.[25]

This Exposition was presented to the legislature of South Carolina in December, 1828. It was not formally adopted, for the state was then looking hopefully to Jackson for redress of grievance. It was now clear, however, that little in the way of tariff reduction could be hoped for from the Hero. The South, it appeared, was doomed forever to pay tariff-protected prices for the manufactured goods it purchased, whether those goods were produced at home or abroad. The national government was discriminating against the southern states, and nullification of the tariff by the state governments became an increasingly popular idea.

The South had another weapon besides nullification in its armory, one that it also proposed to use. This was, in short, a political alliance of South and West. The Westerners favored cheap land, but Jackson had come out in favor of distribution of the government's surplus revenue to the states as soon as the national debt was liquidated. This would make it difficult to reduce the price of public lands, and the West was alarmed at the prospect. It was, then, only natural that West and South should join hands, the latter section supporting the West's desire for cheap land, while the West, as a *quid pro quo,* supported tariff reduction. Such an alliance was clearly forming at the beginning of Jackson's administration. Its outstanding champions were Senators Thomas Hart Benton of Missouri and Robert Y. Hayne of South Carolina.[26]

It fell to the lot of Senator Samuel A. Foote of Connecticut to

[25] Richard K. Crallé (ed.), *The Works of John C. Calhoun* (6 vols., Charleston and New York, 1853–56), VI, 1–57.

[26] Raynor G. Wellington, *The Political and Sectional Influence of the Public Lands, 1828–42* (Cambridge, 1914), pp. 12–13, 18–34; Charles M. Wiltse, *John C. Calhoun* (3 vols., Indianapolis, 1944–51), II, 53–66.

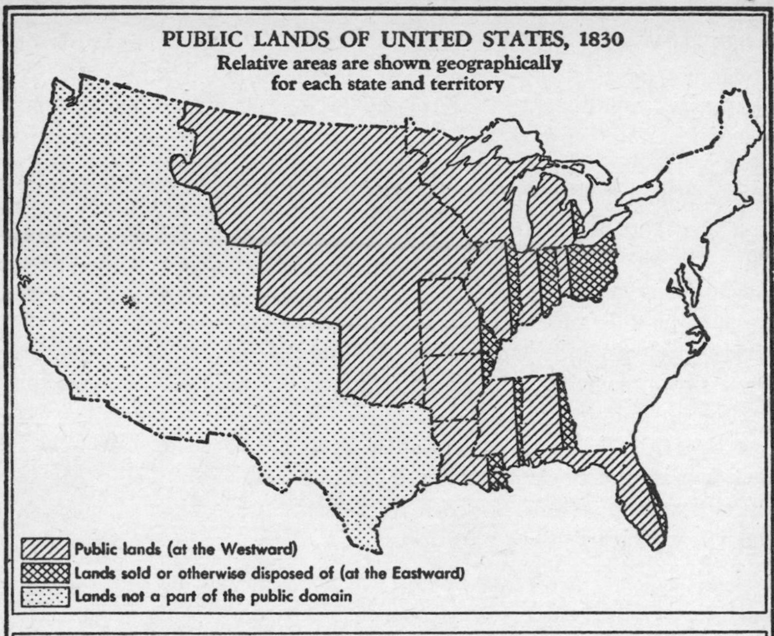
PUBLIC LANDS OF UNITED STATES, 1830
Relative areas are shown geographically
for each state and territory
Public lands (at the Westward)
Lands sold or otherwise disposed of (at the Eastward)
Lands not a part of the public domain

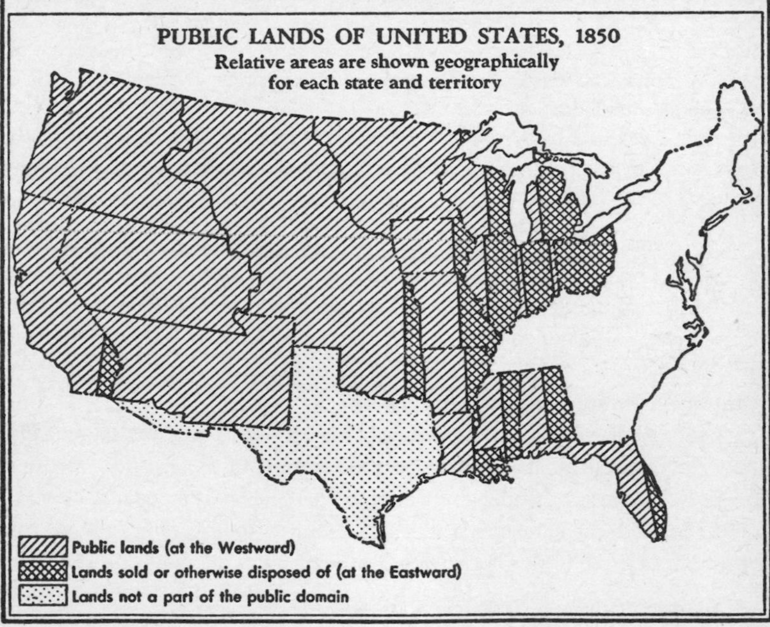
PUBLIC LANDS OF UNITED STATES, 1850
Relative areas are shown geographically
for each state and territory
Public lands (at the Westward)
Lands sold or otherwise disposed of (at the Eastward)
Lands not a part of the public domain

bring this West-South alliance into the open. On December 29, 1829, Foote proposed in the Senate a resolution of inquiry into the expediency of limiting the sale of public lands.[27] Benton, in his rumbling voice, denounced this as an effort to check the settlement of the West so that the East might keep a supply of cheap labor in its factories. Hayne followed with an argument for a cheap land policy, asserting that the national government had dealt in niggardly fashion with the West. He was particularly alarmed at the prospect of using the public lands as a great source of revenue for the national government. Such revenue, he said, was bound to be "a fund for corruption—fatal to the sovereignty and independence of the states. . . . If I had, sir, the powers of a magician, and could, by a wave of my hand, convert this capitol into gold for such a purpose, I would not do it."

Webster, a New Englander and a nationalist, rose to answer both Benton and the South Carolinian. In masterly fashion, the Massachusetts statesman poured scorn upon the states' righters, and upon those who attacked his own section:

> Consolidation!—that perpetual cry, both of terror and delusion—consolidation! . . . The East! the obnoxious, the rebuked, the always reproached East! . . . I deny that the East has, at any time, shown an illiberal policy toward the West. I pronounce the whole accusation to be without the least foundation in any facts, existing either now, or at any previous time. I deny it in the general, and I deny each and all its particulars. I deny the sum total and I deny the detail. I deny that the East has ever manifested hostility to the West, and I deny that she has adopted any policy that would naturally have led her in such a course.

Webster would, he said, offer the public lands at a low but not at a giveaway price. He did not share Hayne's fear of the public revenue becoming a source of corruption. And, far from deprecating the power of the government at Washington, Webster opened up a vista of great and beneficent national government activity, aimed at the development of the nation's wealth and power.

Hayne, high-spirited and eloquent, rose to Webster's challenge. His reply developed the strict constructionist point of view, and defended the right of "interposition" by the states whenever the federal government violated the Constitution. As a counter to the charge that this argument represented a narrowly southern point of view, he dwelt at

[27] *Register of Debates,* 21st Cong., 1st sess., 3–4.

length upon New England's attitude toward the War of 1812, quoting with gusto expressions of antiwar and anti-Union sentiment by various New England politicians and divines, and referring in scathing terms to the Hartford Convention of 1814, where leading New Englanders had defended interposition and had manifested anything but a loyal attitude toward the Union.

Webster, in his famous second reply to Hayne, devoted a part of his speech to Hayne's attack on New England. The Hartford Convention, said Webster, belonged to the past, and it little became the Senator from South Carolina to deride in others the sentiments which he now himself expressed. New England was now thinking, not in terms of sectional or state selfishness, but in terms of the national welfare. Forcefully, Webster went on to denounce nullification as a false and futile doctrine destructive of national unity. He declared that the federal government is the manifestation not of the will of the states but of the people; that the national interest is greater, much greater, than that of any state or section. He closed with his great tribute to the Union, one of the most eloquent passages in all political literature.

> When my eyes shall be turned to behold, for the last time, the sun in heaven, may I not see him shining on the broken and dishonored fragments of a once glorious Union; on States dissevered, discordant, belligerent; on a land rent with civil feuds, or drenched, it may be, in fraternal blood! Let their last feeble and lingering glance, rather, behold the gorgeous ensign of the republic, now known and honored throughout the earth, still full high advanced, its arms and trophies streaming in their original lustre, not a stripe erased or polluted, nor a single star obscured, bearing for its motto no such miserable interrogatory as, What is all this worth? Nor those other words of delusion and folly, Liberty first, and Union afterwards: but everywhere, spread all over in characters of living light, blazing on all its ample folds, as they float over the sea and over the land, and in every wind under the whole heavens, that other sentiment, dear to every true American heart—Liberty *and* Union, now and forever, one and inseparable![28]

Hayne had been right, technically, in contending that the federal government had been created by the states and not directly by the people, but his argument carried conviction only to those whose hearts were with the past rather than with the future. Webster's argument, proceeding from truer vision, found an echo in the minds and hearts of a rising generation that glimpsed, however imperfectly, the outlines

[28] *Register of Debates,* 21st Cong., first sess., 11, 22–27, 31–41, 43–80.

of a mighty nation which they themselves were building for generations yet unborn.

Jackson had at least enough of Webster's vision to abhor a doctrine that would destroy the nation piece by piece. There is some evidence that the old General had expected Webster to demolish the South Carolinian's argument.[29] Certain it is that no commendation of Hayne (a personal friend) came from the Executive Mansion. It is also clear that Van Buren was doing nothing to allay the suspicions forming in Jackson's mind about the nullifiers.

The exponents of states' rights and nullification were planning to use the celebration of Jefferson's birthday (April 13, 1830) as a means of broadening southern support for their movement while at the same time they tightened the alliance between East and West. They found the event, however, a sad disappointment.

The toasts arranged for the Jefferson Day dinner—there were twenty-four of them—were mainly a glorification of states' rights, of the Virginia and Kentucky resolutions, and of Georgia's defiance of the United States government during the preceding administration. Then came the volunteer toasts.

The President, according to Van Buren's recollection,[30] had written out his toast beforehand, and had come to the dinner with feelings more suitable to "the field of battle than to a festive board." Jackson himself declared,[31] a year after the event, that he had had no intimation of what was in the wind for the dinner; that it was not until he had read the prepared toasts that he saw what he must do. Be this as it may, his was the first of the volunteer toasts, and he delivered it with emphasis. "Our Federal Union. It must be preserved." William B. Lewis, who kept a copy of the toast, underscored "Federal" and "It must be preserved," and it is reasonable to suppose that those particular words were stressed in utterance somewhat more than the others.

Jackson had raised his glass as a sign that the toast should be drunk standing, and Van Buren, who was short of stature, climbed on his chair in order to get the full effect. He saw a hitherto hilarious company standing in stricken silence. He probably saw, as Ike Hill did

[29] James Parton, *Life of Andrew Jackson* (3 vols., Boston, 1866), III, 282.

[30] John C. Fitzpatrick (ed.), *The Autobiography of Martin Van Buren* (Washington, 1920), pp. 413–414.

[31] Charles Grier Sellers, Jr., *James K. Polk, Jacksonian, 1795–1843* (New York, 1957), p. 147. I am inclined to accept Van Buren's account, which is very circumstantial.

see, Calhoun standing with the rest, but with a hand shaking so "that a little of the amber fluid trickled down the side" of his glass. There was no mistaking the sensation caused by the President's words.

Calhoun was a veteran of political war, and his succeeding toast was intended to retrieve lost ground. "The Union—next to our liberty the most dear. . . ." But the General had served notice, and the effect of the dinner was far from what had been intended by its sponsors.[32]

The Jefferson Day dinner of 1830 was only one of the more dramatic evidences of the steadily growing breach between Jackson and Calhoun. The Van Burenites now brought to the General's attention evidence that, in 1818, Calhoun, as Secretary of War in Monroe's Cabinet, had urged that Jackson be censured for his conduct in the invasion of Florida. Jackson asked Calhoun for his side of the story. The South Carolinian attempted to explain and defend his attitude in 1818, only to be told that the effort was completely unsatisfactory.

A dispassionate observer would say that Calhoun had cause for his action in 1818, but Jackson never bore criticism gladly. By nature headstrong and violent, his wrath now boiled over. He was sure that Calhoun had not only attempted to "shoot me in the dark" but that he had also been seeking to assail Rachel Jackson by his course in the Eaton affair.[33] Any hopes Calhoun might have had for Jackson's support for the succession were now completely dashed.

The friends of Van Buren were in a position to exploit their success, and they proceeded to do so. Duff Green's *United States Telegraph* was supposedly the organ of the administration, but Green was a supporter of Calhoun. In December, 1830, Francis Preston Blair ("Bla-ar," Jackson called him) was brought from Kentucky to set up the Washington *Globe*. Federal officeholders with salaries of $1,000 or more were warned to take this paper or lose their jobs, and in this and other ways a systematic and largely successful attempt was made to shift the *Telegraph's* subscribers over to its new rival.[34] Less and less patronage fell into the hands of the Calhounites. Finally, in the spring

[32] In addition to the works cited in the two preceding notes, see Thomas H. Benton, *Thirty Years View* (2 vols., Washington, 1920), I, 148–149; Parton, *Jackson,* III, 282–284; Frederick Ogg, *The Reign of Andrew Jackson* (New Haven, 1919), pp. 164–165; Bassett, *Life of Jackson,* II, 554–555.

[33] Jackson Papers (second series), Jackson to Miss Mary Easton, Oct. 24, 1830.

[34] Welles Papers, Kendall to Welles, Jan. 24, Feb. 26, Mar. 2, 10, Apr. 1, 23, 1831; Flagg Papers, William B. Lewis to Flagg, Feb. 14, 1832.

of 1831, Van Buren's skillful machinations brought about a reorganization of the Cabinet. Van Buren and Eaton resigned. Then Jackson requested Ingham, Branch, and Berrien, all of whom had become more or less closely identified with the Calhoun interest, to follow suit. They did so and, save for Barry, the President had a new official family. It consisted of Edward Livingston as Secretary of State, Lewis Cass as Secretary of War, and Louis McLane, Levi Woodbury, and Roger B. Taney, these last three stepping respectively into the Treasury, the Navy, and the office of the Attorney General. The Red Fox himself was appointed Minister to England.[35]

Van Buren was by now firmly ensconced in the President's favor, and his followers dominated the Democratic leadership. But this victory had produced convulsions in the party. Calhoun declared that he would be a candidate for the Presidency in 1832, and said freely that all connection between him and Jackson was forever at an end. The Virginia Democracy, which had been given scant recognition by the administration, was riven by dissension. A Calhoun paper, the *Jeffersonian,* was set up in Richmond. It was supported by dissident Virginians and by such anti-Jacksonians as Senator George Poindexter of Mississippi and George McDuffie, Robert Barnwell, and Judge William Harper of South Carolina. There were defections from the party in Pennsylvania and in Tennessee.[36]

By the end of 1831, the political combination that had brought Jackson into office seemed to be falling apart. But the Democratic party had a stout and determined chieftain who commanded wide support among the people and who could be counted upon to give decisive leadership in the stormy times that lay ahead.

[35] Welles Papers, Kendall to Welles, Apr. 23, June 20, Aug. 1, 1831; Jackson Papers (second series), Jackson to "My Dear Sir," Aug. 4, 1831; Bassett, *Life of Jackson,* II, 520–544.

[36] Ewing Papers, Ewing to Mrs. Ewing, Mar. 5, Apr. 18, 1831, Ewing to Creighton, Mar. 22, 1831; Jackson Papers (second series), William Carroll to Jackson, June 13, 1831, Jackson to J. C. McLemore, June 27, 1831, Eaton to Jackson, July 1, 1831; Duff Green Papers, Green to Richard K. Cralle, Aug. 21, Sept. 5, 1831, Jan. 3, Feb. 17, and Feb. through August, 1831.

CHAPTER 3

The Party Battles of the First Term

BITTER political conflict characterized Jackson's first term in office. The ambitions of rival political leaders furnished part of the motivation for this struggle. In part, also, that motivation derived from the economic aspirations of men and sections—the western farmer's desire for cheap land, the New England industrialist's demand for a protective tariff, the southern planter's interest in seeing the tariff kept low, the need of West and North for internal improvements, the need of the speculator and debtor everywhere for cheap money. Partly, too, the political movements of these years reflected the devotion of the American people to democracy, and to equality of opportunity. Politicians and statesmen—Webster, Clay, Calhoun, Jackson, Van Buren, and their ilk—continually weighed and analyzed these currents of popular feeling and the economic and social conditions that gave them rise as they planned their party programs.

The Democratic party was a coalition of state and sectional interests that were often in conflict, but its two leaders, the Hero from Tennessee and the Red Fox from New York, were in agreement as to certain policies and principles that should be made the basis of party action. They heartily believed in the maintenance of the Union and in that limited sense were nationalists. They were also in general agreement on the necessity for economy in government, and on keeping the activities of the national government restricted to a minimum. They were at one in their dislike of Nicholas Biddle's Bank of the United States, Jackson because he disliked banks in general, and Van Buren because of the jealous hostility of the New York state banks to this powerful national institution. They saw the necessity for being "judicious" in their attitude toward the tariff, primarily because it was a sectional issue and therefore menacing to party unity. They were professedly sympathetic with the West's desire for cheap land,[1] and, for expediency's sake, Van Buren was willing to go along with Jackson in removing the Indians from the lands coveted by their white neighbors to the regions west of the Mississippi.

Against this formidable pair and the party which they led, Henry Clay undertook to marshal the forces of political opposition, for Adams had resigned the National Republican leadership into the hands of the man who had been his Secretary of State. Clay himself had gloomily retired to Ashland at the close of his term of office, and the party had been left dispirited and disrupted by its overwhelming defeat. But the natural ebullience of the Kentucky Hotspur, his ambition for public preferment, and his growing desire for the Presidency did not long permit him to remain aloof from politics. As Jackson and Van Buren began to put into action the policies of the Democracy, Clay summoned his followers to battle.

The National Republican program, as developed by Clay and his supporters, was to a large extent one of attack. Jackson was scored for his use of the spoils system, which was described in exaggerated terms. His vetoes of four internal improvements bills by the close of 1830[2] were portrayed as a dangerous use of the executive power by an ignorant and overbearing "Military Chieftain." And his Indian policy was denounced as arbitrary and ruthless.

The Indians in the South, over 50,000 Cherokees, Creeks, Choctaws, Chicasaws, and Seminoles occupying some 33,000,000 acres of land, had been gradually surrounded by the extension of white settlements down to the Gulf. In the North, the Sacs, Foxes, Kickapoos, Pottawatomies, and other tribes had been pushed steadily westward by the onrushing tide of white settlers. This mounting pressure by the whites was deeply resented by the red men, who saw their hunting grounds disappearing before these waves of intruders.

[1] Raynor G. Wellington, *The Political and Sectional Influence of the Public Lands, 1828–1842* (Cambridge, 1914), pp. 40–42.

[2] James D. Richardson, *A Compilation of the Messages and Papers of the Presidents* (11 vols., New York, 1910), II, 1046–1057, 1071–1073. Jackson regarded these projects as either too local, or extravagant, or dangerously conducive to an increase of power in the central government.

The Cherokees of Georgia, one of the most progressive tribes, attempted to consolidate their position there by setting up a state within a state. They were encouraged to do this by a series of treaties with the United States that recognized them as a nation capable of making peace and war, owning the land within its boundaries and "punishing its own citizens by its own laws."[3] Georgia was bound, like any other state, to observe the treaties concluded by the federal government, but was obdurate where the Cherokee treaties were concerned. It refused to recognize the Cherokees as an independent nation, and pressed them to sell their lands. They turned a deaf ear to this demand and asked for federal protection. In two major cases,[4] the United States Supreme Court upheld the "rights" of the Cherokees against Georgia, only to have the state flout each decision.

Jackson supported Georgia. Whether or not he made the famous comment, "John Marshall has made his opinion, now let him enforce it," the Jacksonian policy was in full accord with the spirit of the remark. His first annual message asked Congress to set aside a region in the Far West to which the Indians might remove. Congress did so by a strict party vote, and the forced migration began, to continue through the decade of the eighteen-thirties.

The removal of the Indians was a major operation. There were no precedents to guide procedure, and the attitude of the whites was callous and indifferent. Politicians were early on the ground, seeking profits out of the funds allocated to finance the migrations. Unscrupulous government agents tricked the Indians into unfair agreements. Grasping white settlers took possession of their property, driving them out before preparations for migration were complete. Lands assigned in the trans-Mississippi West were often far inferior to those vacated by the tribes. State governments defrauded the red men and the federal government made only feeble and ineffective efforts to protect them.

The Indians' situation was tragic in the extreme. The Choctaw migration from Mississippi, undertaken in December, 1831, saw hundreds of Indians, thinly clad and without moccasins, crossing the Mississippi to endure zero cold at Little Rock and then the terrible suffering of what was practically a trail-blazing journey to their new "home" on the Red River. The Creeks and Cherokees in Alabama

[3] Cherokee Nation *v.* State of Georgia, 5 Peters, 17.

[4] *Ibid.;* Worcester *v.* Georgia, 6 Peters, 521–579.

suffered similar hardships as they were forcibly and often fraudulently separated from their homes. Creeks refusing to migrate were marched out of Alabama in chains. The Seminoles of Florida, after having been pushed off their fertile lands in that state, were bribed, threatened, and finally tricked into an agreement to migrate to the West. Force, terror, and fraud compelled the Indian to the white man's desire.

The Indian sometimes fought back against his white tormentors. Individuals went berserk from time to time, murdering and scalping without discrimination. In Illinois the Black Hawk War of 1832 marked a desperate but futile attempt by the Sacs to protest the loss of their lands to the whites. Many of the Seminoles, bitter because of the frauds perpetrated upon them, refused to prepare for migration. The government sent troops and the braves, led by the able young chief Osceola, took to the warpath. So began the Seminole War, which lasted from 1835 to 1838 and cost some $14 million. Osceola died a prisoner in Fort Moultrie in Charleston Harbor.

The hardships of the Indians produced repercussions in a number of quarters. Clay denounced Jackson's attitude as staining the national honor, and urged nationwide meetings of protest. Calhoun, after trouble developed between Jackson and South Carolina over nullification, commented satirically on Jackson's inconsistency in upholding states' rights in Georgia and attacking them in South Carolina. Missionary-minded religious denominations, especially the Methodists and Quakers, belabored the treatment of the red brother.

Such denunciations had a measure of political effect. Van Buren thought that 8,000 votes were lost in the election of 1832 in western New York alone. But Jackson ploughed ahead, unruffled by charges of cruelty and inconsistency, and the country as a whole approved his action.[5]

The National Republicans' policy was not simply one of attack upon executive tyranny and Indian outrage. Constructively, they sought to foster the growth of American capitalism and American prosperity.

[5] Richardson, *Messages and Papers,* II, 1019–1022; Flagg Papers, C. E. Dudley to Flagg, May 21, 1830; Grant Foreman, *Indian Removal* (Norman, Okla., 1932), pp. 46–47, 53–70, 76–78, 99, 121–123, 129–152, 236–251, 315–386; Annie H. Abel, "The History of Events Resulting in Indian Consolidation West of the Mississippi," American Historical Association, *Reports* (Washington, 1908), I, 370–412; Wilson Lumpkin, *The Removal of the Cherokee Indians from Georgia* (2 vols. in one, New York, 1907), *passim.*

Their means to this end came to be identified in the popular mind as Clay's "American system."

As Clay himself used the term, his American system was the opposite of what he was wont to refer to as the "colonial" or "foreign" system of free trade. It meant, basically, the use of the protective tariff to build up American industry. This industrial development would serve as a source of national wealth and as a constant nourishment for an urban population that, in turn, would furnish a steady and reliable home market for the nation's agriculture.[6] Clay's system was the political expression of the economic thought that Mathew Carey was busily spreading throughout the land. It found hearty support among industrialists in all sections of the country, especially in the North and West.

Certain other major policies to which Clay was devoted were often identified as part of his American system. These were internal improvements at national expense, the use of public land revenues for such improvements, the maintenance of the Bank of the United States as essential to a stable and uniform currency. Clay never joined these together into a nicely articulated whole. They were, nevertheless, harmonious and closely related, for underlying all of these proposals was his aim of building up the wealth and power of the Republic, of shaping for the United States a grand destiny that would be carved out in proud independence from old Europe. The system in its broader aspects was a concept that had little room for fear of a strong central government, but rather regarded it as an agency to be used for promoting the public welfare. It was the dream of a nationalist—of nationalist Henry Clay.[7]

The building of roads and canals at national expense was certainly an important part of the American system. Its protagonists early found cause for quarreling with Jackson about his attitude toward internal improvements.

Old Hickory, like most Westerners, favored internal improvements as a general principle. He sanctioned expenditures for transport developments during his first term at a rate nearly double that of the expenditures under Adams. But he was always quick to seize an oppor-

[6] Annals of Congress, 18th Congress, first session, 1961–2001.

[7] Clay's ideas are most easily studied in Calvin Colton (ed.), *The Works of Henry Clay* (10 vols., New York, 1904), VI, 78–80, 108–110, 116–135, 218–237, 254–294; VII, 388–391, 395–400, 437–486, 524–535.

tunity for striking at Clay's system, and such an opportunity presented itself in the Maysville Road.

This highway, some twenty miles long, lay wholly within the state of Kentucky. It connected Maysville on the Ohio with Lexington in the heart of the Blue Grass region. Its advocates regarded it as a part of the national Cumberland Road system. Congress passed a bill in 1830 providing federal aid for building the road. Jackson vetoed it on the ground that federal aid to intrastate projects of this nature was unconstitutional. He also declared that such bills violated the principle that government should be an economical affair, and pointed out that they interfered with the speedy extinction of the national debt.[8]

The veto was largely political, for Jackson signed some internal improvement bills fully as local as the Maysville Road. It was a slap at Clay, who had energetically pushed the Maysville Road, and at the American system. It was also a canny slap. The Maysville Road was primarily a local project, and therefore the veto would, as Van Buren observed, displease the smallest possible number of voters. More positively, the veto pleased New York and Pennsylvania, which were financing their own internal improvements and saw no reason why they should help finance similar developments in other states, and it was balm to state's righters, especially to many southern planters who had no need for building roads and canals. It also served notice that, in Jackson's opinion, the construction of roads and canals lay more within the province of the states than of the nation. Jefferson's belief in limiting the scope of action of the national government was now to be one of the tenets of Jacksonian Democracy.[9]

The Maysville veto evoked a great cry from the ranks of the National Republicans. Clay raged against it, and sought to stir up mass meetings that would condemn the President's action. Whigs met and passed resolutions of censure. Even Madison, though retaining his constitutional scruples against internal improvements at national expense, warned the administration that the national government alone had the power to select the improvements most important to the na-

[8] Richardson, *Messages and Papers,* II, 1046–1056.

[9] John C. Fitzpatrick (ed.), *The Autobiography of Martin Van Buren* (Washington, 1920), pp. 312, 320–380; John G. Van Deusen, *Economic Basis of Disunion in South Carolina* (New York, 1928), p. 128; John S. Bassett, *The Life of Andrew Jackson* (2 vols. in one, New York, 1928), 485–489; Marquis James, *Andrew Jackson, Portrait of a President* (Indianapolis, 1937), pp. 220–222; Glyndon G. Van Deusen, *The Life of Henry Clay* (Boston, 1937), pp. 236–238.

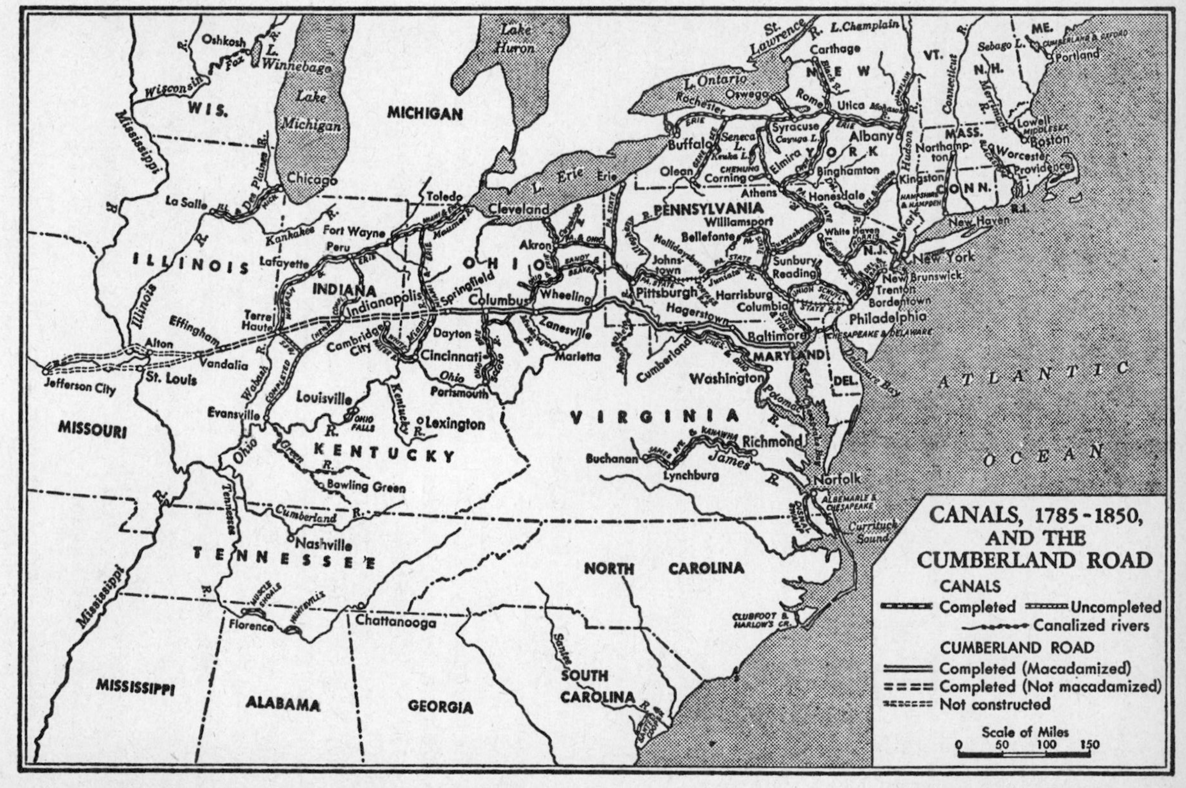
CANALS, 1785-1850, AND THE CUMBERLAND ROAD
CANALS
Completed
Uncompleted
Canalized rivers
CUMBERLAND ROAD
Completed (Macadamized)
Completed (Not macadamized)
Not constructed
Scale of Miles
0 50 100 150
ATLANTIC OCEAN
WIS.
MICHIGAN
ILLINOIS
INDIANA
OHIO
PENNSYLVANIA
NEW YORK
VT.
N.H.
ME.
MASS.
CONN.
R.I.
N.J.
DEL.
MARYLAND
VIRGINIA
KENTUCKY
TENNESSEE
NORTH CAROLINA
SOUTH CAROLINA
GEORGIA
ALABAMA
MISSISSIPPI
MISSOURI
Lake Michigan
Lake Huron
L. Erie
L. Ontario
L. Winnebago
L. Champlain
Oshkosh
Chicago
La Salle
Toledo
Cleveland
Fort Wayne
Peru
Lafayette
Indianapolis
Terre Haute
Effingham
Vandalia
Alton
St. Louis
Jefferson City
Evansville
Louisville
Lexington
Bowling Green
Nashville
Florence
Chattanooga
Cambridge City
Dayton
Cincinnati
Springfield
Columbus
Portsmouth
Akron
Wheeling
Zanesville
Marietta
Pittsburgh
Johnstown
Hollidaysburg
Bellefonte
Williamsport
Harrisburg
Columbia
Hagerstown
Cumberland
Baltimore
Washington
Richmond
Lynchburg
Buchanan
Norfolk
Philadelphia
Bordentown
Trenton
New Brunswick
New York
Newark
New Haven
Reading
Sunbury
White Haven
Honesdale
Athens
Corning
Olean
Buffalo
Rochester
Oswego
Syracuse
Rome
Utica
Albany
Binghamton
Elmira
Carthage
Kingston
Northampton
Worcester
Providence
Lowell
Boston
Portland
Sebago L.
Mississippi
Ohio
Tennessee
Cumberland R.
Kentucky R.
Green R.
Wabash
Illinois
Wisconsin
Hudson
Delaware Bay
Currituck Sound
Santee
James R.
Potomac R.

tional interest, and declared that, with the proper constitutional changes, the revenues from the public lands might well be used for the improvement of communications.[10]

But the administration was not to be deterred from its game of political strategy. As Isaac Hill explained jubilantly to Azariah Flagg, the idea was to identify the American system in the public mind as a policy designed "to impoverish and afterward to corrupt the American people with their own money." If the tariff could be slowly reduced, and the South Carolinians would let nullification alone, Hill foresaw only the rosiest political future for the Democratic party.[11]

There was little likelihood that nullification would be left alone, for there was no substantial abatement of protection.[12] The House, overwhelmingly Jacksonian, decisively defeated McDuffie's effort, in February, 1830, to bring about a general lowering of the protective tariff, the vote being dictated by sectional interests rather than by party affiliations. Since party meant little where the tariff was concerned, Jackson and his lieutenants were willing to bide their time in tariff making.

As Jackson's first term wore on, the Democracy's political position showed elements of great strength. The President was controlling the country by a West-Northeast combination. The West could count on the national government's aid in internal improvements, despite the Maysville veto, for the government was spending about $1 million a year on such projects as were deemed of national importance. It was also clear that the government was actively supporting the West's desire to get rid of the Indians, and that it was at least sympathetic with the West's eagerness for public lands. The Northeast could see that Jackson was no low-tariff man, and that its interests would have voice in the President's inner circle so long as Woodbury was in the Cabinet and Van Buren was the heir apparent. The South, however, might well prove to be the administration's weak point. There Jackson had no leadership support, and Calhoun and his followers were openly disaffected. If nullification flamed up, the party's situation in the South would certainly deteriorate.

[10] *Ibid.;* Van Buren, *Autobiography,* pp. 33–34; Gaillard Hunt (ed.), *The Writings of James Madison* (9 vols., New York, 1900–10), IX, 381–382.

[11] Flagg Papers, Hill to Flagg, July 19, 1830.

[12] The only duty reductions were on salt, tea, coffee, cocoa, and molasses. These were passed in 1830.

The National Republicans were scarcely in the same flourishing condition as the Democracy. They could not establish either nullification or the tariff as an issue. Jackson's use of the veto power had not brought the popular reaction for which Clay had hoped. Van Buren's conduct as Secretary of State had been beyond reproach. The Democratic majority in the Twenty-first Congress was increased in the 1830 elections.[13] And in the Middle Atlantic states and in New England a popular excitement took form and threatened, in its early stages, to challenge the position of National Republicanism as the party of the opposition. This was the Antimasonic movement.

In September, 1826, William Morgan, a brick and stone mason of Batavia, New York, and a member of the Masonic order, was lying in jail in Canandaigua, New York. He was under arrest for a debt of $2.69, but the real reason for his imprisonment was his determination to publish a book containing the secrets of the first three degrees, the so-called Blue Lodge, of Masonry.

Morgan's *Illustrations of Masonry,* which was then in process of publication, did indeed expose the work of the Blue Lodge. It was not the first book to do so. An anonymous work, *Le Tombeau de Jacques Molai,* published in France during the French Revolution, had antedated Morgan's disclosures by more than a quarter of a century.[14] But this book was not known to the Masonic brethren of western New York. To them, Morgan was a traitor of the deepest dye.

Someone paid Morgan's debt. He was released from jail. But as he stepped out into the street, he was seized, gagged, and thrust into a yellow carriage. There was a wild ride, with relays of horses, to the Niagara frontier. There all trace of William Morgan was lost forever.

Morgan's disappearance excited great popular interest. Investigations were set on foot. When it became apparent that these were being obstructed by Masons influential in politics and in the courts, popular indignation reached a boiling point.

Antimasonry, as a political movement, arose out of this popular excitement. It was a protest on the part of the common man against the privileges and power enjoyed in government, in business, and in the

[13] The Democrats had a majority of four in the Senate of the Twenty-first Congress. In the Senate of the Twenty-second Congress, there were twenty-five Democrats, twenty-one National Republicans, and two Antimasons.

[14] A copy of *Le Tombeau de Jacques Molai* is in the Bibliothèque Nationale in Paris.

courts by the members of a fraternity which prided itself on its secrecy and was, at least in the common belief, snobbish and exclusive. Antimasonry put great emphasis on moral conduct, and so fitted nicely into the pattern of the temperance, antislavery, and other moral causes that so easily stirred New Englanders and others of Puritan descent. It stood for the rights of the ordinary citizen and against what its publicists called the "grand kings" of Masonic privilege. As a moral and democratic movement of obvious power, it was taken up by politicians —Thurlow Weed and William Henry Seward in New York, Thaddeus Stevens in Pennsylvania, and others—and skillfully forged into a political party which soon showed remarkable strength in New England, the Middle Atlantic states, and Ohio.

By 1827 an Antimasonic party had been organized in New York State, and in that year it carried several counties in the western part of the state and sent fifteen members to the New York legislature. Similar developments were occurring elsewhere in the East. On September 11, 1830, Antimasonic delegates from eleven states met in Philadelphia and there laid the groundwork for a national nominating convention. This was held at Baltimore, September 26, 1831. It nominated the reluctant William Wirt of Maryland for President and Amos Ellmaker of Pennsylvania for Vice-President, and so brought into being a fashion for nominating presidential and vice-presidential candidates that has been followed ever since.

The Antimasonic nominating convention of 1831 indicated the growing importance of a political movement that, in its early stages, drew considerable numbers of voters from the National Republican ranks, especially in National Republican strongholds such as western New York. Even when, a few years later, the Antimasonic leaders gradually moved into alliance with the National Republicans, they were to bring with them their own political ambitions and thus complicate the problems of National Republican leadership.[15]

Despite the fact that National Republicanism was in the doldrums, Clay determined to re-enter the presidential lists. Ambition, plus the call of numerous legislative and popular meetings throughout the

[15] Flagg Papers, Philander Bennett to Flagg, Nov. 19, 1828, Henry O'Reilly to Flagg Nov. 11, 1829, John Morgan to Flagg, Mar. 27, 1830, George M. Chase to Flagg, Oct. 10, 1830; Charles McCarthy, "The Antimasonic Party," American Historical Association, *Reports* (Washington, 1902), I, 367–550; G. G. Van Deusen, *Clay*, pp. 240–242, and *Thurlow Weed: Wizard of the Lobby* (Boston, 1947), pp. 38–52.

country that nominated him for the Presidency, were irresistible lures. He was convinced, too, that he understood the needs of a rapidly growing capitalistic society much better than did the old pain-wracked General in the Executive Mansion. First Clay sought and the Kentucky legislature gave him election to the Senate. Then, shortly after he arrived in Washington, in December, 1831, a National Republican nominating convention chose him as its presidential candidate for 1832. John Sargeant, a wealthy and conservative Philadelphia lawyer, was named his running mate.

It had been clear for some time that Jackson would be Clay's opponent. The General's health had been so bad in 1829–30 that he had thought his end was near, and had felt constrained to draw up a political will in favor of Van Buren as his successor. But his physical resistance to disease and suffering was enormous. By 1831, the Democratic politicians, and Jackson himself, were determined that he would run for a second term. This determination hardened when, after a bullet had been removed from his left arm, his health began to improve.[16]

The campaign of 1832 began with a flare-up over the conduct of relations with Great Britain. Clay and Adams had been unable to wrest concessions from the British, whether in regard to boundary questions, the free navigation of the St. Lawrence, or trade with the British West Indies. On the West Indian trade, indeed they had maintained altogether too grasping an attitude, and as a consequence that traffic had been closed to American shipping. Van Buren, once he was ensconced in the State Department, took a different tack. He told the British that the preceding administration had adopted a wrong policy, and that the claims it had made would not be revived. This was followed by other diplomatic evidences of moderation, whereupon England opened the West Indian trade in the fall of 1830.

The Democrats hailed the reopening as a triumph of diplomacy. The National Republicans declared that it was decidedly unbecoming conduct to base a diplomatic negotiation upon criticism of a preceding American administration. Clay asserted that it prostrated the American eagle before the British lion. And diplomacy as a subject of

[16] Flagg Papers, Cambreleng to Flagg, Apr. 5, 1830, Charles E. Dudley to Flagg, Apr. 12, 1830; Jackson Papers (second series), William Carroll to Jackson, May 6, 1831; *Niles' Register,* XXXIX (Jan. 29, 1831), 385; Washington *Globe,* Jan. 22, 1831; James, *Andrew Jackson,* pp. 222–223, 291.

political debate received fresh impetus when, in June, 1831, too late for the Senate to act, Jackson appointed Van Buren Minister to England.

The New Yorker went to England, where he dined with Talleyrand and moved with his customary aplomb among the highest political circles in London. But when the Senate came back into session and took up his confirmation, a great clamor arose. The National Republicans pronounced him unfit, as proved by the West Indies negotiation. Calhounites charged him with plotting against their leader, especially in connection with the breakup of the Cabinet. Late in January, 1832, on a bitter cold night, came the vote. It was rigged so that a tie resulted and Calhoun, as President of the Senate, cast the deciding ballot. Jackson's choice was rejected and Van Buren had to return, in ignominy it was hoped, from London.

Van Buren's rejection had significant political consequences. It marked a tendency toward rapprochement between Clay and Calhoun that was to become more pronounced in the near future. Clay pronounced the rebuff to the Red Fox an excellent political stroke. Calhoun exulted. Benton heard the South Carolinian say, "It will kill him, sir, kill him dead. He will never kick, sir, never kick." Democratic leaders, and they proved the truer prophets, believed that it would make Van Buren a martyr and thus ensure his political future.

The rejection enhanced Van Buren's popularity. It determined the President to avenge his favorite. It paved Little Van's way to the White House.[17]

Even while the fight over Van Buren raged, two issues of great economic and political importance engaged Congress in heated deliberation. One was the tariff. The other was public lands.

The South-West alliance of 1830, favoring a lowering of the tariff and cheaper public lands, was still in force. During the winter of 1831–32, the administration showed signs of moving, though cautiously, in that same direction. In response, Clay, as leader of the National Republicans, sought to develop what later became a Whig policy by which the West would receive special benefits from public land

[17] John Spencer Bassett (ed.), *Correspondence of Andrew Jackson* (7 vols., Washington, 1926–35), IV, 401; Thomas H. Benton, *Thirty Years View* (2 vols., New York, 1854–56), I, 219; Nathan Sargent, *Public Men and Events* (2 vols., Philadelphia, 1875), I, 196–200; Charles M. Wiltse, *John C. Calhoun* (3 vols., Indianapolis, 1944–51), II, 125–128; G. G. Van Deusen, *Clay,* pp. 247–248; Schlesinger, *Age of Jackson,* pp. 55–56.

sales, while at the same time the South would be reassured about his party's attitude toward the tariff.

Clay proposed keeping land prices up, but he would give 10 per cent of land sales to the states in which the lands lay. The remainder of the land revenue would be divided among all the states in proportion to their representation in Congress. The West would, then, have a special share in the distribution of land revenue, but the older states would also have a part of the pie. As for the tariff, the South was told that, in Clay's eyes, protection was only "incidental" in tariff making; that the tariff was primarily for revenue; and that he opposed using this revenue for roads and canals.

Conciliation was Clay's motto, conciliation that would enable him to achieve his main purpose, the maintenance of a protective tariff. To preserve his American system of protection, he boasted, he "would defy the South, the President, and the Devil."[18] But here his former chief, John Quincy Adams, was of a different point of view. And Adams was now in a position of power.

For the ex-President was once more in political harness. Public life had become second nature to him and, financially straitened, he needed the eight dollars a day which the munificence of the government awarded to the congressman of that period.[19] He had been elected to the House of Representatives and there the Speaker had made him chairman of the Committee on Manufactures. The framing of the tariff bill was one of his particular concerns.

Adams had never been an extremist on the tariff. Like Jackson, he saw its value, but feared it as a divisive influence. As much a nationalist as Clay, and more farsighted, he took a more intelligent view of protection than did the Kentuckian. Clay inclined to the dogmatic position that high protection was essential to national prosperity. Adams believed that the national interest, broadly considered, now demanded a considerable lowering of the tariff. He undertook to work with the administration in shaping a tariff that would protect where protection was needed, but would be sufficiently reduced to calm the southern mind.

The result of Adams' efforts, much to Clay's disgust, was the tariff

[18] Charles Francis Adams (ed.), *Memoirs of John Quincy Adams* (12 vols., Philadelphia, 1874–77), VIII, 446.

[19] Samuel F. Bemis, *John Quincy Adams and the Union* (New York, 1956), pp. 206, 210–211.

of 1832. It reduced duties to the general level of the tariff of 1824. Jackson signed this bill July 14, 1832, confident that it would end popular discontent in the South.[20]

Meanwhile, a South-West attempt to pass a land bill, one that would graduate land prices and provide a 15 per cent distribution of the proceeds of land sales to the states in which the lands lay, failed by a narrow margin. Clay's own land bill, keeping up prices and providing for a more general distribution of land revenues, was bottled up in the House by the forces of the administration.[21]

There were several items of significance attached to the fate of these various measures. The tariff struggle of 1829–32 had shown the tariff issue to be above all sectional in character. Both parties had split repeatedly in the voting, and along sectional lines. The tariff could not be made into a national party issue. Secondly, southern votes had been lacking at critical times for the bill graduating the price of public lands, and in consequence the South-West coalition now fell apart. Calhoun and his friends had been the spearhead of this coalition. Now, lacking their western anchor, they were more than ever at the mercy of the political winds and therefore the more likely to flirt with Clay and his American system, distasteful though such a flirtation was bound to be in the long run. Thirdly, the administration could feel reasonably well satisfied with the course of events. It had stalled Clay's land bill and in this way had cautiously manifested a sympathy with a cheap land policy that would be gratefully received in the West. It had helped write a tariff which it hoped would placate the South and yet be protective enough to deprive the National Republicans of an issue in the Northeast.

Still another development was pleasing to the friends of the administration. Jackson had said in his annual messages and in the Maysville veto that when the national debt was extinguished, the surplus in government revenue should be distributed to the states. This was designed to allay western suspicion of his opposition to the Maysville Road, and was a skillful counter to Clay's distribution plans.

Clay had, indeed, been defeated, both on the public lands and on the tariff; but where a third aspect of his system was concerned, he had fond hopes of victory. This was the financial issue of a sound and stable

[20] Jackson, *Correspondence,* IV, 462–463.
[21] Wellington, *Public Lands,* I, 183–184.

Lake Superior
Lake Michigan
L. Huron
L. Ontario
L. Erie
MICHIGAN
TERRITORY
ARKANSAS
TERRITORY
FLORIDA TERRITORY
Portland
Portsmouth
Boston
Hartford
Providence
Middletown
New York
Buffalo
Pittsburgh
Baltimore
Washington
Chillicothe
Cincinnati
Richmond
Norfolk
St. Louis
Lexington
Louisville
Fayetteville
Charleston
Augusta
Savannah
Mobile
New
Orleans
BANKS OF 1830
Including All Branches of the
Second Bank of the United States
Bank of the United States
1-5 Banks
Abandoned
Opened late
Branch banks are also indicated
by name of city

currency and credit. At the heart of this problem was the Second Bank of the United States.

This "mammoth monopoly," to use the descriptive phrase of Ike Hill,[22] had been chartered in 1816 for twenty years. It had a capital of $35 million and could issue notes up to that amount which were receivable for United States government dues. It was obligated to maintain specie payment, and to serve as a depository for government funds, this last being a privilege rather than a burden.

The president of the Bank was Nicholas Biddle, scion of a wealthy and distinguished Philadelphia family. Biddle had been born January 8, 1786. A precocious youth, he had graduated from Princeton at the age of fifteen. He had then traveled in Europe and had become much interested in Greece and Greek culture. Diplomacy, too, seems to have attracted him, and he had served for a time as secretary to Minister James Monroe in London. After he came back to the United States, in 1807, he wrote up the Lewis and Clark expedition, a narrative that for a century remained the standard account of the great journey.

Biddle was a Jeffersonian Republican, and stood high in the favor of Jefferson and Monroe. When he demonstrated an interest in and knowledge of banking, Monroe made him (1819) one of the five government directors of the Bank of the United States and in 1823, at the age of thirty-seven, he became its president. Witty, urbane, cultured, basically honest and straightforward, he was also overoptimistic by nature and somewhat naïve. At times he played a conciliatory role. At other times he was arrogant and domineering. But he understood banking and the function of the Bank of the United States in the American economy, and under his leadership the Bank had prospered.[23]

As the Bank prospered, it proved itself to be a valuable institution. It served as a useful market for government bonds and for other Treasury operations. Its swift and cheap exchanges helped to move crops and facilitate commercial operations throughout the country. It furnished, in its own bank notes, a sound currency, and it helped to keep the currencies of the state banks honest. This last was accomplished by peri-

[22] *Register of Debates,* 22nd Cong., first sess., 531.

[23] Bray Hammond, *Banks and Politics in America* (Princeton, 1957), pp. 276–279, 286–298; Ralph C. H. Catterall, *The Second Bank of the United States* (Chicago, 1903), pp. 97, 274–275; Schlesinger, *Age of Jackson,* pp. 75–76, 82, 111–114.

odically presenting the notes of these banks for redemption. Biddle liked to stress the public service which the Bank performed, and, says Walter Buckingham Smith, "the record suggests that up to 1834 the Bank often served the public and on a few occasions this was done at the expense of the stockholders."[24]

The Bank had a large measure of control over foreign and domestic exchange, but it could not justly be called a monopoly. In 1830, when it was very prosperous, it made only 20 per cent of the country's bank loans, its note circulation was only about one-fifth of the nation's total, and it had only about one-third of the total bank deposits and of the specie held by American banks. It was, furthermore, subject to charter revision. These are not the aspects of monopoly banking.[25]

But if the Bank was, in many ways, a national asset, it was also a national liability. It was not subject to anything like effective government regulation. Its power (which lay in its discounts of notes and bills of exchange, its control of the state bank currencies, and the fact that it dominated the domestic and foreign exchange markets) was great. This power was lodged chiefly in the hands of Nicholas Biddle, who knew much more about banking than did the Bank's board, and whose forceful and dominant personality came close to reducing the board to ciphers. Barring revolt by the board, Biddle could exert great influence upon the American economy.

The Bank had another kind of power that was potentially dangerous. Its favors could be and sometimes were extended to important and influential people. Clay and Webster borrowed from the Bank. So did Postmaster General Barry and Amos Kendall. The latter, according to a memorandum in the Biddle Papers, borrowed from the Bank to the amount of $5,375. Seward found the Bank decidedly useful in settling the affairs of the Holland Land Company. Webster not only borrowed $17,782.86 from the Bank during the middle eighteen-thirties, but also acted as its legal counsel. In 1833 he wrote to Biddle that if he were to continue as counsel, it might be well to have his retainer "renewed, or *refreshed* as usual." James Watson Webb of the New York *Courier and Enquirer* was in the Bank's debt in the eighteen-thirties to the

[24] Walter B. Smith, *Economic Aspects of the Second Bank of the United States* (Cambridge, 1953), p. 58.

[25] Thomas S. Berry, *Western Prices Before 1861* (Cambridge, 1943), pp. 414, 424; Catterall, *Second Bank*, pp. 434–449; W. B. Smith, *Economic Aspects of the Second Bank*, pp. 43–63, 69–70, 251.

extent of $18,000, and a number of other newspaper editors supped at the same table.[26] Such favors were conferred with some degree of impartiality, so far as politics were concerned. But of course at any time the Bank could concentrate them in one party or the other.

The powers which the Bank possessed were not used by Biddle, at least down to 1833, in any foolish or vicious way. But the powers were there.

The Bank had many supporters. It also had numerous and powerful enemies. State banks disliked it because of the control it exercised over their note issues. Hard-money men, whether theorists like William Gouge or workingmen who hated all banks because they were frequently paid in state bank notes of fluctuating value, were opposed to this paper-emitting "hydra of corruption." So, too, were western speculators and entrepreneurs who wanted cheap money, honest men who feared the Bank's centralized power as dangerous in a democracy, and politicians who saw it as a whipping boy. Last but not least, there was numbered among the Bank's enemies the President of the United States.

The Old Hero, by his own account, had always been suspicious of banks and of their note issues,[27] and he had been hostile to the Bank of the United States when he took oath as President. Reports reached him, too, from some of his closest associates, that the Bank had played politics in several states in the election of 1828, and it was easy for him to reach the conviction that the Bank was a "hydra of corruption—dangerous to our liberties by its corrupting influence everywhere."[28] By 1832, he was determined that this "Monster," so he called it, should not be rechartered.[29]

Jackson was willing to replace the Bank by one of a much more limited character, which would be tied to the Treasury and could issue no notes and make no loans. This would have destroyed the best

[26] Reginald C. McGrane (ed.), *The Correspondence of Nicholas Biddle* (Boston and New York, 1919), pp. 218, 357–358; W. B. Smith, *Economic Aspects of the Second Bank,* pp. 249–250; Catterall, *Second Bank,* pp. 252–255; Claude M. Fuess, *Daniel Webster* (2 vols., Boston, 1930), II, 8–9.

[27] Samuel R. Gammon, Jr., *The Presidential Campaign of 1832* (Baltimore, 1922), p. 105; Bassett, *Life of Jackson,* II, 591–609.

[28] *Ibid.,* II, 593–597; James A. Hamilton, *Reminiscences* (New York, 1869), p. 167.

[29] Jackson, *Correspondence,* IV, 161–162, 387; Van Buren, *Autobiography,* pp. 625–626; Bassett, *Life of Jackson,* II, 613.

note issue in the country. It would also have created a mighty agent of patronage distribution, which would have been as dangerous an influence as the institution it was designed to replace.

The crisis over the Bank came in 1832. Biddle, who had striven hard to placate Jackson by appointing Democrats to the boards of directors of branches of the Bank, and by presenting to the President a plan for expediting the payment of the national debt,[30] became reluctantly convinced that Jackson was determined upon the Bank's destruction. He then sought the best time to apply for the Bank's recharter, and was assured by Clay, Webster, and his own agent, Thomas Cadwalader, that this year of a presidential election would give him his best opportunity. So the decision was made.

The bill renewing the Bank's charter came to the floor of the Senate on March 13, 1832. As amended and finally passed, it met some of the criticisms leveled against the institution by Jackson and others, for it limited the right of the Bank to hold real estate and establish branches, prohibited branch drafts, reserved to Congress the power to forbid its issuance of small notes, and authorized the President to appoint a member of the board of directors of each branch of the Bank. Framed with a view to meeting the current criticisms of the Bank, the bill curtailed the powers of the institution and improved it in respect to its function of currency regulation. This new bank charter was to run for fifteen years.[31]

The Jacksonians in Congress sought to delay consideration of the bill, and well they might, for one-third of the Democratic party's representatives favored its passage. Really formidable opposition came only from the South and Southwest.

Clay and Webster pushed the measure through. It passed the Senate by a vote of 28 to 20, and the House of Representatives three weeks later by a vote of 107 to 85.

The Senate vote indicated the sectional situation. The South and Southwest voted almost solidly against the bill, casting only three votes in its favor. Save for Kentucky, Illinois, and Missouri, which divided their votes, the West supported the measure. The only vote cast against it from New England was that of Isaac Hill of New Hampshire. New

[30] Catterall, *Second Bank,* pp. 187–192; W. B. Smith, *Economic Aspects of the Second Bank,* pp. 147–151; Hammond, *Banks and Politics,* pp. 371–376.

[31] Senate *Journal,* 22nd Cong., first sess., 451–453; Catterall, *Second Bank,* pp. 235–238, 479–488, 498–500.

York's senators and one from New Jersey voted nay, but the rest of the Middle Atlantic states gave it solid support.[32]

The opposition leadership was jubilant, for it believed that Jackson was confronted by an inescapable dilemma. If he vetoed the bill, he would lose Pennsylvania, a key state where the Bank was very popular. If he signed it, he could be denounced for approving an institution toward which he had repeatedly evinced hostility.

Old Hickory knew what he meant to do. "The Bank is trying to kill me, but I will kill it," he told Van Buren.[33] He had determined to send the bill back to Congress with a ringing message stating the reasons for its rejection, and the veto, framed to compass the death of the "Monster" and the destruction of its political friends, was drawn up with the aid of Amos Kendall, Roger B. Taney, and Levi Woodbury.[34] From a political point of view, it was a devastating document.

The veto declared that the limitations placed upon the Bank by the new charter were "of little value or importance." It then attacked the Bank on a wide variety of grounds. The institution was pilloried as a dangerous centralization of power at the expense of the states. Its proposed capital of $35 million was declared to be far in excess of what was necessary. It was unconstitutional, despite Marshall's pronouncement in *McCulloch* v. *Maryland;* in this connection the highly questionable thesis was advanced that each public official was bound to support the Constitution only as he understood it, not as it was understood by the Supreme Court or anyone else. The veto message stressed repeatedly the dangers inherent in foreigners being holders of the Bank's stock, and the importance of such an institution being "purely American." Toward its close came what was probably the most effective argument with the masses—an impassioned attack upon the bill as a prostitution of government to "the rich and powerful," and a pledge to stand in stalwart fashion against "the advancement of the few at the expense of the many."[35]

Biddle called the veto "a manifesto of anarchy," and Webster denounced it as seeking to "inflame the poor against the rich" and as threatening the very existence of the Constitution. Blair, on the other hand, hailed it as a "Second Declaration of Independence." It was

[32] *Ibid.*, p. 235.

[33] Van Buren, *Autobiography*, p. 625.

[34] Schlesinger, *Age of Jackson*, pp. 89–90.

[35] Richardson, *Messages and Papers*, II, 1139–1154; Henry S. Commager (ed.), *Documents of American History* (New York, 1940), pp. 270–274.

difficult, said Blair, to describe adequately "the sublimity of the moral spectacle now presented to the American people in the person of Andrew Jackson." This sublime chieftain had thrown down his challenge to the "monied aristocracy," that "insidious enemy," that "creeping poison," that "germ of an American nobility," that slavish instrument which was seeking to bring these states once again into dependence on the British Isles.[36]

Despite Blair's encomiums, the veto was weak in its reasoning. Its argument that a national bank in the eighteen-thirties needed no more capital than the one that had existed thirty years before betrayed that reluctance to face realistically the problems of a rapidly developing economy that was so characteristic of the Jacksonians. The veto repeatedly stated that the Bank was a monopoly, which was true only if monopoly were defined in such fashion as to divest the word of its real meaning. It ignored the Bank's enormous services to the national economy. Neither then nor later did the President or his party offer an effective substitute for the Bank, and in the years that followed the veto, despite the fact that there were some painfully slow local improvements in banking practice, the United States sank from a leading to a backward nation in the development of banking techniques.[37] On the other hand, the President had served notice that his administration held the maintenance of economic democracy to be of paramount importance, if social and political democracy was to be preserved. His stand, and that of his party, was a mixture of ignorance and idealistic perception.

The Bank veto ushered in the climactic part of the 1832 campaign. This was a three-cornered affair, made all the more hectic by the first general adoption of the national nominating convention. The Antimasonic nominee, William Wirt, and the party itself, centered their fire upon Masonry, which was pictured as destructive of the very fountainheads of democracy. The National Republican team of Clay and Sergeant offered a wide choice of issues, ranging from spoils and the dangers to democratic government inherent in the veto power to the American system and the recharter of the Bank. The Democracy issued no statement of principles. Jackson was its platform, and the Bank veto was the chief plank.

[36] Biddle Papers, Biddle to Clay, Aug. 1, 1832; Daniel Webster, *Writings and Speeches* (18 vols., Boston, 1903), VI, 180; Washington *Globe,* July 12, 1832.

[37] W. B. Smith, *Economic Aspects of the Second Bank,* p. 263.

The Democrats had assembled at Baltimore, May 21, 1832, to nominate a Vice-President, Jackson being already designated as the head of their ticket by scores of local and state caucuses and conventions held throughout the country. Van Buren was Jackson's choice and, though the Red Fox was definitely unpopular in the South, Jackson's will was decisive. Revolt against the Little Magician was made impossible by the since famous two-thirds' rule, there being no other candidate who could possibly acquire that number of votes.[38]

The result of the campaign was never really in doubt. Jackson was enormously popular, and so was the Bank veto, which the National Republicans, singularly misconceiving its effect, scattered by the thousands of copies throughout the country. The opposition was split by the inability of National Republicans and Antimasons to get together on a compromise candidate, even though some moderately effective state combinations between the two parties were established. But even if these two parties had been able to unite on one candidate, the result would have been the same.[39]

The election was one of the most decisive in the annals of American politics. Clay carried six states: Massachusetts, Rhode Island, Connecticut, Maryland, Delaware, and Kentucky. Wirt carried Vermont. South Carolina voted stubbornly for its own candidate, John Floyd of Virginia. Jackson had the rest. The Old Hero emerged with 219 electoral votes to Clay's 49, and a popular majority of 157,313 out of 1,217,691 votes cast. Local "Workingmen's" parties, organized largely by National Republicans during the preceding two years in an effort to weaken and disrupt Democratic local organizations, had had little or no effect on the national result.[40]

The National Republicans were thrown into the depths of gloom by the election of 1832. Their organ, the *National Intelligencer*, announced darkly that there was "an incendiary spirit abroad," and

[38] Gammon, *Presidential Campaign of 1832*, pp. 100–101.

[39] Flagg Papers, J. H. Keith to Flagg, Oct. 13, 1832, P. N. Nicholas to Flagg, Nov. 14, 1832. Duff Green, editor of the *Telegraph*, opposed Jackson and sought to bring Calhoun and Clay men together, without himself openly coming out for Clay. Duff Green Papers, Green to R. K. Cralle, Aug. 23, 1832, Green to James H. Pleasants, Aug. 27, 1832.

[40] Joseph Dorfman, *The Economic Mind in American Civilization, 1606–1918* (3 vols., New York, 1946–49), II, 643–645, 648–649. The best study of workingmen's parties is in William A. Sullivan, *The Industrial Worker in Pennsylvania, 1800–1840* (Harrisburg, 1955). See especially pp. 101, 162–180, 190–200.

Niles' Register declared that the election doomed not only the Bank but also all federal appropriations for internal improvements. The Democrats were understandably jubilant. It was a "Waterloo defeat" for Jackson's opponents, crowed Ritchie of the Richmond *Enquirer,* who was all the more elated because, in September, he had exactly predicted Jackson's vote in the Electoral College. How had such a feeble minority as the National Republicans been able to make so much noise, sarcastically enquired the New York *Evening Post.*[41] Jackson's supporters harped on the theme that the voice of the people had been heard. So it had. West and South had rallied to the Hero. If Kentucky be considered a southern rather than a western state, the West had gone solidly for Jackson, and in Kentucky itself Jackson had polled almost as many votes as Clay had received in all the rest of the South. Seldom have a party and its leader received a more triumphant vindication at the polls.

The close of 1832 saw the Democratic party stabilized under the leadership of Jackson and Van Buren. Defections had occurred during the past four years from the uneasy combination that had rolled to victory in 1828. Southern nullifiers, Quakers and Methodists embittered by the treatment of the Indians, internal-improvements men alarmed by the Maysville veto, Bank Democrats driven off by the Bank veto, all these had swelled the ranks of the defectors. But those ranks had remained a minority of the voting population. Save in New England, Jackson was still the idol of the people.

The results of the election were speedily manifest. The National Republicans, despairing of victory under their own banner, now sought to rally all opponents of Jackson and his measures under a new standard. The nullifiers, hopeless of relief from the tariff, began turning to extreme measures. As for the General, he felt encouraged to press on to the destruction of Biddle's "Monster." But before the intrepid leader could pursue his warfare against the bank, he had to meet a crisis provoked by the nullifiers of South Carolina.

[41] *National Intelligencer,* Nov. 15, 1832; *Niles' Register,* XLIII (Nov. 17, 1832), 177; Richmond *Enquirer* (semiweekly), Nov. 13, 1832; New York *Evening Post,* Nov. 12, 1832.

CHAPTER 4

Politics, a Tariff, and a Bank

WHILE the election of 1832 brought great joy to the Jacksonians, it also left them facing great responsibilities. The economic discontent of the South remained intense, and there had to be found some means of soothing the turbulent feelings of the plantation gentry. The Bank of the United States, though defeated in its effort to obtain a recharter, was still a power in the land, and many thought it a discordant element in a community where equal opportunity should be the rule of faith and practice. The Bank's influence, in the opinion of some of the most influential Jacksonians, should be restricted at once. It was evident also that the political opposition headed by Clay and orienting around his American system would lose no opportunity of harassing Jackson's administration and disrupting its attempts to formulate specific policies. This opposition must be thwarted.

The tariff, the Bank, and the maneuvering of the opposition party constituted grave problems. It was the South and its attitude toward the tariff, however, that demanded immediate attention.

The editor of the *New Hampshire Patriot,* in 1828, had proclaimed John Quincy Adams an enemy of protection, and had hailed Andrew Jackson as a friend of the tariff and the "True American System." Four years later, after Adams had guided the tariff of 1832 through the House and Jackson had signed it, another Jackson paper, William Cullen Bryant's New York *Evening Post,* had declared itself highly satisfied with this hybrid result. "The long debated question has been decided," said the *Post,* "and many of the animosities to which it gave rise will now be laid asleep."[1] Bryant was arguing on a higher plane than that occupied by his fellow editor, but his comment was as full of error as had been that of Isaac Hill. The tariff of 1832 was not a sign of peace, but of a period of crisis and tension that boded ill for the Union.

This tariff bill, which seemed so reasonable to the President, was deemed utterly unacceptable by the nullifiers, and after its passage resentment against the action of the federal government had steadily increased in South Carolina, the home of nullification. By voting for a man who had no earthly chance of election, the state had scorned the candidates of the contending parties in 1832. Indeed, the election in South Carolina had centered not on the Presidency but on the question of nullification. The "Nullies," as they were called, wanted swift action. They were opposed by a Union party, led by Joel Poinsett, Adams's minister to Mexico but now a Jacksonian Democrat. These Unionists had to face a rising storm of states' rights sentiment, and a lengthy disquisition by South Carolina's leading statesman "On the Subject of State Interposition."

Those who asserted that the Constitution of the United States was made by the people as a whole were wrong, Calhoun wrote to Governor Hamilton of South Carolina: "So far from the Constitution being the work of the American people collectively, no such political body either now or ever did exist . . . the Constitution is the work of the people of the States, considered as separate and independent political communities. . . . The Union, of which the Constitution is the bond, is a union of States, and not of individuals." Calhoun admitted that a state by ratifying the Constitution imposed obligations on its citizens, but he also asserted that it was the state's right to determine the extent of those obligations. When a state held an act of Congress unconstitutional, it could declare that act null and void, and such declaration was binding on the citizens of the state. Conversely, the national government had no authority to control or coerce a state.[2]

Calhoun was arguing for nullification, not for secession. He was, he said, seeking to preserve the Union, a Union that was in essence a confederation, with each state the final judge as to the constitution-

[1] *New Hampshire Patriot,* Apr. 4, 1828; New York *Evening Post,* Aug. 20, 1832.

[2] Richard K. Crallé (ed.), *Reports and Public Letters of John C. Calhoun* (6 vols., Charleston and New York, 1851–55), VI, 144–193.

ality of the acts of the national government. Such an argument was powerful justification for the nullifiers, but it left the form of national government without the substance. Despite Calhoun's intent, it blazed a path toward secession.

The South Carolina election was a victory for the nullifiers. The state might be said to have taken for its motto Judge Clayton's toast to the movement: "He that dallies is a dastard. He that doubts is damned." The nullifiers swept nearly every county and, when the dust of conflict had settled, emerged with more than a two-thirds' majority in both houses of the legislature. Governor Hamilton promptly called that body together in special session and it in turn voted for a convention. On November 19, 1832, 136 nullifiers and 26 Union men met at Columbia. Robert Y. Hayne, George McDuffie, Chancellor William Harper, nullifiers all, were the moving spirits of the convention; the Unionists were helpless.[3]

The nullifiers did their work swiftly. The convention passed an ordinance declaring that the tariffs of 1828 and 1832 were null and void, and that they would not be enforceable in South Carolina after February 1, 1833. The collection of duties by the federal government after that date was forbidden. Appeal of the validity of nullification to the Supreme Court of the United States was prohibited. The ordinance further declared that any forceful attempt by the federal government to coerce the state would dissolve the bonds of South Carolina's allegiance to the Union.

And we, the People of South Carolina, to the end that it may be fully understood by the Government of the United States, and the people of the co-States, that we are determined to maintain this, our Ordinance and Declaration, at every hazard, *Do further Declare* that we will not submit to the application of force, on the part of the Federal Government, to reduce this State to obedience; but that we will consider the passage, by Congress, of any act . . . to coerce the State, shut up her ports, destroy or harass her commerce, or to enforce the acts hereby declared to be null and void, otherwise than through the civil tribunals of the country, as inconsistent with the longer continuance of South Carolina in the Union: and that the people of this State will thenceforth hold themselves absolved from all further obligation to maintain or preserve their political connexion with the people of the

[3] Chauncey S. Boucher, *The Nullification Controversy in South Carolina* (Chicago, 1916), pp. 208–218; David F. Houston, *A Critical Study of Nullification in South Carolina* (Cambridge, 1896), pp. 109–111.

other States, and will forthwith proceed to organize a separate Government, and do all other acts and things which sovereign and independent States may of right do.[4]

This ordinance was a fair representation of the spirit that prevailed among the leaders of the nullifiers. They were ready to fight. "All appear animated," wrote James H. Hammond, editor of the Columbia *Southern Times,* "by the most thorough conviction that we are unconquerable."[5] When the legislature passed the laws necessary to implement the ordinance, it provided money for the purchase of arms and authorized the enlistment of volunteers.

The nullifiers called themselves "whigs" and scornfully applied the term "tory" to the Union men. Blood ran hot between the two factions. James Blair, member of Congress from South Carolina and a Unionist, was so enraged by the "tory" designation that he waylaid Duff Green on the Washington streets and assaulted him with a club.[6]

Jackson's reply to South Carolina's defiance was the adoption of a carrot and stick policy, a blending of conciliation and threat. In his message to Congress, December 4, 1832, the President spoke soothingly of the tariff problem. The rapidly approaching extinction of the national debt, he said, was lessening the importance of the tariff as a source of revenue. Declaring that he was fully aware of the inequities in the existing tariff, he made it clear that he now stood for a substantial reduction of duties. It was his opinion that eventually protection should be limited to articles essential to the nation's safety in time of war. He noted with regret the excitement in South Carolina, but deemed federal laws sufficient for coping with the situation in that state.[7]

Jackson's message was much calmer than the feelings that were stirring in his breast. As he read Poinsett's reports on the doings of the nullifiers, his eyes began to blaze. He wrote Poinsett that Calhoun showed signs of dementia, and that Hayne, McDuffie, and the rest were in a scarcely better condition of mind. South Carolina's attitude, he declared, was worse than rebellion. The raising of troops was

[4] Henry S. Commager (ed.), *Documents of American History* (New York, 1940), pp. 261–262.

[5] Boucher, *Nullification Controversy,* p. 277.

[6] Ewing Papers, Ewing to Mrs. Ewing, Dec. 26, 1832; *Niles' Register,* XLIII (Dec. 29, 1832), 287.

[7] James D. Richardson, *A Compilation of the Messages and Papers of the Presidents* (11 vols., New York, 1910), II, 1160–1162.

"positive treason." Congressmen were assuring him that the legislative branch would sustain him in defending "this union, which alone secures our liberty, prosperity and happiness." He would meet nullification at the threshold "and have the leaders arrested and arraigned for treason. The wickedness, madness and folly of the leaders and the delusion of their followers in the attempt to destroy themselves and our union has not its parallel in the history of the world."[8]

Deeply stirred though he was by the action of the nullifiers, the General moved cautiously. A warning to the people of South Carolina was drawn up, its drafting entrusted to the Secretary of State, Edward Livingston of Louisiana, a distinguished lawyer and politician who had stood shoulder to shoulder with Jackson at New Orleans and was in the President's confidence.

The "Proclamation to the People of South Carolina" was couched in the tones of a father admonishing his children. The South Carolina ordinance, said the President, prescribed a course of action that had as its object the destruction of the Union. The assumption that a state had power to annul a federal law was "incompatible with the existence of the Union, contradicted expressly by the letter of the Constitution, unauthorized by its spirit, inconsistent with every principle on which it was founded, and destructive of the great object for which it was formed." The arguments advanced by the state in justification of its action were inadequate, and he urged its citizens to recognize this inadequacy. Under the Constitution, a government had been formed which represented not the states but the people. No state, therefore, had the right to secede, "because such secession does not break a league, but destroys the unity of a nation. . . . To say that any state may at pleasure secede from the Union is to say that the United States is not a nation. . . ." Nullification, Jackson warned, could end only in failure and worse than failure:

If your leaders could succeed in establishing a separation, what would be your situation? Are you united at home? Are you free from the apprehension of civil discord, with all its fearful consequences? Do our neighboring republics, every day suffering some new revolution or contending with some new insurrection, do they excite your envy? But the dictates of a high duty oblige me solemnly to announce that you cannot succeed. The laws of the United States must be executed. I have no discretionary power on the subject; my

[8] Jackson Papers (second series), Poinsett to Jackson, Nov. 25, 1832, Jackson to Poinsett, Dec. 9, 1832.

duty is emphatically pronounced in the Constitution. Those who told you that you might peaceably prevent their execution deceived you; they could not have been deceived themselves. They know that a forcible opposition could alone prevent the execution of the laws, and they know that such opposition must be repelled. Their object is disunion. But be not deceived by names. Disunion by armed force is *treason*. Are you really ready to incur its guilt?[9]

This Proclamation expounded a political theory strikingly similar to that proclaimed by Daniel Webster in his replies to Hayne, and the Massachusetts statesman gave it his immediate approval.[10] Its explicit and unmistakable warning to the nullifiers was backed by military dispositions and a request to Congress for additional powers for the collection of import duties.[11] These powers were embodied in the Force Bill (South Carolinians dubbed it the "Bloody Bill"), which was reported to the Senate from the Judiciary Committee on January 21, 1833, and which also received Webster's support.[12]

But even as this stick was being brandished, the carrot was again displayed. It took the form of the Verplanck bill, drawn up with the assistance of Secretary of the Treasury Louis McLane and other friends of the administration, and reported out by the Committee on Ways and Means of the House of Representatives on January 8, 1833. This bill proposed immediate and sweeping reductions in duties, with the tariff lowered 50 per cent by 1834.

Jackson and his whole administration supported the Verplanck bill. They were extremely anxious to see the tariff lowered, for the general expectation was that the whole South would go against the Force Bill unless a satisfactory tariff bill was passed. Indeed, Silas Wright wrote to Azariah Flagg from Washington that without such a bill the government would be virtually disbanded.[13]

To make the situation even more difficult, Clay was pushing for the passage of his land bill. This was based on the principle of distribution

[9] Richardson, *Messages and Papers*, II, 1203–1219; Commager, *Documents*, pp. 262–268.

[10] Claude M. Fuess, *Daniel Webster* (2 vols., Boston, 1930) I, 390.

[11] Richardson, *Messages and Papers*, II, 1173–1195.

[12] Commager, *Documents*, pp. 269–270. Duff Green called it "the bill of blunders and of blood." *United States Telegraph*, Mar. 13, 1833.

[13] Flagg Papers, Flagg to Wright, Jan. 27, 1833; Welles Papers, Hill to Welles, Dec. 20, 1832, Wright to Welles, Feb. 13, 1833; *Register of Debates*, 22nd Cong., second session, IX, pt. 1, 150, 958; Jackson Papers (second series), Calhoun to S. D. Ingham (copy), Jan. 16, 1833.

of the land sales revenue to all the states and, it was estimated, would necessitate the raising of some $3 million in additional revenue each year to take the place of the land revenue that would go to the states instead of toward the expenses of the national government. Many members of Congress, including a number of Jacksonian Democrats, were planning to vote for this bill as a means of forcing higher duties than were provided in Verplanck's tariff measure. Greatly distressed by this situation, Wright declared that Clay's proposal was "the most mischievous bill, in my judgment, that ever originated in the Congress of the United States."[14]

As ardent a nationalist as Jackson, Clay reluctantly supported the Force Bill, but the Verplanck measure was anathema to him. Nevertheless, it was obvious that the tariff was going to be lowered and that whoever was responsible for it would gain considerable credit, especially in the South. Clay wanted that credit. He was also moved by a complex of other motives. Dislike and distrust of Jackson, jealousy of Webster, a desire to recoup some of the prestige lost in his recent shattering defeat, all played a part in the thinking of the Kentucky statesman. There was also the possibility of a political alliance with Calhoun and, even more important, the enlisting of broad southern support for the land bill that he was attempting to push through Congress in the face of the administration's outspoken preference for cheap land.[15]

Clay moved cautiously at first. He consulted with John Tyler of Virginia, an ardent states' rights exponent, and with a number of congressional leaders. He conferred with Calhoun, who, having resigned as Vice-President, was now representing South Carolina in the Senate, and who, according to John J. Crittenden, requested Clay's aid in averting Jackson's wrath.[16] The result was the compromise tariff of 1833.

Clay introduced his bill in the Senate on February 12, 1833. It provided for gradual reductions, at two-year intervals, of all tariff schedules in the 1832 tariff that were over 20 per cent. There were to be four of these reductions to 1840. Then, over a two-year period, there would

[14] Flagg Papers, Wright to Flagg, Jan. 27, 1833; *Register of Debates*, 22nd Cong., second sess., IX, pt. 1, 6, 61.

[15] Glyndon G. Van Deusen, *The Life of Henry Clay* (Boston, 1937), pp. 266–267.

[16] George T. Curtis, *Life of Daniel Webster* (2 vols., New York, 1870), I, 444.

be two relatively sharp reductions of the remaining duties above the 20 per cent level. By July 1, 1842, there would be a top-level duty rate of 20 per cent. The bill was amended, at the insistence of protectionist forces, by a salutary provision for the valuation of dutiable goods at the port of entry, thus striking a blow at the fraudulent invoices that had plagued the customs service for many years.

But despite its good features, the compromise tariff of 1833 was not a good bill from an economic viewpoint. It made no provision for specific duties as contrasted with ad valorem, though it was meant to apply to both; the duty reductions were irregular; the 20 per cent level of 1842 set a purely arbitrary and indiscriminate standard of duties. It was a bill framed primarily with an eye to political considerations.[17]

Clay's compromise had heavy going in both houses of Congress. Democratic leaders promptly raised the objection that revenue bills could not originate in the Senate. Clay met this with the ingenious argument that this was a bill not to raise but to lower revenue, since it lowered duties, an argument that apparently baffled his opponents until, objection being again raised, the difficulty was obviated by having the measure introduced in the lower chamber and then promptly reintroduced in the Senate as a House bill. The provision for valuation at the port of entry was most objectionable to Calhoun, for it meant adding freight and insurance to the amount on which the duty was levied, but he had to accept it or lose the vital support for the bill given by moderate protectionist elements in Congress. Webster attacked the measure as a whole, deeming it destructive of industrial interests and an unseemly yielding to the threats of a state. He was joined in opposition by senators from protectionist centers, such as George M. Dallas of Pennsylvania and Asher Robbins of Rhode Island.[18]

The compromise tariff passed the House on February 26, 1833, by a vote of 119 to 85. There the South was almost solidly for the bill. New England was definitely against it, the Middle Atlantic states voted against it three to one, and the North Central states (Ohio, Indiana, and Illinois) split. The Senate vote, on March 1, was twenty-nine for to

[17] Frank W. Taussig, *The Tariff History of the United States* (New York, 1931), pp. 110–111; G. G. Van Deusen, *Clay*, p. 268.

[18] *Register of Debates*, 22nd Cong., second sess., 462–486; John B. McMaster, *A History of the People of the United States* (8 vols., New York, 1883–1914), VI, 166–167; Thomas H. Benton, *Thirty Years View* (2 vols., New York, 1854), I, 324.

sixteen against. The sixteen were almost evenly divided between the followers of Clay and Jackson. Six were from New England, five from the Middle Atlantic states, and five from west of the Appalachians. A better proof that the tariff was a local issue could scarcely be imagined.[19]

The Force Bill passed at the same time as the tariff, and Jackson signed both measures on March 2, 1833. South Carolina promptly nullified the Force Bill[20] but accepted the new tariff, and so, for the time being, the danger of civil war passed away.

The struggle which produced the compromise tariff of 1833 has a considerable significance in American history. The protectionists waxed melancholy over the act. Mathew Carey declared that "to remove the imaginary grievance of a portion of the states, real substantial grievances are inflicted on the remainder, whereby a large portion of their industry and happiness will be blasted and withered."[21] Webster, now the great spokesman of New England's industrial interests, was embittered by the passage of the bill. Almost ten years after the event, he could still say that there was "no measure ever passed by Congress during my connection with that body that caused me so much grief and mortification. It was passed by a few friends joining the whole host of the enemy. . . . The principle was bad, the measure was bad, the consequences were bad."[22] There can be no doubt that this tariff bill did much to widen the breach already opening between Webster and Clay.

The bill had other consequences besides emphasizing the cleavage between Webster and Clay, and between the pro- and antitariff men in the opposition. The industrialists were thrown into an unnecessary panic by the bill's passage. The reductions for which it provided down to 1840 were relatively slight, and there was every reason to anticipate, as Clay did, a revision of the act before its more drastic reductions went into effect. It is true that this revision did not appear, but the final 20 per cent duty for which the measure provided remained in effect only two months, July to September, 1842. Certainly the tariff

[19] *Register of Debates,* 22nd Cong., second sess., IX, pt. 1, 808–809; pt. 2, 1810–1811; Frederick J. Turner, *The United States, 1830–1850* (New York, 1935), pp. 419–420.

[20] Commager, *Documents,* pp. 269–270.

[21] *United States Telegraph,* Mar. 19, 1833.

[22] Daniel Webster, *Writings and Speeches* (18 vols., Boston, 1903), III, 131. Boston speech of Sept. 30, 1842.

of 1833 cannot be regarded as having had an injurious effect upon the national economy.[23]

The conflict over the tariff was also significant for Clay's political future. Even though it sowed seeds of enmity between himself and Webster, it gave a new lease of life to his reputation as the "Great Pacificator." It gave him standing with such states' rights men as John Tyler and Littleton Tazewell of Virginia, men who either became politically neutral or moved into the ranks of the Kentuckian's supporters. And—an anticlimax as it proved—it rallied southern votes to his land bill, which passed Congress only to be pocket-vetoed by the indomitable Chieftain in the White House, who had now reversed himself on distribution as well as on the tariff.

Significant, too, was the emergence from the struggle over the tariff of a working agreement between Clay and Calhoun. The two men had worked together on the compromise, and their *rapprochement* was made all the more evident by the way in which Congress handled the appointments to the lucrative offices of printers to the House and Senate. The House rejected Blair (member of the Kitchen Cabinet and editor of the Washington *Globe*), choosing instead Duff Green, whose daughter had married Calhoun's son and who was a stout supporter of the South Carolinian. Gales and Seaton, the editors of Clay's organ, the *National Intelligencer,* were made printers to the Senate.

The understanding between Calhoun and Clay was to last for the remainder of Jackson's term of office and was to provide formidable opposition, particularly in the Senate, to "King Andrew." Ambition, and hatred of the Hero, had made the great nationalist and the great nullifier lie down together on an uneasy bed of political alliance. It was a combination as opposed to nature as the lion and the lamb of Holy Writ, but while it lasted the opposition to "Jacksonism" could, through astute leadership, challenge the Jacksonians' control of the legislative branch.[24]

[23] *Register of Debates,* 22nd Cong., second sess., 462–486, 718–742; Taussig, *Tariff History,* pp. 116–118.

[24] John S. Bassett (ed.), *Correspondence of Andrew Jackson* (7 vols., Washington, 1926–35), IV, 504–505; Richardson, *Messages and Papers,* II, 1275–1288; Nathan Sargent, *Public Men and Events* (2 vols., Philadelphia, 1875), I, 229–241; Benton, *Thirty Years View,* I, 296–347; Calvin Colton (ed.), *The Private Correspondence of Henry Clay* (Boston, 1856), pp. 347–358, 361–362; William W. Story (ed.), *Life and Letters of Joseph Story* (2 vols., Boston, 1851), II, 113, 119, 121–122; Boucher, *Nullification Controversy,* pp. 286–

While the passage of the compromise tariff was a triumph for nationalism and majority rule, the controversy had been full of sad omens for the future. South Carolina had gone beyond the Virginia and Kentucky resolutions of 1798. The possibility and even the desirability of secession had been openly discussed, and men wore the blue cockade which the nullifiers had adopted as their emblem long after the tempest over the tariff had died down. To all sections the conflict between the free, diversified economy of the North, with its rapidly developing industrial capitalism, and the agrarian, slave-labor economy of the South, with its need for foreign markets, was becoming fearfully apparent.

But despite gloomy portents, the doctrine of "interposition," so stoutly upheld by Calhoun, had been answered with crushing force by Webster and the Unionists. The Constitution is a compact. It must be interpreted in accordance with its provisions for interpretation, that is, by the courts. If it does not properly protect the rights of the states, the remedy is not interposition by them for the purpose of rendering nugatory the decisions of the Supreme Court, or the constitutional acts of any other branch of the federal government. The remedy is amendment of the federal Constitution itself. All other expedients weaken and, if persisted in, destroy both the compact and the Union.

Important as was the conflict over the tariff, it was not the only battle royal in which the administration became engaged during the winter of 1832–33. Jackson was determined to continue his assaults upon the Bank of the United States. Its charter had four more years to run, but this made no difference. The General was moved by dislike and distrust of an institution which he did not understand and which had sought to thwart his will, and the arguments of Taney and Kendall fortified his determination to deprive it of its remaining power in the financial and political community. Taney opposed the Bank on the ground that it had made excessive loans, some of which had been for political support. He also believed it to be unconstitutional—a definitely strict constructionist point of view. Kendall regarded the Bank as a corrupt and dangerously powerful institution which was still plotting for a renewal of its charter. Its destruction, he held, was essential to the preservation of a purely republican government.[25]

Jackson told a Cabinet meeting in November, 1832, that he was

---

313; Frederick L. Nussbaum, "The Compromise Tariff of 1833," *South Atlantic Quarterly,* XI (Oct., 1912), 337–349.

[25] William Stickney (ed.), *Autobiography of Amos Kendall* (Boston, 1872),

convinced the Bank was insolvent, and suggested withdrawing the deposits in it which had been made by the government. Attorney General Taney supported this suggestion. Then the President asked Congress for an investigation to discover whether or not the government deposits in the Bank were safe. The House investigated and replied that they were safe, but the President cared not one whit for this opinion. He next sent Amos Kendall on a mission to bankers in Baltimore, Philadelphia, New York, and Boston to find out if they would take the government deposits. Kendall reported that the bankers would be more than glad to have the funds. It became more and more apparent that removal of the deposits was to be the next step. Such a move, Biddle told Webster, would be "a declaration of war."[26]

The President had Taney and Kendall at his back in removing the deposits, but the Secretary of the Treasury was of another mind altogether. Louis McLane could see no good reason for this step, especially since Congress was opposed, and he said so. It had already been decided to shift McLane from the Treasury to the State Department so that Livingston could become Minister to France. This was now done, and William J. Duane, a Philadelphia lawyer and anti-Bank man was made Secretary of the Treasury.

Jackson took it for granted that Duane would remove the deposits, but he soon discovered that he had caught a tartar. Duane had no more love for state banks than he had for the Bank of the United States and he, too, refused to do the President's bidding. He told the President that the House had voted the public money safe in the Bank (so it had, 110 to 46); that a change to local banks as depositories would shake public confidence; that local banks already had an overinflated currency of better than six dollars in paper to one in silver (the implication being that deposit in local banks would inevitably result in further inflation of the currency).[27]

Duane's arguments, sound though they were, fell upon deaf ears. He was summarily dismissed, and now the President shifted Taney from the Attorney General's office over into the Treasury. At last he had the right man in the right place, so far as his policy was con-

---

pp. 374–375; Carl B. Swisher, *Roger B. Taney* (New York, 1936), pp. 190–193, 212–213, 218.

[26] Reginald C. McGrane (ed.), *The Correspondence of Nicholas Biddle* (Boston and New York, 1919), p. 205; Kendall, pp. 374–376; Bray Hammond, *Banks and Politics in America* (Princeton, 1957), pp. 412–419; Swisher, *Taney,* pp. 210–212.

[27] Kendall, p. 374; Hammond, *Banks and Politics,* pp. 417–418.

cerned. The Treasury continued drawing on its balance in the Bank for current expenses, but it now made its deposits in a number of state banks, the "Pets," located in the principal cities in the country. Its balance in the Bank of the United States grew steadily smaller.

Biddle, meantime, had determined to do the sensible thing—contract the Bank's obligations as the funds at its disposal diminished, and at the same time make the institution ready to repel any other assaults that might be made upon it. He also cherished the hope that, by utilizing the power the Bank still had left, he might yet be able to effect a recharter.[28] During the winter and spring of 1834, the cultured banker and the fiery, iron-willed President confronted one another like two armed and implacable enemies.

The deterioration of relations between the government and the Bank was illustrated by Biddle's handling of the administration's attempt to collect money from the French government. In 1831, a treaty had been signed by France and the United States by which France agreed to pay 25 million francs for damages inflicted upon American commerce during the Napoleonic Wars. The treaty had been ratified February 2, 1832, and payment was supposed to begin a year from that date. As February, 1833, approached, the United States undertook to collect and, on Biddle's advice, a draft was drawn on the French government. The Bank purchased the bill at the day's highest price and forwarded it to London for collection. France refused payment on the ground that no appropriation for that purpose had been made by the French chambers. The bill was then taken up by the Bank's continental agent, Hottinguer and Company. As was customary in such cases, Biddle presented to the American government a claim for interest and for 15 per cent damages. The claim amounted to $170,041.18.

The government denied the justice of the Bank's claim, characterizing it as extortion, and there was much bad feeling on both sides. The Bank collected its claim in 1834 by deducting the sum from the government's dividend. The government charged the Bank with seizing public funds and the case moved into the courts. Eventually, in 1847, the Supreme Court found against the Bank.[29]

[28] Biddle, *Correspondence*, pp. 219–220, 222; Walter B. Smith, *Economic Aspects of the Second Bank of the United States* (Cambridge, 1953), pp. 164–165.

[29] 5 Howard 380–409; Ralph C. H. Catterall, *The Second Bank of the United States* (Chicago, 1903), pp. 299–302; W. B. Smith, *Economic Aspects of the Second Bank,* pp. 159–160.

While this dispute over the payment of the French claim was going on, the removal of the deposits had begun, and Biddle was calling in the Bank's loans and restricting its discount of notes. This policy of contraction, at its beginning, was thoroughly justifiable. No one could tell what measures Jackson might take in his drive to cripple the Bank's power. It was only right that Biddle should guard against all contingencies. He continued the contraction, however, into the winter and spring of 1833–34, when it was no longer necessary in order to safeguard the Bank. This was done with the design of forcing a recharter. Both Biddle the banker and Clay the political leader believed that the general distress occasioned by calling in loans and refusing credit in the name of the Bank's safety would create a demand for rechartering the Bank, a demand that in the long run would prove irresistible.[30]

The effects of the contraction of credit are not easily determined. There was some credit stringency, some tightness in the money market. The administration at first denied that there was anything the matter with the financial situation, then pointed to the Bank as the cause of all the trouble. The pro-Bank forces claimed that the financial status of the country was precarious, that it was growing worse, and that it was all Jacksons' fault. Hundreds of petitions for relief flooded Congress and deputations of businessmen waited on Jackson to beg for relief.

They found the President adamant. Trembling with rage and with the intensity of his convictions, he told the suppliant businessmen to "go to the Monster, go to Nicholas Biddle," if they wanted relief. "I never will restore the deposits," he stormed at the New York committee. "I never will recharter the United States Bank, or sign a charter for any other bank, so long as my name is Andrew Jackson." He told the Baltimore committee that "the failures that are now taking place are amongst the stock-jobbers, brokers, and gamblers, and would to God, they were all swept from the land! It would be a happy thing for the country." The Hero wrote to Van Buren that he was "fixed in my course as firm as the Rocky Mountain . . . Providence has a power over me, but frail mortals who worship Bale [sic] and the golden calf, can have none."[31]

[30] W. B. Smith, *Economic Aspects of the Second Bank,* pp. 160–167; Catterall, *Second Bank,* pp. 289–299; G. G. Van Deusen, *Clay,* p. 283.

[31] *Register of Debates,* 23rd Cong., first sess., X, pt. 3, 3071–3075; Flagg Papers, Jackson to Van Buren, Feb., 1834.

Actually, the crisis in financial affairs seems to have been exaggerated by both sides for the purposes of political war. There was some unemployment and some decline in stock values in the winter of 1833–34, but imports, commodity exports, and internal commerce all increased during that period. John A. Dix wrote to Wright and Van Buren from Albany in February, 1834, that times were better than they had been in the previous year, and that the only people being hurt by the contraction were gamblers in stocks and commodities. Isaac Hill believed that the Bank's contraction policy would, at most, create only a temporary distress. So thought Robert Rantoul in Boston. Even the New York *Evening Post,* which was disposed to cry havoc about the Bank's policy, admitted that the decline in cotton prices abroad, the exaction of cash duties on imported goods, and the failure of the sugar crops at the South were in part to blame for the tight money market in the winter of 1834.[32]

The chief result of the pressure exerted by Biddle was a marked lessening of the Bank's popularity. The contraction, as the Richmond *Enquirer* put it, had given the Jacksonians an opportunity to view with alarm. This they had done, calling upon the people to "tremble at the enormous power of this mammoth institution,"[33] and the people's response had been that anticipated by the Democratic politicians.

The government now deposited its money in the "Pets." Some of these were well chosen, others not. They all promptly expanded their loans, and in this way fostered the speculative craze that characterized the eighteen-thirties and terminated in the depression of 1837.

In 1836 the Bank received a new charter as the United States Bank of Pennsylvania. This charter committed it to pay a bonus of $2 million to the state, to make loans to the state for internal improvements, and to purchase the state's public utility stocks. Biddle estimated that the cost of the charter to the Bank was $5,775,000, a price that he did not regard as high but that proved to be a heavy financial burden.

The United States Bank of Pennsylvania soon found itself in other difficulties than those imposed by its charter. While times were yet

[32] Flagg Papers, Dix to Wright, Feb. 11, 1834, Dix to Van Buren, Feb. 16, 1834; Welles Papers, Isaac Hill to Welles, Apr. 22, 1834; Luther Hamilton (ed.), *Memoirs, Speeches, and Writings of Robert Rantoul, Jr.* (Boston, 1854), pp. 535–537; New York *Evening Post,* Jan. 14, 21, 25, Feb. 4, 1834; W. B. Smith, *Economic Aspects of the Second Bank,* pp. 170–172; Thomas S. Berry, *Western Prices Before 1860* (Cambridge, 1943), p. 410.

[33] Richmond *Enquirer,* Jan. 18, Apr. 18, 1834.

good, it began borrowing heavily abroad, a debt that proved embarrassing in the depression years. It also became involved in a disastrous cotton corner, this being the result of Biddle's effort to support the price of United States cotton in the face of a falling world market. As cotton prices continued to sag and the Bank found itself more and more heavily involved, it sought salvation by raiding the New York, Boston, and Baltimore money markets. Its credit became more and more shaky. Wise investors disposed of their holdings in its stock. Early in 1841 it closed its doors forever, a bankrupt institution.

On March 29, 1839, Nicholas Biddle resigned as president of the United States Bank of Pennsylvania, but nevertheless he was closely associated with the last disastrous phases of the Bank's career. He continued to advise his successors in the Bank after his retirement and was heavily involved in the cotton corner. As this corner failed and the Bank's financial situation deteriorated, stockholders in the institution sued Biddle for $240,000, and he and four other former officers of the Bank were arrested on charges of criminal conspiracy. They were exonerated in court procedings. Other court actions ensued, but Biddle was not long involved. He died February 27, 1844, at the age of fifty-eight.

The career of the United States Bank of Pennsylvania has often been used to support the argument that the Jacksonians were justified in destroying the Second Bank of the United States. Certain it is that the same management developed the policies of both institutions. The Bank of the United States, however, had been a central bank, operating under a federal charter and vested with great responsibility for the public welfare. This was not the case with the United States Bank of Pennsylvania. There the public responsibility was gone and with it the restraint upon daring speculative enterprise. Biddle, as head of the Bank of the United States, had been a conservative and conscientious banker. When he became head of a state bank, he made errors of judgment that were disastrous to the institution he served. Such capacity for error was, perhaps, inherent in his character, but it had not been apparent before the Jacksonians leagued to destroy him and the Bank of the United States together.[34]

Such was the story of the Second Bank of the United States and its

[34] The best analyses of the course of the United States Bank of Pennsylvania are to be found in Hammond, *Banks and Politics,* pp. 451–548, and W. B. Smith, *Economic Aspects of the Second Bank,* pp. 178–263.

tragic aftermath. The Bank had been given too much power by the charter granted it in 1816. Had it been rechartered, this power could have been curbed by regulatory provisions; indeed, some attempt at this had been made by the Bank's friends. The idea of charter modification was much in the air during the early eighteen-thirties. Hezekiah Niles, Nathan Appleton, Daniel Webster, Horace Greeley, even Jackson himself, projected such plans. The modifications in the Bank's charter provided by the recharter bill of 1832 were constructive. They would have made for a better institution. But when the Bank became a political football, the issue was no longer susceptible to rational analysis. Its destruction as a federal bank fostered speculation, was a blow to the development of a sound credit policy, and contributed materially to the currency chaos that characterized the succeeding decades. The economic development of the United States along sound and constructive lines was clearly hindered by the destruction of the Bank.

Politically, the Jacksonians profited by the Bank war. Clay, Webster, and their followers generally had rallied to the Bank's support, and this gave the Jacksonians an opportunity to pillory their political opponents as the lackeys of a "mammoth corporation," friends of the wealthy and powerful, exploiters of the masses. Whig leaders, such as Thurlow Weed and William Henry Seward, sought to dissociate themselves from the "Monster," but it was uphill work. The Jacksonians knew a good thing when they saw it. Isaac Hill told Gideon Welles that the Bank issue between the parties was "primarily the question that democrats should most desire," and Van Buren wrote gleefully to Jackson in July, 1834, "The Opposition labor hard to shake off the Bank, but we are determined to hold them to it. A fitter union was never formed."[35]

The struggle over the deposits was only one aspect of the political conflict that raged during Jackson's second term. The Twenty-third Congress had a House of Representatives that could generally be counted safe by the administration, but the Clay-Webster-Calhoun group could muster a majority in the Senate.[36] This opposition took away from the Senate's presiding officer the power of appointing com-

[35] Welles Papers, Hill to Welles, Apr. 11, 1834; Jackson Papers (second series), Van Buren to Jackson, July 22, 1834.

[36] The House had 147 Democrats, 43 National Republicans, 53 Antimasons, 7 nullifiers, and 10 states' rights members. The Senate had 20 Democrats, 20 National Republicans, 2 nullifiers, and 6 states' rights members.

mittees which he had exercised since 1828, restoring it to the body of the Senate, that is, to the anti-Jackson coalition. The President's opponents were out to embarrass the administration in every possible way, as was soon to be shown by their assaults upon the Cabinet and upon Old Hickory himself.

The opposition knew what it wanted, but its great handicap was a lack of discipline. It held together only through its detestation of the Old Hero. Clay commanded great loyalty among the lesser lights, but Webster could not always be counted upon to support him. Calhoun was but a recent convert, and both the rival chieftains found the Kentuckian's imperious manner difficult to bear. There could always be defection, too, where economic or other sectional interests were at stake. Clay counted himself, rightly, as the leader, but he never knew from day to day whether his shaky coalition would hold firm.[37]

When Congress convened on December 2, 1833, Clay lost no time in taking the offensive. He offered a resolution requesting the President to furnish the Senate with a paper he had read to his Cabinet on the removal of the deposits from the Bank of the United States. The pretext was Clay's desire for an authentic copy of what had already been published in the press. This time his coalition held together. The resolution passed the Senate by a vote of twenty-three to eighteen. Jackson refused to accede, alleging, quite correctly, that the request was an infringement of the Executive's prerogative.[38] Then Clay, in the midst of attacks against the inefficient Postmaster General Barry and Secretary of the Treasury Taney, undertook to persuade the Senate to condemn the President's course regarding the deposits. On December 26, 1833, he dramatically offered two resolutions of censure. One declared that, by dismissing Duane and appointing Taney in order to effect the removal of the deposits, Jackson had assumed a power not granted him by either the Constitution or the laws, and dangerous to popular liberty. The second declared the reasons assigned for removal of the deposits to be "unsatisfactory and insufficient."[39]

The country, Harry of the West charged, was in the midst of a revolution, "hitherto bloodless," that was rapidly changing the government from a republic to a dictatorship. Jackson's use of the veto, his frequent and arbitrary appointments and removals of government

[37] Clayton Papers, Clay to Clayton, Dec. 12, 1833.
[38] *Register of Debates,* 23rd Cong., first sess., 30–37.
[39] *Ibid.,* 58–59.

functionaries, his contemptuous disregard of the judiciary, his attitude toward the American system, and the union of the purse and the sword that was being effected by the subjection of the Treasury to the Executive will constituted Clay's evidence in the case. If the trend continued until March 4, 1837, said Clay, the government would become an elective monarchy—"the worst of all forms of government." Lengthily, Clay argued that the Constitution and the Fathers had lodged the power of the purse in the hands of Congress; that the Secretary of the Treasury was responsible to Congress, not to the President. The function of the Chief Executive was to execute the laws, not to interpret or override them. His office was one "of observation and superintendence," not of dictation to other officials of the government. The Western Hotspur closed his speech with a darkly shadowed verbal picture of the contemporary scene:

> We behold the usual incidents of approaching tyranny. The land is filled with spies and informers; and detraction and denunciation are the orders of the day. People, especially official incumbents in this place, no longer dare speak in the fearless tones of manly freedom, but in the cautious whispers of trembling slaves. The premonitory symptoms of despotism are upon us; and if Congress do not apply an instantaneous and effective remedy, the fatal collapse will soon come on, and we shall die—ignobly die! base, mean, and abject slaves—the scorn and contempt of mankind—unpitied, unwept, unmourned![40]

A running debate of three months' duration followed Clay's onslaught. Benton, Wright, and Forsyth bore the brunt for the administration. Webster and Calhoun supported Clay. The latter reiterated his concern over "the rapid strides of Executive power." Webster declared that the country's welfare, its Constitution, and its laws were at stake. Calhoun, proclaiming himself independent of both the major parties and an impartial judge, asserted that the removal of the deposits was an unconstitutional act and an alarming portent of "the approach of despotic power." What was it, asked the South Carolinian, but a distribution through the pet banks "in the shape of discounts and loans to corrupt partisans as a means of increasing political influence?" The crisis was a fearful one, he said, and there was danger of both dissolution and despotism.[41]

[40] *Ibid.;* Calvin Colton (ed.), *The Works of Henry Clay* (10 vols., New York, 1904), VII, 575–620.

[41] *Register of Debates,* 23rd Cong., first sess., 222–223, 475, 1172–1184.

The Jacksonians vigorously fought back. Wright defended removal of the deposits as both constitutional and wise, and made an impassioned plea for the Hero of New Orleans, the Indian fighter, the people's choice, who was now being condemned without trial. Benton declared that all the pother trumped up by the opposition was for the purpose of obtaining a recharter of the Bank of the United States. The Bank was the head of the American system. If rechartered, it would re-establish that system—tariffs, local internal improvements, and all—in greater power and glory than ever before. Forsyth pooh-poohed the dire predictions of calamity and despotism that accompanied the removal of the deposits. For years such predictions had been the stock in trade of congressmen, but the crisis predicted had always vanished and the pictures exhibited had always turned out to be "fancy sketches."[42]

The administration forces fought a losing battle against Clay's resolutions. On March 28, 1834, the resolutions, their phraseology slightly softened, passed the Senate by votes of twenty-six to twenty and twenty-eight to eighteen.[43]

The debate had centered around the powers and prerogatives of the President. Here the opposition was on dangerous ground, particularly in regard to the Treasury, for the Chief Executive had always appointed the Secretary of the Treasury, and had been expressly given the right to remove him from office.[44] It was only when the President's critics assailed his destruction of the Bank and the removal of the deposits that they were on safe ground. It was better to question the wisdom of Jackson's acts than their constitutionality.

Jackson indignantly protested the censure in a special message and asked that this be entered in the Senate journal.[45] The Senate rejected the request. The House, where the Jacksonians could muster a majority, refused to concur in the censure, and also turned down a Clay-inspired resolution for the restoration of the deposits to the Bank of the United States. But the opposition had a triumph of sorts when the Senate

[42] *Ibid.*, 342–343, 1159–1167, 1242–1247.

[43] *Ibid.*, 1187.

[44] *The Laws of the United States of America* (3 vols., Philadelphia, 1796), I, 36–40, "An Act to Establish the Treasury Department," Sept. 2, 1789, sec. 7: "That whenever the Secretary shall be removed from office by the President of the United States, or in any other case of vacancy . . . the assistant [to the Secretary] shall . . . have the charge and custody of the records, books, and papers appertaining to the said office."

[45] Richardson, *Messages and Papers*, II, 1288–1312.

rejected a long list of presidential nominations, including that of Roger B. Taney as Secretary of the Treasury.

The Democrats emerged from the elections of 1834 with an increased majority in the House, where they now numbered 145 as against 98 Whigs, and triumphantly elected one James K. Polk of Tennessee as Speaker. Twenty-seven Democrats confronted twenty-five Whigs in the Senate. All the efforts of the opposition had failed to stay the march of the Bank toward destruction, and even Clay could see that it was doomed. So too was his land bill, which he repeatedly introduced and which as repeatedly failed of passage. Only the vote of censure remained as a blot on the administration's record, and this was but temporary, for in January, 1837, a Democratic majority expunged the resolution, drawing black lines around the offending words while the General's enemies uttered mournful but futile cries of protest. Small wonder that Clay, at the end of Jackson's second term, was to comment that the President had "swept over the Government, during the last eight years, like a tropical tornado."[46]

Clay's impassioned description of the effect of Jacksonism was, of course, exaggerated. It took no account of the interest in preserving equality of opportunity which was at least one basis of the Jacksonian war on the Bank. It ignored that devotion to the rights of the common man which the Jacksonians proclaimed, and which in part underlay rotation in office, their inclination toward a cheap land policy, and their ready acceptance of white manhood suffrage. But in the realm of finance Jacksonian influence had been destructive, while the introduction of the spoils system had had a deteriorating influence on the public administration.

And in still another way Jacksonism had meant a retrograde movement. This was in science and scientific discovery. The first Presidents of the United States had been men of broad culture, interested in the advancement of science and learning. Washington and Madison and John Quincy Adams had advocated a national university. John Adams had been an intellectual and a scholar. Jefferson was one of America's early scientists, interested in Virginia's flora and fauna and in the scientific possibilities of the Lewis and Clark expedition. From 1797 to 1815 he was president of the American Philosophical Society, and his correspondence with foreign scientists was voluminous. John Quincy Adams, in his first message to Congress, urged contributions to geo-

[46] *Register of Debates,* 24th Cong., second sess., 438.

graphical and astronomical science, the outfitting of scientific expeditions, the establishment of an astronomical observatory (he mentioned these "lighthouses of the skies" in flattering terms), and an examination of the patent laws with a view to stimulating scientific invention.[47] These men gave a tone to the national administration which, had it been continuous, would have given a constant stimulus to the development of scientific research.

Jackson's administration ushered in a change of view at Washington in connection with science, to say nothing of the other aspects of intellectual life. The triumph of an administration whose principal organ declared that the world is governed too much, the devotion to governmental economy, the lack of intellectual interest characteristic of the Old Hero and many of those who surrounded him, diminished the likelihood of assistance for scientific learning from the national government. Jackson did sign a bill for exploration of the Pacific that eventually resulted in the despatch of the Wilkes expedition of 1838, but aside from this the record was mainly negative. The federal government refused to take any practical steps to safeguard public health, this at a time when local government was becoming increasingly concerned with health problems. Jacksonians such as Benton and Silas Wright were fearful of another centralizing agency like the Bank that they had just destroyed. Consequently, they defeated a proposal by Whig Senator Asher Robbins that Englishman James Smithson's $500,000 bequest to the United States should be used to create a scientific and literary institution in Washington, and it was not until 1846 that the efforts of men like John Quincy Adams and Joel Poinsett established the Smithsonian Institution. The idea of a national university was abandoned. A national observatory went by the board. The conclusion is inescapable that the advent of Jacksonian Democracy delayed the advance of scientific thought and experimental research in the United States.[48]

[47] Richardson, *Messages and Papers,* II, 878–882; A. Hunter Dupree, *Science in the Federal Government* (Cambridge, 1957), pp. 1–43.

[48] William J. Rhees (ed.), *The Smithsonian Institution* (2 vols., Washington, 1901), I, 171–182; Dupree, *Science,* pp. 66–79; Charles A. Beard (ed.), *A Century of Progress* (New York, 1932), pp. 291–295, 323–324; Dirk J. Struik, *Yankee Science in the Making* (Boston, 1948), pp. 181–202, 337–345, 355; Bernard Jaffe, *Men of Science in America* (New York, 1944), p. xxxi; Thomas C. Johnson, Jr., *Scientific Interest in the Old South* (New York, 1936), p. 199; Samuel F. Bemis, *John Quincy Adams and the Union* (New York, 1956), pp. 501–523; Richard Shyrock, *American Medical Research, Past and Present* (New York, 1947), *passim.*

CHAPTER 5

The Close of a Reign

WHILE the lines of battle over tariff and Bank formed and reformed, a political transformation of considerable magnitude took place. One of the major parties cast off some of its elements. Two parties died. A fourth party was born.

These political changes were in part due to maneuverings by master craftsmen in politics like Thurlow Weed and Martin Van Buren of New York. They were also due to the aspirations of the common man and of the hustling, bustling middle-class entrepreneurs, urban and rural, who were constantly seeking economic advantage through political alignments. The development of a rising moral tumult over slavery, a tumult that boded ill for the nation's future, also played a part in the political movements of this period.

The Democratic party of Jackson's second term was emerging more and more clearly as the party of the ordinary run of citizens. In New England and the Middle Atlantic states, Jackson's championship of the poor against the rich, and the activities of local Democratic organizations such as New York's Tammany Hall, brought the foreign-born, particularly the Irish, into the ranks of the Democracy. A majority of the small farmers and fishermen, and at least some city laborers, joined the Jacksonians. Considerably above these groups in the social and economic scale, but on the same side of the political fence, were state bankers hostile to the Bank of the United States and commercialists dependent upon foreign trade.

In the South, the large planters and the states' rights elements which had supported Jackson in 1828 could no longer be counted among his adherents. But he did command the support of a majority of the smaller planters and the grain-growing, nonslaveholding farmers—in short, the support of those who wanted a social equality expressed in terms of an unlimited franchise, free public schools, and equitable legislative apportionment.

In the West, the frontiersmen and small farmers, with their passion for free land and tax-supported public schools, tended to gravitate into the Democracy. And in all sections Jackson probably numbered supporters in the thousands who voted for him as a military hero or simply as a man of courage and integrity, a real tribune of the people.

Jacksonian Democracy, as a movement, accented liberty and equality. It was, in the eyes of such leaders as Jackson, Benton, Silas Wright, and Azariah Flagg, a "crusade," aimed at establishing and maintaining equality of opportunity for all, and imbued with a highly realistic sense of the political power of the masses. This crusading spirit helped to give it vitality, for, while the party contained many conservative and quasi-conservative elements, its leaders kept on the alert for causes which would enable them to portray the party as the protector of the common man against aristocracy and privilege. Six years after Jackson had entered the Executive Mansion, the party could still be described as moving, slowly and spasmodically, to the left.

But the Democracy was not in any real sense a party that actually arrayed or sought to array the masses against the classes. It was, rather, a party dominated by a passion for justice and equality that was essentially middle class in its nature. It is significant that that fervent Democrat and hater of monopoly, Robert Rantoul, said in an "Address to the Workingmen of America," which was published in the Workingmen's Library in 1833, that he acknowledged "all those to be workingmen who *do something for a living*," and that he listed as workingmen such individuals as the Philadelphia banker Stephen Girard, Shakespeare, Franklin, Mirabeau, Washington, and Lafayette. This was scarcely a twentieth-century concept of the laboring class. For most of these early nineteenth-century politicians, class lines were considerably blurred.[1]

[1] Flagg Papers, Bryant and Leggett to Flagg, Jan. 6, 1834, Levi Woodbury to Flagg, Jan. 22, 1834; William M. Gouge, *A Short History of Paper Money and Banking in the United States* (Philadelphia, 1833), pp. 91–100; Joseph Dorf-

One of the best evidences of the modestly liberalizing tendency in the Democratic party was the change in the Supreme Court's climate of opinion that took place beginning with the eighteen-thirties. During his two terms of office, Jackson appointed a new Chief Justice and no less than seven associate justices, thus effecting a considerable modification of the court's viewpoint on social and economic questions. The effect of these appointments became apparent under the Chief Justiceship of Roger Brooks Taney, who succeeded Marshall as Chief Justice. Under Taney's leadership, the Court demonstrated a much less rigid respect for the sanctity of contracts than had been evident when Marshall was at the judicial helm.

In the famous *Charles River Bridge* v. *Warren Bridge* decision (1837), Taney proclaimed the great principle that where the rights of private property collide with those of the community, the rights of the community are paramount, and that owners of private property have duties and obligations to society which, if necessary, must be established and enforced by the courts.[2] This decision was a blow to the "sanctity of contracts" doctrine, but, unlike some of the political policies of the Democracy, it facilitated the nation's economic expansion. Had the contention been upheld that the Charles River Bridge Company had a monopoly of bridging the Charles River, the consequences in an era which demanded the rapid development of means of transportation would have been serious indeed. As it was, the decision, by freeing the initiative of a host of internal improvement companies, opened the way for a rapid development of transportation facilities.

Taney shared the left-wing Democracy's distrust of corporations as aggregates of wealth that were dangerous because of their power, but he also accepted corporations as necessary instruments of society, a point of view not relished by the rigid antimonopolists of the Democratic party. He was also more regardful of states' rights than Marshall had been. Taney held that the states could prohibit corporations from outside their borders doing business within their limits; he asserted

---

man, *The Economic Mind in American Civilization* (2 vols., New York, 1946), II, 296–306, 601–636; Richard Hofstadter, "William Leggett, Spokesman of Jacksonian Democracy," *Political Science Quarterly,* LVIII (Dec., 1943), 581–594; Luther Hamilton (ed.), *Memoirs, Speeches, and Writings of Robert Rantoul, Jr.* (Boston, 1854), pp. 219–220.

[2] Charles River Bridge *v.* Warren Bridge, 11 Peters 420. The most significant parts of the decision are given in Henry S. Commager (ed.), *Documents of American History* (New York, 1940), pp. 285–287.

that, in the absence of federal regulation, the states could regulate interstate commerce. But, though by predilection a strict constructionist, he nevertheless recognized that the national government was inevitably increasing its sphere of influence, and that both state and national governments must protect the interests of society rather than of privilege.[3]

The slow drift to the left of the Democratic party in the middle eighteen-thirties was emphasized by the emergence of Locofocoism. This movement developed first as a split in the Democracy's ranks in New York City, where such leaders as the agrarian George Henry Evans, William Leggett (an editor of the New York *Evening Post*), a philosophical writer named John W. Vethake, a politician and would-be office holder named Alexander Ming, Jr., and others set up in the name of equal rights a political opposition to the banking and commercial elements that controlled the party's local and state organization. The Locofocos, so named because of their use of "locofoco" matches to light candles at a meeting where the conservative Democrats had turned off the gas lights, opposed monopoly in any form. They were hard-money men, distrusting the paper currency of the banks and heartily detesting banks themselves as agencies of corruption and oppression. They were the enemies of corporations, believing them to be not only inequitable but dangerous, and they advocated unlimited liability for corporation stockholders. They were free traders, foreign and domestic, some even going so far as to oppose usury laws on the ground that they limited freedom of trade in money. They also opposed imprisonment for debt and, though not abolitionists, were hostile to slavery. They sought, in short, to purge American democracy of the inequities that had crept into its midst and, as a means to that end, to free Jacksonian Democracy from any taint of privilege. They were principled equalitarians, neo-Jeffersonians, men filled with a high sense of justice and fair dealing; and could they have had their way, the economic development of the United States would have been long delayed. As it was, they gave the Democracy a flavor of radicalism, and in economic matters of negativism, which became more and more apparent in the middle eighteen-thirties and which tended to split the Democracy into radical and conservative wings.[4]

[3] This analysis of Taney's point of view is based on Carl B. Swisher, *Roger B. Taney* (New York, 1935), *passim.*

[4] F. Byrdsall, *The History of the Loco-Foco or Equal Rights Party* (New

The Democratic party's great rival in the middle period, the Whig party, might almost be said to have been born to fill a vacuum, for it emerged out of the wreck of two other national political organizations. The National Republican party had never had a strong national organization, and the jealousy of its rival leaders, Webster and Clay, during the early eighteen-thirties had been an unsettling influence. Its disastrous defeat in 1832 had been a crushing blow, virtually ending its existence. The Antimasonic party, despite its mushroom growth in New England and the Middle Atlantic states, was too narrowly based and had too many bitter opponents among the National Republicans to make it acceptable as the party of the opposition. The logic of circumstance indicated the necessity of a new party, one that could rally all of the opponents of Jacksonian Democracy into some semblance of national organization.

The Whig party that clearly emerged during 1834 was, politically speaking, a coalition of the great majority of National Republicans and Antimasons, together with an increasing leaven of disgruntled Democrats. In other words, it was a coalition of anti-Jackson forces. It probably owed its name to James Watson Webb of the New York *Courier and Enquirer,* who, together with others, sought thus to give the party a sound middle-class identity and, by implication, to stigmatize the followers of "King Andrew" as Tories. The word "Whig" first appeared on a ballot in the New York City elections of 1834, and its use spread rapidly to Pennsylvania and other states.

A host of economic interests marched under the Whig banner. New England and Middle States Whigs numbered industrialists, commercialists, and much of native labor in their ranks, together with a respectable number of conservatively minded farmers. In the Ohio Valley, the pushing, ambitious, go-ahead bankers and businessmen, canal promoters, land-owning interests, lawyers with an eye to the main chance, and farmers anxious for internal improvements were more apt than not to be found in the Whig ranks. In the South, one

York, 1842), pp. 13–28 and *passim;* Arthur M. Schlesinger, Jr., *The Age of Jackson* (Boston, 1945), pp. 132–143, 177–209; Francis P. Weisenburger, *The Passing of the Frontier, 1825–1850* in (Carl Wittke [ed.], *The History of the State of Ohio* [6 vols., Columbus, 1941]), III, 308–313; Wilfred E. Binkley, *American Political Parties* (New York, 1943), pp. 120–145; Arthur B. Darling, "The Workingmen's Party in Massachusetts," and "Jacksonian Democracy in Massachusetts," *American Historical Review,* XXIX (Oct., 1923; Jan., 1924), 81–88, 271–287.

source of Whig strength lay in the urban commercial and banking interests. These men, many of them quondam Democrats who had deserted Jackson on the Bank issue (it is significant that twenty-eight of the forty-one Democrats in Congress who voted to recharter the Bank of the United States in 1832 had joined the Whig party by 1836), carried with them their economic associates, many of whom were their economic dependents, the big cotton, tobacco, and sugar planters who owned perhaps two-third of the slaves in the South. And in all sections there were local groups and individuals who disliked Jackson and the Democratic party for a wide variety of reasons—states' righters like Calhoun and Tyler, disappointed aspirants for the succession (again Calhoun, or men like John Bell of Tennessee), followers of magnetic leaders like Clay and John J. Crittenden of Kentucky and Tom Corwin of Ohio, or solid businessmen and yeoman farmers[5] deeply alarmed by Jackson's financial policies. Such were the elements which constituted the Whig party.

Whiggery had certain general characteristics. It was socially conservative. Dominated by those with vested interests, those who had "arrived," it distrusted the city rabble, the backwoodsmen, the illiterates in general. The ignorant and the vicious, said the Whig editors of the *American Review,* should not feel that they had a right to vote. They had it simply because there was no remedy that was not worse than the disease.[6] Social conservatism also manifested itself in a certain smug consciousness of superiority. There was a saying in Virginia, and probably elsewhere, that "Whigs knew each other by the instinct of gentlemen."

But if Whiggery attracted the socially conservative and the smug, it also drew men of vision, especially economic vision. This was what caught the imaginations of Horace Greeley, William Henry Seward, Abraham Lincoln, and the captains of industry in the East and in the Ohio and Mississippi valleys—men who saw the vast national potential and the possibilities in Clay's American system, men who were respectful of the Jeffersonian tradition but impatient of Jacksonian equalitarianism and negativism. For Whiggery was national in its outlook. Clay's system was a national system, and the vision of the business lead-

[5] The southern Whigs were by no means confined to the planter class or the business elements. See the interesting article by Grady McWhiney, "Were the Whigs a Class Party in Alabama?" *Journal of Southern History,* XXIII (Nov., 1957), 510–522.

[6] *American Review,* II, 446–448; IV, 29, 442; V, 626.

ers, North and South, was a national vision. Eastern businessmen like Abbott Lawrence and Nathan Appleton were always adjuring the South to industrialize and the West to grow so that all could enjoy the results in a developing harmony of interests. In the South the states' rights element was only an appendage of the Whig party, an appendage that dropped away until, by 1841, the southern Whigs stood almost solidly in support of Clay's nationalistic policies. The Whig party in its days of power was a nationalist party, a soother of sectional jealousies, a barrier to fratricidal strife.[7]

Andrew Jackson thought he knew what a Whig was, but his definition only made up in vigor and directness what it lacked in depth. A Whig, said Jackson, was a man devoid of principle and honesty, a man completely untrustworthy. This illustrates the General's capacity for rancorous judgment. It also illustrates the bitter partisanship of the times. It was as unfair and misleading as was John Quincy Adams' description of Jackson as an "illiterate barbarian."[8]

The man who was now rounding out his second term in the Presidency would, and often did, take valuable counsel from his political advisers. He had always possessed a frontiersman's rough-and-ready sense of justice and, as his party's leader, he had developed a passion for serving the people well. He was personally without fear. But he lacked the capacity for that slow and often painful balancing of opposite viewpoints, the fruit of philosophic reflection, which is the

[7] Duff Green Papers, Thomas Cooper to Green, Apr. 30, 1834, George Sharswood to Green, May 22, 1834; Richmond *Enquirer,* July 11, 1834; Henry R. Mueller, *The Whig Party in Pennsylvania* (New York, 1922), pp. 236–246; Charles M. Thompson, *The Illinois Whigs Before 1846* (Urbana, 1915), pp. 42–44; Paul Murray, *The Whig Party in Georgia, 1825–1853* (Chapel Hill, 1948), pp. 1–3; B. Malcolm Carroll, *Origins of the Whig Party* (Durham, 1925), pp. 1–40; Arthur C. Cole, *The Whig Party in the South* (Washington, 1913), pp. 1–38; Weisenburger, *Passing of the Frontier,* pp. 271–285; William A. Sullivan, *The Industrial Worker in Pennsylvania, 1800–1840* (Harrisburg, 1955), pp. 159–207; Charles G. Sellers, Jr., "Who Were the Southern Whigs?" *American Historical Review,* LIX (Jan., 1954), 335–346; Edward Pessen, "Did Labor Support Jackson: the Boston Story," *Political Science Quarterly,* LXIV (June, 1949), 262–274; William Trimble, "Diverging Tendencies in New York Democracy in the Period of the Locofocos," *American Historical Review,* XXIV (Apr., 1919), 396–421; Harold E. Davis, "Economic Basis of Ohio Politics," *Ohio State Archeological and Historical Quarterly,* XLVII (1938–39), 288–318.

[8] Jackson Papers (second series), Jackson to Blair, Dec. 8, 1838; Charles Francis Adams (ed.), *Memoirs of John Quincy Adams* (12 vols., Philadelphia, 1874–77), VIII, 546.

characteristic of the man of culture. His emotions were volcanic. They easily rose to the surface and, when they erupted, were overpowering in their intensity.

An interesting commentary on Jackson's character was made at this time by Nathaniel Niles, New England Democrat and diplomat, an observer who was close to the leading members of his party in Washington. Niles was convinced that those who had a real hold on Jackson's affections held that status not because they liked but because they hated the same persons and things that the General hated. "This is not meant as a libel on the General," Niles told William Cabell Rives, "but merely the expression of an opinion founded upon a careful analysis of his conduct and the emotions which govern it. For his whole course in life has been dictated by emotion in contradistinction to reason."[9] This judgment was too extreme, but it contained a large element of truth.

Both Jackson's fearlessness and his penchant for intense emotional conviction were well illustrated by an incident that took place early in 1835, and of which Niles has left a moving account. It was January 29, 1835, and Jackson was at the Capitol. As he started from the rotunda and through the piazza on the east side, one Richard Lawrence, a painter by trade, snapped a percussion pistol at him from a distance of about eight feet. It missed fire. Jackson, who was leaning on Woodbury's arm, started toward his assailant, cane upraised, as Lawrence aimed a second pistol which also missed fire. Had Woodbury not restrained the General, he would have reached and caned his would-be assassin.

Jackson, in commenting to Niles on the attack, remarked that he had received over 500 letters threatening his life. But he did not worry about assassination, said the President, since he meant always to live and act in such a way as to be ready at all times to die. "The manner in which this sentiment was expressed," said Niles, "excited my admiration." The General was convinced, however, that Lawrence had been hired to do the deed by Whig Senator George Poindexter of Mississippi, who, said Jackson, "would have attempted it himself long ago, if he had had the courage." Jackson undertook to obtain evidence of Poindexter's complicity, and the latter asked the appointment of a special Senate committee of investigation. The committee was appointed and found him innocent. Duff Green gave the incident still

[9] William C. Rives Papers, Niles to Rives, June 14, 1835.

more of a partisan flavor by spreading the report that the whole thing had been a fake, *two* pistols missing fire being altogether too much of a coincidence. Lawrence was found to be insane.[10]

Jackson's penchant for deep emotion, together with his strong national patriotism, were dominant aspects of his foreign policy. He took an active part in the conduct of foreign affairs. During his administrations, the United States endeavored unsuccessfully to conclude naval conventions that would guarantee respect for American neutral rights. More successfully, a number of reciprocal trade agreements were negotiated, in addition to that with Great Britain concerning West Indian trade, thus providing a basis for American commercial expansion. A treaty with Siam was signed in 1833, the first such agreement between the United States and an Asiatic nation.

Jackson was wont to tell American representatives abroad to seek their objectives patiently and tactfully; but when no results were obtained by these methods, the General was perfectly willing to resort to threats of reprisal. Now and then the appearance of an American frigate in a foreign country's principal port would lend tone to the representations being made by the American Minister to that particular state. This combination of methods resulted in the collection of over $12 million for damages inflicted by various nations upon United States shipping during the Napoleonic Wars, and kept American prestige in good standing among the nations of the world.[11]

The Jacksonian method of handling foreign affairs is well illustrated by Jackson's policy in regard both to the West Indian trade and the French debt question. The West Indian trade was closed when Jackson became President. Adams had attempted to negotiate its reopening, but he had done so in a tactless manner and had obtained no concessions. Van Buren, with Jackson's consent, appeased the British by frankly acknowledging that the approach to the problem by Clay and Adams had been rejected by the American people, a statement that had some semblance of truth, since Adams had been reproached in the 1828 campaign for his failure to reach an agreement with the

[10] Rives Papers, Niles to Rives, Jan. 30, 1835; Duff Green Papers, "Communications" (1835), Poindexter to Van Buren, Feb. 21, 1835; Jackson Papers (second series), affidavits of David Stewart and Mordecai Troy, Feb. 4, 1835.

[11] For Jackson's foreign policy, see Frank L. Benns, *The American Struggle for the British West India Carrying Trade, 1815–1830* (Bloomington, 1923), pp. 163–188; Samuel F. Bemis (ed.), *The American Secretaries of State and Their Diplomacy* (10 vols., New York, 1927–29), IV, 161–332.

British. This conciliatory approach pleased the English government, but Canadian protests over the advantages American shippers would derive from the West Indian trade delayed the negotiation of a settlement.

As months went by without any move by the British, Jackson's patience began to wear thin. He told Van Buren in April, 1830, that if England was not willing to negotiate, the United States should act "with that promptness and energy due to our national character." He proposed that Congress be asked to pass a nonintercourse law with respect to "Canaday," together with provision for sufficient revenue cutters to enforce it. Fortunately, such vigorous measures were unnecessary. Acting on a hint from McLane in England, Congress passed a law authorizing the President to grant certain trading privileges to British ships as soon as England gave the same privileges to American ships trading with the West Indies. The British thereupon removed the restrictions on tonnage and place of departure that had hampered American trade and, October 5, 1830, Jackson proclaimed trade with the West Indies open.[12]

The Jacksonian approach to problems in foreign affairs was even better illustrated in the case of the French debt question, which threatened to provoke an international crisis in 1834–35. The United States had been disappointed in 1833 in its effort to collect the first installment of the 25 million francs agreed upon by the two nations as indemnity for the losses suffered by Americans at the hands of the French during the Napoleonic Wars. The French Chambers again refused to make the necessary appropriations in 1834. Jackson's anger smoldered, then flared. In his message to Congress, December 1, 1834, Old Hickory put the matter up to that body. It could, he said, continue to wait, if it wanted to do so. He believed, however, that the United States should insist upon the prompt execution of the treaty. If this was refused, if the approaching session of the Chambers did nothing, he recommended passage of a law that would authorize reprisals upon French property. Churchill C. Cambreleng, a Jackson leader in Congress, wrote to William Cabell Rives that the time had come to treat France "as a nation with whom we may be compelled to go to war."[13]

[12] Benns, *West India Trade,* pp. 107–162; John S. Bassett, *The Life of Andrew Jackson* (2 vols., New York, 1911), II, 656–663.

[13] James D. Richardson, *A Compilation of the Messages and Papers of the Presidents* (11 vols., New York, 1910), II, 1325–1326; Rives Papers, Cambreleng to Rives, Feb. 1, 1835.

The President's minatory tone excited resentment in France and alarm at home. War loomed in the offing, or so it seemed. Livingston, from Paris, advised delay, and the Whigs, always seeking political capital, began taking a pacific tone. Clay, as chairman of the Senate Committee on Foreign Affairs, reported a resolution on January 6, 1835, to the effect that it was inexpedient to threaten reprisals, although our claim was undoubtedly just. The Whigs were taking their stand for peace, but the Democrats in the Senate were not far behind them, for the resolution was unanimously adopted.

The House Democrats and John Quincy Adams rallied a little more strongly to Jackson's support, and the House passed a $3 million fortifications bill, to be used in the nation's defense should need arise before the next session. This bill was lost, due to Whig opposition in the Senate, to a delay in Senate-House conference proceedings at the very end of the session, and to a quibble on the part of the Democratic leadership in the House, the argument being that the House could not transact business after midnight and therefore had to adjourn without taking action on the results of the conference. Each party blamed the other for the loss of the bill, Adams again siding with the Democrats.

In April, 1835, the French Chambers passed the appropriation, with the proviso that it should only be paid if there was some satisfactory explanation of the language of Jackson's message. Jackson was adamant. It was high time, he told Amos Kendall, that French arrogance should be put down, and all Europe taught "that we will not permit France or any, or all European governments to interfere with our domestic policy or dictate to the President what language he shall use in his Message to Congress. . . ."[14] Diplomatic relations with France were suspended. But Jackson's first draft of his message in December, 1835, was toned down by his advisers and contained a disclaimer of any intention to menace or insult France. British mediatory efforts had a generally soothing effect. France found the language of the 1835 message satisfactory, and payment of the debt began in 1836.[15]

The merits of the French debt controversy can be endlessly debated, and to little effect. Jackson had used threatening language in an effort

[14] Jackson Papers (second series), Jackson to Kendall, Oct. 31, 1835.

[15] *Register of Debates,* 23rd Congress, second session, 104–108, Appendix, pp. 208–219; 24th Congress, first session, 163–178, 366, 2605, 2799, 3594; Richard A. McLemore, *Franco-American Diplomatic Relations, 1816–1836* (University, Louisiana, 1941), pp. 128–209; Samuel F. Bemis, *John Quincy Adams and the Union* (New York, 1956), pp. 305–322.

to obtain satisfaction of a just claim. This was "big-stick" diplomacy. The Whigs paraded themselves in all the panoplies of moderation. Both sides angled for political advantage, and each sought, with some reason, to blame the other for the loss of the fortifications bill. The evidence indicates that Whig policy, in the initial stages of the controversy, may have had a beneficial effect in preventing a war of reprisals. On the other hand, the satisfactory settlement of the controversy in the spring of 1836 was a feather in the administration's cap, and deprived the Whigs of a campaign issue for that year.

The excitement created by the French debt question obscured the fact that the crusade of the national administration on behalf of liberty and equality had somewhat subsided with the close of its victorious war against the Bank. Thereafter the battle for economic democracy was carried on chiefly in states such as Massachusetts, New York, and Pennsylvania. There the Locofocos, or their equivalents, waged sometimes effective, though not always constructive, war against banks and other corporations, and fought for hard money and the right of labor to a more equitable share in the nation's wealth and opportunity.[16] But even though the states now bore the brunt of the fight, the tone of the national administration remained distinctly Locofocoish in character.

Jackson's annual messages to Congress showed where the heart of the administration lay. Repeatedly the General denounced legislation for special interests, invoking the concept that that government governs best that governs least; repeatedly he recommended a cheap land policy, criticized the protectionist philosophy, and blasted the spirit of monopoly in the name of justice for all and privilege for none. Distribution of the surplus revenue was wrong, he now asserted, for it took one man's property and gave it to another. In December, 1835, he urged the suppression of all bank bills below twenty dollars. A hard-money circulating medium for the farmers and mechanics, he declared, would "revive and perpetuate those habits of economy and simplicity which are so congenial to the character of republicans . . ." and would "form an era in the history of our country which will be dwelt upon with delight by every true friend of its liberty and independence."[17]

[16] Welles Papers, Kendall to John M. Niles, May 13, 1835, C. C. Cambreleng to Welles, Apr. 15, 1835; Schlesinger, *Age of Jackson*, pp. 144–209.

[17] Richardson, *Messages and Papers*, II, 1380–1381, 1383–1386, 1459–1465, 1467–1469, 1471–1472.

Administration supporters in and out of Congress voiced sentiments similar to those of the President. John A. Dix of New York was certain that the people of that state were "animated by a revolutionary spirit" in regard to "all monsters in a monied shape," and Azariah Flagg reported joyfully the death in Albany of scores of applications for bank charters. Robert Rantoul, Boston Democrat, looked with deep suspicion upon all applications for corporation charters, from business firms to musical societies. It was the principle, he said, that was wrong. James Buchanan joined the President in damning all bank notes under twenty dollars in value. Ike Hill proudly told Gideon Welles that he had never voted for a bank, and never would do so. Churchill C. Cambreleng declared that the best remedy for the small-note evil was to abolish bank notes altogether. Such being the spirit of the Democratic leaders, it was not surprising that the coinage act of 1834 sought to bring more gold into the country and thus facilitate the elimination of small notes, nor that by October, 1836, no less than thirteen states had prohibited their banks from issuing bank notes of less than five dollars in denomination.[18]

The Specie Circular of 1836 was a move made in conformity with this general Locofoco trend, for it was a typical hard money reaction to the inflation that had swept over the country. During the middle eighteen-thirties, the purchase of public lands increased by leaps and bounds. In 1834 some 4,500,000 acres were sold, the largest amount, save for one year (1819), that had yet been sold by the government. In 1835 nearly three times this amount of the public domain was purchased, and in 1836 the staggering total of 20,074,871 acres passed into private hands.[19] President Jackson was at first delighted with these sales, viewing them as evidence of an unexampled prosperity,[20] but by the close of 1836 he had awakened to the dangerous situation which the sales represented.

[18] Flagg Papers, Dix to Wright, Feb. 11, 1834, Flagg to ———, Feb. 14, 1834; Welles Papers, C. C. Cambreleng to Welles, Apr. 15, 1835, Hill to Welles (Jan., 1836); Rantoul, *Memoirs,* pp. 313–317, 320–321, 336; John B. Moore (ed.), *The Works of James Buchanan* (12 vols., Philadelphia, 1908–11), III, 255; *Niles' Register,* LI (Oct. 1, 1836), 80; *Congressional Globe,* 24th Cong., second sess., Appendix, pp. 36–37; Davis R. Dewey, *Financial History of the United States* (New York, 1934), p. 211. The coinage change defeated its own purpose. It undervalued silver. Most silver dollars were out of circulation by 1840, and even fractional coins tended to disappear.

[19] Fred J. Guetter and Albert E. McKinley, *Statistical Tables Relating to the Economic Growth of the United States* (Philadelphia, 1924), p. 291.

[20] Richardson, *Messages and Papers,* II, 1367, 1381.

The truth was that these public land sales, which supposedly poured millions into the Treasury each year, were really based on bank credits of a highly questionable character. Speculators were obtaining huge blocks of western lands, using political influence, outright bribery, and very doubtful forms of currency and credit. Bank credits had become superabundant, due to government deposits in the "Pets," to wildcat banking, and to the optimism engendered by good times. The currency, which in 1834 amounted to some $124 million, had increased by 1836 to over $200 million, and much of it lacked any backing that could be safely counted upon to redeem it. The banks, particularly in the West, had extended their loans beyond all reason. Much of the payment for government lands consisted of nothing more than the paper of shaky banks, paper that was loaned out, returned to the banks, and again loaned out in a vicious circle. The lack of the restraining influence of the Bank of the United States was already beginning to be felt, and the government was all the more willing to step into the picture because, in so doing, it could emphasize the superior value of a hard-money currency.

The administration had begun using land sales as a means of exhibiting its hard-money tendencies in 1835. In April of that year the Treasury had ordered the land offices to receive no bills of less than five dollars in payment for public lands, and had intimated that this limit would soon be raised to ten dollars and that banks issuing smaller notes would not be used as fiscal agents. One year later the government announced that it would pay out no bank notes of any denomination, save such as were readily convertible into specie.

The Specie Circular of July 11, 1836, was, in one sense, only a culmination of a general policy, although it was also the result of public outcries against speculators and of an awakening to the danger of uncontrolled inflation. It prohibited all federal government receivers of public money from accepting anything but specie in payment for the public lands.[21]

The issuance of the Circular was a well-meant move. It served notice to land speculators that the government wished to be no longer

[21] *American State Papers. Public Land* (8 vols., Washington, 1832–61), VIII, 910. Under certain circumstances, Virginia land scrip would also be received in payment for the lands. Also, up to December 15, purchases by actual settlers, or bona fide residents of the state where the sale was made, could continue to be made as before.

a silent partner in their schemes. It brought the country's attention to a dangerously inflationary situation. But it also had other and less fortunate effects. The Circular drained specie from the East to the West. Ironically, it aided speculators, for the average purchaser of land had little specie. He therefore could no longer buy land from the government and was forced into the clutches of the speculator. This made the Circular highly unpopular in the West. But Jackson had made his decision, and all protests fell on deaf ears.

The Whigs denounced the Circular and Senator Ewing of Ohio offered a joint resolution annulling it. Clay supported this move, suggesting that the government be obligated to accept, in payment of its debts, bank notes that were of par value at the place where payment was made. Senator Rives of Virginia, though still a Jackson man, proposed that the bills of banks not issuing notes under certain denominations be accepted by the government. The Whigs liked this idea, for it virtually annulled the Specie Circular, and a combination of Whigs and eastern Democrats pushed it through both houses of Congress. Jackson pocket-vetoed it. Its passage was ominous, however, so far as the hard-money men were concerned, for it represented the feeling of a growing number of Democrats who were sympathetic with state banks and who held, quite truly, that as it was there was simply not enough specie in the country to meet currency needs.[22] Restrictions on the note issues of specie-paying banks only made a bad matter worse.

The Specie Circular remained the law of the land. It was finally made inoperative by a joint resolution of Congress, May 21, 1838.[23]

While the administration was manifesting its sympathy with Locofoco tenets, politicians of both parties were demonstrating their awareness of the fact that 1836 was a presidential year. The subject of the demonstration was the surplus.

The government of the United States was out of debt in 1836, and money was beginning to pile up in the Treasury. The quarrel over land policy had resulted in a deadlock, neither Clay's plan of distribution nor the administration's cheap land proposal being able to pass both houses of Congress, and receipts from land sales mounted. In

[22] *Congressional Globe,* 24th Cong., second sess., pp. 22–23, 44, 61, Appendix, pp. 36–37, 100–105; Frederick J. Turner, *The United States, 1830–1850* (New York, 1935), pp. 445–446; Glyndon G. Van Deusen, *The Life of Henry Clay* (Boston, 1937), pp. 288–289.

[23] William MacDonald, *Jacksonian Democracy* (New York, 1906), p. 291.

1836, the land receipts exceeded those from customs, and the government had an excess of receipts over disbursements of almost $20 million.[24]

The surplus was largely paper, but the states yearned for it and the politicians longed to satisfy their yearnings. In June, 1836, with the blessing of both the administration and the Whigs, Congress passed a bill which distributed all of the surplus over $5 million to the states, in proportion to their representation in Congress. This pork-barrel legislation stimulated an already unhealthy inflation. Clay supported it against his better judgment. The administration claimed credit for its passage, only to be critical of it after the election was over. It was a voters' market in a presidential year, and the surplus was the lure.[25]

The approach of the national election also brought out the fact that slavery was threatening to become a political question. Antislavery agitation, stimulated by the activities of Benjamin Lundy, William Lloyd Garrison, Theodore Dwight Weld, and the American Antislavery Society, had become a formidable force in the North by the middle eighteen-thirties. One of its most objectionable forms, from the southern point of view, was the presentation of antislavery petitions in Congress, especially petitions for abolishing slavery in the District of Columbia. As antislavery voters grew in numbers, more and more congressmen were willing, and eager, to present these petitions. The more petitions, the more the South's rancor grew and the more determined it became to end what it regarded as an intolerable situation.

For the South was becoming more and more self-conscious about slavery and slaveholding. Antislavery pamphlets, such as *Walker's Appeal* with its threats of violence, and, much more significantly, Nat Turner's rebellion of 1831 in Virginia with its massacre of between fifty and sixty whites had alerted the South to the frightful menace of a slave uprising. By the middle eighteen-thirties, with abolitionist pamphlets and petitions steadily increasing, southern white public opinion was becoming more and more violent in tone. The South's leading demand, Thomas Cooper wrote to Van Buren, was to be let alone on slavery, and it would persevere in this demand at the expense,

[24] Guetter and McKinley, *Statistical Tables,* pp. 15, 29; Edward G. Bourne, *The History of the Surplus Revenue of 1837* (New York, 1885), pp. 12–13.

[25] John S. Bassett (ed.), *Correspondence of Andrew Jackson* (7 vols., Washington, 1926–35), V, 409; G. G. Van Deusen, *Clay,* pp. 286–287; Bourne, *Surplus Revenue,* p. 23.

if necessary, "of separation and war."[26] Calhoun, probably hoping to unite the South under his leadership and obtain enough antiabolition votes in the North to carry him into the Presidency, urged Congress to refuse all action hostile to slavery.

The House finally took middle ground between Calhoun and the abolitionists. It established a rule which automatically laid on the table all antislavery petitions, but merely affirmed the inexpediency of interfering with slavery in the District of Columbia. Offered by a southern man, this compromise was a typical Van Buren maneuver and was probably engineered by his supporters. Calhoun and his followers did not like it, for it did not preclude the possibility of legislative action that would destroy slavery in the District of Columbia. It also dissatisfied the southern extremists because it gave the abolitionists an opportunity to invoke the right of petition guaranteed in the First Amendment to the Constitution. It had, however, taken some of the abolitionist pressure off Van Buren's shoulders and, by dividing southern opinion, weakened Calhoun in the South.[27]

If Van Buren weakened Calhoun in the South by his treatment of antislavery petitions, Calhoun did the same for his rival in the North when it came to dealing with incendiary literature. Abolitionists were flooding the southern mails with matter calculated to cause unrest among the slaves, and this literature made the South furious. President Jackson proposed a law prohibiting, under heavy penalty, the circulation through the mails of publications intended to excite slave insurrections,[28] but the South thought this vested too much power in the federal government and preferred a bill forbidding postmasters to deliver such literature when it was barred by state laws. Webster and Clay opposed this bill as vague and also as dangerous to the freedom of the press. It was not a strictly party matter, the Senate was evenly divided, and the Calhoun forces engineered a tie vote on the engrossment of the bill, thus compelling Van Buren, as President of the Senate, to cast the deciding vote. The Little Magician voted for the measure.

[26] Van Buren Papers, Thomas Cooper to Van Buren, Apr. 14, 1837.

[27] Daniel Webster, *Writings and Speeches* (18 vols., Boston, 1903), VI, 11–12, 14; Charles M. Wiltse, *John C. Calhoun* (3 vols., Indianapolis, 1949), II, 278–286; Turner, *United States,* pp. 431–445. The Senate used a different kind of gag, simply providing that the question of reception of antislavery petitions should automatically be laid on the table.

[28] Richardson, *Messages and Papers,* II, 1394–1395.

Thus his strength in the South, what there was of it, was conserved, but his action was distinctly unpopular with the abolitionists.[29]

Slavery and politics also figured in the government's attitude toward Texas in 1836. Americans, mainly Southerners and slaveholders, had been moving into Texas for fifteen years, attracted by fertile cotton lands, an attractive climate, and their ability to evade Mexican laws against slavery by introducing their Negroes as indented servants. There were over 30,000 of these settlers by 1836, hardy pioneers who had grown increasingly restive as Mexico, belatedly recognizing the danger to its sovereign control that was presented by this foreign immigration, had tried ineffectually to abolish slavery in Texas and stem the onrushing tide of frontiersmen. That same year the grievances of the American settlers came to a head.

The Mexican dictator, General Antonio Lopez de Santa Anna, attempted to establish a rigid, centralized control over the troublesome gringos north of the Rio Grande. The Texan response, March 2, 1836, was a declaration of independence. Santa Anna promptly took his army into Texas. The garrison of the Alamo at San Antonio was exterminated; 350 prisoners were summarily executed at Goliad. Then, April 21, 1836, the little Texan army, led by Sam Houston, struck in its turn, completely routing the Mexicans and taking Santa Anna prisoner. He was forced to sign treaties (which he had no intention of keeping) by which he agreed to evacuate Texas and use his influence to obtain Mexican recognition of Texan independence, with the Rio Grande as the southern boundary of the new state. The Mexican army was drawn back south of the Rio Grande, and for the moment the Texans were free.

Texas claimed freedom, and Mexico, while refusing to recognize the claim as either just or valid, showed no immediate disposition to contest it by force of arms. What would be the attitude of the United States toward recognition? Here much depended upon the attitude of President Jackson.

Old Hickory had been interested in Texas for some time. He had been willing to spend $5 million for it, and for years had tried to interest the Mexicans in such a deal. Sam Houston, leader of the Texas revolt, was his close friend. The President now moved cautiously, however, for Webster and Adams were opposing recognition, and charges

[29] Thomas H. Benton, *Thirty Years View* (2 vols., New York, 1854), I, 585–587; Webster, *Writings,* IV, 134.

of a southern conspiracy were in the air. It would not do to make a move that would weaken Van Buren as a presidential candidate in the North. Recognition, therefore, was deferred until after the election. It was actually given on March 3, 1837, when Jackson nominated a chargé d'affaires to the Republic of Texas.[30]

While Texas and abolitionism had been moving toward the center of the national stage, the Democrats had held their second national convention. This was rigged for Van Buren's nomination, for Jackson had thrown the full power of the Executive patronage behind his favorite. The convention met at Baltimore, May 20, 1835, and named the Red Fox as its unanimous choice for the highest office in the land, in bland disregard of the fact that both the Alabama and Tennessee legislatures had already repudiated him. The vice-presidential nomination was a contest between Richard M. Johnson of Kentucky and William Cabell Rives of Virginia. The former gained the prize, much to the rage of the Virginians who refused to support him in the campaign. There was no platform, only an address to the people prepared by a special committee.

The Whigs, not yet well organized as a party and full of conflicting views, declared that a national convention was only "King Caucus" revived and refused to hold one. Neither did they draw up a platform of principles. Clay wanted the nomination again, but the prevailing Whig sentiment opposed running a candidate who had been so disastrously defeated on the Bank issue. The strategy was adopted of putting up candidates who were regarded as the strongest in the various states. Jackson had declared that the Whigs would have to look for a general to lead them, and this prophecy was at least partially fulfilled. The principal Whig candidate was the sixty-three-year-old William Henry Harrison, whose chief claim to fame was the military reputation he had gained in the War of 1812. Webster was nominated by the Massachusetts legislature. In the South the Whigs' choice was Hugh

[30] John S. Bassett, *The Life of Andrew Jackson* (2 vols., New York, 1911), II, 682; Justin H. Smith, *The Annexation of Texas* (New York, 1911), pp. 54–57, 60–62. Jackson seems also to have considered the possibility of enlarging the United States at the expense of Texas, if the latter did not maintain her independence. At least he criticized General Gaines, who crossed the border into Texas in 1836 on the pretext of keeping order, for wanting to help Texas rather than helping establish the old claim of the Sabine as the rightful United States boundary. See Jackson Papers (second series), Kendall to Jackson, July 30, 1836; Jackson, *Correspondence*, V, 420–421.

1. Andrew Jackson in the uniform of Major General, U.S.A.

By Ralph E. W. Earl (The Smithsonian Institution)

2. J. C. Calhoun

(The Berkshire Museum, Pittsfield, Mass.)

3. John Quincy Adams

By G. P. A. Healy
(Archives Photographiques d'Art)

4. "King Andrew"

5. "The rats leaving a falling house"

(The New York Historical Society, New York City)

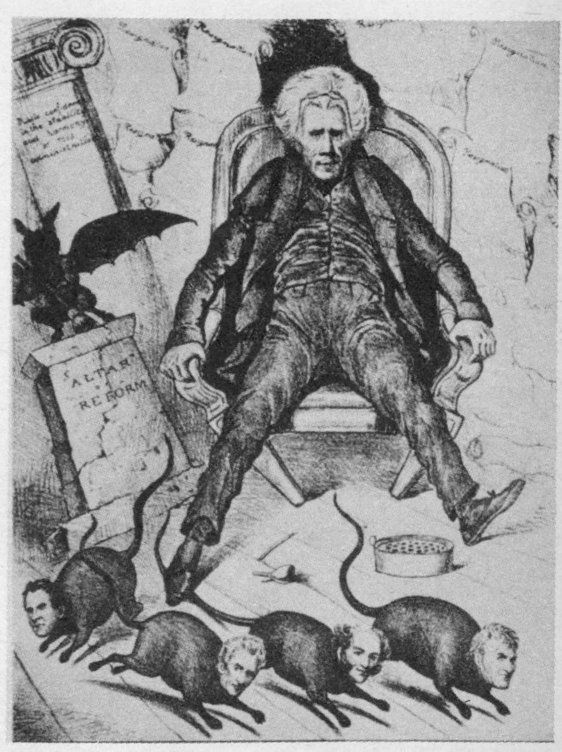

6. City of Washington in 1833

(The New York Public Library)

7. Boston in 1832

(The New York Public Library)

8. John Tyler

By G. P. A. Healy
(Frick Art Reference Library)

9. Martin Van Buren

By G. P. A. Healy
(Frick Art Reference Library)

10. "The effect of Loco Foco Pledges" (The New York Historical Society, New York City)

11. "Santa Anna declining a hasty plate of soup at Cerro Gordo"

12. Cincinnati in 1841

(The New York Public Library)

13. Buffalo from Lake Erie in 1835

(The New York Public Library)

14. Henry Clay

By Rembrandt Peale (The Pennsylvania Academy of the Fine Arts)

15. James K. Polk

(The New York Historical Society, New York City)

16. Daniel Webster

By Joseph Alexander Ames (Yale University Art Gallery)

17. William Henry Harrison

By James Reid Lambdin (National Gallery of Art, Washington, D.C.)

18. Broadway, New York City, 1834

19. Arrival of the *Great Western* steamship off New York, April 23, 1838

20. Detroit in 1834

(The New York Public Library)

21. Cleveland in 1833

(The New York Public Library)

22. Winfield Scott

By G. Callen (The New York Historical Society, New York City)

23. Zachary Taylor

By J. H. Bush (Frick Art Reference Library)

24. Columbia College, c. 1833 (The New York Public Library)

25. "The Polka"

(The New York Historical Society, New York City)

26. New Orleans, 1846-1847

(The New York Public Library)

27. Yale College and State House, New Haven, Connecticut, in 1832

(The New York Public Library)

28. Natchez, Mississippi

(The New York Public Library)

29. St. Louis in 1847

(The New York Public Library)

Lawson White of Tennessee, an erstwhile Democrat who as a strict constructionist had become increasingly critical of Jackson's policies, and who heartily disliked Van Buren.[31]

In the campaign of 1836 the Democrats were riddled by factionalism. In Tennessee, John Bell joined White in directing the anti-Jackson forces that opposed the administration on grounds that varied from states' rights theory to quarrels over the patronage. In the South, generally, White became the choice of those numerous Democrats who loathed Jackson on account of the Force Bill and disliked and distrusted Van Buren. The Virginia followers of Rives were in anything but a conciliatory mood. Factionalism was also rife in such northern states as New York and Illinois. Madison, in 1834, had predicted the early demise of the Democratic party because of Jackson's widespread unpopularity, and party strife had increased after this prediction was made.[32]

There was no bank to quarrel about in the campaign of 1836, nor was there any other issue of transcendent importance. Harrison and Van Buren were interrogated about their attitudes on national questions by one Sherrod Williams, a member of Congress from Kentucky, and both responded at length. Harrison favored the distribution of proceeds from land sales, opposed internal improvements at national expense (save for works of great national importance), and straddled on the question of establishing another Bank of the United States. Van Buren, although cautiously as was his wont, opposed distribution, internal improvements at national expense, and a national bank. At the same time, he indicated that he favored a currency largely composed of gold.[33] He also explicitly declared against the abolition of slavery in the District of Columbia without the consent of the South, and announced his opposition to the slightest interference with slavery in the states where it existed. The Little Magician was continuing to

[31] Arthur C. Cole, *The Whig Party in the South* (Washington, 1913), pp. 41–45; Turner, *United States,* p. 428; William G. Sumner, *Andrew Jackson* (Boston, 1910), p. 443.

[32] Jackson Papers (second series), Jackson to Andrew Jackson, Jr., May 20, 1835; Flagg Papers, P. Reynolds to Flagg, Nov. 12, 1836, C. C. Cambreleng to (Flagg), Nov. 21, 1836; Rives Papers, J. H. Smoot to Rives, May 27, 1835, H. A. Garland to Rives, May 29, 1835, C. W. Gooch to Rives, Oct. 20, 1835; Gaillard Hunt (ed.), *The Writings of James Madison* (9 vols., New York, 1900–10), IX, 540; Thompson, *Illinois Whigs,* p. 56; Ulrich B. Phillipps, *Georgia and State Rights* (Washington, 1902), pp. 138–139.

[33] *Niles' Register,* LI (Sept. 10, 1836), 23–30.

curry favor with the distrustful Southerners. But it was the shadow of Old Hickory that loomed largest across the national stage, and the campaign really centered on approval or disapproval of the record he had piled up during his eight years in the White House.

Van Buren gained a clear but by no means overwhelming victory. White carried Georgia and Tennessee. South Carolina voted for Willie P. Mangum. Webster received the electoral vote of Massachusetts. Harrison carried Ohio, Indiana, New Jersey, and Vermont. Van Buren had the rest, with 170 electoral votes to 124 for his combined opponents. No vice-presidential candidate received a majority and that election, for the first and only time, went to the Senate, which chose Richard M. Johnson.[34]

The triumphant Democracy, however, had no great cause for self-congratulation. It had a majority of only 25,688 out of 1,505,290 popular votes. It carried only 557 counties in the nation to 485 for the Whigs. And, while it had a comfortable majority in the Senate, the House was an open battleground, with conservative Democrats and "radical" Whigs holding the balance of power.

The election of 1836 was not an overwhelming vindication of Jacksonian Democracy. It was, rather, a clear-cut evidence of the emergence, in nearly every state in the Union, of a fairly evenly balanced two-party system. Those voters, especially in the South, who had stayed at home in 1832 rather than vote for Andrew Jackson came out in 1836 and voted Whig. The Jacksonian movement to the left, with all its talk of hideous monsters, evil corporations, and the parlous state of liberty and equality, was not winning votes. The wave of Jacksonian "reform" had spent much of its force.[35] Van Buren, according to Churchill C. Cambreleng, one of his most ardent followers, came into office supported in fact by only a minority of the people.[36]

[34] The Whig vice-presidential candidates were Francis Granger of New York, John Tyler of Virginia, and William Smith of Alabama.

[35] W. Dean Burnham, *Presidential Ballots, 1836–1892* (Baltimore, 1955), pp. 1–10, 15–20, 163 ff.; Carroll, *Origins of Whig Party*, pp. 140–151; Cole, *Whig Party in the South*, pp. 39–45.

[36] Van Buren Papers, C. C. Cambreleng to Van Buren, Nov. 18, 1837.

CHAPTER 6

The Little Magician Takes the Reins

THE RED FOX of Kinderhook began his Presidency with uncertain popular support. He was soon to find himself harried by a host of troubles. By its shortsighted financial measures Jackson's administration had sown the wind. Van Buren was to reap the whirlwind of a severe depression.

Martin Van Buren was fifty-five years old when he took oath, as President of the United States, to preserve, protect, and defend the Constitution. Somewhat below middle height (hence the sobriquet "Little Van"), balding, and slightly inclined to corpulence, he wore habitually a cheerful countenance, and was noted for suavity and tact. Van Buren liked people and under his benign sway the social life of the White House increased in tempo. He relished being on good terms with his political opponents, Clay among the rest. Stanch Whig Philip Hone, who on a visit to Washington sat in Van Buren's pew at St. John's Church, held that the President had detestable associates but was himself a gentleman.

Opinions differed then, and have continued to differ, about Van Buren's qualifications for his high office. He has been acclaimed for his wisdom, and for his skill in the management of men. On the other hand, he has been criticized for superficiality and for failure to control his subordinates. He has been accused of stubbornness, of possessing, as Virginia Governor David Campbell expressed it, a vein of "mere animal obstinacy, such as you would see in a buffalo bull." Contrariwise, he has been characterized as a man whose habitual indecision revealed itself in a vacillating noncommittalism.

Despite this welter of charge and countercharge, certain aspects of Van Buren's character and presidential career stand out with clarity. It is true that his general conduct of office showed him to be much under the shadow of his predecessor. It is true, as John Randolph said, that he had a penchant for "rowing to his object with muffled oars." It is true that at times his control over his subordinates was lax. But with all his weaknesses, the fact remains that Van Buren was honest; that he knew the value of and habitually sought counsel; that he deliberated before making decisions; and that his four years in the White House demonstrated, for better or for worse, a perfectly logical development of the left-wing tendencies of Jacksonian Democracy, a development which it took courage to foster in the face of a catastrophic depression.[1]

The new President displayed little ingenuity or resourcefulness in making up his Cabinet. He offered William Cabell Rives the post of Secretary of War, an offer promptly refused by the proud Virginian. He approached Benton on the subject of a Cabinet position, only to suffer a similar rebuff. In the end, he contented himself with the almost complete reappointment of Jackson's Cabinet. The only new face was that of Joel Poinsett, the South Carolina Unionist, who became Secretary of War.

It was not a distinguished Cabinet. John Forsyth in the State Department had had considerable diplomatic experience. He was celebrated for his wit. But he was a courtier by nature, "irresistible to the ladies," and spent altogether too much time in social gaiety. As head of the State Department, he was scarcely top flight. Levi Woodbury, a conservative by nature and somewhat stodgy, was hardly big enough for his job in the Treasury. Mahlon Dickerson in the Navy Department lacked energy. Kendall, the Postmaster General, and Benjamin F. Butler, the Attorney General, were politicians rather than statesmen. Neither was the Cabinet well distributed geographically. The West

[1] Rives Papers, D. Campbell to Rives, Sept. 15, Nov. 17, 1837, Rives to Mrs. Rives, Sept. 25, 1837; Nathan Sargent, *Public Men and Events* (2 vols., Philadelphia, 1875), II, 22; Allan Nevins (ed.), *The Diary of Philip Hone, 1828–1851* (2 vols., New York, 1927), I, 244–246; II, 65; Edward M. Shepard, *Martin Van Buren* (Boston and New York), pp. 449–467; Holmes Alexander, *The American Talleyrand* (New York, 1935), pp. 177, 253–254; Arthur M. Schlesinger, Jr., *The Age of Jackson* (Boston, 1945), pp. 47–52, 263–264.

had no representation and Pennsylvania, despite great pressure from some of her leading politicians, had failed to gain a foothold in the administration's inner circle. That circle was Jackson's more than it was Van Buren's own. The most that could be said for it was that it enveloped the new administration in an odor of Jacksonian sanctity.[2]

March 4, 1837, in Washington was a day of brilliant sunshine. A great crowd gathered early before the east portico of the Capitol. It was there to see Van Buren take the oath of office and, even more, to pay its respects to the Old Hero, who had left a sickbed to be present at the ceremony. When all was over, and the cavalcade started back down Pennsylvania Avenue, the departing leader received a great ovation from the crowd. For once, as Benton remarked, "the rising was eclipsed by the setting sun."[3]

The inaugural message itself was clothed in a humility that gave every appearance of being sincere. It professed to see nothing save what was bright in the American future, either at home or abroad. It pledged the carrying out of pre-election promises and praised Jackson's leadership, promising to follow in his footsteps. But it was mainly devoted to stressing the importance of national unity and the values to be derived from that unity's preservation. In this same connection, Van Buren reiterated his pre-election stand on slavery—his opposition to its abolition in the District of Columbia without the consent of the southern states, his determination to resist any attempt at interference with slavery in the states where it existed. "No bill," he declared, "conflicting with these views can ever receive my constitutional sanction." The highlights of the message were Jacksonism and satisfaction to the South on slavery. It was obvious that Van Buren was planning to base his administration on a union of planters and plain republicans.

The declaration on slavery outraged the abolitionists. It seemed to them an unnecessary commitment on a great moral question, and they paid little attention to the succeeding passages in which the President, by pledging that he would not meddle in foreign disputes, intimated he would not push for the annexation of Texas. They were not in a mood to appreciate the fact that Van Buren was doing his best to

[2] Rives Papers, 1834–40, Feb. 1, 1837; Van Buren Papers, C. J. Ingersoll to Van Buren, Mar. 3, 1837, Buchanan to Van Buren, Feb. 19, 28, 1837, S. Cameron and O. F. Johnson to Van Buren, Feb. 24, 1837 (Van Buren to Forsyth), Mar. 9 (?), 1837, J. D. Hammond to Van Buren, May 26, 1838; Thomas H. Benton, *Thirty Years View* (2 vols., New York, 1854), II, 9, 11.

[3] *Ibid.*, I, 735.

guard the government from any involvement in the slavery controversy, an involvement which, once it became political, would shake the nation to its foundations.[4]

Despite Van Buren's preoccupation with the slavery question, it was not slavery that was shortly to absorb the nation's startled attention. The first and greatest problem of the administration was posed by the country's financial situation.

The panic and depression that started in the winter of 1836–37 derived from a number of causes. "Overbanking and overtrading," as various Democrats labeled it, was undoubtedly a factor. Banks had multiplied and bank loans and note issues, especially in the South and West, had expanded in the riskiest sort of fashion. Many planters, plunging heavily into debt for land and slaves, had borrowed at rates as high as 30 per cent. Speculation in land had become a veritable mania, and prices had risen to dizzying heights. A Hartford speculator told of making 75 per cent annually on an investment of $1,000 in Michigan lands. Philip Hone, noting the skyrocketing of real estate values in and about New York City, cited as an example a farm three miles from Brooklyn. It had been offered at $20,000 in 1831 with no takers, but had sold in 1835 for $102,000. Other evidences of the inflationary wave were the state internal improvement programs, which, too often unproductive of returns in revenue, had cost hundreds of millions of dollars. These improvement programs had fostered the creation of state banks that made the riskiest sort of loans. Trading in stocks on Wall Street, responding to the speculative mania, had reached dizzying heights.

By 1837, overexpansion had created a mountain of debt and bad currency. The situation had been made worse by Jackson's monetary policy. The destruction of the Bank of the United States had removed the one real control over the state banks' emission of paper, and thus had fostered bad banking practice. The Specie Circular of 1836 had drained gold and silver from the East to the West, made money very tight on the eastern seaboard, forced western banks to curtail their discounts, and spread a sudden wave of doubt about the soundness of the nation's banking structure.

A situation already grave was made worse by a depression in Eng-

[4] James D. Richardson, *A Compilation of the Messages and Papers of the Presidents* (11 vols., New York, 1910), II, 1530–1533, III, 1534–1537; Jabez D. Hammond, *Political History of the State of New York* (3 vols., Cooperstown and Syracuse, 1846–48), II, 466–467.

land which lowered the price of cotton from seventeen and one-half to thirteen and one-half cents, and started a drain of specie from the United States as foreign investors began curtailing their commitments in the New World.

And now the mood of America began to change. From being a nation of people who would boast, with Philip Hone, that they could "run faster, sail smarter, dive deeper, and fly farther than any other people on the face of the earth," Americans began exhibiting a spirit of doubt and hesitation. Creditors rushed to foreclose; planters and farmers were in despair as they looked for additional sources of credit; businessmen and laborers became alike distrustful and uneasy.[5]

The outlook, in fact, had been ominous for months before Van Buren's calm assumption of general prosperity in his inaugural. *Niles' Register* had begun warning of disaster as early as April, 1836. In December of that year, Benton in the Senate had referred satirically to reports of a little, starveling panic, "a mere church-mouse concern," a comment rebuked by John J. Crittenden of Kentucky, who declared that the panic was real and was spreading. Two months later, Benton himself sought to convince Van Buren of the imminence of financial collapse, only to be told that "your friends think you a little exalted in the head on that subject," a remark that mightily offended Old Bullion's *amour-propre*. By April, 1837, there was no question in anyone's mind that a great deflation had begun. Hundreds of failures were being reported in New York City. Plantations were selling at a tithe of their value. Factories were closing down. Unemployment was spreading. May 10, 1837, the New York City banks, after a run had taken at least a million in specie out of their vaults, suspended specie payments, and the banks in other parts of the country speedily followed suit. The country was entering a depression from which it did not fully recover for some seven years.[6]

The situation in which Van Buren and the Democratic party were placed by the onset of the panic was, as the President wrote to his

[5] Welles Papers, Ellsworth *Prospectus,* Mar. 18, 1835; Hone, *Diary,* I, 131, 140, 167, 200, 240; Samuel Rezneck, "The Social History of an American Depression, 1837–1843," *American Historical Review,* XL (Oct., 1934), 662–687; Reginald C. McGrane, *The Panic of 1837* (Chicago, 1924), *passim;* Van Buren Papers, Jackson to Van Buren, Mar. 30, 1837.

[6] *Register of Debates,* 24th Cong., second sess., XIII, 1, 22, Dec. 19, 1836; Van Buren Papers, J. F. Claiborne to Van Buren, Apr. 10, 1837; E. T. Throop to Van Buren, Apr. 29, 1837; Benton, *Thirty Years View,* II, 10–11; McGrane, *Panic of 1837,* p. 93.

former chief, "one of peculiar delicacy and difficulty." For as the depression deepened, its calamitous political consequences became more and more apparent. The Whigs seized every opportunity to lay the blame for the distress upon Jackson's financial policies, a strategy that paid rich dividends. State and local elections in 1837 showed tremendous Whig gains, those in New York being especially disastrous from a Democratic viewpoint. In that state the Assembly, which in 1836 consisted of 34 Whigs and 94 Democrats, changed in 1837 to 101 Whigs and 27 Democrats. It was obvious that there were rough years ahead for the Democratic party.

The depression, and the political debacle that it threatened, also fanned into flame long-smouldering differences of opinion in the Democracy over hard money, banks, and other aspects of Jacksonian policy. New York's Democratic party split wide open. Its pro-bank, paper money, anti-Locofoco element, dubbed the Conservatives and led by United States Senator Nathaniel P. Tallmadge, refused to follow the lead of the national administration in financial matters, and often aligned with the Whigs in the state elections. Tallmadge, moreover, established a close correspondence with William Cabell Rives in Virginia, where another powerful group of Conservatives bade defiance to the Van Buren leadership and worked in more or less harmonious collaboration with the Whigs.[7] The Pennsylvania Democracy was likewise cursed by factional strife, and this was also the case in New Jersey and South Carolina. The party's main leaders tried, and with some effect, to pull the state organizations together as the campaign of 1840 loomed, but factionalism was a major problem throughout Van Buren's troubled four years.

The chief reliance of the Whigs during the Van Buren regime was the inescapable fact that times were hard. There was no general Whig agreement on such major issues as a national bank, the tariff, or internal improvements, southern Whigs being mainly against and northern and western Whigs preponderantly for all three. But they could and did unite in blaming the depression on Democratic financial measures and in promising relief if Whigs were elected to office. Generally speaking, the Whigs were respectful of banking and business interests, and they were optimistic as to the nation's economic development. This they were anxious to foster by providing a sound, specie-

[7] Some of these dissident Virginians, Rives being an outstanding example, became Whigs by 1840.

backed currency and ample supplies of credit. Save for the states' rights Whigs, these being mainly of southern extraction, the party remained strongly nationalist in its thinking. Its leaders emphasized their zeal for the education of the people and for a general social and economic program that would, as the Springfield *Republican* put it, "level up, not down."

The Democrats who were loyal to the administration kept declaring that the depression was not due to Jacksonian policies, but to overbanking and overtrading. They explained Whig victories by allegations of fraud and corruption. The electorate was warned that there was a Whig plot to bring back the Bank of the United States. The loyal Democrats were also bitter in their attacks on the Conservatives, who were charged with wrecking the party for selfish purposes. Administration supporters were furiously critical of banks, bankers, speculators, and monopolies of economic privilege (by which they usually meant banking corporations). More zealous for the maintenance of equality of opportunity and for social justice than they were to foster economic development, wedded to the idea that the world was governed too much, they clung doggedly to a hard-money policy and to a concept of the government's role as that of a passive policeman. The advisers closest to Van Buren looked upon the financial crisis as a healthful deflation that would rid the country of speculators and gamblers and restore the economy to stable levels. This would take place naturally, without any intervention by the national administration.[8]

No sooner was Van Buren in office than he was assailed by demands for the repeal of the Specie Circular. Democrats as well as Whigs swelled this chorus. They declared that the Circular had spread fear and distrust; that its rescission would restore confidence, increase land values, and bolster the revenues of the government. Even some stanch admirers of Jackson held that while the Circular had been of good effect in checking the orgy of speculation, it was now exerting a dangerously deflationary effect. On the other hand, Van Buren was

[8] Van Buren Papers, Flagg to Van Buren, Apr. 13, May 26, 1837, Polk to Van Buren, May 29, 1837, Cambreleng to Van Buren, Apr. 8, 1837, Jackson to Van Buren, Oct. 24, Nov. 19, 1838, J. D. Hammond to Flagg, Oct. 7, 1837, Richmond *Enquirer,* Aug. 14, 1837, Springfield *Republican,* July, Aug., 1839; Hone, *Diary,* I, 277; Glyndon G. Van Deusen, *Thurlow Weed: Wizard of the Lobby* (Boston, 1947), pp. 86–104, *Horace Greeley, Nineteenth Century Crusader* (Philadelphia, 1953), pp. 25–32, and "Some Aspects of Whig Thought and Theory," *American Historical Review,* LXIII (Jan., 1958).

told by men like Cambreleng and Taney that repeal would set off another wave of inflation, flood the Treasury with currency of dubious value, and be generally hailed as a betrayal of Jackson and a victory for the Whigs.

The pressure for repeal mounted. The Cabinet was divided on the subject. Even Silas Wright, though himself not in favor of repeal, reported that it was advocated by some of the best people in New York and that the majority were clearly for it. Jackson's letters to Van Buren indicate the General's conviction that the Little Magician needed some strong encouragement if he was to be held true to the Circular.[9]

For some weeks Van Buren pondered. He even drew up a list of questions on repeal to be submitted to the Cabinet, only to hold them back in the knowledge that the Cabinet was divided on the subject and that, after all, his was the final responsibility. By April 1 he had made his decision. It was that the Circular should remain in effect.[10]

Van Buren's determination to stand by the Specie Circular was significant in several ways. In the face of great pressure, he had remained true to what had become the most unpopular act of Jackson's administrations. The business community was affronted. Rives, Tallmadge, and the Conservatives generally were alarmed and disgruntled.[11] The Whigs cried havoc—and Locofocoism. The President had given a clear indication that the government's trend of the past five years toward hard money was not to be reversed.

Maintaining the Specie Circular was well enough in its way, but it was scarcely sufficient as a means of meeting the situation produced by the panic, and the first weeks of the President's administration saw him forced into calling an extra session of Congress. The suspension of specie payment by the banks at once rendered them ineligible as custodians of the government's funds, since they were by law obliged to return these deposits to the government in specie if such demand should be made. This fact, plus fears that the depression, by drying up the revenue, would leave the Treasury without sufficient funds to meet

[9] Van Buren Papers, C. P. White to Van Buren, Mar. 14, 1837, Levi Woodbury (?) to Van Buren, Mar. 19, 1837, Wright to Van Buren, Mar. 21, 1837, Jackson to Van Buren, Mar. 22, 30, 1837.

[10] Van Buren Papers, "Questions to the Cabinet," Mar. 21, 1837, Taney to Van Buren, Apr. 1, 1837.

[11] Van Buren Papers, Rives to Van Buren, Apr. 7, 1837; Rives Papers, Tallmadge to Rives, May 1, 1837, W. M. Peyton to Rives, June 27, 1837.

ordinary expenses, made an extra session necessary. Van Buren issued the call May 15, 1837, the time of meeting was fixed as September 4, and on that date the first session of the Twenty-fifth Congress assembled in Washington.[12]

Van Buren's message to the special session makes curious reading today. He made it clear that Congress had been called together rather to solve the embarrassments of the national government than to cope with those of the country. He began with an explanation of the depression as due to overbanking and overtrading, and then suggested the advisability of certain courses of action. He proposed passage of a law throwing into bankruptcy the banks which suspended specie payment; postponement of the distribution of the surplus still in the Treasury (so that it might be used to cover the estimated deficit for 1837); postponement of the payment of bonds posted for duties by the politically powerful importing merchants of New York and other ports; the issuance of Treasury notes to meet the immediate needs of the government; and the passage of a law providing that the government keep its own receipts in its own Treasury vaults, thus completely divorcing its fiscal operations from the banks of the country.

In his argument for the Independent Treasury, which occupied the major part of the message, the President made clear his narrow view of governmental responsibility. It was not the function of government, he declared, to manage domestic or foreign exchange. He was opposed to any such "blending [of] private interests with the operations of public business" as would be involved in the re-establishment of a national bank. The expense of government should be limited to its actual wants, and its revenues to its expenses. He wished to avoid a new national debt. He favored a narrow construction of the government's power over commerce and currency, and paid no attention at all to the general-welfare clause of the Constitution.

Van Buren did hope that the measures he proposed would be of some assistance to the country at large, but he expressly cautioned citizens against looking to the government for relief in their distress. The government had not been created for any such purpose, he declared. The Founding Fathers had "wisely judged that the less government interferes with private pursuits the better for the general prosperity." Government aid to any class or group "would be substantially to use

[12] Van Buren Papers, Van Buren to Jackson, May 23, 1837; Richardson, *Messages and Papers,* III, 1538–1539, 1541.

the property of some for the benefit of others," and he had refrained from suggesting any interference with the exchanges or with commerce, or any plan for "relieving mercantile embarrassments," in the belief that such measures would be unconstitutional and "would not promote the real and permanent welfare of those they might be designed to aid."[13]

This was not such a message as a Whig President, at least a northern Whig, might have sent under similar circumstances. Webster denounced it. "I feel," he said, "as if I were on some other sphere, as if I were not at home, as if this could not be America when I see schemes of public policy proposed, having for their object the convenience of Government only, and leaving the people to shift for themselves. . . ."[14] A Whig message would probably have suggested some form of aid for business (such as tariff or currency legislation), and would have been predicated on the neo-Hamiltonian assumption that what was good for business was good for the country. Van Buren's message was a very fair representation of the ideas of a party that was the heir not only to Jeffersonian idealism but also to Jeffersonian agrarianism and strict construction, and to the neo-physiocratic concepts of John Taylor of Caroline.

The Democracy's laissez-faire attitude toward government was applied only at the nation's capital. In the states, as, for example, in Pennsylvania and Massachusetts, the party took a much more positive attitude toward the stimulation of the economy by governmental activity. The granting of corporation charters, the use of mixed (state and private) enterprise, the aid given to railroad and canal companies, gave striking evidence that in local areas the Democrats could vie with the Whigs in expanding the role of government to meet the needs of the people. It was chiefly at Washington that the Democrats persisted in applying the Jeffersonian concept that that government governs best which governs least.[15]

As soon as Van Buren's message had been received, the Congress

[13] *Ibid.*, III, 324–346.

[14] *Congressional Globe,* 25th Cong., second sess., Appendix, p. 606, col. 3, Webster on the Subtreasury, Jan. 31, 1838.

[15] Louis Hartz, *Economic Policy and Democratic Thought: Pennsylvania, 1776–1860* (Cambridge, 1948), pp. 62–125, 289–295, and *The Liberal Tradition in America* (New York, 1955), pp. 89–142; Oscar Handlin, *Commonwealth: A Study of the Role of Government in the American Economy, Massachusetts, 1774–1861* (New York, 1947), pp. 218–263.

went to work. The Judiciary Committee of the House reported against a bankrupt law, and this punitive proposal regarding the banks was heard of no more; but out of the Senate Committee on Finance came legislation designed to meet the other requests made by the President. One bill postponed indefinitely the payment of the surplus; another authorized the issue of $10 million in Treasury notes bearing interest at not more than 6 per cent; still another gave six months' grace for the payment of duty bonds; and finally came a bill providing for what came to be known as the Subtreasury, or Independent Treasury, a bill that divorced the government from all connection with the nation's banks.

Putting this program of legislation into effect was not an easy matter. Clay, who in the Senate naturally assumed the leadership of the Whig forces, pronounced it barren and pointless. And as each proposal came before Congress, the Whigs submitted it to a barrage of withering criticism.

The Whigs declared that postponement of the "surplus" distribution was bad because it would embarrass the states. The prospect of this $9 million being added to the national debt depressed them not at all, particularly since the government had ended the year 1836 without any debt whatsoever. The Democrats argued that the surplus had, in effect, already been swallowed up by the needs of the government.

In the altercation over distribution of the surplus, the Whig case was not without strength. Flagg, the Democratic New York State comptroller, had warned Van Buren that failure to distribute would be very embarrassing, as loan certificates based on the promise of distribution had been handed out in the state by the thousands. This was evidently the case in other states, as well as in New York. There was also, as Senator Rives remarked, something to be said for action by the national government that, by affording some measure of relief, would help to restore confidence. But the ending of surplus distribution was an administration measure, and it passed both houses by comfortable majorities.[16]

As Clay had castigated the postponement of distribution, so he denounced the issuance of Treasury notes, declaring that it would put the Treasury into competition with all the banks of the country. It was, he said, a national bank in disguise, run by the Treasury. But this line

[16] Van Buren Papers, Flagg to Van Buren, May 26, 1837; *Congressional Globe,* 25th Cong., first sess., 28, 29.

of argument was futile; the need was real; and the bill passed the Senate by a vote of thirty-five to six.[17] The bill authorizing postponement of the payment of duty bonds also passed Congress without difficulty. The Independent Treasury was another matter.

On June 20, 1834, William F. Gordon of Virginia had proposed that the government separate its financial operations completely from the banks, and on February 10, 1835, he had proposed an amendment to that effect for the deposit bill then under discussion.[18] Gordon was an ardent advocate of states' rights and a follower of Calhoun, who had previously suggested the same procedure, and the Democrats had had no patience with this proposal. Three years later, they were ready to see it in a different light.

The Independent Treasury bill was introduced in the Senate September 14, 1837, by Silas Wright from the committee on finance. On the following day Churchill C. Cambreleng reported a similar bill from the House Committee on Ways and Means. It was thus sponsored by two of Van Buren's New York henchmen. It ordered collectors of the customs, postmasters, and other receivers of public money to hold their receipts until ordered to pay them out or transfer them. It also ordered the Secretary of the Treasury to withdraw the government's funds as expeditiously as possible from the "pet" banks and place them with the depositories established by the act.[19]

Wright's bill did not forbid the payment of paper money to the government, and Calhoun, already committed to the idea of an Independent Treasury, offered an amendment known as the "specie clause." This provided that, beginning after January 1, 1838, there should be a gradual reduction in the amount of bank notes receivable by the government from specie-paying banks, and that after January 1, 1841, the only money receivable other than coin should be notes, bills, or paper issued under the authority of the United States. The amendment also provided that after January 1, 1841, federal disbursements should be only in gold or silver, or in such notes or paper as would be authorized by law.[20] These provisions were accepted by Wright and incorporated in the bill, which was thereafter supported by Calhoun.

[17] *Ibid.*, 120, 121. It had passed the House on the previous day by a vote of 127 to 98.

[18] *Register of Debates,* 23rd Cong., first sess., 219, 4640–4641; second sess., 1282–1288.

[19] *Ibid.*, 27, 33.

[20] *Ibid.*, 44.

This move by Calhoun was politically significant, for it heralded his separation from the Whigs, and his return, after a fashion, to the ranks of the Democracy. Never at ease among the centralizing Whigs, even though on occasion he had professed himself to be one of them, deeply suspicious of Clay's American system and leadership, he was once more aligning himself with the party whose narrow view of the national government's power was in harmony with his own. At the same time, convinced that neither major party could long endure as a national entity, he was hoping for a general political melee in which the South, under his leadership, would hold the balance of power.[21]

Calhoun's defection angered the Whigs. His fellow senator from South Carolina, Preston, charged him with desertion (to which Calhoun blandly replied that he had never been a Whig or anything else save "an honest Nullifier"). On the other hand, the Van Buren Democrats were scarcely uplifted by this accession to their ranks. It was, of course, a relief to be free from the attacks of publicists like Duff Green and Richard K. Crallé, and some Democrats wanted to welcome the South Carolinian with cordiality. Others felt that no good could come from such a somersault, and Jackson warned that those who confided in Calhoun's support of the administration were bound to be disappointed.[22]

Calhoun's support of the Independent Treasury was counterbalanced by the open opposition of the Conservatives. Rives introduced a bill that would make government receipts payable in the notes of specie-paying banks, and he and Tallmadge, as the battle developed, led the Conservatives into an alliance with the Whigs.

The Independent Treasury bill, with the specie amendment, satisfied several administration needs. It manifested the party's devotion to the hard-money antibank policy of Jackson, for it removed the government deposit basis for expanding the money supply, and thus promoted a larger use of specie in monetary transactions. It helped propitiate labor leaders who wanted to reduce the importance of state bank notes in the currency. It permitted the Democrats not only to get out from under the onus of being "bank-governed" (a charge that had been

[21] American Historical Association, *Annual Report* (Washington, 1900), II, 371–410; Frederick J. Turner, *The United States, 1830–1850* (New York, 1935), pp. 462–463; Charles M. Wiltse, *John C. Calhoun* (3 vols., Indianapolis, 1944–51), II, 354–356.

[22] Jackson Papers (second series), W. B. Lewis to Jackson, Oct. 2, 1837; Rives Papers, W. B. Lewis to ———, Nov. 3, 1837; Wiltse, *Calhoun,* II, 355.

used with much effect by Weed and the New York Whigs) but also to shift that charge over against the opposition. It offered, in the opinion of Silas Wright, the only means of vanquishing the Whig doctrine that Congress could constitutionally regulate all the currency, not just the coinage. It would help, as Cambreleng put it, to keep the government "in the hands of the planting, farming, and laboring classes and save it from becoming a mere gambling machine to fill the country as in England with 'palaces, poorhouses, and prisons.'" The struggle between aristocracy and democracy, said Cambreleng, would go on; but with the suffrage as it was, the triumph of the Democracy would be certain.[23]

The lengthy battles in forensics that followed the introduction of the Independent Treasury bill found its Whig opponents denouncing it as a measure bound to stifle recovery. It would, they asserted, draw specie out of circulation and curtail loans and credit; it would increase executive patronage, provide one kind of currency for the government and another for the people, and promote peculation. They also argued at length that it was a withdrawal of the government from the country. Webster thundered that it was the government's duty to establish and maintain a sound national currency. Clay declared that the government should provide relief for the country's plight, and it was clear that the primary means of relief which he had in mind was the re-establishment of a national bank. In the course of a four-hour speech in the Senate, September 25, 1837, he remarked that Van Buren had no more right to infer from his election that the people were opposed to a bank than he had to infer that the people considered a little man of five feet, with red face, sandy-colored whiskers, head inclined to baldness, and downcast look, a model of human perfection. The fastidious Rives found the logic of this speech doubtful, and its personal allusion to Van Buren in very bad taste.[24]

The supporters of the bill found no difficulty in refuting some of the arguments against it. They pointed out that it would not sensibly increase the Executive patronage; that it would not dry up the country's supply of specie, since the government would be paying out at least as much money as it took in; that it would not promote peculation, if the

[23] Van Buren Papers, Wright to Van Buren, June 4, 1837, Cambreleng to Van Buren, Nov. 18, 1837.

[24] Rives Papers, Rives to Mrs. Rives, Sept. 25, 1837; *Congressional Globe*, 25th Cong., first sess., 67–68, 94, and *passim.*

standards of governmental appointment were kept as they should be kept. The bill's sponsors also denied that it would furnish two kinds of currency, one for the government, the other for the people, their argument being that the national government had no power over anything save coinage and that, therefore, it was up to the states to see to it that the state banks furnished a currency equally as valid.

The Whig argument about the government's responsibility for affording relief was more difficult to counter. Often the Democrats took refuge simply in violent denunciations of the banks. Once again the Bank of the United States was held up to view as a horrible menace to the independence of government, while the state banks were portrayed (with considerable justice) as grasping, selfish institutions which were profit- and privilege-minded to the nth degree. Their activities made the currency and the whole credit system "as unsteady and as uncertain as April weather," said one Democratic congressman. "I defy the art of man," said James Buchanan, "to devise a worse banking system than that which prevails throughout this country." Far from doing anything about this situation, however, they retreated into a narrow construction of the Constitution, and from that vantage point extolled the Independent Treasury.

Van Buren's proposal, said his supporters, would keep the government independent and the revenue safe. It would exert a healthful moral influence, since it would diminish the opportunity for speculation. It would not artificially stimulate trade, for its insistence on specie and specie-backed notes in payment of government dues would improve the condition of the currency and tend to check unwise bank expansion.

The Conservatives joined the Whigs in viewing the Independent Treasury with abhorrence, but they saw it as really a Treasury bank, another national bank in disguise. Zealous for maintaining the rights of the states, the best plan that they could devise was to keep the government's money in carefully selected and supervised state banks.

The congressional struggle over the Independent Treasury demonstrated the even balance of the two great parties. In the Twenty-fifth Congress (1837–39) the Democrats had a clear majority in the Senate, but the House was almost evenly divided. In the latter body, the Whigs and the Conservatives, joined by some western Democrats, defeated the Independent Treasury bill, 120 to 106. Whig maneuvers, furthermore, ousted Blair (whose Washington *Globe* had remained the administration organ and reflected its views on the currency) as printer of the House, that post being given to Allen of the *Madisonian,* a spokesman for the Conservatives.[25] But when Clay made an effort to obtain congressional approval for another national bank, he failed ignominiously in both houses, many of those who had voted against the Independent Treasury also voting against his proposal.

At the beginning of the regular session of the Twenty-fifth Congress, Van Buren again urged passage of the Independent Treasury bill, remarking dryly that since the suspension of specie payment, the government had been keeping its own funds willy-nilly. This clearly indicated, it seemed to him, that his proposal was a practical one. Again Wright introduced the necessary bill and again there was great argument. This time it was only by eliminating the specie clause that the bill could be pushed through the Senate, and even thus modified it failed in the House. At this same session, Clay and Webster pushed through the rescission of the Specie Circular. The administration's course was being charted in the path of very heavy weather.

Van Buren might never have secured the passage of the Independent Treasury bill had it not been for the depression itself. This had moderated somewhat during 1838, and in May of that year the banks had resumed specie payments. But conditions became worse toward the close of 1839 and once again the banks suspended. This demonstration of their instability was a powerful argument for steering clear of their clutches. It was reinforced by the collapse of Biddle's United States Bank of Pennsylvania, and the consequent decline of his influence, which had been vigorously cast against Van Buren's plan. Under these circumstances, an Independent Treasury bill passed both houses of Congress by the end of June, 1840, though by narrow majorities. The Democrats rejoiced mightily. Blair had characterized it as the second Declaration of Independence and so, to many left-wing Democrats, it seemed. Van Buren signed it July 4, 1840.[26]

The Independent Treasury had none of the calamitous and positive

[25] William E. Smith, *The Francis Preston Blair Family in Politics* (2 vols., New York, 1933), I, 106–107.

[26] The course of this struggle may be followed in the *Congressional Globe.* See also Benton, *Thirty Years View,* II, 39–42, 124–125, 164–167; and Reginald C. McGrane (ed.), *The Correspondence of Nicholas Biddle* (Boston, 1919), pp. 270–310, and *Panic of 1837,* pp. 209–236. For a sympathetic view of Van Buren's policy in this struggle, see Schlesinger, *Age of Jackson,* pp. 227–241, 250–252, 264–265.

effects that the Whigs had predicted in their more impassioned moments. It has been argued that it was a necessary step because the state banks were untrustworthy as places of deposit, and a national bank was unsuited to the growing needs of the country. There is some justice in this contention, but the fact remains that the Independent Treasury made no fundamental contribution either to financial stability or to the search for a uniform currency. Under it, Benton later declared, "paper money and even broken bank paper money" was daily paid out to the government's creditors. Instead of developing the great principle of governmental regulation of the currency urged by the Whigs, which was at least implicit in the charter of the Second Bank of the United States, and which is today recognized as a legitimate and necessary province of the national government, that function had now been largely surrendered to the states. This was a backward step, but it was a logical one to be taken by the party in power.[27]

Closely connected with the struggle over the Independent Treasury bill was the land question, out of which everybody wished to make political capital. The main body of Whigs, led by Clay, and a good many eastern Democrats as well, wanted to distribute the proceeds of the sale of public lands to the states. Westerners generally were cool to this idea. Their idea of a good land program consisted of restriction of land sales to actual settlers; the right of states to tax land as soon as the government sold it; permanent pre-emption (safeguarding of squatters' rights); graduation of land sales so that the longer lands remained unsold, the cheaper they would become; and, eventually, control by the western states of the lands within their limits. This program, summed up, meant cheap land, easily obtainable. The great spokesman for the land-hungry West was Old Bullion Benton of Missouri, whose remedy for the depression was graduation, plus confidence in the farmers.[28]

Van Buren had opposed Clay's land bill, but otherwise, in the years before he became President, his ideas on the land question had not been made clear. By December of 1837, however, he saw that his best hope of passing the Independent Treasury bill was to curry favor with

[27] *Congressional Globe,* 29th Cong., first sess., Appendix, p. 820; A. T. Huntington and Robert J. MaWhinney, *Laws of the United States Concerning Money, Banking, and Loans, 1778–1909* (Washington, 1910), p. 126; David Kinley, *The Independent Treasury of the United States and Its Relations to the Banks of the Country* (Washington, 1910), pp. 51–52.

[28] Van Buren Papers, Benton to Van Buren, May 31, 1837.

the West. This meant, as Benton put it, infusing "new life into the bosoms of the [western] delegations" by supporting their views on land policy. In his annual message that year, the President came out for the Bentonian scheme of graduation. He also asked for a pre-emption law benefiting squatters not covered by such previous legislation.[29]

To Whigs like Clay and John Quincy Adams, the President's proposals were no better than attempts to buy western votes by the plunder of western lands. They denounced pre-emption as a measure that would despoil the national government of its land, and termed graduation wasteful, unfair to older states, and conducive to speculation. In these attacks they were joined by Calhoun, although his objectives were not the same as their own. The Whig leaders envisioned using the revenue from the public lands for promoting and developing a great government-sponsored program of internal improvements which would revolutionize transportation, increase domestic markets, stimulate agricultural and industrial production, and bind the nation together in a great harmony of interest. Calhoun wanted outright cession of the lands to the states in which they lay, with compensation to the older states for their attendant loss in revenue. Both the Whigs and Calhoun, however, hoped to make political capital out of their stand, and they were generally able to get enough eastern Democratic support so that they could slow down or defeat administration land measures.

The battle over land policy resulted in the passage of a pre-emption bill in 1838, but graduation was defeated in the House. Early in 1840, the Democrats passed another graduation bill in the Senate, but once again it failed in the House. At the same time they passed another pre-emption bill extending the pre-emption act of 1838 to 1842.

By 1840 the struggle over the public lands was exhibiting still another phase. Many of the states were in grave financial difficulty, due to a combination of hard times and overambitious programs of internal improvements. As a remedy for this situation, various Whig organs began proposing the assumption of state debts by the national government. This would be done indirectly, through distribution of the land sales proceeds.

Assumption had certain points in its favor. It would be welcomed by investors, domestic and foreign, in state obligations. It would stimu-

[29] Richardson, *Messages and Papers,* III, 1601–1606; William N. Chambers, *Old Bullion Benton, Senator from the New West* (Boston, 1956), p. 226.

late the transportation revolution and thus foster confidence and bring about an improvement in business conditions and in employment. It was really based on the old Federalist "trickle down" concept of the national economy.

But assumption was also vulnerable at several points. It was not attractive to the West, which feared that it would endanger pre-emption and graduation. Neither was it attractive to the South, which believed that exhaustion of land revenues in this manner would result in a higher tariff. Both Benton and Calhoun attacked it vigorously. Whig resolutions in its favor were defeated in the Senate in March, 1840, and the Whigs did not seek to make it an issue in the 1840 presidential campaign.[30]

By 1840, Van Buren had succeeded, against heavy odds, in securing the passage of the Independent Treasury bill and in making some progress toward implementing a "cheap and easy" land policy. But vexing problems still confronted his administration. There were irritating and potentially dangerous diplomatic troubles. The slavery question would not down. The depression hung like an albatross around the neck of the Democracy. Eighteen hundred and forty was a Presidential year, and the outcome of that quadrennial conflict appeared dubious in the extreme.

[30] Raynor G. Wellington, *The Political and Sectional Influence of the Public Lands* (Cambridge, 1914), pp. 64–82; Wiltse, *Calhoun,* II, 398–400; Chambers, *Benton,* pp. 227, 235; Van Deusen, *Clay,* pp. 306–307.

CHAPTER 7

Slavery, Patriotism, Ballyhoo

AS VAN BUREN'S Presidency was rapidly confronted with a severe depression, all the grievances and animosities bred of nearly twelve years of Democratic rule, combined with the growing tumult over slavery, came to focus in a spreading discontent with the reigning party and its hapless chief. The administration's problems were further complicated by a series of border incidents on the Canadian frontier that made for strained relations with Great Britain. The Red Fox strove to pick a careful way through this maze of difficulties. The Whigs, on their part, tried to turn the country's sufferings to their own advantage, and looked with rising hopes to the election of 1840.

Where the Independent Treasury was concerned, the Whig and Democratic parties had clearly differentiated policies. Sectionalism, where it did appear in the voting on this issue, played only a minor role. Land policy was much more subject to the play of sectional interest. And sectional division was still more evident in the rising clamor over slavery and freedom of speech which repeatedly agitated Congress during Van Buren's term of office.

The President, still clinging to his hope of building his party's strength upon an alliance of the planters of the South and the plain republicans of the North, was loath indeed to see the rise of slavery agitation. But the growing power and aggressive tactics of the abolitionists were continually bringing the question of slavery to the fore. The abolitionists were bent on kindling fires. The South, keenly aware of its vested interest in slaves and as keenly sensitive about its honor, seemed bent on fanning the flames.

The gag rules earlier established by the House and the Senate had by no means eliminated congressional consideration of slavery. Petitions against it, particularly against slavery in the District of Columbia, kept putting in an appearance in both houses. The excitement roused by these efforts of the abolitionists was by no means allayed when, early in Van Buren's term of office, the government of the Republic of Texas began making clear the fact that the Texans were favorably disposed toward annexation by the United States.

In December, 1837, Calhoun undertook to define the ultra-southern position regarding slavery and the annexation of slaveholding territory in a series of resolutions that he presented in the Senate. These declared that, in adopting the Constitution, the states had acted "as free, independent, and sovereign states"; that they had retained "exclusive and sole" control of their domestic institutions where power over these had not been delegated, and that interference with such control emanating from other states was dangerous to the Union; that the national government was obligated to safeguard the states' control of their own institutions; that domestic slavery was an important part of these institutions and that attacks upon it were violations of the most solemn religious and moral obligations; that any attempts to abolish slavery in the District of Columbia or in the territories would be "a direct and dangerous attack" upon the institutions of the slave states; and that to refuse (on the ground that slavery was immoral or sinful) to "strengthen" the southern and western states or to increase their limits or population by the annexation of new territories or states would, in effect, disfranchise the slaveholding states.[1]

Clay attacked the last two of these resolutions as dangerously extreme. If the annexation of Texas and abolition were to be coupled in the same set of resolutions, he said, "then indeed there will be too much reason to apprehend that the North, at no distant day, will be united as one man."

The Kentuckian's argument, and that of others, resulted in the modification of Calhoun's resolutions. The reference to annexation was stricken out, as was the one about the national government being obligated to safeguard state institutions. Even so, they remained the

[1] *Congressional Globe,* 25th Congress, second session, 55.

sternest kind of admonition to the foes of slavery. They passed by ample majorities.

The zeal of senators, Whig as well as Democratic, for exorcising the specter of conflict over slavery was further demonstrated when the Senate tabled, twenty-three to twenty-one, a resolution introduced by Senator Allen of Ohio to the effect that nothing in the Calhoun resolutions should be construed as an abridgment of the freedom of speech or press, or of the right of petition. But the sectional aspect of the vote on Allen's resolution was little short of startling. Twenty of the twenty-three voting to table were from slaveholding states. Nineteen of the twenty-one voting against tabling were from free states. Such a division on such an important issue made the menace of sectional conflict very clear indeed.[2]

In his speech on Calhoun's resolutions, Clay had remarked that the abolitionist movement was spreading, and that one reason for its spread was the arbitrary way in which antislavery petitions were being tabled by the Senate. This was a statement of fact, not only for the Senate but for the House, but southern control of Congress prevented any improvement in the situation. In December, 1838, the problem of handling such petitions was again debated in the House of Representatives. A New Hampshire Democrat presented a resolution directing that all antislavery petitions should, on their presentation, be laid on the table "without being debated, printed, or referred." The House passed this gag, dividing chiefly along sectional lines. A year later (January, 1840), by a vote of 114 to 108, a resolution was adopted to the effect that antislavery petitions should not even be received by the House. Here again the vote was markedly sectional rather than partisan.[3] In all, five successive gags were passed by the House during this controversy.

The South had clearly triumphed in the matter of petitions, but the triumph was not to be a lasting one. John Quincy Adams, who had

[2] *Ibid.*, 25th Cong., second sess., 74, 80–81, 96–97, 98, Appendix, p. 58. Benton of Missouri and Clayton of Delaware, one a Democrat, the other a Whig, were the only senators from slaveholding states to stand up for the right of free speech. The three senators from the free states who voted to table (Niles of Connecticut, Norvell of Michigan, and Pierce of New Hampshire) were balanced against their opposite numbers. That is to say, the senatorial delegations from those three states were split on the motion.

[3] *Ibid.*, 25th Cong., third sess., 21–22; 26th Cong., first sess., 150–151. Frederick J. Turner, *The United States, 1830–1850* (New York, 1935), p. 468.

already made himself the great defender of this basic right, continued to lead the fight against the gag. Gradually, as the abolitionists became better organized, and as the northern representation increased, the southern hold on Congress loosened in the matter of petitions. It was peculiarly fitting that when, December 3, 1844, the gag rule was finally rescinded in the House, it should be on the motion of Old Man Eloquent.[4]

Adams' triumph came almost four years after Van Buren had left the Presidency. During the reign of the Red Fox, the South continued to control Congress where slavery was concerned. Aroused by the deluge of abolitionist propaganda and the increasing activities of the Underground Railroad, stung by the refusal of Governor Seward of New York to allow extradition to Virginia of three Negroes charged with slave stealing and of the governor of Maine to extradite the captain and mate of the schooner *Susan* to Georgia on a similar charge, Southerners became more and more violent in defense of slavery, and Congress, in its zeal to avoid sectional conflict, bent repeatedly to their will. A signal evidence of this congressional attitude was furnished by the case of the *Enterprise.*

The *Enterprise* was an American brig engaged in the coastal slave trade. She was forced into a Bermuda port by bad weather and there the slaves she was carrying were freed. The United States demanded an indemnity, which Great Britain refused. Thereupon, March 4, 1840, Calhoun introduced in the Senate a series of resolutions which declared that Great Britain had acted in violation of the law of nations and in a manner "highly unjust" to the owners of the slaves.

Calhoun's case was by no means a strong one. The *Enterprise* had been sailing from one southern port to another. Slavery was a local institution, and the states which recognized it had no jurisdiction on the high seas. The slaves had been freed by a habeas corpus proceeding in a country where slavery was unlawful. Where was the law of nations, generally recognized, which identified slaves as property? There was no such law. The Senate blandly overlooked these considerations and by a vote of thirty-three to nothing (though with eleven abstentions) adopted Calhoun's resolutions.

[4] *Congressional Globe,* 28th Cong., second sess., 7; Russell B. Nye. *Fettered Freedom* (East Lansing, 1949), pp. 32–54; Samuel F. Bemis, *John Quincy Adams and the Union* (New York, 1956), pp. 334–347, 350–351, 370–373, 420–439, 446–448.

That the administration was almost as complaisant as the Senate where the feelings of the slaveholders were concerned was indicated by its attitude toward the African slave trade. This traffic was far from dead. Carried on by ships that were, or purported to be, under American registry, it was bringing hundreds, if not thousands, of slaves every year to the North American continent. Van Buren, in his message to Congress in 1839, condemned this trade, pointed out the way in which it flourished as a result of loopholes in American laws relating to the sale and transfer of American vessels abroad, and urged remedial legislation. Nothing was done. Indeed, the government was so zealous to deny the right of search, or even the right of visit, that British efforts to stop the trade were rendered largely ineffectual. And the American naval force which was finally sent to the African coast was too small to have any real effect.

The administration's attitude toward the slave trade came out clearly in the case of *L'Amistad.* This Spanish ship was carrying fifty-three Negroes, illegally imported from Africa into Cuba and there designated as slaves. In June, 1839, while sailing from one Spanish port to another in the Caribbean, the Negroes seized the ship. They sought to force one of the ship's company to sail the vessel back to Africa, but, under cover of night, the ship was edged toward the North American mainland. Coming to anchor at length off the coast of Connecticut, *L'Amistad* and its cargo were picked up by a federal revenue cutter.

Van Buren was more than willing to surrender the Negroes on *L'Amistad.* Indeed, he gave instruction that if the United States District Court for Connecticut found for the Spanish "owners," the Negroes were to be hurried on board an armed ship that had been sent to New Haven to carry them to Cuba. There was to be no opportunity for appeal. In defiance of the President's wishes, however, the case was carried to the Supreme Court, which declared the Negroes free men.[5]

[5] *Congressional Globe,* 26th Cong., first sess., 327–329; James D. Richardson, *A Compilation of the Messages and Papers of the Presidents* (11 vols., New York, 1910), III, 538; George W. Julian, *The Life of Joshua R. Giddings* (Chicago, 1892), pp. 73–84; Wilbur H. Siebert, *The Underground Railroad* (New York, 1898), pp. 17–22, 33–44; W. E. Burghardt Du Bois, *The Suppression of the African Slave Trade* (New York, 1904), pp. 141–146, 154–156, 161–162, 293; Hugh Soulsby, "The Right of Search and the Slave Trade in Anglo-American Relations 1814–1862," Johns Hopkins University, *Studies,* LI, No. 2 (Baltimore, 1933), 39–58.

Difficult as was Van Buren's position vis-à-vis the southern slave interest, it did not involve the wholesale violence and even threat of war created by conditions on the Canadian frontier. There a situation had developed by the latter eighteen-thirties that led many to believe a third armed conflict inevitable between the United States and Great Britain.

Class discrimination, religious dissensions, and political despotism had combined to produce a fever of discontent in Canada. William Lyon Mackenzie, a "wiry and peppery little Scotchman" and a born agitator, spearheaded a movement for independence in Upper Canada. A similar movement in Lower Canada was headed by a vain though brilliant orator and politician, Louis Joseph Papineau. On December 4, 1837, Mackenzie raised the standard of revolt. The movement fizzled and its leader escaped to the United States. Papineau, after leading a similarly abortive attempt in Lower Canada, also fled to the United States with a price on his head.

The Canadian rebels, especially the exiles, found much sympathy and support on the southern side of the border. The stirrings of what was later to be called Manifest Destiny were already apparent. Despite the fiasco of the attempt at conquest in the War of 1812, many Americans persisted in wishing to see Canada annexed. As one enthusiast put it, the dominion of the United States ought to extend "not only from the Atlantic to the Pacific, but also from Tierra del Fuego to the aurora borealis." Many believed that it was an American duty to extend the area of freedom. How could this be better done than by giving help to the oppressed Canadians? Not a few venturesome spirits, thrown out of employment by the depression, found it easy to enlist in secret societies bearing such alluring titles as "The Patriots" or "The Hunters," and pledged to all kinds of daring exploits on behalf of downtrodden fellow human beings. The insurgents found it easy to recruit men and supplies at Buffalo, Rochester, Montpelier, and ten or a dozen other places along the frontier. They also established a base on Navy Island, a Canadian possession in the Niagara River not far above the falls.

The Canadian government, and the great majority of Canadian citizens, viewed these proceedings with alarm and disgust. Some Canadian Loyalists cherished bitter memories or traditions of the American Revolution from which they or their ancestors had fled. Canadian patriots in general suspected that the United States had fell designs on Canada. The press on both sides of the border fed the excitement. Then came the *Caroline* affair.

The *Caroline* was a steamer used by the insurgents to transport supplies from the American side of the Niagara River to Navy Island. On December 29, 1837, Canadian soldiers crossed the Niagara and, after a skirmish in which at least one American citizen was killed, towed the ship out into the river, where it was set ablaze and adrift. It sank a mile or two above the falls.

The seizure of the *Caroline* produced great excitement on the American side of the frontier. The insurgents multiplied their recruiting activities, with a good deal of success. The following year saw a number of raids into Canada with considerable blood spilled, both by Canadians and Americans. A British steamer, the *Sir Robert Peel,* was seized and burned and a United States boat was fired on in the St. Lawrence. Hunters' Lodges in the United States and Canada dedicated themselves to Canadian freedom. In September, 1838, some 160 Hunters from both sides of the border attended a convention in Cleveland, where they elected one Smith, a resident of that city, President of the Republic of Canada.

The government of the United States looked askance upon these stirring events. Van Buren declared that expressions of sympathy for the cause of freedom were only natural among Americans, but he also stated unequivocally that Americans had no right to invade a friendly power, and warned that United States citizens who fought against the Canadian government and were captured would be left to their fate. Existing laws, he said, would be enforced.[6]

The enforcement of such laws was another matter. On November 30, 1837, the actual strength of the military forces of the United States was less than 10,000, perhaps not much over 5,000 men, and most of these were in the South and West fighting the Indians. Shortly after the burning of the *Caroline,* the President sent General Winfield Scott to the frontier. He had only a paltry force at his command, but with incredible energy he moved back and forth along an 800-mile frontier, urging the citizenry to remember the duties of good republicans and to avoid hostile acts toward a friendly power. These exhortations had considerable effect in allaying the excitement.

The United States demanded reparations for the *Caroline*. These were refused by Great Britain and once again relations on the border

[6] Richardson, *Messages and Papers,* III, 1699–1700, 1702–1704.

became tense. Then, on November 12, 1840, one Alexander McLeod, a Canadian deputy sheriff, boasted in an American tavern that it had been he who had killed the American citizen on the *Caroline*. McLeod was promptly arrested and thrown into a Lewiston, New York, jail to stand trial for murder. Great Britain protested this seizure, but the United States government, quite properly, took the position that it could not interfere with the jurisdiction of the New York State courts. McLeod's trial was still pending as Van Buren's administration came to an end, and it was generally feared that his conviction would cause a marked deterioration in United States-British relations and might even lead to war.[7]

At the same time that these events were vexing the border from Michigan to Vermont, the United States became involved in a contention with the Canadians and Great Britain over the northeast boundary between the United States and Canada. The language in the Treaty of Paris defining the line of demarcation between Maine and Canada was decidedly ambiguous, and in consequence the boundary itself had been a matter of dispute since 1783. The treaty declared that the boundary, in part, was to run "along the Highlands which divide those rivers that empty themselves into the River St. Lawrence from those which fall into the Atlantic Ocean." This was obviously an attempt to give the land on the south side of the watershed to the United States, on the north side to Canada. A difference of opinion arose concerning the St. John River and the territory through which it runs, for the St. John empties into the Bay of Fundy. Was this bay to be regarded as, to all intents and purposes, the Atlantic Ocean? Britain said no. The United States said yes. Upon the final decision hinged the possession of some 12,000 square miles of land, some of it rich in ship timber. Both sides had maps and written documents supporting their point of view.

In 1826, Great Britain and the United States had agreed upon the King of the Netherlands as arbiter of this boundary dispute. Having

[7] Winfield Scott, *Memoirs of Lieutenant General Scott, LL.D.* (2 vols., New York, 1864), I, 301–317; II, 331–334; Orrin E. Tiffany, "Relations of the United States to the Canadian Rebellion of 1837–1838," Buffalo Historical Society, *Publications,* VIII (1905), 7–147; Wilson P. Shortridge, "The Canadian-American Frontier during the Rebellion of 1837–1838," *Canadian Historical Review,* VII (1926), 13–26; Alastair Watt, "The Case of Alexander McLeod," *Ibid.,* XII (1931), 145–167; Albert B. Corey, *The Crisis of 1830–1842 in Canadian-American Relations* (New Haven, 1941), pp. 1–45; Hugh Ll. Keenleyside and Gerald S. Brown, *Canada and the United States* (New York, 1952), pp. 80–92.

heard both sides, *ad nauseam,* he declared the treaty of 1783 "inexplicable and impracticable," and fixed an arbitrary boundary line which gave 7,908 square miles to the United States and 4,119 square miles to Canada. Great Britain signified its acceptance of this award. The State of Maine protested the decision and the United States Senate refused it, a refusal that later cost the United States 900 square miles of territory.

During the period from 1828 to 1838, popular feeling in Maine on the one hand and Nova Scotia and New Brunswick on the other rose to a higher and higher pitch. Overt acts were committed by both sides. Britain withdrew her acceptance of the Dutch award in 1838, and Canadians entered the disputed territory and began cutting timber in the valley of the Aroostook River. Maine thereupon became belligerent. The Maine legislature voted $800,000 for defense, and Governor Fairfield called out the state militia, took forcible possession of most of the land in dispute, and set up forts therein. The "Aroostook War" was on.

These proceedings had reverberations in Congress, which authorized Van Buren to call out 50,000 volunteers and voted $10 million for defense. Meantime, antipathy for the United States became rampant in Nova Scotia and New Brunswick, and they also hurried military preparations.

Scott, America's ace trouble shooter at the time, was now sent by Van Buren to Maine. There, with some difficulty, he persuaded Governor Fairfield to withdraw his troops from the Aroostook region. New Brunswick also agreed not to take military possession of this no man's land. Tempers cooled, and diplomatic negotiations were resumed. But no settlement had been reached by the end of Van Buren's term of office.

The President's attitude during these trying events was, on the whole, admirable. He told Scott that his objective was "peace with honor," and this was borne out by his conduct. The Maine boundary dispute provided occasion for floods of oratory in Congress, with each side trying to make political capital out of the situation, but the cool firmness of the administration kept the situation there from getting out of hand. Van Buren's neutrality was unpopular on the border, however, and undoubtedly contributed to Seward's election as governor of New York State in 1838.[8]

[8] Corey, *Crisis,* pp. 50, 64, 114–115, 159–162; Keenleyside and Brown, *Canada,* pp. 138–152.

While the Van Buren administration struggled to make its views prevail in domestic and foreign matters, the campaign of 1840 began to assume a larger and larger place in the thoughts of politicians. There was little doubt of Van Buren's renomination. His rejection as the party's standard bearer would have been tantamount to a repudiation of Jacksonism and to a confession of defeat. But the choice of his Whig opponent was by no means such a foregone conclusion.

Clay's ambition burned as brightly as ever, and his inveterate optimism fed the flame. It was evident, he wrote, as early as August, 1837, to Whig journalist George D. Prentice, "that I shall be again forced into the Presidential arena." He had heard, and he believed, that he was the favorite candidate in New York City, in New England, in western New York, in Louisiana, and in Ohio. James Watson Webb had told him that the North certainly would not go for General Harrison. Clay's friends, so thought the master of Ashland, needed only to point to his record in order to ensure his nomination. It was rumored in Washington that Clay had visited the White House to determine whether it "would be likely to be in a tenantable condition about three years hence."[9]

There was good reason for Prince Hal's optimism. His personal popularity among the northern Whigs was of long standing. He had carefully sought favor in the South (among Democrats perhaps as much as among Whigs) by indicating his acceptance of the tariff as it was, his belief that internal improvements were no longer a great national issue, and his willingness not to press too hard for a national bank. In consequence of this temporizing, the southern Whigs had come to regard him as an acceptable candidate for 1840. James K. Polk, a shrewd observer, wrote to Jackson from Washington in January, 1838, that all parties there believed Clay would be the next Whig candidate for the Presidency.[10] That same year he was endorsed by the legislatures of Kentucky, Rhode Island, and Maryland, and by many local meetings throughout the country.

But these political omens were not as auspicious as they appeared to be. It was true that the southern Whigs were for him as the party's candidate, but there were not many of them who believed that he could carry the South and their pessimism in this regard was shared

[9] Thomas J. Clay Papers, Henry Clay to G. D. Prentice, Aug. 14, 1837; *Congressional Globe,* 25th Cong., second sess., 54.

[10] Jackson Papers (second series), Polk to Jackson, Jan. 7, 1838.

by northern Whigs. Webster, who had ambitions of his own, was cool to Clay's candidacy, and Webster had influence in New England. Harrison early showed great strength in the West, and in Pennsylvania as well. And in the critical state of New York the Whig boss, Thurlow Weed, looked the situation over with a cold, calculating eye and came to the conclusion that the Kentuckian would not do.

As Weed saw the situation, Clay lacked availability. Antimasons were cool to the Kentucky Hotspur. The abolitionists, a growing coterie in New York State, disliked him as a slaveholder who had denounced them in Congress. The Democrats were continually pillorying Clay as a bank man, and Weed knew the effectiveness of this argument from his own utilization of the state bank issue against the Democrats in the state campaign of 1838. What was needed, Weed felt, was a military hero. His thoughts turned to Harrison and, more particularly, to Winfield Scott.

The hero of Lundy's Lane had recently gained fresh popularity in New York State and in New England by the tactful way in which he had handled the situation on the Canadian frontier. He was a native of Virginia, and therefore blessed with a southern background. He had had no connection with any of the issues on which the Whigs had lost the last two national elections. Weed's preference was for Scott.[11]

Evidence began to multiply that New York was not right for Clay, and in the late summer of 1839 the Kentuckian made a pilgrimage in that direction, ostensibly for a vacation. His route lay from Buffalo through central New York, then to Montreal and Quebec, then down to Saratoga Springs, and finally to New York City.

Clay's trip was something in the nature of a royal progress and it raised hopes already buoyant. New York's Whig leadership, however, remained cool. Clay saw Seward in northern New York and Weed at Saratoga. Both attempted to persuade him to withdraw, but without success. While at the famous watering place, news came that Tennessee was giving him only equivocal support, and thereafter he appeared to one observer to be somewhat "discountenanced and chopfallen."[12] But his determination to be a candidate remained adamant.

The Whig convention at Harrisburg met on December 4, 1839. Clay

[11] Rives Papers, Thos. Allen to Rives, Sept. 23, 1839; Glyndon G. Van Deusen, *The Life of Henry Clay* (Boston, 1937), pp. 320–327, and *Thurlow Weed: Wizard of the Lobby* (Boston, 1947), pp. 110–111.

[12] Rives Papers, Hugh S. Legaré to Rives, Aug. 16, 1839.

had a plurality of the delegates, but much of his strength came from states that the Whigs could not carry. The supporters of the two generals were active and astute. The convention adopted a complicated system of balloting by states that neutralized Clay's plurality, and it early became apparent that the hopes of Harry of the West were doomed.

But was it to be Scott or Harrison? The former was the candidate of Weed and Seward and had better than half of the New York delegation. The New York Conservatives were for him and he had considerable support among northern congressmen. Both of these facts were useful at the convention. On the other hand, Harrison had the prestige of his strong showing in 1836. Webster was for him, as were the Antimasons, and he had not aroused the deep hostility of the abolitionists. He was also strong in the West and in Pennsylvania. Arguments based on these grounds proved decisive. The Scott delegates swung to "Old Tip" and on December 6, 1839, he received the nomination.

Harrison being a northern candidate, it was necessary to balance the ticket. What was needed was a man who could command southern votes, especially of the states' rights variety, and rally the Clay supporters who were chewing the cud of bitterness. Such a man was John Tyler of Virginia.

Tyler was a states' rights, strict constructionist. He was very popular with those southern Whigs who still looked askance at the aims and ambitions of their northern brethren. He had worked for Clay's nomination and reportedly had cried when the Kentuckian had gone down to defeat. He seemed an admirable choice, and the convention rallied to him with unanimity.

"We took Harrison," Hugh Legaré later wrote of the South's attitude, "because Tyler was his endorser—and it was known we would take him on no other condition." This assertion reflects admirably the state of mind in which the southern Whigs entered the campaign. It is noteworthy that four southern states (South Carolina, Georgia, Tennessee, and Arkansas) sent no delegates to the convention and that of Louisiana's eleven delegates, only one appeared. The rest of them felt that it was more important to tend to their cotton and sugar crops. But this southern Whig apathy tended to disappear as the campaign gave increasing promise of success.[13]

[13] Rives Papers, Thos. Allen to Rives, Sept. 23, Oct. 12, 1839, Hugh S.

Since the Whigs represented a combination of views on national issues, and since it was hoped to gather in a considerable number of votes from without the party fold, it was thought best to adjourn without drafting a platform.

The Democrats professed joy over Clay's rejection, and declared that the nomination of "Granny" Harrison, that "old Lady" (he was sixty-seven), was a hopeful sign for them. A friend of Clay was represented in a Democratic paper as having said that if Harrison was given a pension of $2,000 a year, a barrel of hard cider, and a log cabin to live in, he would never bother anyone about the Presidency. The Whigs took up this remark, and the log cabin and the cider barrel at once began to figure in the campaign.

Four months after the Whig convention had met, a group of New York state abolitionists issued a call for a political convention. They proposed to form a new party. William Lloyd Garrison, Theodore Dwight Weld, and other prominent abolitionists opposed this move. It was alleged that it would mean abandoning the high religious and moral ground taken by the opponents of slavery; that even abolitionists, when the chips were down, would cling to their old party allegiances; that Whig abolitionists, particularly, would vote for Harrison on account of their hatred of Van Buren. The counterargument was that under the old party system no progress had been made toward abolition; that, on the contrary, fundamental rights such as petition and free speech had been repeatedly invaded without redress. Advocates of a new party pointed to the murder of Elijah Lovejoy at Alton, Illinois, in 1837, and to countless other unpunished outrages against abolitionists as evidence of the failure of the old parties to safeguard human freedom. They declared that the only way to control the slave power, to keep it from dominating the government, was to form a northern party dedicated to the great principle of freedom. They also blamed slavery for the depression, at the same time pointing out the need for political action as a means of lessening the slavery South's injurious control over national financial policies.

On April 1, 1840, antislavery delegates from six states met at Albany, New York. They nominated for President James G. Birney, a Kentuckian who had been converted from slaveholder to abolitionist

---

Legaré to Rives, Sept. 2, 1841; Springfield *Republican,* Dec. 7, 1839; *Niles' Register,* Dec. 14, 1839; Oliver P. Chitwood, *John Tyler* (New York, 1939), pp. 167–173.

by Theodore Dwight Weld. Thomas Earle of Pennsylvania was Birney's running mate. The meeting adjourned without a platform, without even giving the party a name, but Gerrit Smith called it the Liberty party and so it was to be called throughout the nation.[14]

The Democrats met in national convention at Baltimore, May 5, 1840. Van Buren was unanimously renominated, but there was considerable difference of opinion as to the Vice-Presidency. Formidable opposition had developed to the renomination of Richard M. Johnson, and the convention was unable to agree on Jackson's choice, the recently elected governor of Tennessee, James K. Polk. The nomination of a Vice-President was finally left to the states.

The Democrats, unlike the Whigs and the Liberty party, adopted a platform. It emphasized the limited powers of the national government; it pronounced against internal improvements at national expense and the assumption of state debts; it asserted that a national bank and protection for manufacturers were in the black books of the Democracy. The platform declared that Congress had no power to interfere with slavery in the slave states, and that it should not interfere with slavery in any way whatever. It endorsed the Independent Treasury, and condemned restrictions on naturalization.

The Democratic convention adjourned on Wednesday, May 6, in a somewhat sober mood. "We have, after many embarrassments and difficulties," wrote John A. Dix to Flagg, "brought matters to a satisfactory conclusion." The convention, he added, "broke up in harmony and with the very best feeling." It had not, however, been a very happy gathering, and the delegates did not depart in a rosy glow of confidence over the prospects of the campaign.[15]

The weekend before the sober Democrats gathered at Baltimore, thousands of Whig young men had come to that city to ratify the Harrisburg proceedings. On Monday, May 4, they had held a monster parade, with bands, banners, transparencies, cider barrels, and log

[14] Dwight L. Dumond, *Antislavery Origins of the Civil War in the United States* (Ann Arbor, 1939), pp. 87–93; Gilbert H. Barnes, *The Antislavery Impulse, 1830–1844* (New York, 1933), pp. 176, 177; Alice F. Tyler, *Freedom's Ferment* (Minneapolis, 1944), pp. 498–499, 501–508; Theodore C. Smith, *The Liberty and Free Soil Parties in the Northwest* (New York, 1897), pp. 27, 37–39; Julian P. Bretz, "The Economic Background of the Liberty Party," *American Historical Review,* XXXIV (Jan., 1929), 250–264.

[15] Jackson Papers (second series), Jackson to Kendall, Apr. 16, 1840; Flagg Papers, Dix to Flagg, May 6, 1840; *Niles' Register,* May 9, 1840.

cabins. Liquor flowed freely; joy abounded. Clay and Webster spoke to the cheering throng, and even though a raging northwest wind carried away their words, they were acclaimed with frenzy. As one delegate to the Democratic convention later remarked, it was obviously going to be hard money against hard cider.

The campaign was not quite as simple as that. The Democratic campaign was a combination of abuse and solid argument. Harrison was labeled an illiterate, a defaulter, a man who had sold white men into slavery for debt. Postmaster General Amos Kendall used local postmasters and census takers to distribute Democratic literature. But the Democrats also tried to inject a serious note into the campaign. They talked a good deal about the Independent Treasury. They denounced the assumption of state debts and tried, none too successfully, to make out that this was a cardinal Whig policy. They extolled Van Buren's establishment, March 31, 1840, of a ten-hour day for federal employees.

The Whigs, in their turn, were not entirely devoid of solid argument. Greeley in the *Log Cabin* argued for protection, a sound and uniform currency, distribution, and a restriction of Executive influence in the government, the while he denounced the ten-hour day as an electioneering trick. The New England Whigs took a strong stand for freedom of speech and press. Webster pleaded repeatedly for a national government that would take an active part in establishing a national currency and sound credit facilities for a growing country. Harrison announced that he was for a strong union, for a protective tariff and internal improvements, for a national bank if the public interest demanded it, for military training, a limited Chief Executive, and honest republican government.[16] But the great emphasis of the Whigs was not on issues or principles of government. They went for the spectacular.

Just as the Democrats had created a Jackson myth, so the Whigs undertook to create a Harrison myth during the campaign. They glorified Old Tip as being a man of sound health, strong constitution, and magnificent principles. He was an honest, God-fearing farmer, the latchstring of whose log cabin (he really lived in a commodious farmhouse) was always out for the ever-welcome visitor. March 4, said the Springfield *Republican*, was to be a great day in the annals of the

[16] Dorothy B. Goebel and Julius Goebel, Jr., *Generals in the White House* (New York, 1945), pp. 112–114; Dorothy B. Goebel, *William Henry Harrison, a Political Biography* (Indianapolis, 1926), pp. 361–364.

Republic. "Then will the farmer of North Bend strike his plough into the soil of corruption at Washington, and turn it to the light of the sun."

Van Buren was scarcely a paragon of virtue in Whig eyes. They never tired of heaping scorn and derision upon him. He was "Matty," or "Martin Van Ruin," or "Sweet Sandy Whiskers." He was declared to cherish a policy of "fifty cents a day and French soup," in contradistinction to the Whig policy of "two dollars a day and roast beef." Thus the Whigs appealed to the labor vote.

Another Whig method of attack on "Sweet Sandy Whiskers," one calculated to appeal to all classes, was to picture him as being grossly extravagant with public money. Wild charges along this line, made by the Democrats against Adams in 1828, were now returned with dividends. Under Van Buren, declared the Springfield *Republican,* the national government paid a gardener a salary of $1,000. This was as much as the governor of Ohio received! When Van Buren had come to New York City in 1839, it was said, the champagne had flowed like water. "How the long necks had popped!" The hotel bill for six days of this Republican simplicity had been $675, and the total cost of the visit $5,000! Congressman Charles Ogle of Pennsylvania, a Jacksonian turned Whig, delivered an oration on "The Royal Splendor of the President's Palace" in which, with the aid of a bill of particulars ludicrous in its exaggeration, Van Buren was pictured as lolling in silken splendor. Another Whig congressman, Levi Lincoln of Massachusetts, exposed this speech for the buncombe that it was, but it was widely reprinted, and Whig orators echoed its charges throughout the country.

Along with tales of Harrison's simplicity and Van Buren's extravagance, the Whigs made heavy use of other propaganda instruments. They brought out fake Indians, to remind people of Harrison's record in the War of 1812. Whig orators boasted of humble log-cabin origins, to bring home the fact that Whiggery was of the common people. Whig stalwarts marched thousands of miles in parades replete with bands, flags, and transparencies. The voice of the cannon was constantly heard in the land. Huge victory balls were rolled miles along the highways by perspiring bands of stalwarts. Log cabins multiplied. Cider barrels were everywhere, with sweet cider for the temperance man and hard cider for the rest. According to one report, Old Cabin Whisky was distributed in bottles shaped like a cabin by the E. C. Booz

Company of Philadelphia, thus originating the word "booze." And always there were the Whig songs.

From the White House, now Matty,
turn out, turn out,
From the White House, now Matty,
turn out.

This was the "Turn Out Song." Another owed at least part of its inspiration to Scotland's favorite poet.

We can na' longer go ye, Martie
Where are ye gangin' now, wee Martie?
Ye've got sae fitty an' sae starty,
Scarce ken we o' Auld Jackson's party
Which way ye sped;
Tho' once ye promis'd strang an' hearty,
His steps to tread.

Ye've missed ye're predecessor's track,
An' make sa mony a crooked tack,
We're fearfu' ye are slidin' back,
To thrones and kings;
In Ogle's tale we see nae lack
O' ye'r fine things.

The Whig campaign of 1840 indicated the party's realization that it could not afford to let the Democrats monopolize the credit for being the friends of the people. It was a bold attempt to array the major part of the wealth and social standing of the country in the panoplies of democracy as the ordinary man understood the meaning of that term. That it was effective became apparent early in the campaign. "We have taught them to conquer us!" said the *Democratic Review* in June of 1840. It was, said the *Review,* "the out-Heroding of Herod," a steal that was "nothing short of High Treason."[17]

The Whigs emerged from the campaign of 1840 with a clear-cut victory. Harrison carried nineteen of the twenty-six states, including

[17] Flagg Papers, J. K. Kane to Flagg (May 7, 1840), S. R. Hobbie to Flagg, Aug. 27, 1840; Daniel Webster, *Writings and Speeches* (18 vols., Boston, 1903), III, 41–52, 55–79; Springfield *Republican,* Dec. 21, 1839, June 2, July 20, Oct. 17, 1840; Nathan Sargent, *Public Men and Events* (2 vols., Philadelphia, 1875), II, 105–111; *Democratic Review,* VII (June, 1840), 486; VIII (Sept., 1840), 198; *Congressional Globe,* 26th Cong., first sess., Appendix, pp. 701–703.

every northern state except New Hampshire and Illinois. They had majorities in both House and Senate. While their plurality was only 146,843 in a total of 2,408,630 votes cast, they had 53 per cent of the two-party vote, almost a landslide for those days. They had even shown very considerable strength in the South, where they had carried no less than seven states.

Party moods varied with the result of the campaign. Elation ruled among the Whigs. "The honest old Farmer of Ohio," said the Springfield *Republican,* "takes the reins of government into his own pure hands. The voice of the People wills it. . . . The charms of despotic power are broken. . . . Let the People—the whole People—rejoice." The Charleston, South Carolina, *Courier,* which had held aloof from the contest, struck a more sober note—"God grant that it may be for the welfare of our beloved country." Jackson, at the Hermitage, laid the Whig victory to corruption and to the interference of England in the election. Britain had sought a President who would "unite with her in her corrupt views, put down our republican system, and build upon its ruins a great, consolidated government to be ruled by the corrupt money power of england [*sic*] and america [*sic*]." The *Democratic Review* accused the Whigs of having taken advantage of human suffering, of turning price and credit collapse into political advantage. This was not surprising, said the *Review* bitterly. The "bastard Federalists" would stoop to take any advantage, however low.[18]

While one of the major parties rejoiced and the other lamented, the third party that had been in the field ruefully surveyed its situation. The Liberty party's campaign, in terms of ballots, had been a dismal failure. It had polled a total of only 6,225 votes. It had failed to capture a single county in the whole nation. Even in New York, its center of greatest strength, it had mustered less than 3,000 supporters. This scarcely looked like the beginning of a political revolution.

In its larger significance, the election of 1840 demonstrated once more that there were two fairly well-balanced parties contending for political control. It found Calhoun and his followers back in the ranks of the Democracy, and the erstwhile Democratic Conservatives gravitating into the Whig fold. It demonstrated a tendency (that has become traditional) for the American electorate to blame hard times upon

[18] Springfield *Republican,* Nov. 14, 1840; Charleston (S.C.) *Courier,* Nov. 11, 1840; Jackson Papers (second series), Jackson to Amos Kendall, Jan. 2, 1841; *Democratic Review,* VIII (Nov.–Dec., 1840), 387 ff.

the party in power. It also indicated that the Jacksonian Democracy's crusade against oppression by powerful wealthy interests was in process of devitalization. This was so because of the depression itself, with its debilitating effect upon the party in power, and also because the party had lacked a constructive economic program with which to meet the challenge of an America whose dynamic was only briefly smothered by hard times. From this point on, the Democracy began searching for other issues, and the proponents of slavery began assuming a larger and larger place in its councils. And indeed, from this point on, human bondage began to plague both parties, Whig as well as Democratic. Both parties claimed to be national; both had a national organization. Slavery was sectional; the opposition to it was sectional. That opposition was now beginning political organization, and this effort was to continue until it destroyed one of the old parties and wrought drastic changes in the other. Even worse was in store. The shadow of the Liberty party was now scarcely larger than a man's hand, but it was the shadow of civil war.

CHAPTER 8

The Advent of "His Accidency"

THE Whigs were now in a position to demonstrate their capacity for leadership, and to translate the economic theory of the American system into specific legislative measures. It remained to be seen whether they were capable of the concerted action necessary to these ends. The most immediate problem was to determine the real head of the new administration.

Would Harrison be President in fact, or would someone lead the nation's new leader? There was a Kentuckian who had decided aspirations in the latter direction. Harrison visited Kentucky shortly after the election of 1840. Fearful of being thought Clay's pawn, he made it clear that he desired to avoid even meeting the Millboy of the Slashes. This attitude on the part of the President-elect was blandly ignored by Clay. He saw to it that Harrison was publicly invited to Lexington, an invitation that for obvious reasons could not be declined. There Clay was master of ceremonies. There was much feting of Old Tip, with plenty of conversation on the side. While Harrison was still in Lexington, Clay left for the lame duck session of the Twenty-sixth Congress, obviously satisfied with the new White House occupant.

The short session of the Congress in the winter of 1840–41 was chiefly notable for the arrogance of Clay's leadership. He made it his business to taunt the fallen foe with their defeat, and he and his henchmen turned the knife in the wound by forcing the dismissal of Blair and Rives as printers to the Senate. So far as constructive legislation was concerned, the session was barren of result.

Not so barren were the efforts of the leaders, especially Clay and Webster, to influence the selection of the Cabinet. Here Webster carried off the honors, being himself chosen to head the State Department and having an important influence on the choice of the other members of the President's official family. Clay was not, however, without friends in the inner circle. John J. Crittenden, the Attorney General, was Clay's long-time associate and supporter, and both Ewing of Ohio in the Treasury and Bell of Tennessee in the War Department were well disposed toward the Kentuckian.

It was not alone in the Cabinet that Clay had influence. Everyone looked to him to lead the Whig forces in the Senate. Not a few, including Clay himself, believed that his, rather than Harrison's, would be the guiding hand.

Old Tip's inaugural, delivered on March 4, 1841, deplored the tendency that had been lately exhibited to concentrate the power of the federal government in the executive branch. He believed in only limited use of the veto, and in a clear separation of powers. There was unconscious irony in his statement that he was a one-term President; that he would never consent to serve a second term.

As became a good Whig, Harrison criticized the Independent Treasury. He also frowned upon the spoils system, which was already producing a deluge of office seekers wearing down his health and strength. He scolded the abolitionists for weakening the bonds of the Union, and closed with a plea for the mitigation of party bitterness and an expression of his reverence for the Christian religion. It was the message of one who looked back fondly to the days of ancient Roman virtue (it was full of classical allusions), of one whose primary interest was in a calm and peaceful Presidency. It was the message of a warrior crying peace when there was no peace. His month's reign was a continuous series of contentions and frustrations.

Clay urged, vehemently, a special session of Congress. To this the President reluctantly consented. But despite strenuous efforts, Clay was unable to prevent the followers of Webster from taking over the rich plum of the New York port collectorship, together with practically all the other important appointments in that city. In the course of the struggle over these spoils, the President accused Clay of attempting dictation, there was a stormy scene at the White House, and the President later informed the senator that he wished communication between them to be restricted to the written word.[1] More and more Old Tip came to resent the imperious manner of the masterful Kentuckian.

Clay's overbearing manner was not the only problem confronting the new President. Harrison was literally overwhelmed by office seekers, to say nothing of being flooded by the tearful entreaties of those who were turned out of office to make room for deserving Whigs. He also faced the rising discontent of the Conservatives, who felt that they were being cold-shouldered by the Whigs in the matter of appointments. Harrison naïvely added fuel to this flame by telling Rives that the latter had been his choice for Secretary of State; that the Whigs had overruled him in his intended action; and that he, Harrison, did not share the Whig jealousy of these erstwhile Democrats. The Whig-Conservative alliance seemed to be trembling in the balance. "I feel sometimes," wrote Thomas Allen of the *Madisonian* to Rives, ". . . as though we were on a volcanoe."[2]

How the aging and infirm Chief Executive would have handled all these problems must remain a matter of conjecture. The never-ending quarrels among the Whigs and their allies, the constant importunities of the hordes of office seekers and office losers, sapped the veteran's strength. It may well be that he caught the cold which resulted in his death when, with his vitality at a low point, he went out, as was his wont, bareheaded and without an overcoat, to the Washington meat and fish markets in search of White House provender. On April 1, 1841, the news spread that the President was ill. It soon developed that he had pneumonia. In his last hours, as he lay sick and weak, he was heard to mutter, "Sir, I wish you to understand the true principles of government. I ask nothing more." Then, at half-past twelve on the morning of April 4, he died. Two days later John Tyler, the "friend" of Henry Clay, summoned in haste from Williamsburg, took the oath of office as tenth President of the United States.

John Tyler was fifty-one years old when he was summoned to the highest office in the land. No other man had become President at so early an age. Suave and genial in manner, he had a deserved reputation for honesty and conscientiousness. Very popular in Virginia, he

[1] Nathan Sargent, *Public Men and Events* (2 vols., Philadelphia, 1875), II, 115–116.

[2] Rives Papers, Rives to Mrs. Rives, Feb. 15, 1841, William B. Lewis to Rives, Mar. 26, 30, 1841, Thomas Allen to Rives, Dec. 21, 1840, Mar. 21, 1841.

had held almost every office which the Old Dominion could bestow, and this popularity had extended beyond the confines of his native state. Under great stress, as the events of the succeeding months were to show, he could be tortured by indecision, and it was a commonplace among his erstwhile Democratic comrades that he lacked firmness of character. But if his career had proved anything, it had shown that he had great regard for consistency and great devotion to the doctrine of states' rights. It was this states' rights Democrat, turned Whig because of Andrew Jackson, who had now been thrust by fate into the highest office in the land.

Since Harrison was the first President to die in office, a question arose over Tyler's exact status as his successor. Was the Virginian indeed President, or was he simply the Vice-President assuming the duties and responsibilities of the President's office? Tyler insisted that he had become President in every sense of the word. This was not effectively challenged, and thus a precedent was established which has endured down to the present day.

But even though all agreed that Tyler was now President, there still remained the question of who should be the real leader of the government and of the Whig party. The Whigs had had much to say, during the past eight years, about the overweening power of the Executive in the national government. If they now tamely submitted to the leadership of a man who had never assumed to voice the sentiments of more than a minor faction in the party, and who, moreover, had been put on the ticket because of practical politics, rather than with any thought to the succession, would they not be stultifying one of their great principles? Was not this the time, if ever there was to be a time, when the congressional leadership of the party ought to be asserted? Not a few of the Whigs thought so, and none thought so more vehemently than did Henry Clay.

The statesman from Ashland regarded himself, and the majority of Whigs regarded him, as the real head of the Whig party. Despite the fact that he had long been on good terms with Tyler, his views on government policy had differed widely from those of this strict constructionist Virginian, and Clay was determined that his own opinions should prevail. There was an additional consideration. Harrison, in his inaugural, had pledged himself not to seek a second term. Tyler's brief inaugural contained no such pledge. It was only natural that Clay, whose eyes were closely fixed on 1844, should wish to prevent the emergence of a lion in his path.

When Congress met in extra session, May 31, 1841, Clay's leadership became immediately and sometimes painfully apparent. He differed violently and volubly with states' rights Whigs on tariff and bank policy; but even while he rode roughshod over the states' rights element of his party, he was made chairman of the Committee on Finance in the Senate, and charge of the Committee on Public Lands was given to one of his trusted followers. His friends also dominated the most important committees in the House, and the Speaker of that body, John White of Kentucky, was a Clay man.

Clay's tendency to be imperious, to hold his party to his will with a rough and almost brutal rein, was never more marked than in the Twenty-seventh Congress. Perhaps it was the gnawing sense of opportunity missed, of the fact that had his party willed it he would now be in the White House, which spurred him on to carry things with a high hand. Be that as it may, Whigs who opposed the master's plans were assailed with jibe and sneer, to say nothing of even rougher handling in the frequent Whig caucuses. But the Kentuckian clearly sought to restrain himself when directing his remarks to the Democratic side of the Senate, for he knew that he would have to have considerable support from that party to secure passage of the bills that he was determined to present to the President.[3]

Within a week after the opening of Congress, Clay outlined his program. The Independent Treasury Act, he declared, should be repealed and a national bank should be re-established. The tariff should be adjusted to provide more revenue, and provision should be made for distributing the proceeds of the sales of public lands.[4] This looked like a revitalization of the American system, and the states' rights Whigs, especially the little coterie from Virginia, became more and more uneasy.

During June, 1841, Clay pushed through the Senate the repeal of the Independent Treasury. He then turned his attention to a plan for a "Fiscal Bank" which had been sent down from the Treasury Department by Secretary Ewing.

[3] Rives Papers, Rives to Mrs. Rives, June 20, 1841; Van Buren Papers, Wright to Van Buren, June 21, 1841; Glyndon G. Van Deusen, *The Life of Henry Clay* (Boston, 1937), p. 345.

[4] *Congressional Globe,* 27th Congress, first session, 22.

The Treasury plan provided for the incorporation of the new bank in the District of Columbia. It would be a bank of discount and deposit and, where the states consented, it could establish branches. Its provision for discount and deposit was obnoxious to Tyler, but the evidence indicates that he would nevertheless have signed the Treasury bill, had it been promptly passed and presented to him.[5]

But Clay was determined not to have the Treasury bill. He denounced Ewing's plan as ineffectual and dangerous, and committed all of his splendid oratorical powers to supporting the passage of his own bank bill, which provided for a bank with unlimited branching power. This, rather than the Ewing bill, became the center of congressional action.

June and July, 1841, brought much argument and negotiation in their train. Rives, with the White House blessing, attempted, in effect, to substitute Ewing's bill for Clay's by an amendment to Clay's bill which made the establishment of branches of the bank conditional on the assent of the states concerned. Webster supported this move. Clay raged and stormed, but finally assented to a modification of his bill giving the states an opportunity to prevent the establishment of branches of the bank within their borders by having the state legislatures pass prohibitory acts at their first sessions after the bank bill had passed Congress. Even in such a case, Clay's bill still provided that if Congress deemed it necessary, it could establish a branch of the bank within the borders of a recalcitrant state. This was as far as he would go, and on this point the Tyler Whigs deserted him. But he was able to obtain consent to the amendment embodying this stand by a vote in the Senate of 25 to 24. The following day, July 28, 1841, Clay's amended bill passed the Senate by a margin of three votes. The House passed it nine days later, 128 to 98.[6] Now it was Tyler's to accept or reject.

While Clay was marshaling his bank bill through Congress, Tyler had become a prey to conflicting emotions. He wanted peace and harmony in his administration, but he had the same hearty dislike as

[5] *Congressional Globe,* 27th Cong., first sess., 48–49; Tyler Papers, Tyler to Tazewell, Oct. 11, 1841; Lyon G. Tyler, *The Letters and Times of the Tylers* (3 vols., Richmond, 1884–96), II, 53–54; George R. Poage, *Henry Clay and the Whig Party* (Chapel Hill, 1936), p. 46.

[6] *Congressional Globe,* 27th Cong., first sess., 256, 260, Appendix, pp. 351–354; Rives Papers, Rives to Mrs. Rives, June 27, July 4, 1841; Ewing Papers, Webster to ——— (July 15, 1841).

Harrison for the Kentuckian's domineering ways. He also felt insecure, being isolated from the leadership at the other end of Pennsylvania Avenue. Indeed, Rives at one time was the only member of Congress with whom he was in confidential communication.[7]

The President had no enthusiasm whatever for Clay's bill, and told Rives as early as June 1 that the Congressional Whigs would have to accept state consent for branching or face a veto.[8] There can also be little doubt that Tyler's ambition to be the real rather than the titular head of the Whig party was a growing thing which influenced his attitude in the dispute over the bank. The bank bill which Congress had sent up to him was indubitably Clay's bill. If, despite his known objections, he signed it, his own claim to party leadership would be seriously impaired, and his chances for the Whig nomination in 1844 correspondingly dimmed.

There was much speculation as to what Tyler would do. Wright had believed, in June, that Tyler would sign the bill Clay put before him, even if it contained no restriction on branching power. Calhoun, on the other hand, was convinced that Tyler would veto the bill as passed, and that division and discord would reign in the Whig ranks.

The Cabinet urged the President to sign the bill. Threats swirled in the air. Clay declared at a dinner party which Rives attended that if the bill was vetoed, he would live a hundred years and devote them all to the extermination of Tyler and his friends. But Tyler's Virginia friends exhorted him to stand firm and veto.

It is small wonder that Tyler was tortured by doubts and indecision, but at length he made up his mind. On August 16 he sent the bill back to the Senate, disapproved.[9]

The veto opened a breach between the President and the congressional Whigs, but it was not yet evident that this breach was past all healing. Tyler told Rives that he was still in favor of a fiscal agency. It should be, he felt, established in the District of Columbia, where Congress indubitably had power to establish a bank. It should be enabled to branch, with the consent of the states, but it should not have the

[7] Rives Papers, Rives to Mrs. Rives, June 17, 1841.

[8] *Ibid.*, Rives to Mrs. Rives, June 1, 20, 1841.

[9] J. Franklin Jameson (ed.), "Correspondence of John C. Calhoun," American Historical Association, *Annual Report,* 1899 (Washington, 1900), II, 484, Calhoun to Hammond, Aug. 1, 1841; Van Buren Papers, Wright to Van Buren, June 21, 1841, Woodbury to Van Buren, Aug. 7, 1841; Rives Papers, Rives to Mrs. Rives, July 25, Aug. 1, 22, 1841.

power of making local discounts. This would be a bank of more restricted powers than the one under the Ewing plan to which he had originally assented. A bill embodying these provisions was drawn up after numerous consultations between Tyler, his Cabinet, and certain members of the House.

What followed the concoction of this second bank bill is not altogether clear. It may be that Tyler's views on the measure had not been outlined as lucidly as he thought they had been. It is also possible that the Clay Whigs, determined to "head" the President, slipped into the measure last-minute changes that were designed to make it unacceptable at the White House. As the bill made its way through Congress, the President began to express doubts and dissatisfaction concerning it. He sought to postpone its passage, but this Clay refused. The Kentuckian appeared determined to force the issue.

Tyler may not have been as reluctant to see the bank bill pass as he professed to be. He was revolving plans for reorganizing his Cabinet and for the formation of a new party with himself at the head. The evidence indicates that Tyler was as determined to find fault with the bill as Clay was to force its passage.

The result was a foregone conclusion. The bill passed the House by what was largely a party vote, the Whigs supporting and the Democrats opposing it. The Senate passed it by an almost strictly party vote, Rives alone among the Whigs voting in the negative. Six days later, Tyler returned it to the House of Representatives with his veto.[10]

The second bank veto precipitated a Cabinet crisis that had long been brewing. Most of the Cabinet members were Clay partisans. They had failed in their efforts to construct a bank bill acceptable both to President and to Congress. They were conscious of the President's lack of confidence in them. Whig congressional leaders were exerting pressure upon them to resign. On September 11, 1841, all of the Cabinet, save Webster, sent in their letters of resignation.

Tyler received these resignations in a philosophical spirit. When he

10 Marcy Papers, Marcy to Wetmore, Aug. 22, 1841; McLean Papers, J. E. Miller to McLean, Aug. 25, 1841, Green to McLean, Aug. 26, 1841; Thomas H. Benton, *Thirty Years View* (2 vols., New York, 1854), II, 345–349; Rives Papers, Rives to Mrs. Rives, Aug. 27, 1841, Duff Green Papers, John McLean to Green, Sept. 6, 1841; T. Ewing, "Diary of Thomas Ewing," *American Historical Review,* XVIII (Oct., 1912), 99–105; James D. Richardson, *A Compilation of the Messages and Papers of the Presidents* (11 vols., New York, 1910), III, 1921–1925.

had sought advice in the summer of 1841, it had been from a small group of friends such as Rives, Henry A. Wise, and Duff Green, rather than from the members of his official family. As the weeks had passed, his suspicions of the Cabinet had deepened, and sometime between the first and second bank vetoes he had determined to turn them out, lock, stock, and barrel. He had called upon Rives, and probably upon other members of his inner council as well, for advice, and a new slate had been gradually drawn up. The resignations only anticipated action by the President.[11]

Webster alone of the Cabinet had not resigned. He had plans for negotiations with Great Britain that he did not wish to abandon, and the prospect of a delightful social season in Washington was always alluring to him. The Massachusetts delegation in Congress urged him to stay at his post. Tyler, the Massachusetts statesman felt certain, wanted him to stay on. He was with Tyler when Ewing's letter of resignation arrived. He knew its contents and, as an opportunity presented itself, he asked, "Where am I to go, Mr. President?"

The President had earlier decided that Webster should be thrust into outer darkness with the rest. Taking Rives' advice, he had offered the State Department to Louis McLane, but McLane had turned it down, and there was no other likely candidate at hand. Webster did not know it, but he was only second choice.

To the "Godlike's" query, Tyler replied, "You must decide that for yourself, Mr. Webster."

"If you leave it to me, Mr. President," said Webster, "I will stay where I am."

At this reply Tyler rose, hand outstretched, and said, "Give me your hand on that, and now I will say to you that Henry Clay is a doomed man from this hour."[12]

It was not Clay who was doomed at this juncture. The Whigs were to rally behind the standard of the Kentucky Hotspur with remarkable unanimity. But the new Cabinet did signalize Tyler's complete breach with his enemy. There was not a Clay Whig in the group, and the new

[11] Van Buren Papers, Woodbury to Van Buren, Aug. 7, 1841, ——— to (Van Buren), Aug. 22, 1841; Rives Papers, Rives to Mrs. Rives, Aug. 27, 1841.

[12] Rives Papers, Rives to Mrs. Rives, Aug. 27, 1841; Tyler, *Letters and Times,* II, 122 and note; Charles Francis Adams (ed.), *Memoirs of John Quincy Adams* (12 vols., Philadelphia, 1874–77), XI, 14; Claude M. Fuess, *Daniel Webster* (2 vols., Boston, 1930), II, 98–99; Oliver Chitwood, *John Tyler* (New York, 1939), p. 280.

Postmaster General, Charles A. Wickliffe of Kentucky, was Clay's mortal enemy.[13]

During the struggle over the bank bills, the remainder of Clay's legislative program had not been forgotten by the Whigs, least of all by their impetuous leader. Clay was determined to realize his long-cherished project for distribution of the proceeds from public land sales. He was the more set upon this proposal in 1841 because it would afford relief to the debt-burdened states, and would thus be an effective substitute for the politically vulnerable idea of assumption of state debts which had found considerable favor among the Whigs before the campaign of 1840. The master of Ashland could see that such distribution might well necessitate a raising of the tariff to provide for the government's expenses if the land sale proceeds were drained away by distribution, but as a long-term friend of protection such a prospect did not frighten him in the least. Distribution there must be.

Tyler liked the idea of distribution. He saw it as affording relief to the debt-burdened states. It would, he believed, relieve the citizens of what must otherwise be heavy state taxation, and would thus foster the return of prosperity.[14] For once it looked as though Tyler and Clay might be able to co-operate. There was only one obstacle to such harmony. The President was willing to distribute land sale proceeds only if such action did not bring a higher tariff in its train.

There was still another difficulty in the way of distribution. To Westerners, and to an increasing number of Easterners as well, the most attractive land policies were ease of occupation and cheapness of price. Without support from such elements of the voting population—especially without western votes—distribution could not pass. In order to ensure its passage, Clay had to accept what he had long opposed, namely, pre-emption.

With pre-emption tied to distribution, a considerable number of new state Whig votes could be counted on that would go against distribution alone. Hence there appeared the Pre-emption Act of 1841. This established permanent pre-emption. It gave bona fide settlers the right to "squat" on 160 acres of land and, when the land was opened to purchase, to buy it, free from competitive bids, at the minimum government price. This measure had been called into being by the growing

[13] *Ibid.*, pp. 280–281; Poage, *Clay*, pp. 16–17, 104.

[14] Richardson, *Messages and Papers*, III, 1900.

political power of the West. Benton called it the "Log Cabin" bill. It was a step toward the democratization of land holdings that Jackson, Van Buren, and Benton had long favored, and Clay had long opposed. It rallied votes for distribution, but Clay received little credit for it in the West.

But even the combination of pre-emption with distribution was not enough to ensure the passage of the distribution bill. It turned out that something had to be done for bankrupts as well.

A bankruptcy act had been passed in 1800, but it had been unsatisfactory and had lasted only three years. From time to time since then there had been discussion of the need for another bankruptcy law, and in 1827 there had been an unsuccessful attempt to enact such a measure. States' rights principles, to say nothing of relief laws passed by the states, had intervened, and nothing had been accomplished. But now the widespread loss of fortune, the many failures, and the burden of indebtedness which accompanied the depression of 1837 revived a demand for federal relief legislation.

Van Buren's proposal, in his message to the special session of Congress in 1837, of a bankruptcy law for banks had resulted in much argument but no legislation. The demand for relief of debtors increased. A bankruptcy law was reported out of the House Judiciary Committee in the spring of 1840, but it failed to pass. By 1841, however, the distress of an estimated 400,000 bankrupts had become a potent political force, and the pressure for a bankruptcy law, emanating from such states as New York, Massachusetts, Michigan, Mississippi, and Louisana, had intensified. If a bankruptcy bill should now be sponsored by the father of distribution, additional votes for the latter measure could almost certainly be obtained.

With Clay's emphatic approval and support, and with the backing of Webster, a bill was introduced in the Senate providing for both voluntary and compulsory bankruptcy. Only banking corporations were exempted from its provisions. It was a strictly Whig measure.

The bankruptcy bill passed the Senate July 25, 1841, by a party vote, but its sponsors could not command sufficient votes for its passage in the House. There it was tabled. Then came a masterly logrolling operation. Just as western votes had been gained for distribution by accepting pre-emption, so eastern votes were now gained for distribution by the promise of western votes for the bankruptcy measure.

One of the master strategists in this operation was the New York Whig boss, Thurlow Weed, who had come down to the nation's capital for a week of political maneuvering. He had access to the floors of both houses of Congress and, "as busy and mischievous as the devil," to quote William Learned Marcy, could be seen in confidential conversation with members, his long arms draped over their shoulders, or walking the streets locked arm in arm with Webster and Francis Granger of New York. Weed claimed credit for the passage of the bankruptcy bill, and Marcy was sure that he would have credit for the passage of the distribution bill as well.

But even with bankruptcy and pre-emption votes in his pocket, Clay had to make still another concession before he could assure the passage of his distribution bill. A number of southern Whigs in the Senate, Archer, Berrien, and Rives in particular, were determined to vote against distribution unless they had assurances about the tariff legislation that was in the offing. To appease them, Clay agreed to an amendment to the distribution bill. This amendment provided that distribution would be suspended if future tariff duties went above the final 20 per cent level provided by the Compromise Act of 1833. With this proviso, the distribution bill passed, and along with it the bankruptcy law.

The great log roll was over.[15] It had been a success in the sense that bills had been passed because of it. But the success had been purchased by an amendment that had taken the heart out of the distribution bill, an amendment accepted by Clay because he knew only too well that Tyler would use the veto unless distribution was coupled with a promise not to push the tariff above 20 per cent.

The difficulties experienced by Clay in securing the passage of the distribution bill served to emphasize the extraordinary situation in which the Whig party now found itself. Clay and his supporters were for open war with "His Accidency," as they now termed the President, and more and more the party inclined to this position despite all the dangers involved in such repudiation of its titular head. There were

[15] *Congressional Globe,* 27th Cong., first sess., 349–370, 388; Van Buren Papers, Wright to Van Buren, June 26, 1841; Flagg Papers, Marcy to Flagg, Aug. 23, 1841; Washington *Globe,* June 24, 1842; Raynor G. Wellington, *The Political and Sectional Influence of the Public Lands, 1828–1842* (Cambridge, 1914), pp. 96–103; Charles Warren, *Bankruptcy in United States History* (Cambridge, 1935), pp. 49–79.

some Whigs who wished to chart a middle course, but they were soon alarmed by Tyler's apparent interest in currying favor with the Democrats in the matter of appointments, and by rumors that he and his friends were planning a new party. By the beginning of 1842, Tyler's hold on the Whig party in Congress had, to all intents and purposes, disappeared. This was illustrated by the fate of his plan for a National Exchequer.

In his message to Congress, December 7, 1841, the President had outlined a plan for a "Board of Exchequer." This plan, developed by the Secretary of the Treasury, Walter Forward, reached the Senate on December 21. Under its provisions, the Board, consisting of the Secretary of the Treasury, the Treasurer of the United States, and three commissioners appointed by the President with the advice and consent of the Senate, would establish agencies throughout the country. These agencies would handle the public moneys. They would also accept deposits of specie up to $15 million and issue certificates against these deposits. The government would likewise issue Treasury notes up to a $15 million limit. The agencies of the Board would operate on a specie basis, and deal in bills of exchange.[16]

This "Fiscality" was at least a step in the direction of a sound currency and a system of swift and cheap exchange. Webster gave it his emphatic endorsement, declaring that a trial of three years would prove it to be of the greatest value. Greeley, visiting Washington in December, 1841, found a great deal of sentiment among congressional Whigs for something of this nature, sentiment that might easily have been marshaled behind the proposal had party harmony prevailed. But Clay, still savage for a national bank, would have none of it, and when it emerged from committee in a mutilated state it was promptly defeated.[17]

Clay resigned from the Senate in March, 1842. In a winning speech, he asked forgiveness for his arrogance, pleading in self-defense his

[16] Richardson, *Messages and Papers,* III, 1937–1938; *Congressional Globe,* 27th Cong., second sess., 34–39. The Board could set up two agencies in each state or territory. If state law prohibited, agencies were forbidden to receive deposits other than those of the United States, or make or sell drafts or purchase bills, other than those necessary for the collection, transfer, or disbursement of the public funds.

[17] Weed Papers, Greeley to Weed, Dec. 15, 1841; Daniel Webster, *Writings and Speeches* (18 vols., Boston, 1903), III, 134–137; Joseph Dorfman, *The Economic Mind in American Civilization* (3 vols., New York, 1946), II, 618.

anxiety for the nation's good. He looked old and careworn; but if the Whig party still had a leader, the Sage of Ashland was the man.

When Clay resigned from the Senate, the program that he had announced so proudly at the beginning of the Twenty-seventh Congress had been realized only in very small part. The Independent Treasury, it was true, had been repealed, but no national bank had been created, distribution had been limited by a crippling proviso, and there was still no new tariff bill. To this latter objective the congressional Whigs now turned, albeit in bitterness and uncertainty of spirit. Provision for additional revenue had become a pressing matter.

To the statesmen of the pre-Civil War period, a national government deficit was a fearsome thing, and ever since 1837 deficits had been of annual occurrence. These had been partially met by annual issues of Treasury notes, but of course these were only a form of government debt. That debt, extinguished in 1836, had risen by 1842 to the awesome total of $13,500,000, and gave every appearance of going higher still.[18] The need for additional government revenue was made even more painfully apparent by the precipitate drop in duties scheduled for 1842 under the Compromise Act of 1833.

The government's financial need was not the only argument advanced on behalf of tariff revision. The act of 1833 had been badly drafted, especially its provisions for the sudden reductions to the 20 per cent level, which were to be completed on or by July 1, 1842. There was even some doubt that under its provisions, so loosely worded were they, any duties at all could be collected after June 30 of that year.

Under these circumstances, a tariff bill was prepared by the Secretary of the Treasury, the effect of which was to restore the tariff to the general level of the tariff of 1832. This bill was introduced in the House by Millard Fillmore from the Committee on Ways and Means, but, as it was anticipated that there would be lengthy discussion of its provisions, a so-called "Little Tariff" was also introduced. This latter bill, which was designed to extend the operation of the existing tariff levels until August 1 and so prevent the July 1 reductions, was introduced by Fillmore on June 7, 1842.[19]

[18] Fred J. Guetter and Albert E. McKinley, *Statistical Tables Relating to the Economic Growth of the United States* (Philadelphia, 1924), pp. 13–14. The deficit, on July 1, 1843, was $32,742,992, a per capita debt of $1.75.

[19] *Congressional Globe,* 27th Cong., second sess., 591.

The Little Tariff was a congressional Whig measure, and it contained a provision which was full of dynamite. Clay's distribution bill, which had been enacted into law, included the proviso that distribution would not take place if the tariff stood above 20 per cent. The Little Tariff was framed to keep the duties at the June 1 level (that is to say, considerably above 20 per cent) until August 1, and it contained a statement that nothing in the act suspended distribution. This was plainly a move toward eliminating the barrier to distribution-plus-higher-protection which Clay had been forced to accept in the summer of 1841.

Discussion of the Little Tariff in Senate and House centered on this proviso. All attempts to eliminate it were beaten down, and the bill was passed by narrow majorities in both houses. Tyler thereupon vetoed it, on the ground that it did not suspend distribution.[20] The congressional Whig leadership was unable to pass the bill over his veto and for a short time duties, though sharply diminished after July 1, continued to be collected under the act of 1833. But protectionists noted, with considerable relief, that in his veto message Tyler not only accepted the necessity of raising the tariff above the 20 per cent level but also gave his assent to the principle of "incidental" protection.

Meanwhile the House had taken up the measure which was eventually to become the tariff of 1842. This was pushed through both branches of Congress by very narrow margins and sent off posthaste to the President, who as promptly vetoed it.

The reason for the President's veto (it was the fourth time he had used this weapon so abhorrent to the Whigs) was that the bill, like the Little Tariff, attempted to maintain distribution while raising the tariff substantially above the 20 per cent level. Tyler was vigorous in his objections. He spoke out the more strongly because it was patently an attempt to coerce him by grafting distribution upon a sorely needed revenue bill.[21]

The veto was referred to a select committee of the House, of which John Quincy Adams was chairman. Adams brought in a report harshly censuring the President. It called for a constitutional amendment giving Congress power to override vetoes by a simple rather than a two-thirds' majority, and suggesting the possibility of impeaching

[20] Richardson, *Messages and Papers,* III, 2033–2036.
[21] *Ibid.,* III, 2036–2042.

Tyler. The House adopted this report. The President protested its adoption. The House refused to accept his protest. But the veto stood. There was no possibility of mustering the two-thirds' majority necessary either to override the President or to impeach him.[22]

There were heartburnings among the Whigs, but they were helpless. The tariff bill, minus any attempt to keep distribution, was now passed in both houses by narrow margins. It was largely a sectional measure. The New England and Middle Atlantic states were heavily for it; the South and Southwest were heavily opposed; the western area was split but was mainly for the bill. Some thirty southern House of Representatives Whigs voted against it, and it could not have passed either house without the aid of the Democrats.[23] Tyler signed it, August 30. The duty level was thereby restored approximately to the status it had had with the passage of the 1832 bill. But distribution, despite the frantic efforts of the Whigs, was a thing of the past.

The passage of the tariff of 1842 coincided with the beginning of a gradual rise in American prosperity. Business conditions became perceptibly better the following year, and by 1844 the economy was once more on an even keel and forging rapidly ahead. Whether or not this was the result of the tariff, no man can tell. The most that can be said with any degree of certainty is that its passage probably exerted a good psychological effect upon the industrial community, especially upon the textile and iron manufacturers.[24]

The Whig achievement in legislation under Tyler had not been a brilliant one. The hated Independent Treasury was no more, and a higher tariff had been enacted, but there was no national bank. Distribution, which Greeley regarded with justice as the very heart of the Whig program, had gone down to defeat. For this sorry record, the Whigs had to thank the gentleman from Virginia, and they thanked him with bitterness and a hearty dislike. In September, 1842, the New

[22] Samuel F. Bemis, *John Quincy Adams and the Union* (New York, 1956), pp. 440–442; Leonard D. White, *The Jacksonians: A Study in Administrative History, 1829–1861* (New York, 1954), p. 30; Edward Stanwood, *Tariff Controversies in the Nineteenth Century* (2 vols., Boston, 1903), II, 20–28.

[23] Webster, *Writings,* III, 30.

[24] Walter B. Smith and Arthur H. Cole, *Fluctuations in American Business, 1790–1860* (Cambridge, 1935), pp. 87–105; Stanwood, *Tariff Controversies,* II, 30–37; Frank W. Taussig, *The Tariff History of the United States* (New York, 1923), pp. 113–14; Frederick J. Turner, *The United States, 1830–1850* (New York, 1935), pp. 505–507.

York *Tribune* identified two recent post-office appointments as having been made by "Judas Iscariot."[25]

But if Clay's program had suffered disastrous defeats, his leadership of the Whig party had been established beyond question. Southern Whigs generally, save for the Virginia group, had supported Clay's bank bill and criticized Tyler's vetoes. A general feeling, fostered by the hard times of the depression, that the home market should be built up had stimulated the growth of protectionist sentiment in all sections. Even in the South, there was a general Whig willingness to accept Clay's leadership in tariff legislation. In that section, too, sentiment was growing for internal improvements, sentiment most clearly evident among the members of the Whig party. It was significant that the southern Whigs were now rallying to the basic features of the American system—that body of doctrine which had always constituted one of the main bases of the Kentuckian's strength in the North and West. Even a politician like Thurlow Weed, who had always sensed to the full Clay's weaknesses as a presidential aspirant, was constrained to admit that he was the logical Whig candidate for 1844.[26]

Clay's star was indeed rising, but that of the great American democratic experiment was showing some signs of going into eclipse. As vested interests increased in wealth and in the power to corrupt, and as the full impact of universal manhood suffrage with its masses of ignorant voters began to be felt, there was noticeable a serious decline in the manners and morals of the congressional solons. This was the era of "Sausage Sawyer," member of the House from Ohio, who ate his sausages sitting at the Speaker's rostrum, and who demanded the abolition of West Point because it was a useless extravagance, even though hostilities with Mexico had begun and it was by no means clear that a war with Britain could be avoided.[27] Drunkenness more and more disgraced the congressional halls. Champagne flowed in the cloakroom of the Senate, and Senate President pro tem Willie P. Mangum, doubtless with a wry smile on his face, shifted its cost from the Senate's stationery fund to that of the fuel account.

As the level of congressional manners declined, violence and unseemly personal altercations became more and more frequent on the

25 New York *Tribune*, Sept. 16, 1842.

26 Arthur C. Cole, *The Whig Party in the South* (Washington, 1913), pp. 64–103.

27 *Congressional Globe*, 29th Cong., first sess., Appendix, p. 585.

floor of the House of Representatives. These outbreaks varied in intensity from mere vituperation to such scandalous proceedings as the fight which took place on April 23, 1844, between Democratic Representative Rathbun of New York and Whig Representative White of Kentucky. The two men were trading blow for blow when a fellow Kentuckian of White's came charging in to his support and fired a pistol, breaking the leg of an officer of the House.[28]

As if low manners and unseemly brawls were not enough to bring the national legislature into disrepute, it also became apparent that many congressmen could be tempted by what a later generation was to term a "fast buck." Lobbies for patent renewals and for grants of various kinds increased in number, and lobbyists who had money to spend found congressmen eager to earn it. The "Mileage-elongators," as Greeley called another brand of erring congressmen, took as much as $50,000 a year out of the Treasury by presenting fraudulent claims for mileage expenses. Suspicion of corruption was on the increase.

There were, of course, many men of high standards and marked ability in both houses of Congress, but the number of political nonentities and individuals on the make was undoubtedly increasing in alarming fashion.[29]

It was not only in Congress that democracy seemed on the decline. The malaise was affecting the Land Office, the customhouses, and other branches of government. The South, increasingly sensitive on the subject of slavery, and not for conscience's sake, was violating the fundamental rights of free speech and petition, and slavery champions such as Thomas R. Dew and William Harper were formulating a political philosophy that threw overboard the doctrine of natural rights and glorified the mudsill theory of society. In the North, it was true that the Dorr rebellion in Rhode Island, the antirent disturbances along the Hudson, and the ofttimes fervent defense of free speech and free press gave proof that democratic idealism was far from dead. But even in the North, the rise of a bigoted nativism that found refuge in the bosom of the Whig party, the grinding poverty that lowered living standards among the textile workers, and the growth of sweatshop conditions in the great cities showed that there also the dignity of the

[28] Rives Papers, Rives to Mrs. Rives, Apr. 23, 1844.

[29] Whie, *Jacksonians,* pp. 25–27, 414–430; Glyndon G. Van Deusen, *Horace Greeley, Nineteenth Century Crusader* (Philadelphia, 1953), pp. 126–128.

individual was by no means safe and that democracy, whether political, social, or economic, was not assured.

Were the politicos going to grapple with these fundamental problems of the democratic order, or were they to turn to more spectacular and eye-catching issues? The answer was soon to come.

CHAPTER 9

Expansion and Election

THE currents of national affairs, like the Mississippi River, sometimes cut stream beds that shift the flow of events. Old channels remain but new ones appear, and the nation's course is altered. The advent of the eighteen-forties brought just such alterations in American life. In the Tyler administration the nation began shaking off the depression that still clung to it in leechlike fashion, and economic development began moving forward at an accelerated pace. As this happened, America turned its gaze more and more intently upon the West and Southwest, and the national government's policies harmonized with this shift in popular interest.

The diplomacy of John Tyler's administration illustrates the nation's shift in course. While the congressional Whigs were quarreling over domestic legislation, Tyler's foreign policy was settling old differences of opinion, establishing agreements as to long-disputed boundary lines, and setting the stage for an expansionist movement that was to rival in significance the acquisition of Florida and Louisiana.

It is one of the ironies of history that these preparations by a Whig President were to be utilized to the full by the Democratic party. That party was itself in a process of reorientation. For the Democracy of the eighteen-forties was consecrating itself to new objectives and new ideals.

Confused, disheartened, stultified by the Whig victory of 1840, the Democratic Left, with its emphasis on individual rights and equality of opportunity, was gradually beginning to lose control over the counsels of the party. Its place in party leadership was being taken by a somewhat different breed of men from those who had listened to the siren song of Locofocoism. These men were Southerners, or southern sympathizers, anxious to satisfy the demands of that section of the country, and at the same time alert for any movement or trend in national thinking that would have widespread popular appeal. That Robert J. Walker, James Buchanan, James K. Polk, and their ilk were soon to seize the reins of leadership in the Democracy indicated that a new spirit was pervading that party's ranks. The new spirit which these men snuffed in the breeze of party politics was that of expansionism.

The expansionist movement that was to dominate the decade arose from a multiplicity of causes. It was a manifestation of the same urge that had set statesmen to purchasing Louisiana, browbeating Spain for Florida, and vainly attempting to purchase Texas. Back of it lay certain concepts and influences long present in American life but now reaching new heights of intensity.

Pride in America and its potentialities was a factor in expansionism. Fear of foreign influence posted on American borders was another cause of the movement. Land hunger, coupled with contempt for the supposedly "lesser breeds without the law," played a part in the thinking of the time. And there was always the pushing force of the frontier, its numbers swelled by native farmers and planters seeking greener pastures as the exhaustion of eastern soils and the inrush of hordes of immigrants complicated the problems of life in the older regions of the country.

As expansion had its causes, so it had its justification. Some of its sponsors declared that the natural rights of man included a right to safety which could only be achieved by acquiring areas in which strong foreign powers might easily gain menacing positions of strength. The doctrine of "natural frontiers," such as the Rio Grande and the Pacific Ocean, was given adequate, and more than adequate, recognition. Those more religiously inclined were sure that God intended the soil of America for the most productive use, and it went without saying that those who could use it most effectively were the citizens of the United States. Others declared that it was our duty to carry freedom, that precious gift which every American knew was the peculiar trust of his countrymen, into areas where it had not hitherto flourished.

Others still, in more matter-of-fact fashion, defended expansionism as based on the natural growth of the country, thus anticipating Alfred Thayer Mahan's dictum that a nation must either grow or die.

The whole concept of expansion was summed up in the words "Manifest Destiny," first used in 1845 by the Democratic editor and publicist John L. O'Sullivan in the *Democratic Review.* But the idea back of those mouth-filling words had been germinating in the national consciousness for some time before it thus burst into the open.[1]

Bold and dramatic though the expansionist movement of the eighteen-forties turned out to be, it had a modest beginning. It was ushered in by a diplomatic bargain which was not motivated in any primary fashion by a desire to expand the territory of the United States. This bargain was little more than a compromise settlement of areas in dispute. It did, nevertheless, establish the American flag in a hitherto disputed region. It also helped clear the way for further territorial adjustments which increased the size of the country.

When Daniel Webster became Secretary of State in Harrison's Cabinet, relations with Great Britain had become strained indeed. The dispute over responsibility for the *Caroline* incident remained unsettled. McLeod had not yet been tried and, to the great disgust of the British, lay languishing in a New York State jail. Slave traders were using the American flag with impunity and laughing at the efforts of British warships to interfere with their vicious traffic. Tempers were flaring in Canada and the United States over the northeast boundary dispute.

The governments and the peoples of England and the United States were glowering at one another across the Atlantic. Britain's powerful and truculent Foreign Minister, Lord Palmerston, was reinforcing the British troops already in Canada. Feeling in America ran high as Americans read or heard of savage British criticism of our manners and morals. Englishmen jealously watched America's growing power, even as they commented bitterly on the losses they had suffered through repudiation of state debts and by bankruptcy proceedings in the United States. There was real danger of a third Anglo-American war.

But with the advent of Tyler's administration there came a decided improvement in the relations of the two countries. Secretary of State Forsyth, Van Buren's spokesman in foreign affairs, had been an Anglophobe. Webster was an Anglophile, and his guiding principle in

[1] The best analysis of expansionism is Albert K. Weinberg, *Manifest Destiny: A Study of Nationalist Expansionism in American History* (Baltimore, 1935).

the State Department was peace with England. It was also fortunate that 1841 saw the fall of the Melbourne ministry in England. It was succeeded by the ministry of Sir Robert Peel, and the pacific Lord Aberdeen replaced the bristling Palmerston in the Foreign Office. This was a happy omen indeed.

Since both Webster and Aberdeen wished to avoid war, arrangements looking to that end were soon forthcoming. Aberdeen appointed a special representative to the United States, and his choice was significant. The sixty-seven-year-old Alexander Baring, Lord Ashburton, was a personal friend of Daniel Webster. Ashburton had an American wife, a keen sense of humor, and a great desire to promote good relations between Great Britain and the United States. He arrived in Washington April 4, 1842, empowered to negotiate a settlement of all disputes that existed between the two countries.[2]

One of the first subjects of negotiation between Ashburton and the American Secretary of State was the troublesome McLeod case. Webster took it up in conciliatory fashion, the more confidently because of private assurances from New York's Governor Seward that there was evidence that McLeod had had no direct connection with the *Caroline* affair. The trial, in fact, proved McLeod an outrageous liar. He had not been within half a dozen miles of the *Caroline* when that vessel had been seized by the Canadians, and when his alibi was proven he was speedily acquitted.

The McLeod acquittal paved the way for other developments of a constructive nature. Ashburton was prevailed upon to express regret that "some explanation and apology" for the sinking of the *Caroline* had not been made by Great Britain. As a *quid pro quo,* Webster obtained from Congress a law giving federal courts power to grant writs of habeas corpus where states like New York arrested aliens for acts perpetrated under the authority of the alien's own country. So far as the slave trade was concerned, it was agreed that it should be brought under control by each nation providing a fleet of at least eighty guns in African waters, these to co-operate, where exigency required, in suppressing the illegal use of the American flag. The negotiators agreed upon a compromise boundary line extending from Lake Superior to the Lake of the Woods. They also agreed on rectifications of the Vermont and New York boundaries. By the latter of these,

[2] George T. Curtis, *Life of Daniel Webster* (2 vols., New York, 1870), II, 94–125.

strategic Rouse's Point was awarded to the United States. The most significant settlement, however, concerned the Maine-Canadian frontier.

Webster proposed that they settle the Maine-Canadian boundary by a compromise line. He was able to make this proposal because he had obtained the assent of commissioners representing Maine to such action. This had been achieved in part by the use of federal money in organizing propaganda in Maine for the treaty, and in part by the utilization of a clever stratagem.

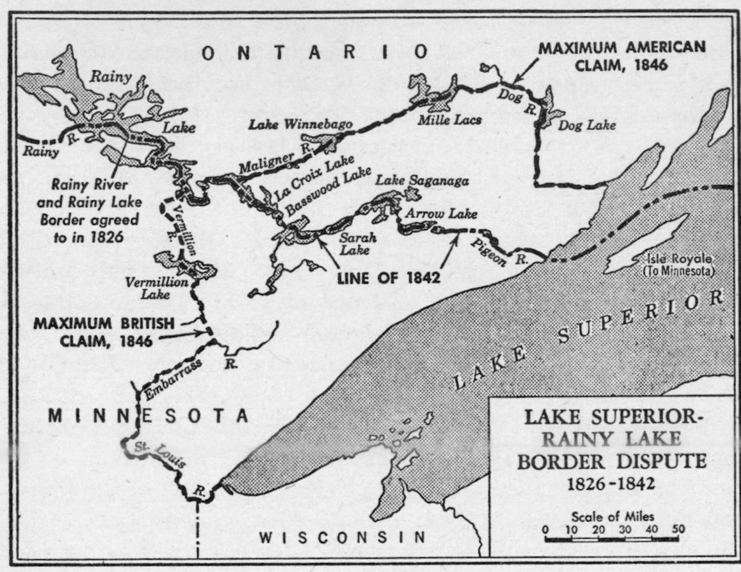

Jared Sparks, that indefatigable historian, had discovered in the Archives des Affaires Étrangères in Paris a map on which the Maine-Canadian boundary was marked by a red line. This line had been supposedly drawn by Benjamin Franklin, when he was one of the American peace commissioners in 1783, to represent the preliminary boundary agreement between the British and American peace commissioners. Sparks appeared before the commissioners armed with a copy of this map. It gave most of the territory in dispute to the British; with this evidence staring them in the face, the partisans of Maine agreed to a compromise settlement.

The agreement finally reached gave Maine some 7,000 of the 12,000 square miles in dispute. The feelings of Maine and Massachusetts (which also claimed an interest in the area) were salved by a grant of $150,000 to each.

The Senate ratified the Webster-Ashburton Treaty by a vote of 39 to 9. All save one of the opponents were Democrats, and there was considerable Democratic opposition from other quarters as well. James Buchanan denounced the treaty as "unjust to Maine and dishonorable to the whole country." Andrew Jackson declared that it was "disgraceful, and disreputable to our national character." Such partisan denigrations, however, had relatively little effect.[3]

The treaty did not settle all outstanding difficulties between the United States and Great Britain. Nothing was done about the old question of impressment; the northwest boundary was discussed but not determined; Ashburton, pleading lack of instructions, refused to negotiate on the *Creole* case (another instance like *L'Amistad* of slaves mutinying on board ship and gaining their freedom by taking it into a British port). It can also be argued, with some justice, that the United States had a very good claim to all of the disputed area.

The treaty was, nevertheless, a substantial achievement. It provided a useful agreement on extradition. Its joint cruising convention for the suppression of the African slave trade gave promise of ending that traffic and would have done so had not succeeding administrations allowed its provisions to become dead letters. It satisfied strategic sensibilities by giving Rouse's Point to the United States, the while it safeguarded the British line of communications between Halifax and Quebec. It gave the United States the immensely valuable iron ore deposits of northern Minnesota, including a large part of the Mesabi Range.[4] Best of all, it ended some very troublesome border difficulties and ushered in a period of improved Anglo-American relations. Whig businessmen, Democrats from the northeastern part of the country, and southern planters approved of the agreement. Attacks upon it by Benton, Cass, Jackson, and others in the West bore little fruit. It was a triumph for the principle of compromise. It meant peace. The fact that, while under attack in the United States, it was stigmatized in

[3] John B. Moore (ed.), *The Works of James Buchanan* (12 vols., Philadelphia, 1908–11), V, 342, 384; Rives Papers, William B. Lewis to Rives, Sept. 3, 1841.

[4] Webster and Tyler knew of the existence of this mineral wealth; Ashburton, apparently, did not.

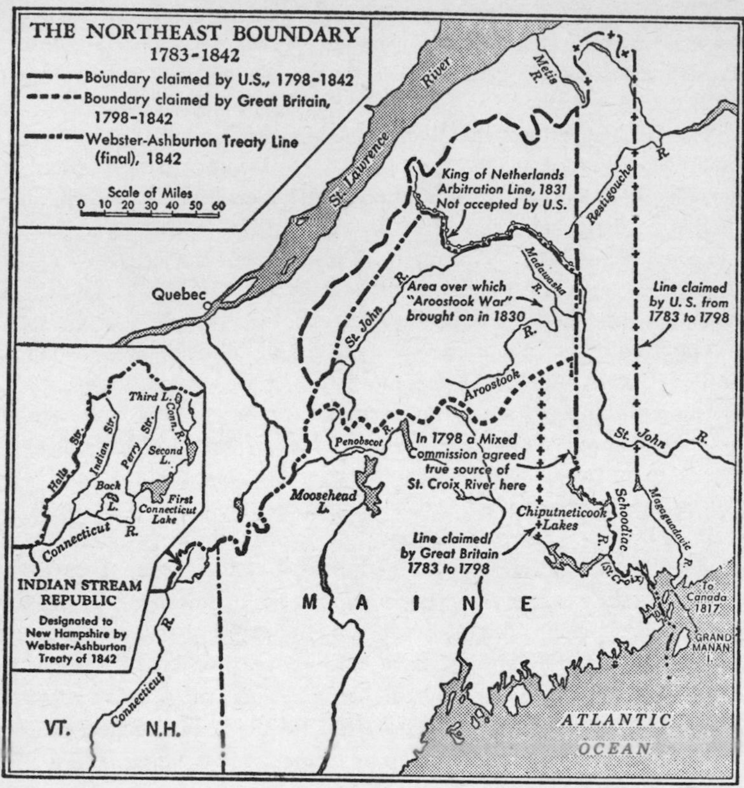

England as "Ashburton's Capitulation" was perhaps the best proof of its essential fairness.[5]

The tense situation that had developed between the United States and Great Britain having been eased by the treaty of 1842, Tyler now felt free to turn his attention to a project that had interested him

[5] Albert B. Corey, *The Crisis of 1830–1842 in Canadian-American Relations* (New Haven, 1941), pp. 161, 168, 181–182; Richard N. Current, "Webster's Propaganda and the Ashburton Treaty," *Mississippi Valley Historical Review,* XXXI (Oct., 1947), 187–200; Samuel F. Bemis, *John Quincy Adams and the Union* (New York, 1956), pp. 456–462. Bemis's criticism of Webster in connection with this treaty is unnecessarily harsh.

almost from the beginning of his administration. This was the annexation of Texas.

Texas had offered itself for annexation during Van Buren's term of office, but the Lone Star State's proposal had produced no tangible results. Both political parties, in fact, had shied away from a project of such explosive potential. When Tyler took office, his Secretary of State was cool to the idea of annexation, and whatever interest the President had was dampened by the fact that Webster and his following constituted, outside Virginia, Tyler's one real source of strength in the Whig party.

When it became evident that Clay, not Tyler, was the real head of the Whigs; when the Whig legislative program, such as it was, had been disposed of; and when the Webster-Ashburton treaty had been signed and ratified, Webster's usefulness to the administration had largely ended. The President, therefore, felt much freer to pursue the Texas matter, especially since the proposal of annexation had been renewed by the Texas representative in Washington in March of 1842. Tyler had, moreover, become alarmed by reports of English designs on Texas. Evidence was accumulating that the British were seeking the elimination of slavery in Texas, and that they were much interested in the establishment of commercial supremacy in that region. There was also the possibility that, by putting himself at the head of annexation, he might become the leader of a great popular movement that would develop into a third party and sweep him into the White House in 1844.

The more Tyler thought about the situation, the more he felt impelled to act. He was confirmed in this disposition by his close friends Henry A. Wise and Thomas W. Gilmer of Virginia, both influential members of the House, and by Robert J. Walker of Mississippi, the administration's unofficial spokesman in the Senate of the United States.

Webster knew that annexation was very much in the air. He also knew that with the Ashburton treaty concluded, his further stay in the State Department would compromise his standing with the Whigs. On May 8, 1843, he resigned, and President Tyler appointed in his place Abel P. Upshur, another member of that Virginia group which was now very nearly the President's sole support.[6]

[6] Charles M. Wiltse, *John C. Calhoun* (3 vols., Indianapolis, 1944–51), III,

Upshur was a man of strong convictions. Devoted to slavery, and to Jeffersonian agrarianism, his ardent nature yearned for the acquisition of this empire in the Southwest which, it now appeared, was to be had for the asking. He was convinced that England was determined to abolish slavery in Texas, and that this would be detrimental to southern agriculture and, therefore, to northern manufactures as well. He was equally convinced that Mexico had to be dealt with vigorously where Texas was concerned. The result of all this was ten months of rather truculent diplomacy.

The Mexicans were told that they must either reconquer Texas immediately or recognize its independence, and that the United States had full right to negotiate with Texas on any subject whatever. England was informed in no uncertain terms that the extradition clauses in the Webster-Ashburton Treaty covered all cases of runaway slaves, and that the United States was not disposed to yield an inch in protecting the property interests of its citizens. At home, Upshur worked closely with Tyler, seeking to whip up popular opinion for annexation and thus lay the basis for a treaty that would bring the Lone Star State into the Union. Texas, meanwhile, was informed that the United States government was busily preparing the ground in the United States for a favorable reception of the proposal.

The attitude of the Texas government, especially of Sam Houston, toward annexation has never been absolutely clear. Houston himself, an adept at the game of bluff, was enthusiastic by turns over annexation and over the glorious future of a Texan Republic and an empire in the Southwest, dreams of which danced before his eyes as they had before the eyes of Aaron Burr. "The Raven" had many things to consider—the Mexican threat of reconquest, England's attitude, America's policy—and his cards had to be carefully played. The one outstanding fact is that under his leadership Texas moved, if somewhat coquettishly, into the American orbit.[7]

150–156; Justin H. Smith, *The Annexation of Texas* (New York, 1941), pp. 103–115; James C. N. Paul, *Rift in the Democracy* (Philadelphia, 1951), pp. 23–29; Clyde A. Duniway, "Daniel Webster," in Samuel F. Bemis (ed.), *The American Secretaries of State and Their Diplomacy* (10 vols., New York, 1927–29), V, 59–60.

[7] Llerena Friend, *Sam Houston* (Austin, 1954), pp. 84–86, 138–139, 145, 146, 152–153, 155, 159; Eugene C. Barker, "The Annexation of Texas," *The Southwestern Historical Quarterly* (July, 1946), 51; Marquis James, *The Raven* (Indianapolis, 1929), pp. 272, 333, 338, 346, 349; Smith, *Texas,* pp. 147–156.

The attitude of the American people and their leaders toward annexation began to crystallize in the winter of 1843–44. There was some small sentiment for it in the North, much more in the West, and much, much more in the South. The northern abolitionists were up in arms against it and John Quincy Adams and twelve of his colleagues in the House of Representatives had declared that it would be "identical with dissolution" of the Union. (This statement had been made as early as March, 1843.) Benton, viewing the Tyler movement with suspicion, labeled it an intrigue for the Presidency and a scrip and land speculation. Webster came out strongly against annexation. But Robert J. Walker of Mississippi, a most managing man, was just as strongly for it. Andrew Jackson from the Hermitage and Supreme Court Justice John Catron (also of Tennessee) were pushing it. Upshur believed that two-thirds of the Senate favored annexation, and there was considerable evidence to support this belief.[8]

Acting on the supposition that his estimate of the Senate's views was correct, but that the balance was delicate and must not be disturbed, Upshur secretly undertook to negotiate a treaty of annexation with Isaac Van Zandt, the Texan chargé at Washington. This instrument was nearly completed when, February 28, 1844, the Secretary of State was killed by the explosion of a new cannon on board the battleship *Princeton.*[9] One week later, Tyler sent to the Senate, as his nominee for Secretary of State, the name of John C. Calhoun. The Texas negotiation, so the President thought, admitted of no delay, and he knew that Calhoun was an ardent annexationist.[10]

Calhoun had twice refused efforts by Tyler to lure him into the Cabinet, for he had had no desire to serve as an aid to Tyler's search for the Presidency. But the South Carolinian's presidential hopes for 1844 had been extinguished by defeats in New York and Massachusetts, to say nothing of a decisive beating administered by the Van Buren forces in the organization of the House of Representatives in 1843. In December of that year, Calhoun had withdrawn from the race. Now, his ambition for the White House momentarily thwarted, he thought he saw an opportunity to serve his section and the nation, while gaining

[8] Smith, *Texas,* pp. 139–146, 156–163.

[9] Randolph G. Adams, "Abel Parker Upshur," in *American Secretaries of State,* V, 68, 124; Smith, *Texas,* pp. 169–170.

[10] As to whether Tyler really wanted Calhoun or was tricked into appointing him, *cf.* Wiltse, *Calhoun,* III, 161–163, and Paul, *Rift,* pp. 106–107.

kudos that would serve him well in 1848. His aim was to exploit what he believed to be the growing expansionist sentiment of the country. He would join the interest of the West in Oregon (an interest which was steadily increasing as settlers moved in increasing numbers across the Great Divide) to that of the South and West in Texas; do what he could to satisfy both urges; and in the process reforge the old South-West alliance, destroy the protective tariff, and open up the markets of England and the United States to an increasingly lucrative trade.[11]

Calhoun reached Washington March 29, 1844, and the following day had a two-hour interview with Tyler. It was high time. Closely guarded though the treaty negotiations had been, news of them had leaked and for the past few weeks the opposition press, abolitionist, Whig, and Democratic, had been thundering against the project. Mexico's attitude could scarcely be termed enthusiastic, and Britain was distinctly miffed by the news. It seemed to both the President and his Secretary of State that time was of the essence, and they proceeded to move.

The treaty of annexation was speedily completed. Texas was to come into the Union as a territory. Its public lands were to be ceded to the United States, and the national government was to assume the Texan public debt up to $10 million. The instrument was presented to the Senate on April 22, 1844, nine days before the Whig national convention was to meet in Baltimore.

The Texas treaty was now indeed a political question. Both parties were on the verge of naming their candidates. The attitudes of those candidates, and the positions on annexation taken by the parties, would obviously be major factors in the campaign.

The presidential campaign had begun as early as 1841. The Whig political stalwarts had begun rallying to Clay as soon as his breach with Tyler had become apparent, and the movement thus inaugurated had spread. In the North, even Thurlow Weed was convinced that Clay was the man for 1844. The southern Whigs, certain that their party was a bulwark against the leveling tendencies of the radical Democracy, resisted Tyler's efforts to lure them into a separate party under his leadership and rallied behind Harry of the West. Over 200 Whig newspapers had declared for him by August, 1842. During the next year and a half, Whig conventions or legislatures in no less than seven-

[11] Wiltse, *Calhoun,* III, 164–165; William E. Dodd, *Statesman of the Old South* (New York, 1919), pp. 144–146.

teen states had come out for him. His nomination was assured at least three months before the Whigs met in national conclave. The other Whig aspirants, Winfield Scott, Judge John McLean, and Webster, had been left hopelessly behind.[12]

The Democratic nomination had likewise attracted a number of contenders; but as the spring of 1844 dawned, Van Buren appeared to be far in the lead. Calhoun was out of the race. Great as was his talent for logical exposition, clearly as his mind worked in the realms of abstract thought, the very fervor of his devotion to the South and the basically narrow conservatism of his social and political philosophy limited his appeal in any national contest.[13] The growth of national power and of a national interest, the swelling tide of democracy itself, worked powerfully against him in the North and West. Even in the South, outside his own state, his support was negligible. With Calhoun out of the picture, Van Buren's triumph was complete. Or so it seemed.

Other candidacies than that of Calhoun sprang up to flourish like the green bay tree and then wither away. Lewis Cass of Michigan and Richard M. Johnson ("Old Dick") of Kentucky both had support from conservative elements within the Democracy. There was a momentary movement for James Buchanan, Pennsylvania's favorite son. But none of these hopefuls gathered the force necessary for a serious challenge to the Red Fox. He seemed to hold the northern Democracy in the hollow of his hand, and Tom Ritchie, the powerful editor of the Richmond *Inquirer,* appealed for his nomination on the ground of party harmony. Jackson was for Van Buren, and southern Jacksonians followed their old leader in raising the New Yorker's standard. Western politicians, such as Senator Ben Tappan of Ohio, rallied to the man from Kinderhook.

A menacing shadow, however, was looming on the horizon of Van Buren's hopes. Greeley, visiting Washington in December, 1841, had found both southern and western Democrats cool to Van Buren. They "mean to throw Van overboard," Greeley wrote to Weed. "There is music ahead."[14] Now Calhounites and Tylerites, avid for Texas,

[12] George R. Poage, *Henry Clay of the Whig Party* (Chapel Hill, 1936), pp. 107–112; Glyndon G. Van Deusen, *The Life of Henry Clay* (Boston, 1937), pp. 358–359; Arthur C. Cole, *The Whig Party in the South* (Washington, 1913), pp. 64–103.

[13] For a suggestive exposition of this philosophy, see Richard Hofstadter, *The American Political Tradition* (New York, 1948), pp. 68, 79–91.

[14] Weed Papers, Greeley to Weed, Dec. 15, 1841.

hurried on the annexation project, a project toward which the Red Fox had always been cool. They enlisted Jackson's support. Senator Robert J. Walker also persuaded Silas Wright, the close friend and trusted adviser of Van Buren, to support a "late" convention. This fatal blunder, from Van Buren's point of view, ensured the injection of Texas into the struggle over the nomination.

Van Buren had made a fence-building western tour in the spring of 1842. He had visited Jackson at the Hermitage, there receiving the old General's blessing upon his candidacy, and had then journeyed on to Ashland for a two days' stay with Henry Clay. No record of their conversations remains, but they must have touched upon Texas, and it is at least reasonable that they then and there agreed to take that "common ground" which Clay later told Crittenden they would take as the crisis came upon them.[15]

On April 27, 1844, five days after the annexation treaty reached the Senate, letters from Clay and Van Buren regarding Texas were published in Washington. Both opposed annexation, though in qualified fashion. Clay was the more outspoken in what became known as his "Raleigh letter," due to the place of its origin. "Annexation and war with Mexico are identical," he declared, and he insisted that the agitation for Texas derived mainly from government circles and from holders of Texas bonds and scrip. What the United States most needed, Clay believed, was "union, peace, and patience." He held up the possibility of the United States co-operating peacefully with Canada and Texas as friendly neighboring republics and ended by declaring that annexation "at this time, without the assent of Mexico," was inexpedient.

Van Buren said substantially the same thing in a letter three times as long as Clay's. It took the New Yorker three columns of *Niles' Register* to state that annexation was constitutionally possible, but that it was inexpedient because it involved the danger of war with Mexico. If Mexico recognized Texan independence, the situation would change; if public opinion came to be overwhelmingly in favor of annexation, Van Buren would bow to the mandate of the people. But under existing circumstances he was opposed to taking Texas into the Union.

While the prospective candidates of the two major parties were

[15] Paul, *Rift,* p. 38, note 4.

framing their statements on Texas, Secretary of State Calhoun had sent to Sir Richard Pakenham, the British envoy at Washington, a statement that was to have significant consequences for the coming political campaign. In this note, which was a response to one in which the British government had avowed its interest in abolishing slavery throughout the world, Calhoun undertook to defend it as a beneficial institution. He declared that where the American Negro had been freed he had sunk into vice and pauperism and, in consequence, into deafness, blindness, insanity, and idiocy "to a degree without example." Experience therefore proved, said the Secretary of State, "that what is called slavery is in reality a political institution, essential to the peace, safety, and prosperity of those states of the Union in which it exists." Calhoun also asserted that the annexation of Texas was a step necessary to the security and peace of the United States, since the abolition of slavery in Texas so much desired by Great Britain would be a danger to both the South and the Union.[16]

Calhoun's defense of slavery, so closely coupled with his justification of annexation, was forwarded to Congress as well as to the British envoy, and Senator Benjamin Tappan of Ohio gave it to the press. In effect, it made it apparent that annexation was being undertaken, not, as might have been supposed, from the point of view of great national interests, but simply for the protection of the South's peculiar institution. It was couched in such terms, Blair wrote to Jackson, as to "drive off every northern man from the support of the measure." It certainly fostered the development of sectional conflict over slavery.[17]

Clay and Van Buren both hoped that their letters would eliminate Texas as a campaign issue. The Whig convention, which opened in Baltimore May 1, 1844, did nothing to disabuse them of this notion. The city was a riot of bunting, flags, placards, parading delegates, and live coons and little foxes, caged but "raising the old Harry." Clay was unanimously nominated for President, with Theodore Frelinghuysen of

[16] Richard K. Crallé (ed.), *The Works of John C. Calhoun* (6 vols., Charleston and New York, 1851–56), V, 333–339.

[17] John S. Bassett (ed.), *Correspondence of Andrew Jackson* (7 vols., Washington, 1926–35), VI, 281; Rives Papers, Rives to Mrs. Rives, Apr. 3, 1844; Smith, *Texas,* pp. 201–202; Poage, *Clay,* p. 131. Rives favored annexation, believing that it would result in the destruction of slavery by drawing Negroes from the South into Texas and fostering a flow of them into Mexico, "to mix with the Indians and Creole races of that border country." See also Wiltse, *Calhoun,* III, 165–171; Oscar Handlin, *Chance or Destiny* (Boston, 1955), pp. 68–73.

New Jersey as his running mate. The Whig party organization obviously had no qualms about its candidate's stand on Texas, and its resolutions simply omitted all reference to expansion. But the Democracy was yet to be heard from.

Van Buren never really achieved that smooth combination of southern planters and northern plain republicans for which he yearned. The South was still cool to him in 1844. It regarded him not only as a beaten candidate but also as the representative of a northern radical wing of the Democracy, a wing whose zeal for equality and human rights made its dominance in the party councils something not easily to be borne. The conviction had been growing for some time among southern Democrats that they must assert their control over the fortunes of their party, and when they saw his attitude toward Texas, revolt against his candidacy quickly spread among their ranks.

Jackson helped to turn the tide against his former lieutenant by first announcing that he was for both Texas and Van Buren (which was simply not practical), and then by abandoning the New Yorker's candidacy. Ritchie executed a *volte-face,* coming out against Van Buren in the Richmond *Inquirer.* The Mississippi delegation in Congress turned against the Red Fox, as did those of Indiana and Illinois. This movement was being spearheaded from the South. "The present state of things here," Benton wrote to Jackson from Washington, May 3, 1844, "have now taken an aspect which looks beyond *men* and parties, and reaches the *Union* itself. The Texas issue is now perverted to fearful purposes, and your name . . . is used against your friends."[18]

The Democrats, and the Tylerites also, gathered at Baltimore on May 27. Tyler was nominated by his disorganized followers, but there was no chance of the Democrats accepting the Virginian. Various rumors were afloat as to the Democracy's course of action. Van Buren had a majority of the delegates, but Rives, viewing the situation from Washington, thought Cass had the best chance of nomination. Buchanan and Johnson were also possibilities, but no man could predict with any certainty what might develop when the convention began to ballot.

The result was an unexpected one. By clever management, the ex-

[18] Duff Green Papers, Rhett to Green, Feb. 2, 1844; Van Buren Papers, Blair to Van Buren, Mar. 18, 1844; Blair Papers, Benton to Jackson, May 3, 1844; Flagg Papers, Preston King to Flagg, May 7, 8, 1844, O. Hungerford to Flagg, May 6, 1844; Paul, *Rift,* pp. 114–143.

pansionist forces succeeded in getting the convention to adopt what had become, in Democratic conventions, the usual two-thirds' rule for nomination. This rule, which had been used to secure Van Buren's nomination to the Vice-Presidency in 1832, and had been jammed through the Democratic convention of 1836 by his friends, now deprived him of much of the advantage that was his at the beginning of the proceedings. He simply could not command a two-thirds' majority of the delegates, and the convention deadlocked.

Then, due to George Bancroft of Massachusetts and Gideon Pillow of Tennessee, a dark horse was brought forward in the person of James K. Polk. A former governor of Tennessee, congressman, and Speaker of the House, a hard-money, Independent Treasury Jacksonian, Polk had been a Democratic stalwart ever since the rise of the party to power. He was known to be in the confidence of the Old Hero at the Hermitage. He was also an expansionist.

The swing to Polk began. On the ninth ballot New York went to him, though sullenly and in bitterness of spirit, and thus was nominated the first dark-horse candidate in American presidential history.[19] Within ten seconds, the news was flashed on Mr. Morse's "electro-magnetic telegraph" to the basement room in the nation's Capitol where the wondrous machine had been set up. The room was crowded, both House and Senate having adjourned to hear the report from Baltimore, and to marvel at this clicking instrument which represented a major advance in man's never-ending effort to annihilate the barriers of time and space. For the moment, at least, the amazement of the congressmen at the news of the nomination almost equaled the awe with which they regarded the invention of Mr. Samuel F. B. Morse.

With the presidential hurdle cleared, the convention hurried through its remaining business. Silas Wright was nominated for Vice-President, a sop to the New Yorkers, but declined to run on a Texas ticket. The convention then settled on Senator George M. Dallas of Pennsylvania. It also denounced distribution and, possibly as the result of a bargain between northern and southern delegates, demanded "the reoccupation of Oregon and the reannexation of Texas at the earliest practicable period. . . ." Adjournment was then the order of the day, but the work started at Baltimore was far from finished. It was to go on until

[19] Eugene I. McCormac, *James K. Polk* (Berkeley, 1922), pp. 236–240; M. A. DeWolfe Howe, *The Life and Letters of George Bancroft* (2 vols., New York, 1908), I, 248–255; Paul, *Rift*, pp. 88–89, 144–165.

the Democracy, its humanitarian pretensions left hopelessly behind, was dedicated to expansionism and was driven into proslavery policies by the increasing dominance of southern interests in its counsels.

The course of presidential politics had made the fate of the annexation treaty in the Senate a foregone conclusion. There the treaty had been attacked by Crittenden, Clay's spokesman, and by Thomas Hart Benton, who, as a defender of the small-farmer class against the planter expansionists of the South, took up the cudgels for Van Buren's position. The ensuing debate brought out the fact that Tyler had ordered troops and a naval unit to the Southwest. Benton declared that the United States had loaned its Army and Navy to Houston. The *Tribune* and other Whig papers began calling for Tyler's impeachment.

When the treaty came up for passage, June 8, 1844, there were only sixteen votes in the affirmative. Twenty-eight Whigs (all the Whigs in the Senate, save one from Mississippi) voted against the treaty. Seven Democrats (all left-wing agrarians) voted against it in defiance of Jackson's expressed wishes. In the days that followed, McDuffie of South Carolina, a leading annexationist, practically read Benton out of the Democracy and the Missourian, in an empassioned rejoinder on the floor of the Senate, charged that the movement for Texas was a movement for the dissolution of the Union.[20]

And now the parties became locked in the fateful campaign of 1844. The first impulse of the Whigs was to deride the Democratic choice. The polka had invaded Washington earlier that spring, and William Cabell Rives wrote to his wife: "the polk-a dance will now be the order of the day, which I understand is two steps *backward* for one in advance." Other Whigs raised the scornful cry, "Who is James K. Polk?" and a Whig senator, when it seemed that Wright would have the second place, exclaimed, "A Kangaroo ticket, by God! Strongest in the hind legs."

Nor were the Democrats united in their enthusiasm for the results of their convention. Benton felt that the party had been betrayed by a bunch of "damned fools." The New Yorkers were more than unhappy. William Cullen Bryant, David Dudley Field, Azariah Flagg, and others

[20] *Congressional Globe,* 28th Cong., first sess., 652; William N. Chambers, *Old Bullion Benton, Senator from the New West* (Boston, 1956), pp. 273–279; Smith, *Texas,* pp. 221–233; St. George L. Sioussat, "Calhoun," in *American Secretaries of State,* V, 159.

circulated a proposal to support the nominations but reject the convention's resolutions on Texas. Wright waited until he had heard from his political friends, then wrote a letter to Polk that was full of distilled bitterness of spirit. He promised to work for the ticket, but declared that "upon every principle of democracy" Van Buren had been nominated on the first ballot, and charged that the South had acted "in bad party faith" and, for the sake of "sectional issues," was abandoning the Union. "In my deliberate judgement," added Wright, "our Union was never so much in danger as at this moment."[21]

There were four tickets as the campaign of 1844 opened, for the Liberty party, late in 1843, had nominated James G. Birney, with Thomas Morris of Ohio as his running mate. This number, however, was soon reduced to three. Tyler's candidacy was hopeless from the start. Now, wooed by the Democrats and urged by Jackson, anxious to defeat Clay and to support annexation, "His Accidency" withdrew from the race on August 20, 1844. Birney, however, kept up the fight to the bitter end, and exerted a crucial influence upon the result.[22]

It was a vicious campaign. The Democrats attacked Clay as immoral, a duelist, a friend of the abolitionists. They raked up against him from 1824 the old cry of "bargain and sale." The Liberty party zealots, fearful that antislavery people would vote for Clay as the best means of preventing the annexation of Texas, pilloried him as a "man-stealer" and gambler. The Whigs retorted to these attacks in kind. They singled out Polk as a man who came of Tory stock and, being a free trader, was tied to Britain's chariot wheels; they denounced Birney as a fanatical extremist, a vote for whom was a vote for Polk and Texas. Name calling became the order of the day. But there was also a more serious side to the contest.

A number of fundamental issues were discussed by the leaders of the parties. The Whigs avowed their devotion to distribution, a sound currency, and restrictions on the veto power. The Democrats opposed distribution, hedged on the tariff, and upheld the use of the veto. Such policies, however, paled into insignificance before the Texas question.

[21] Flagg Papers, Flagg to O. Ungerford, May 11, 1844, also Circular of 1844; Rives Papers, Rives to Mrs. Rives, May 29, 1844; Polk Papers, Wright to Polk, June 2, 1844; Paul, *Rift,* pp. 165–168; G. G. Van Deusen, *Clay,* p. 367.

[22] Oliver Chitwood, *John Tyler* (New York, 1939), pp. 377–385; Theodore C. Smith, *The Liberty and Free Soil Parties in the Northwest* (New York, 1897), p. 68.

Clay's Raleigh letter and the party's silence on expansion made it clear that under Whig leadership there would be little immediate chance of acquiring Texas. The Democrats and their candidate were for the acquisition of Texas as soon as it was practicable, which obviously meant in the very near future. Therein lay the crucial difference between the two party positions.

As the campaign wore on, the Clay forces found the going increasingly difficult. The tendency of Whigs to ally with nativist movements that were anti-immigrant and anti-Catholic was used by the Democrats to good effect, especially in New York City. It was difficult for the New York State Whigs to make headway against the popular Silas Wright, who was running for governor on the Democratic ticket. The Pennsylvania Whigs tried hard to carry that state on the tariff issue, but the so-called Kane letter, written by Polk, was couched in such ambiguous terms that he could be portrayed in the Keystone State as a friend of a protective tariff, and the Whig effort ended in failure.[23] The main issue, however, was expansion.

Cleverly, the Democrats joined together Oregon and Texas. Skillfully they portrayed the Whig candidate as absolutely opposed to the acquisition of Texas, and as the weeks went by Clay saw his southern strength beginning to slip away. To counteract this drift, he wrote the "Alabama letters." In these labored missives, he explained that he had no personal objections to annexation; that, indeed, he would like to see Texas annexed, slavery and all, if it could be done without dishonor or war. These letters probably did some good in the South, but they caused the Liberty people to redouble their execrations, and undoubtedly cost him votes among both the extreme and moderate antislavery people of the North.

New York was the pivotal state. There the Liberty party votes, recruited largely from among the Whigs, cost Clay the state. And with New York went the election.

Even so, the middle ground that Clay took came close to giving him the victory. Out of 2,700,560 votes cast, Polk received only 38,367 more than did Clay. The Democratic percentage of the two-party vote was 50.7, and Polk ran only 5,106 votes ahead of Clay in New York

[23] Malcolm R. Eiselen, *The Rise of Pennsylvania Protectionism* (Philadelphia, 1932), pp. 158–171.

State. Had it not been for Birney's 15,814 votes in New York, it is altogether likely that the eleventh President of the United States would have been Henry Clay.[24]

While the major parties had been contending in the national arena, a series of local political movements that were portents of things to come had developed in various parts of the country. Nativism had been gathering strength for some two decades. The nativists were now viewing the incoming bands of shillelagh-swinging Irishmen and beer-guzzling Germans with feelings born of anger and fear. During the election of 1844, local nativist parties in the South, the West, and the East demanded twenty-one years' residence before naturalization and the restriction of authority over the naturalization process to the federal courts. In the election itself, the nativists swept the New York City government and elected three out of four congressmen from the Philadelphia area. The movement languished during the next four years, but it was the harbinger of a great native American crusade that was to swell into a roaring tide during the following decade.[25]

The election of 1844 disheartened the Whigs and their chieftain. It encouraged the Liberty party men, who had seen their national vote swell from 6,225 to 61,999, despite the logical Whig argument that the only effective way to stop the annexation of Texas and the expansion of slavery was to vote for Clay. It brought more joy, though joy mixed with foreboding, to the ranks of the Democracy.

Superficially, at least, the outlook for the Democratic party seemed bright. It had recouped the numerical losses it had suffered in 1840, and was demonstrating great strength in the West and South. Buchanan, viewing the result with an ecstasy that may have been in part artificial, declared that God had preserved Andrew Jackson's life so that he could help Polk achieve victory. Kendall reported jubilantly to Old Hickory that the Whigs had "bet like madmen and lost their money like fools." But there were many bitter spirits among the northern Democrats, men whose feelings were expressed by Preston King when he wrote to Azariah Flagg, "Calhoun has designedly put slavery in the foreground for mischief. . . . One year ago I had great

[24] W. Dean Burnham, *Presidential Ballots, 1836–1892* (Baltimore, 1955), pp. 27–33; Paul, *Rift*, pp. 173–177; G. G. Van Deusen, *Clay*, pp. 367–376.

[25] Ray A. Billington, *The Protestant Crusade, 1800–1860* (New York, 1938), pp. 193–211, 238–239.

confidence in Southern faith and Southern honor. Now I have none."[26] The South, where the great planters and also the small farmers were now beginning to drift back into the Democracy,[27] was on the whole pleased by the result, and southern orators began carrying things with a high hand in the House of Representatives.

John Tyler, grimly exultant, proclaimed the election a mandate for annexation and urged Congress to act. Texas, Preston King wrote to Azariah Flagg, was being pushed by the present administration, by "all the promise of patronage from the next, [and by] the immense pecuniary interest of somebody I do not know who in the Texas scrip."[28] There was also steadily mounting pressure for annexation from the South and West, and even from the North, for the false rumor was spreading that England and France were going to guarantee the independence of Texas, if necessary by war. Even so, the legislative wheels moved slowly, and there were weeks of debate.

Late in January, 1845, the House passed a joint resolution for the admission of Texas as a state. It became evident that such unilateral action by the United States would be defeated in the Senate. The proponents of annexation, therefore, attached to the House resolution an alternative proposal by Senator Benton, providing for the admission of Texas through negotiation between it and the United States. It was obvious that Benton hoped to delay annexation, though some of the sponsors of his proposal felt that it would be soothing to Texan honor and would help to propitiate Mexico. Benton later charged that he and several other senators voted for the resolution only on the assurance that the choice between the alternatives would be left to Polk, after he became President, and that Polk would choose negotiation of a treaty of annexation. The weight of historical evidence indicates that this assertion by the senator from Missouri was correct.

[26] Major A. Davezac folder, National Archives, Buchanan to Davezac, Nov. 25, 1844; Jackson Papers (second series), Kendall to Jackson, Nov. 12, 1844; Flagg Papers, King to Flagg, Dec. 21, 1844.

[27] Cole, *Whig Party,* pp. 112–117.

[28] Flagg Papers, King to Flagg, Jan. 11, 1845; Elgin Williams, *The Animating Pursuits of Speculation* (New York, 1949), pp. 98–100, 162, 165–166, 168, 175. H. Donaldson Walker, "A Politician of Expansion: Robert J. Walker," *Mississippi Valley Historical Review,* XIX (Dec., 1932), 365, states of Robert J. Walker, one of the prime movers in the annexationist movement, that "even in his years of particular glory he was generally regarded as 'odorous of Texan scrip.' " Walker denied financial interest in Texas properties, but did not deny that his father-in-law lived in Texas.

The joint resolution, in this alternative form, passed the Senate by the narrow margin of twenty-seven to twenty-five. The House promptly accepted it. Tyler and Calhoun thereupon proceeded to act under only one of the alternatives, the House proposal, and an invitation to enter the Union as a state was forwarded to Texas on March 3, 1845. When Polk became President, he permitted this action to stand. Thus, in the midst of circumstances fraught with the suspicion of double dealing, the Lone Star State was invited to become a part of the Union.[29]

[29] For the controversy over these circumstances, see Thomas H. Benton, *Thirty Years View* (2 vols., New York, 1854), II, 635–638; Milo M. Quaife (ed.), *The Diary of James K. Polk during his Presidency, 1845–1849* (4 vols., Chicago, 1910), IV, 38–47; Richard R. Stenberg, "President Polk and the Annexation of Texas," *Southwestern Social Science Quarterly,* XIV (Mar., 1934), 333–356. Senator King's comments to Flagg are to be found in the Flagg Papers, King to Flagg, Jan. 11, 1845.

CHAPTER 10

The New Jacksonians

THE chief aspects of the "New Democracy"—its neo-Jacksonian leadership, its opposition to a high tariff and a centralized banking system, its indifference to hard money, its growing zeal for territorial expansion—were soon to become apparent. Andrew Jackson faded out of the picture, dying in the full hope of immortality on a hot Sunday afternoon in June, 1845. Martin Van Buren still lived, but the Democratic faction of which he remained the chief would never again control the party, and ten years later would furnish many a stout adherent to the Republican cause. Thomas Hart Benton was a Democrat still, but his views on expansion were now more Whiggish than he would have thought possible even four years previously, and the gaze he bent upon the new administration was full of deep suspicion.[1] The fact was that a refurbished Democratic party was now starting out, with at least a new leadership.

The head of the New Democracy was James Knox Polk. Somewhat below middle size, but erect in carriage and dignified in manner, Polk was an industrious politician, tough, determined, and full of drive. Neither warm nor outgoing by nature, lacking the easy camaraderie of Clay, he had trained himself to be affable, to remember names and faces, to use wit and sarcasm and grimaces in a way that delighted the audiences on the Tennessee hustings. His large steel-gray eyes and compressed lips contributed to that air of power held in restraint which

[1] William N. Chambers, *Old Bullion Benton, Senator from the New West* (Boston, 1956), pp. 292–296, 301.

was one of his most impressive characteristics. Secretive by disposition and often slow in decision, when he was seized by a conviction he would cling to it with ferocious tenacity. A doctrinaire believer in political democracy and in the principles of Thomas Jefferson, he had been a loyal supporter of King Andrew, but he was now king in his own right and determined to hew his own way.[2] That way was not always along the path marked out by the Old Hero. Polk was a Jacksonian with a difference. There would be times when the voice would indeed be Jacob's voice, but the hands would be those of Esau.

Polk emerged from the campaign of 1844 unencumbered by pledges to any wing of the party, or to the Tylerites. As a consequence, he possessed a freedom of action that was not altogether pleasing to the ambitious politicians who sought influence with him. Tyler and his friends felt aggrieved as they saw themselves ignored by the new administration. Calhoun and his henchmen were almost equally disappointed, both in the matter of appointments and in some of the policies that developed under Polk's guidance.[3] Bitterest of all were the followers of Van Buren, for to their memories of the nominating convention and their fears of southern influence was added now a realization of the fact that they were deriving scant support from the national administration in a fight which they were waging for control of the Democratic party in the Empire State itself.

The Van Burenites were known in New York politics during the eighteen-forties as the Barnburners, a designation which indicated that if they could not own the Democratic barn, they would willingly burn it down. They had for some years been engaged in a running battle with a rival wing of the state Democracy, called Hunkers, a term as uncomplimentary as that borne by their opponents and which indicated that those it designated were "hunkering" for office. The followers of the Red Fox, the Barnburners, had in general distinguished themselves by their hostility to banks, canal enlargement, increasing the state debt, and, in a larger field, to the expansion of the power of the slaveholding South. The Hunkers' attitude was more or less clearly defined in opposition to the Barnburners on all of these counts. There was also

[2] Charles G. Sellers, Jr., *James K. Polk, Jacksonian, 1795–1843* (New York, 1957), pp. 40–41, 74, 91–92, 276–278; Eugene I. McCormac, *James K. Polk* (Berkeley, 1922), pp. 4, 7–9, 25, 69, 139, 283.

[3] Oliver Chitwood, *John Tyler* (New York, 1939), pp. 383–385; Charles M. Wiltse, *John C. Calhoun* (3 vols., Indianapolis, 1944–51), III, 217–224; McCormac, *Polk,* p. 339.

ferocious strife between the two factions over the spoils of office. During the winter of 1844–45, the Van Buren-Wright-Flagg-Preston King group successfully withstood a Hunker attempt to elect Henry A. Foster to the United States Senate seat that had been vacated by Silas Wright when he ran for governor of the state. The Barnburners put John A. Dix in the Senate, but Daniel S. Dickinson, a Hunker, was elected as Dix's fellow senator. The Van Burenites were in for the battle of their lives, and the attitude of the Polk administration was to them a matter of the utmost importance.[4]

The manner of Polk's Cabinetmaking did nothing to heal the wounds which had been sustained by Van Buren's followers at the Baltimore convention. Wright was offered the Treasury. He declined it on the reasonable ground that he could not abandon the governorship. Polk then asked him to propose a candidate either for the State Department or for the Treasury. Thereupon Wright and Van Buren suggested the same men (Benjamin F. Butler for State and Azariah Flagg for the Treasury). But as things turned out, New York was given neither post, and the War Department was handed over to William Learned Marcy, a Hunker. The Van Buren wing was out in the cold. It received the news sullenly, and by a natural association of ideas it became more and more convinced that the South and those favorable to slavery were to have an altogether sinister influence upon the national administration.

"New York is, I fear, betrayed," wrote John A. Dix to Flagg, the day before Polk's inauguration. "I only desire to say that the President acts with full knowledge of the probable consequences and with a view of the whole ground." Dix had gone straight to Polk and had minced no words, but his warnings had been useless.[5]

The unhappiness of the Van Buren wing of the party was soon to be deepened. Frank Preston Blair was the close friend of Jackson and Van Buren. From near the beginning of Jackson's first term, Blair's news-

4 Flagg Papers, Preston King to Flagg, Dec. 31, 1844, Jan. 8, Feb. 8, 1845; Herbert D. H. Donovan, *The Barnburners* (New York, 1925), pp. 23–33, 48–73. The Tyler Administration had aided the Hunkers. Preston King believed that Foster's victory "would destroy the northern Democracy."

5 Flagg Papers, L. Stetson to Flagg, Dec. 31, 1844, Jan. 25, 1845, Flagg to Stetson, Feb. 2, 1845, Poinsett to Flagg, Dec. 6, 1844, Preston King to Flagg, Dec. 21, 1844, John A. Dix to Flagg, Mar. 3, 1845; Joseph G. Rayback, "Martin Van Buren's Break with James K. Polk," *New York History,* XXXVI (Jan., 1955), 51–60; McCormac, *Polk,* pp. 291–297, 338. McCormac believes that the Van Burenites had no cause for complaint. They thought otherwise.

paper, the Washington *Globe,* had been the mouthpiece of successive Democratic administrations, the organ of the Democracy at the Capital. Blair was sympathetic with the Barnburners. He and his paper were now discarded by Polk. A new administration organ, the *Union,* was established at the capital, with Tom Ritchie as editor. This step, taken over the objections of the dying Jackson, was a grievous blow to the New Yorkers. Once again, the southern influence appeared to be triumphant.[6]

From time to time, Polk made gestures toward healing the breach with the New Yorkers. Van Buren, and later Dix, were offered the London mission. Both declined. Flagg was sounded out on a possible Cabinet post, but was unreceptive to the idea. The Barnburners' view was that relations with Texas and Mexico were being handled with special consideration for "peculiar institutions and *peculiar men,*" and they were determined to retain their freedom of action. Their relations with the administration grew worse instead of better. In August, 1846, Dix wrote to Flagg that the presidential patronage was all going to the Hunkers, and that the President paid no attention, "even in the smallest matters," to the wishes of himself and his friends.[7] The Democratic party was in process of fragmentation. It was being slowly and inexorably pried apart by the leverage of local issues, the rivalries of ambitious men, and the growing divergence of sectional interest.

The Cabinet which Polk gathered about him was scarcely of distinguished caliber. Buchanan in the State Department was obstinate, petulant, and often timid in the face of responsibility. He longed for the Presidency, and was not above using his office to push himself toward his desired goal. Walker in the Treasury was able and industrious, but a speculator par excellence. Suspicion of involvement in the schemes of moneyed men hung over him like a cloud. Marcy was tactful and had ability, but was scarcely first rate. Bancroft had few qualifications for his post, the Navy, and left for a diplomatic mission after having been the prime mover in the founding of the Naval Academy at Annapolis. John Y. Mason of Virginia as Attorney General and Cave Johnson of Tennessee as Postmaster General were perfectly

[6] William E. Smith, *The Francis Preston Blair Family in Politics* (2 vols., New York, 1933), I, 156–157, 166–167, 170–175, 178–181; McCormac, *Polk,* pp. 299–300, 331–333; Wiltse, *Calhoun,* III, 222–224.

[7] Flagg Papers, Jn. Yawrence to Flagg, Oct. 23, 1845, John A. Dix to Flagg, July 17, Aug. 13, 1846; McCormac, *Polk,* p. 338.

respectable appointments, but that was all. It was scarcely a Ministry of All the Talents. Polk dominated it, seeking its advice, but rarely changing his views because of its counsels. It had, however, one outstanding feature. It was overwhelmingly expansionist.

March 4, 1845, was a dark and rainy day and Polk, as John Quincy Adams put it, delivered his inaugural "to a large assemblage of umbrellas." The new President made it clear that he disliked both abolition and disunion, and that he had no use for protective tariffs, a national bank, or a national debt. On the other hand, a tariff for revenue was strongly endorsed, the annexation of Texas received emphatic approval, and the United States' title to the Oregon country was declared to be "clear and unquestionable." It was evident that "Young Hickory," as his admirers called him, had a far-ranging gaze.

The program outlined in the inaugural received significant emphasis, a few days later, in a conversation between Polk and his Secretary of the Navy. Smiting his thigh for emphasis, the President told Bancroft that his administration would have four great measures. The tariff would be reduced, the Independent Treasury re-established, the Oregon boundary question settled, and California brought into the Union.[8] Texas, not yet admitted, was obviously taken for granted. If a President's quality is to be measured by the attainment of his goals, Polk should be rated as one of the greatest of America's Chief Executives.

Success in practical achievement is, however, only one measure of historical significance. Fully as important is the philosophy which underlies the action. The philosophy of the Polk administration is exemplified by the thinking of the President himself and that of his Secretary of the Treasury, Robert J. Walker. These men well represented the New Democracy of the eighteen-forties.

Polk's Jacksonianism appears on the surface to have been clear and unmistakable. His very nickname was significant. He had always been a foe of the Bank of the United States. He had been consistently opposed to internal improvements at national expense. He was a friend of graduation and pre-emption. The true policy of the government, he said in his first message to Congress, should be to help its citizens "to become the owners of small portions of our vast public domain at low and moderate rates." He feared Clay's American system, and an

[8] James Schouler, *History of the United States* (7 vols., New York, 1891–1913), IV, 498.

analysis of it, in one of his messages to Congress, throws considerable light upon his social and economic philosophy.

The exponents of the American system, Polk declared, were dazzled by the authority and glitter of European aristocracies. They were seeking to create a similar aristocracy in the United States. Hence they championed a powerful national bank, and the maintenance of a national debt that would furnish "aliment" to the bank. They also urged high protection, internal improvements, and distribution of the proceeds of land sales. These policies meant big government expenditures. Therefore, they also meant the maintenance of "a rich and splendid government at the expense of the taxed and impoverished people." The system would produce a "consolidated empire" instead of a federal union.

This Whig dream, said Polk, was vicious. In the first place, it was unconstitutional. It would also make the rich richer and the poor poorer. It would create distinctions in society based on wealth. Fortunately, of its various parts, only internal improvements remained a clear and present danger. But all aspects of the system must be sternly resisted; for if they were not, the whole evil framework would be established and "commercial revulsions, depression of prices, and pecuniary embarrassments" would again be the order of the day.[9]

Such was Polk's description of the core of Whiggism. It was scarcely the concept of Whig intent that was held by Horace Greeley and Abraham Lincoln.

Polk's regard for the poor was expressed in phrases reminiscent of those used by Jackson in his Bank veto. But when Young Hickory's humanitarianism came into conflict with his ideas about frugal government, his sympathy for the masses was not so evident. In 1831 he had opposed a congressional resolution which approved the giving of firewood to the Georgetown poor, lest it develop a lamentable tendency on the part of poor people to look to the government for relief, and a year later he had taken similar ground regarding a quasi-philanthropic project in silk culture. In Polk's opinion, congressmen were in Washington "to legislate on the great concerns of the Union, and not to give away the public property."[10]

[9] James D. Richardson, *A Compilation of the Messages and Papers of the Presidents* (11 vols., New York, 1910), IV, 2504–2512.

[10] Thomas H. Benton, *Abridgment of the Debates of Congress from 1789 to 1856* (16 vols., New York, 1857–61), XI, 306–307, 691–692; McCormac, *Polk,* pp. 657–658.

In his views of the scope and character of government, in his attitude toward the Union, Polk was in general a good Jacksonian. But his zeal for expansionism, as his administration was to show, went far beyond anything in the administrations of his two Democratic predecessors.

Robert John Walker was a more complex individual than Polk. A little man, weighing under a hundred pounds, plagued by a wheezy voice and chronic bad health, Walker had nevertheless an active mind, indomitable energy, and at times a mordant wit. His career abounded in contradictions. It showed more than a trace of antibankism, but at various times he avowed himself a friend of banks, worked closely with the banking fraternity, and was sometimes involved in unsavory banking deals. His land speculations were notorious, but he had also been an ardent advocate of the Jacksonian land policies which were supposedly for the benefit of the settlers. One of his main arguments for reduction of the tariff was that such a reduction would give the poor a better chance in the struggle of labor with capital, and yet he was more than anxious to raise some $3 million in revenue by a duty in the tariff of 1846 on tea and coffee, a duty that would have fallen very largely on the poorer classes of society.[11]

Walker was an ardent advocate of expansion, one of the prime movers in Texas annexation. He was also possessed of a healthy sense of skepticism, so far as the Jacksonian hard-money policy was concerned. He had fought to have the Specie Circular rescinded, and a clash with Benton in the middle eighteen-thirties had given him an opportunity to exercise his satirical gifts at the expense of Old Bullion's monetary concepts, in a fashion much enjoyed by the readers of the period.

> The distinction of the Senator in this respect was as incomprehensible to him [Mr. Walker] as he believed it was to every Senator, and, indeed, was discernible only by the magnifying powers of a solar microscope. It was a point-no-point, which, like the logarithmic spiral, or asymptote of the hyperbolic curve, might be forever approached without reaching; an infinitesimal, the ghost of an idea, not only without length, breadth, thickness, shape, weight, or dimensions, but without position . . . a mere imaginary nothing, which flitted before the bewildered vision of the honorable Senator, when traversing,

[11] H. Donaldson Jordan, "A Politician of Expansion," *Mississippi Valley Historical Review,* XIX (Dec., 1932), 363–365, 374–375; John S. Bassett (ed.), *Correspondence of Andrew Jackson* (7 vols., Washington, 1926–35), VI, 405.

in his fitful somnambulism, that tesselated pavement of gold, silver, and bullion which that Senator delighted to occupy. Sir, the Senator from Missouri might have heaped mountain high his piles of metal; he might have swept, in his Quixotic flight, over the banks of the states, putting to the sword their officers, stockholders, directory, and legislative bodies by which they were chartered; he might, in his reveries, have demolished their charters, and consumed their paper by the fire of his eloquence; he might have transacted, in fancy, with a metallic currency of twenty-eight millions in circulation, an actual annual business of fifteen hundred millions, and Mr. Walker would not have disturbed his beatific visions nor would any other Senator . . . for they were visions only, that could never be realized.[12]

Both Polk and Walker may be called Jacksonian Democrats without unduly perverting the meaning of the term. But it was a Jacksonianism in which the sense of values had shifted. Hard money had lost its fascination, expansionism, while not unknown to the Democrats of the eighteen-thirties, had become predominant in the thinking of the New Jacksonians. They were also inclining toward domestic policies that aligned them somewhat more clearly with southern desires than had been the case with the Jacksonians of the preceding decade. In accordance with southern sentiment, they were dedicated to a distinctly lower tariff. In harmony with the southern viewpoint, they were turning a deaf ear to the demands for internal improvements and for free lands that were welling up more and more strongly from the North and West. The West could be temporarily appeased for the failure to satisfy these aspirations by administration support for the acquisition of California and Oregon, especially since California was also a lodestar for southern eyes, but the immutable fact remained that the Democratic party organization was beginning to pass under the rod of southern influence.

More and more Northerners were becoming alarmed by these trends in administration policy. New York's Democratic congressman, Lemuel Stetson, expressed the views of these northern Democrats when he told Azariah Flagg that by 1846 the Democratic party would have "so strong a smell of Nigger" that a quarter of its northern adherents would go abolitionist and the 1848 election would see "a great sectional war between the North and the South for control of the country." There was some ground for such forebodings.[13]

[12] *Congressional Globe,* 29th Congress, first session, Appendix, p. 821. Benton's speech on a proposed amendment to the bill for an Independent Treasury.

[13] Flagg Papers, Stetson to Flagg, Dec. 31, 1844.

It was inevitable that tariff reduction should be a prime consideration of the administration's policy. Polk had always been an opponent of protection. The support given him by Calhoun in the election of 1844 had been due to South Carolina's expectation that a Democratic victory would mean not only the acquisition of Texas but a lowered tariff as well. This point of view was shared, although somewhat less fervently, in other parts of the South. The lower-tariff drive was also aided by the fact that 1845 had seen an excess of government receipts over expenditures, and a similar situation was anticipated for the ensuing year. Protectionists were in a decided minority in the Twenty-ninth Congress, where a free trader, John W. Davis of Indiana, was elected Speaker, and the Committee on Ways and Means had a majority favoring tariff reduction. Something was going to be done about the tariff, something that Whigs and Pennsylvania and New York Democrats were not going to like.[14]

When Congress assembled in December, 1845, Polk's message asked for a revenue tariff bill, with incidental protection. A revenue tariff meant, to the President, at its maximum a duty level which, if raised only 1 per cent, would result in a lowering of receipts. Polk did not want such a maximum tariff, for he believed that it would result in an excess of revenue over needs. Neither did he want a horizontal scale. He held that the more generally an article of necessity was used, the lower should be the duty, a point of view which certainly showed consideration for the wants and needs of the masses. Finally, Polk held that such incidental protection as the tariff afforded should apply equally to agriculture, manufacturing, commerce, and labor. If it did not do so, the protection given would be inequitably applied. This was the theory of a perfectionist and, strictly interpreted, would have resulted in little protection indeed.

The President's request for a revenue tariff was supplemented by Secretary Walker's report, an able argument for the reduction of duties. In general agreement with the President's position, it made certain additional points. A maximum revenue duty, Walker held, should be imposed on all luxuries. Minimum duties based on artificial

[14] McCormac, *Polk*, p. 656; Wiltse, *Calhoun*, III, 185; William M. Meigs, *The Life of John Caldwell Calhoun* (2 vols., New York, 1917), II, 248–262; Davis R. Dewey, *Financial History of the United States* (rev. ed., 1934), p. 249; Edward Stanwood, *Tariff Controversies in the Nineteenth Century* (2 vols., Boston, 1903), II, 69–70.

valuations, and all specific duties, should be abolished. He denounced the tariff of 1842 as discriminatory and socially unjust. The tariff should show no favoritism for any class or section, he declared, and he stressed the importance of using lowered duties to give labor a better chance in its unequal struggle with capital for a higher standard of living.[15]

Able and persuasive as Walker's argument was, it was vulnerable in certain aspects. It is not necessarily true, as he declared it was, that the price of an imported article, enhanced by duty, *ipso facto* raises the price of the like domestic product. His claim that if England would repeal her duties on our agricultural products the overthrow of the American protective system would be the inevitable result was to be proven historically inaccurate. Walker disclaimed any prejudice against manufacturers, but his decided preference was for an agrarian society. "Agriculture," he declared, "is our chief employment; it is best adapted to our situation, and if not depressed by the tariff would be most profitable." Remove the tariff, Walker asserted, and the American agricultural output would break down foreign tariffs and "would feed the hungry and clothe the poor of our fellow men throughout all the densely populated nations of the world." The little Secretary of the Treasury was dreaming of a nation that would develop along lines that had been dear to the heart of Thomas Jefferson.

On April 14, 1846, Chairman McKay of the House Ways and Means Committee reported a revenue bill based on the recommendations of Polk and Walker. All duties were to be put on an ad valorem basis. Commodities were organized in schedules, ranging from a group of luxuries with duties at 100 per cent to a group on the free list. As time was to prove, the duty rate averaged about 25 per cent.

The debate that followed the introduction of this bill ranged the whole gamut of national welfare, but it was heavily imbued with politics and local interest. War with Mexico broke out while the bill was under consideration, and its opponents declared that it would diminish the now much-needed revenue. It was asserted that the ad valorem duties were certain to invite customhouse frauds, and that they would protect the manufacturer least when he needed protection the most. Protectionists maintained that lowering the duties would be

[15] *Congressional Globe,* 29th Cong., first sess., Appendix, pp. 1–13; Richardson, *Messages and Papers,* III, 2253–2256; Frank W. Taussig, *State Papers and Speeches on the Tariff* (Cambridge, 1892), pp. 219–251.

sure to unsettle the business community, damaging some industries and ruining others. It would expose American labor to the competition of underpaid European labor.

Whigs and not a few Democrats joined in this assault on the Walker bill. Secretary of State Buchanan opposed it, as did Senators Simon Cameron of Pennsylvania and John M. Niles of Connecticut. Buchanan preferred the tariff of 1842 to the pending bill. David Wilmot of Pennsylvania was the state's only Democratic member of the House delegation who favored the bill, and even he wavered in his loyalty. The New York Democratic delegation was decidedly unenthusiastic. They favored a measure known as the McKay bill of 1844, a moderate, compromising reduction of the tariff of 1842 that had stirred ultra-Southerners to deep resentment. There was also dissatisfaction with the measure among the Democratic members of the House from Virginia.[16]

The proponents of the Walker tariff, as it was called, were not slow in rallying to its defense. They denounced the tariff of 1842 as a "tariff of abominations." Protection was derided as rank favoritism to the wealthy and privileged. Specific duties were declared, with reason, to discriminate against the poor. The supporters of the bill denied that it would damage the industrial interests of the country. On the contrary, they prophesied, it would have a most healthful influence on the national economy.

The outcome in the House was never really uncertain. The bill passed that body, July 3, 1846, by a vote of 114 to 95, a vote cast mainly along party lines. Eighteen Democrats, including eleven from Pennsylvania and four from New York, voted against it. Only two Whigs, both from the South, voted for it. The slaveholding South gave fifty-six votes for the bill to twenty against it, eleven of the twenty coming from Kentucky and Tennessee.

The Senate took up the tariff bill on July 6. The fight in its behalf was led by Senator Dixon H. Lewis, a veritable mountain of a man weighing 450 pounds, a devoted exponent of states' rights, whose views on the tariff and internal improvements coincided with those of Polk.

[16] Flagg Papers, Dix to Flagg, July 30, Sept. 7, 1846; Daniel Webster, *Writings and Speeches* (18 vols., Boston, 1903), IV, 63–66; Ann M. B. Coleman (ed.), *The Life of John J. Crittenden* (2 vols., Philadelphia, 1871), I, 248; McCormac, *Polk*, pp. 251–252; Malcolm R. Eiselen, *The Rise of Pennsylvania Protectionism* (Philadelphia, 1932), pp. 184, 192–193; Stanwood, *Tariff Controversies,* II, 39, 72–73; Dewey, *Financial History,* pp. 251–252; Wiltse, *Calhoun,* III, 173–174.

Once again the Whigs swarmed to the attack, and here the outcome was more doubtful. The bill would not have passed but for the casting vote of Vice-President Dallas on some of the crucial ballots, a vote which was cast in obedience to party dictates, for Dallas was a protectionist. Finally, modified by an amendment offered by Webster which guarded against the undervaluation of imports, the measure was accepted by a vote of twenty-eight to twenty-seven. The House concurred in the amendment and Polk signed the bill July 31, 1846.

The tariff of 1846 had neither such dismal effects as had been predicted by its foes nor such happy consequences as were foretold by its proponents. Prosperity and adversity being always the result of a complex of factors, the Walker tariff was at most only a contributory cause of the economic developments of the succeeding years. Statistics for the eighteen-forties are inadequate, but such as there are indicate that this measure, like the tariff of 1842, had only a negligible effect upon prices and wages. The finer grades of woolen manufacture in the United States were apparently destroyed by the lower duties of 1846, but the manufacture of the cheaper grades, and of all grades of cotton goods, steadily expanded. It is possible that the manufacture of iron was somewhat retarded, but, on the other hand, the lower tariff facilitated the import of iron sorely needed for railroad expansion and helped to eliminate inferior methods of iron production in the United States. Greeley, who had made dismal prophecies about the effects of the measure, privately confessed in 1847 that within ten years the need for a protective tariff would have largely disappeared.

The tariff of 1846 had no profound effect upon the national economy, but in two respects it was historically significant. It was primarily responsible for introducing the warehouse system of handling imports that is still in use. Secondly, it resumed the trend toward free trade that, only temporarily halted in 1842, lasted until the outbreak of the Civil War.[17] Such a trend was natural, almost inevitable, in view of the general movement toward free trade that was then developing in the western world. It also harmonized with America's need for markets in which to dispose of its rapidly growing agricultural sur-

[17] Fred J. Guetter and Albert E. McKinley, *Statistical Tables Relating to the Economic Growth of the United States* (Philadelphia, 1924), p. 46; Stanwood, *Tariff Controversies,* II, 64; Taussig, *Tariff,* pp. 128–135, 140–148, 152; Dewey, *Financial History,* p. 252; Glyndon G. Van Deusen, *Horace Greeley, Nineteenth Century Crusader* (Philadelphia, 1953), p. 105.

pluses. Clay's American system, had it been fully applied, would have experienced difficulty in maintaining a high degree of protection against European manufactured goods, while at the same time the American farmer was seeking to dispose in foreign markets of the flood of agricultural products resulting from the rapid development of the frontier areas and the tremendous strides that were being made in transportation.

While the Walker tariff was wending its way through Congress, the administration was also pushing toward its second domestic objective, the reinstitution of the Independent Treasury. In vain Polk's friend, Supreme Court Justice Catron, had warned against the idea of separating the government from the banking operations of the country, calling it an "absurd shadow"; in vain Catron had described the hard-money concept as one "deemed a feeble and exploded theory, by the people." The President was a neo-Jacksonian and a determined man. His advocacy of what he called a "constitutional treasury" in his message to Congress in December, 1845, was a call to battle for an institution dear to the hearts of the left-wing Democracy. It was also a propitiatory offering to Van Buren and his followers.[18]

On March 30, 1846, the Independent Treasury bill made its appearance on the floor of the House. Once again the government was to be separated from the banks. Under the measure, government dues could be collected only in gold, silver, or Treasury notes, and disbursements could be made only in gold, silver, or drafts on the various places of deposits.

In the House, and later in the Senate, the Whigs concentrated some of their heaviest fire on the bill. Caleb B. Smith of Indiana offered an amendment authorizing the government to deposit its money in banks, and to receive government dues in the paper of specie-paying banks. There was no hope for this amendment and it was soon withdrawn,[19] but Smith and the other Whigs continued their attacks. They declared that the bill would encourage defalcations by placing large sums of money in the hands of government employees; that, as a result of its passage, millions of dollars would lie idle in government vaults instead of being put to use in developing the nation's economy. Smith correctly pointed out that both of these arguments had been used by Polk him-

[18] Polk Papers, Catron to Polk, Jan. 2, 1842; Flagg Papers, Dix to Flagg, Dec. 26, 1845; McCormac, *Polk,* pp. 660–661, 663, 667.

[19] *Congressional Globe,* 29th Cong., first sess., 594.

self in 1835, when William F. Gordon had proposed an Independent Treasury and Polk and the other administration Democrats would have none of it. The Whigs also charged that the bill would result in millions of specie being locked up in the Treasury, thus creating an abnormal demand for specie and greatly diminishing bank-note circulation; that it would destroy confidence and paralyze enterprise; that it was a "cruel, wanton, and wicked" plot to destroy the banks of the country.

The Democrats repelled these charges with scorn. They described the measure as a high-principled effort to destroy the monstrous evils of paper money and financial privilege. It would serve as a healthful deterrent to the inflationary and dishonest propensities of the state banks. Far from being dangerous or extreme, it was conservative of the best in American financial practice. "Our radicalism," said Representative Charles J. Ingersoll of Pennsylvania, with perhaps more truth than he realized, "has never gone beyond restoration."

The bill was not a 100 per cent hard-money measure. It provided for the use of Treasury notes in the payment of government dues. Walker, himself no hard-money man, even asked for an amendment permitting Treasury agents to use in their disbursements drafts that could not be exchanged at par. Benton pounced on this as providing for a "federal paper money currency," and the proposal was modified, but the bill still did not prohibit Treasury drafts being used as currency.[20]

The Independent Treasury Act passed the House on April 2, 1848, by a vote of 122–66. It was shepherded through the Senate by Calhoun's follower, the mountainous Dixon H. Lewis. It passed the Senate August 1, with some fairly insignificant amendments, by a vote of 28–25. The House concurred in the amendments and President Polk signed the bill on August 8.

The Independent Treasury Act represented a roundabout and largely ineffectual effort to obtain the benefits of a central banking service without having a central banking system. By this act, the Treasury became virtually a bank of issue. From 1846 to 1848, it put out over $32 million in Treasury notes, retiring all but $200,000 of

[20] *Congressional Globe,* 29th Cong., first sess., Appendix, pp. 582–583, 592–594, 820–821, 1176; A. T. Huntington and Robert J. MaWhinney, *Laws of the United States Concerning Money, Banking, and Loans, 1778–1909* (Washington, 1910), pp. 136–141; Coleman, *Crittenden* I, 249; United States, *Statutes at Large,* IX, 59 ff.

these by 1850. It probably helped to prevent an inflationary movement during the Mexican War, but during the balance of the nineteenth century it exercised relatively little influence on business conditions. This was due to the fact that, save during wartime, government receipts and expenditures were more often than not on a fairly even balance. The development of a public debt and wise administration of surplus revenue prevented the hoarding of gold and silver that could logically have been expected to derive from the act.[21]

Polk's zeal for the Independent Treasury was only equaled by his dislike of internal improvements at the expense of the national government. The demand for such improvements was on the increase, and Horace Greeley beat a strident drum for action in the columns of the New York *Tribune.* As the national population mounted by leaps and bounds, as national prosperity increased, and as American territory expanded to the Pacific, it was only natural that the clamor for government aid in hastening the transportation revolution should rise.

In December of 1844, Asa Whitney of New York presented the first well-developed plan for a railroad to the Pacific. A year later, Stephen A. Douglas proposed a similar project. Both depended to a considerable extent on government aid. In the summer of 1847, at a great Rivers and Harbors Convention held in Chicago, some 20,000 Americans expressed the growing demand for federal aid in internal improvements, and once again the building of a Pacific railroad was given prominent attention.[22]

But despite the signs of the times, Polk remained obdurate. Governor Polk had urged upon the Tennessee legislature the immense importance of clearing navigable rivers and making other improvements in transportation. President Polk remorselessly vetoed rivers and harbors bills

[21] Esther R. Taus, *Central Banking Functions of the United States Treasury, 1789–1941* (New York, 1943), pp. 50–51; Henry P. Willis, *The Theory and Practice of Central Banking* (New York, 1936), pp. 61–62; John J. Knox, *United States Notes* (New York, 1884), pp. 61–70; William G. Sumner, *A History of American Currency* (New York, 1874), pp. 166–167; David Kinley, "The Influence on Business of the Independent Treasury," *Annals of the American Academy of Political and Social Science,* III (Sept., 1892), 180–210.

[22] *Niles' Register,* July 31, Aug. 7, 1847; Robert R. Russell, *Improvement of Communications with the Pacific Coast as an Issue in American Politics, 1783–1864* (Cedar Rapids, 1948), pp. 10–16; Albert J. Beveridge, *Abraham Lincoln* (2 vols., Boston, 1928), I, 386–388; George R. Taylor, *The Transportation Revolution, 1815–1860* (New York, 1951), *passim.*

passed by Congress. When, in October, 1848, Buchanan proposed that a survey be made for a railroad or canal across the Isthmus of Panama (where a recent treaty with New Grenada had given United States citizens the right of passage), Polk quashed the idea by remarking that no constitutional authority existed for either a survey or the construction of such a road. The government, said the President firmly, had no more right to make external improvements than it had to make them within the country. If any such bill passed Congress, he would veto it.[23] Polk had come to regard internal improvements by the national government with a dislike that was fanatical in its intensity.

[23] Milo M. Quaife (ed.), *The Diary of James K. Polk* (4 vols., Chicago, 1910), IV, 139–140; Richardson, *Messages and Papers,* IV, 2310–2319, 2460–2476; Sellers, *Polk,* p. 396; McCormac, *Polk,* pp. 683–684.

CHAPTER 11

Dangerous Diplomacy

THE DEVELOPMENT of domestic policy, important though it was for the country's future, absorbed only a minor portion of the time and energy of the Polk administration. As befitted an era of expansion, when frontiersmen were pushing into Texas and Oregon and California, and Yankee skippers were trading from California to Zanzibar and the ports of southeast Asia, 1845 to 1849 were years of intense diplomatic activity which made American influence felt in various quarters of the globe. Though unwilling to survey a route across the isthmus of Panama, the United States government did guarantee the neutrality of the isthmus by its treaty with New Grenada, and was quick to show its displeasure when Latin American states manifested a disposition to establish close relations with France or England. Reciprocity treaties stimulated trade with Latin America, and with Europe as well, and the government in Washington demonstrated an increasing interest in developing trade relations with China and Japan. It looked with longing upon Cuba, a longing stimulated by the fear that Spain might sell that island to a foreign power, and, only to be rebuffed, Polk offered $100 million for this Pearl of the Antilles. By methods diplomatic and military, Washington gained sole title in the Northwest as far as the Straits of Vancouver and acquired an empire in the Southwest that stretched from Texas to California.

Oregon was the object of Polk's greatest attention at the beginning of his administration. The treaty between the United States and Great Britain in 1818 had left that area in the joint occupation of the two powers, both of which, by the eighteen-forties, had claims to the region by virtue of exploration and settlement. Joint occupation had been extended indefinitely in 1827, with the proviso that it might be terminated by either party on a year's notice. Such was the situation when Polk took office in 1845. By that time a variety of factors had made the status of Oregon an explosive issue.

The country around Vancouver was a fur-trading region and the Hudson's Bay Company, a British concern, occupied a strategic position in the area. It had established a trading post on the Columbia River. It had also developed a policy of encouraging agricultural settlements in the surrounding territory, glowing reports of which had aroused the interest of American pioneers. By 1843, hundreds of bold and hardy spirits had taken the Oregon Trail that stretched from the wide Missouri across the Great Divide and into this land of promise. These Americans settled principally in the Willamette Valley, south of the Columbia.

Out of the interest aroused by this settlement and the expansionist fever of the eighteen-forties, especially as manifested in the western states, came a rising American clamor for an end to joint occupation and for the assertion of America's claim to the entire region from the lower borders of Oregon to the southern limits of the Alaska Panhandle. "Fifty-four forty or fight" was the cry. The Democratic demand in the election of 1844 for the "reoccupation" of Oregon had reflected this clamor, and Polk declared in his inaugural that the title of the United States to Oregon was "clear and unquestionable." This statement aroused a storm of anger in Great Britain.[1]

Interest in Oregon increased from year to year. In vain South Carolina's George McDuffie declared in the Senate that Oregon was unfit for settlement; that all the wealth of the Indies could never build a railroad to the mouth of the Columbia; that people living 5,000 miles apart could not possibly be under the same government; that he would not give a pinch of snuff for the crops that could be raised in the territory.[2] Three thousand eager Americans moved into the new land in 1845, and the population of the Willamette Valley doubled. More

[1] James D. Richardson, *A Compilation of the Messages and Papers of the Presidents* (11 vols., New York, 1910), III, 2231; Frederick Merk, "British Government Propaganda and the Oregon Treaty," *American Historical Review,* XL (Oct., 1934), 38–42.

[2] *Congressional Globe,* 27th Congress, third session, 199–200.

and more attention was also paid to the Vancouver region as a base for expanding commercial activity in the northern Pacific area.

The fact that Monroe's administration, and each that succeeded it, had offered the 49th parallel as a compromise dividing line for the territory established a precedent for American action. This precedent had weight with Polk, as did the critical state of relations that was rapidly developing between the United States and Mexico. Privately, hc was for compromisc, and in July, 1845, he and Buchanan offered the 49th parallel, together with the freedom of any ports on Vancouver Island that Britain might desire. No mention was made in this offer of the free navigation of the Columbia which had been proposed in previous American proposals.

Pakenham, the British envoy at Washington, refused Polk's offer. It was thereupon withdrawn, the President falling back upon his claim to the whole territory. He went even further, and in his message of December, 1845, advocated giving the stipulated year's notice of termination of joint occupation. Compromise on British terms, he declared, was impossible. At the end of the year's notice, Congress should decide whether to abandon or maintain our rights in Oregon. They could not be abandoned, he told Congress, without sacrificing both national honor and national interest.[3]

This was bold talk. Its effect was heightened when, a few weeks later, Polk told a Congressman who feared that the government's course was leading to war that "the only way to treat John Bull was to look him straight in the eye." Any other course, said Polk, made the British government more arrogant and grasping in its demands.

As the President had requested, a resolution was passed by both houses of Congress authorizing Polk to give notice of the abrogation of the convention of 1827. This was done only after bitter wrangling that threatened to tear the Democratic party to pieces. Democrats from the Old Northwest, such as Senator Edward A. Hannegan of Indiana, were vociferous in support of a strong and peremptory statement, while Calhoun and the southern Democrats in general favored a more conciliatory attitude toward Great Britain. Those who followed Calhoun joined with the Whigs (who often represented financial and commercial interests that were interested in preserving good relations with England) in so modifying the resolution in the Senate that it expressed

[3] Richardson, *Messages and Papers,* III, 2247.

a hope of compromise, a promise of the Senate's co-operation in an amicable adjustment. Thus amended, the notice passed both houses, April 23, 1846.[4]

Polk signed the resolution passed by Congress, though without much enthusiasm. He confided to his diary that he would have preferred "a simple naked Resolution," and the notice he sent to England a few days later was merely a formal announcement that notice was thereby given.[5] McLane was also told that any further proposal for adjustment of the Oregon question must come from Britain.

The President was still, apparently, looking John Bull straight in the eye. This was, however, a nineteenth-century game of "brinkmanship," something that Henry Clay would have characterized as a game of bluff or "brag." Polk undoubtedly saw that persistence in an ultra stand would mean running a greater risk of splitting his party than would final recourse to compromise. He was definitely alarmed by reports of military and naval preparations in Great Britain, where the Foreign Minister, Lord Aberdeen, though desirous of peace, was preparing for the worst because of his uncertainty as to the real designs of the United States government. Simultaneous war with England and Mexico was not pleasant to contemplate, and as early as February, 1846, war with Mexico was almost a certainty. Finally, the American President must have been aware of the rapidly growing opinion in influential quarters outside of Congress that ports on the Pacific were more important than territory; that the area north of the 49th parallel was not worth a war, so long as the United States had access through the Vancouver Straits to the ocean; and that compromise with the British in Oregon was necessary, if they were to be kept from getting a slice of a greater prize, California.[6]

Before February, 1846, was over, Secretary Buchanan had told Louis McLane in London that if Britain made a new offer, it would be submitted to the Senate. A few weeks later the British government was

[4] *Congressional Globe,* 29th Cong., first sess., 678–683, 716–721; Milo M. Quaife (ed.), *The Diary of James K. Polk* (4 vols., Chicago, 1910), I, 155.

[5] *Ibid.,* I, 360–363.

[6] *Ibid.,* I, 153–156; Julius W. Pratt, "James K. Polk and John Bull," *Canadian Historical Review,* XXIV (Dec., 1943), 341–349; Robert L. Schuyler, "Polk and the Oregon Compromise of 1846," *Political Science Quarterly,* XXI (Sept., 1911), 443–461; St. George L. Sioussat, "James Buchanan," in Samuel F. Bemis (ed.), *The American Secretaries of State and Their Diplomacy* (10 vols., New York, 1927–29), V, 261; Norman A. Graebner, *Empire on the Pacific* (New York, 1955), pp. 126–137.

again informed that a proposal of the 49th parallel by Britain would in all probability be placed before the Senate by the President. This, coupled with the tone of the notice resolution as it had been amended by the Senate, was not as wide as a church door, but it would serve.

Britain responded positively to the American suggestions. The only area really in dispute was that between the Columbia and the 49th parallel. The Hudson's Bay Company, due to the pressure of the United States settlements, had shifted its main depot from the Columbia to the tip of Vancouver Island, and had thus eliminated one of the main reasons for Britain's insisting upon the Columbia as a boundary. Edward Everett's skillful diplomacy had prompted the English Whig leader, Lord John Russell, to give Aberdeen assurance that he would not make giving up the Columbia a party question. This had relieved the British government of much of its fear of denunciation by that "half hornet, half butterfly," Lord Palmerston. Aberdeen and those supporting a peace policy could and did point out that the fur trade in the Pacific Northwest was a dying industry; that the Columbia was not the western outlet of Canada; that concession harmonized with the prospective British reversal of tariff policy and with the promotion of international good will.[7]

It was under these circumstances that Britain once again advanced the proposal of a compromise at the 49th parallel. On June 10, 1846, Polk submitted the British offer to the Senate without recommendation. The United States was then at war with Mexico. The Senate acted swiftly and affirmatively. The treaty was signed by Buchanan and Pakenham on June 15, and three days later the Senate sanctioned ratification by a vote of forty-one to fourteen. The only opposition which was at all formidable came from a small group of ultra-expansionists representing the Old Northwest.

The Oregon treaty made the 49th parallel the dividing line between Canada and the United States in the region west of the Rockies. This line extended "to the middle of the channel" separating the continent

[7] *Ibid.*, pp. 137–149; Henry S. Commager, "England and Oregon Treaty of 1846," *Oregon Historical Quarterly,* XXVII (Mar., 1927), 18–38; Frederick Merk, "The British Corn Crisis of 1845–46 and the Oregon Treaty," "British Government Propaganda and the Oregon Treaty," "British Party Politics and the Oregon Treaty," and "The Oregon Pioneers and the Boundary," in, respectively, *Agricultural History,* VIII (July, 1934), 95–123; *American Historical Review,* XL (Oct., 1934), 38–62, XXXVIII (July, 1932), 653–677, XXIX (July, 1924), 681–699.

from Vancouver Island and thence (in a line that later had to be arbitrated) to the Pacific. It made navigation of the Columbia free to the Hudson's Bay Company, and guaranteed respect for the property rights of British subjects in the territory appropriated by the United States.

Viewed in the large, the negotiation of the treaty and the terms of the settlement itself were creditable to Polk and his administration. Both parties to the agreement viewed the result with general satisfaction. It was a milestone in what was to be a lasting era of peace between

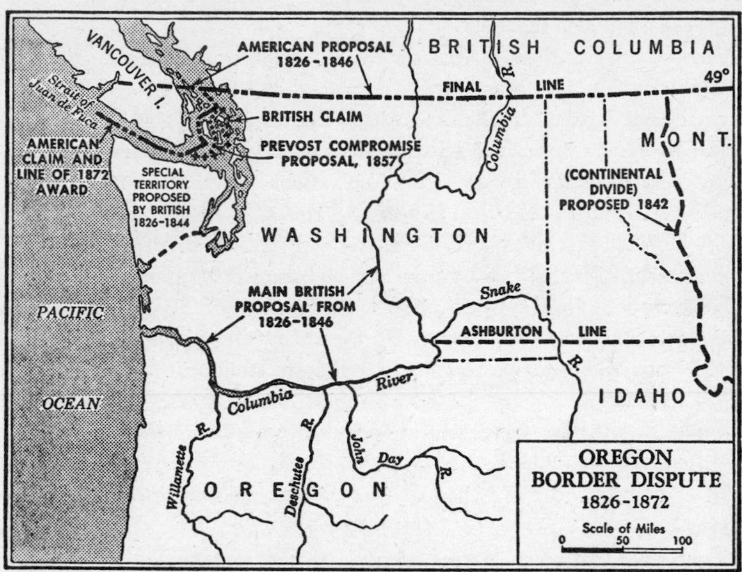

the two great English-speaking countries. And it freed the American government for full concentration upon the war with Mexico.

That war had been brewing ever since the joint resolution for annexing Texas had passed Congress, early in 1845. Promptly upon that passage, special agents had carried to Texas the invitation to join the Union. Both President Anson Jones of Texas and Sam Houston were disappointed that there was no opportunity to arrange terms by negotiation. Both disliked the terms offered.[8]

[8] Llerena Friend, *Sam Houston, the Great Designer* (Austin, 1954), pp. 138–139; Herbert P. Gambrell, *Anson Jones* (New York, 1948), pp. 394–404.

England tried to prevent annexation by urging Mexico to recognize Texas, on condition that the Lone Star State refuse the American offer. France seconded England. But Polk's agents came bearing gifts in the shape of lavish promises of fortifications and internal improvements, and popular opinion in Texas was overwhelmingly in favor of joining fortunes with the United States. The offer of annexation was accepted by the legislature and a state convention in the summer of 1845. A state constitution was then framed. It was approved by the United States government on December 29, 1845. In February, 1846, the old Texas government was replaced by a state government. Texas had at last entered the Union.[9]

Mexico was ridden by foreign debts, its credit was exhausted and its government was weak and trembling on the verge of chaos. It nevertheless reacted violently to the Texas developments. Weak as Mexico was, its mood and attitude were warlike. Its leaders apparently believed that its army was better and its soldiers braver than those of the United States; and that if war did come, it could count on assistance, perhaps on military support, from abroad. General Almonte, the Mexican Minister to the United States, broke off diplomatic relations on March 6, 1845, in protest against the joint resolution of annexation. The Mexican press resounded with cries for war. By the first of April, 1845, Polk had information leading him to believe that Mexico had 8,000 to 10,000 men on the Rio Grande. On July 20, 1845, as it became apparent that Texas would accept annexation, President Herrera of Mexico recommended that the Mexican Congress declare war as soon as annexation was concluded, or at least as soon as United States troops "invaded" Texas.[10]

The American government did not quail before the Mexican threats. Quite the contrary. Buchanan told Almonte, before that gentleman left his post in Washington, that the annexation of Texas was irrevocable. The tone of this communication was not minatory, but strong naval detachments were sent to the Mexican coasts, and on June 15, 1845, General Zachary Taylor was ordered from Fort Jesup, on the

[9] Richard R. Stenberg, "President Polk and the Annexation of Texas," *Southwestern Social Science Quarterly,* XIV (Mar., 1934), 351–355; Eugene C. Barker, "The Annexation of Texas," *Southwestern Historical Quarterly,* L (July, 1946), 70–72; Sioussat, "Buchanan," V, 245–246.

[10] Russell B. Nye, *George Bancroft* (New York, 1944), pp. 151–152; Justin H. Smith, *The War with Mexico* (2 vols., New York, 1919), I, 87–88; George T. Curtis, *Life of Daniel Webster* (2 vols., New York, 1870), I, 589.

western border of Louisiana, to such stations "on or near" the Rio Grande as would be best suited to repel invasion. He took his stand at Corpus Christi, on the south side of the mouth of the Nueces River, with some 1,500 troops under his command. By November, 1845, his force had been recruited to about 4,000 men.

Taylor's move south of the Nueces highlighted a controversial problem—the boundary between Texas and Mexico. The Texans asserted that the Rio Grande was the boundary. Mexico, still claiming all of Texas as her territory, defined the southeastern limit of Texas Province as the Nueces River.

As a Mexican department, Texas had extended only to the Nueces. West and south of that river the land had belonged to the department of Tamaulipas. Certainly Texas had never established either a government or even a settlement between the two rivers. So clear was the evidence that even some of the Americans supporting annexation of Texas had held that acceptance of Texas' boundary claims would be an injustice to Mexico.[11] To say the least, the claim of Texas to the Rio Grande as a boundary was highly doubtful. Taylor's move across the Nueces was a move into disputed territory which was properly subject to negotiation rather than occupation.

Polk did not think so. He was determined to maintain Texas' claim to the Rio Grande boundary. The evidence indicates that he, or at least agents of his administration, urged Texas to occupy the area between the two rivers even before Texas had been admitted into the Union. Certain it is that Texas was informed from Washington that the claim to the Rio Grande boundary would be upheld, and Taylor was told to regard any Mexican crossing the Rio Grande as an act of war.[12] By August, 1845, the Whig *National Intelligencer* in Washington was declaring that Polk intended to make war on Mexico.

Polk did not believe that he was provoking Mexico into war. He

[11] McCormac, *Polk,* p. 408; William C. Binkley, *The Expansionist Movement in Texas* (Berkeley, 1925), pp. 124–129; Leroy P. Graf, "Colonizing Projects in Texas South of the Nueces, 1820–1845," *Southwestern Historical Quarterly,* L (Apr., 1947), 431–448.

[12] Gambrell, *Anson Jones,* pp. 400–401; Stenberg, "The Failure of Polk's Mexican War Intrigue," *Pacific Historical Review,* IV (1935), 39–68, and "Intrigue for Annexation," *Southwest Review,* XXV (Oct., 1939), 58–69; Binkley, *Expansionist Movement,* pp. 125–126; McCormac, *Polk,* pp. 377, 381–382; Charles M. Wiltse, *John C. Calhoun* (3 vols., Indianapolis, 1944–51), III, 274.

seems to have felt that a show of force would prevent, rather than provoke, war. "We shall not be the aggressors upon Mexico," he told a congressman in August, 1845. He knew that Mexico was weak, that it had no money with which to pay the claims of American and British nationals, and that any payments that might be made would have to be in land. His strategy seems to have been to take a strong stand as to the Rio Grande boundary, the while he protested his peaceful intentions, and at the same time to keep up a steady pressure for the satisfaction of American claims, this pressure being accompanied by dangling a bait of millions of dollars for additional territorial cessions. California was especially on his mind. He would run the risk of war for the sake of the potential gains involved. Polk was now looking the Mexicans in the eye, but this time the result was to be war.[13]

American interest in California was increasing in the early eighteen-forties. By the middle of that decade California possessed a population of 7,000 to 8,000 residents of Spanish descent and 800 or 900 American pioneers. Mexico's hold upon the province had always been weak. It was now growing weaker, just at a time when the fever of expansionism was sweeping over the United States. Tales of the beauty and fertility of the Californian paradise filtered back into the East. San Francisco Bay was already important for the California trade in hides. The prospective transcontinental railroad stimulated dreams of the Golden Gate as an entrepôt for trade with the Orient. Polk's interest in expansion to the Pacific centered to a large extent in ports, commerce, and whale fisheries. He was motivated, as the instructions of the administration to its agents show, by the commercial opportunities available on all sides of that vast ocean.

Fear of California's falling into other hands stimulated desire for its possession. During the summer and autumn of 1845, disquieting reports reached Washington from United States officials in England, Mexico, and California as to English and French interest in this prize. These reports were exaggerated. The European powers, while distinctly loath to see California acquired by the United States, had no intention of seizing it for themselves. But Washington regarded the danger of a

[13] Graebner, *Empire,* p. 114; Nye, *Bancroft,* pp. 151, 153–154. The diplomatic negotiations of this period and the outbreak of hostilities are well described from the Mexican point of view in Vito Alessio Robles, *Coahuila y Texas* (2 vols., Mexico, 1945, 1946), II, 303–336.

foreign, and especially of a British, lodgment on the California coast as being very real indeed.

Polk had a twofold policy regarding California. One policy was that of purchase. There was always the possibility that Mexico's empty treasury, its need for American gold, might result in the sale of the territory to the United States. The other possibility was that of watchful waiting, with perhaps a little covert encouragement, for California to follow the path marked out by Texas and separate itself from Mexican control. Annexation might then easily follow.

The Californians of Spanish descent were not really loyal to Mexico. The American pioneers had no love for Mexican control. Buchanan told Thomas O. Larkin, the American consul and later secret agent at Monterey, that while of course we would take no part in any conflict between California and Mexico, if the former became independent we would welcome her as a sister republic and render her all the kind offices within our power. The obvious implication here was that, within the limits of discretion, Larkin could exercise considerable latitude in fostering revolution in California. Secretary of the Navy Bancroft ordered Commodore Sloat, who was cruising with a squadron off Mazatlán on the west coast of Mexico, to keep in touch with Larkin and assist him in his California maneuvers. The dashing John Charles Frémont was sent from Washington in the spring of 1845 to survey a route to the Pacific coast that would run deep into the Mexican possessions. He was ordered to visit California as far south as the mouth of the Colorado River. Nobody bothered to obtain a passport for him. There is no evidence that he had instructions to stir up revolt, but private advices from Bancroft suggested that, if necessary to prevent England's seizing California, he might carry into California territory any war that broke out between Mexico and the United States.[14] One way or another, sooner or later, Polk was determined that California should become a part of the United States.

The California situation was the immediate inspiration for Polk's

[14] *Senate Executive Documents,* 30th Cong., first sess., No. 52, pp. 78–79; Graebner, *Empire,* pp. 63, 99, 108–112, 119; Ephraim D. Adams, "English Interest in California," *American Historical Review,* XIV (July, 1909), 748–763; Smith, *War with Mexico,* I, 324–325; Jesse S. Rives, *American Diplomacy Under Tyler and Polk* (Baltimore, 1907), pp. 278–280; Nye, *Bancroft,* p. 153; Allan Nevins, *Frémont, Pathmarker of the West* (3rd ed., New York), pp. 201–205; George Tays, "Frémont Had No Secret Instructions," *Pacific Historical Review,* IX (1940), 157–171.

reassertion of what has come to be known as the Monroe Doctrine. President Monroe, alarmed by the specter of Russian colonization on the California coast, and by the possibility of an attempt by the European continental powers to restore Spanish control of South and Central America, had declared in his message to Congress in 1823 that the American continents were free and independent, no longer subject to colonization by any European power. He had further asserted that interference with any of the Latin American republics would be regarded as dangerous to America's peace and safety and as "the manifestation of an unfriendly disposition toward the United States." Sometime in October, 1845, Polk told Senator Benton that he thought of reasserting the principles of Monroe, his immediate object being to forestall possible British colonization in California. He was doubtless also thinking of the Oregon question, as yet unsettled, of British opposition to American expansion, and of the declaration (June 10, 1845) by French premier François Guizot that it was in the interest of France to preserve the existing balance of power in the New World.

Polk's restatement of Monroe's principles was made in his first annual message to Congress, December 2, 1845. It warned Europe against entertaining schemes of colonization in North America and against attempts to establish any "balance of power" there. In effect, Polk told Europe that its interference with the expansion of the United States would not be tolerated. At the same time, by applauding the wisdom of Monroe's statements, Polk placed a fresh seal of approval on the Monroe Doctrine's warning to Europe to keep hands off the countries of the Western Hemisphere.

The notice thus served on Europe was scarcely necessary, so far as repelling aggressive European action was concerned. Neither France nor Great Britain were planning any colonization in the New World at this time. It was, nevertheless, an important document. It indicated that the fear of European action was playing a very considerable role in shaping American policy. It was also a significant testimonial to the growing American conviction that expansion on this side of the Atlantic, even expansion by transfer from one country to another, was an American and not a European prerogative.[15]

During 1845, while Polk was busy with the Oregon question and

[15] Henry S. Commager, *Documents of American History* (New York, 1940), pp. 309–310; Dexter Perkins, *The Monroe Doctrine, 1826–1867* (Baltimore, 1933); McCormac, *Polk,* p. 386.

with "safeguarding" California and other parts of North America against European interference, he also attempted to re-establish relations with Mexico. Here he had two objectives. He wished to settle questions in dispute between the two countries, especially the long-standing question of American claims. He also wished to purchase large portions of Mexico's territory.

The ship that bore General Almonte from American shores after he had asked for his passports in March of 1845 also bore an American secret agent, one William S. Parrott, a dentist, merchant, and *bon vivant,* who for some time had been a resident of Mexico. Parrott's mission was to discover whether Mexico would reopen diplomatic relations with the United States.

The United States' secret agent was a none too savory character. He had dabbled in Mexican politics during the eighteen-twenties, and his extravagant claims against the Mexican government (eventually scaled down some 90 per cent by the claims commission) had made him *persona non grata* in Mexico City. Of these things Polk and Buchanan appear to have been ignorant. They seem to have believed that his residence in Mexico had given him easy access to the highest officials of the government.

Parrott investigated the situation, so far as he was able, and came to the conclusion that an American envoy would be well received. On the basis of his report, and that of two American consuls in Mexico, Polk and his Cabinet agreed that the time had come to reopen diplomatic relations and to attempt the purchase of New Mexico and California. For these provinces, together with the Rio Grande boundary for Texas, the President and his counselors were willing to go as high as $40 million.[16]

The man chosen for the Mexican mission was John Slidell, a states' rights Democrat from Louisiana who was blessed with a fluent command of Spanish. His commission as envoy extraordinary and minister plenipotentiary to Mexico was signed by the President on November 10, 1845, and that same day he resigned his seat in Congress and began making preparations for his departure from the United States. Dr. Parrott was appointed his secretary of legation.[17] In anticipation of the

[16] Polk, *Diary,* I, 33–35; James M. Callahan, *American Foreign Policy in Mexican Relations* (New York, 1932), pp. 37, 119, 146–148; *Rives, American Diplomacy,* pp. 269–270; Smith, *War with Mexico,* I, 88–89.

[17] Polk, *Diary,* I, 93, 100.

event, Slidell had already been ordered to proceed to Pensacola. His commission and certain additional instructions were forwarded to him there in the care of Dr. Parrott, and from that point the mission went on to Mexico City.

Slidell's office, his instructions informed him, was one of "vast importance." He was to counteract the hostile influence of foreign powers upon Mexico, and restore good relations between that country and the United States. In addition, he was to press for satisfaction of the claims of American citizens, claims amounting to well over $6 million and long evaded by the Mexican government. These, said Buchanan, "must" be speedily adjusted. The obvious way for Mexico to do this was by the grant of territory, with the United States assuming the debts due American claimants as a *quid pro quo.* Such territorial cession could not involve the area between the Nueces and the Rio Grande. That belonged to Texas. It would involve New Mexico and possibly California.

Slidell was to offer the assumption of American claims by the United States for a boundary running from the mouth of the Rio Grande to its source and thence north to the 42nd parallel of latitude. In addition, $5 million would be paid for the balance of New Mexico territory. The acquisition of California as well would be an "immense service." Slidell was authorized to offer $25 million for it if the cession involved the area as far south as Monterey, $20 million if it included only the bay and harbor of San Francisco. In conclusion, he was adjured to deal tactfully with a jealous, feeble, and distracted Mexico.[18]

Slidell's instructions made it evident that his mission would be judged successful if he obtained Mexican recognition of the Rio Grande boundary and the satisfaction of American claims. The tone of the instructions was perhaps a trifle condescending, but it was peaceful.

Somewhat different was the tone of the President's message to Congress, three weeks later. There Polk referred darkly to "unredressed injuries," which included insults offered to American citizens and to the American flag. He quoted Jackson, with approval, as having declared in February, 1837, that these injuries "would justify in the eyes of all nations immediate war." If the Slidell mission failed, Polk indicated that he would recommend to Congress "such ulterior measures of redress" as would be fitting under the circumstances. If this was not mere empty verbiage, it meant that Slidell's failure to obtain recog-

[18] *Senate Executive Documents,* 30th Cong., first sess., No. 52, pp. 71–80.

nition of the Rio Grande boundary and satisfaction of American claims would result in war. It also indicated that Polk was not prepared to go to war for either New Mexico or California.[19]

As Slidell and Parrott neared the Mexican coast, the weak Mexican government under President José Joaquín Herrera felt that it was being subjected to severe pressures. The attitude of the American government was disquieting. So was that of "public opinion" in Mexico, where posters appeared declaring that Slidell had come to buy Texas and California and that negotiation with him would be treason. Herrera's government appealed fruitlessly to England and France for aid. It did not dare receive Slidell, who, during the latter part of December, withdrew from Mexico City to Jalapa, near Vera Cruz.

Herrera resigned under pressure on the night of December 29–30, 1845, and General Mariano Paredes assumed control of Mexican affairs. His motto was no concession to the United States. On January 12, 1846, word from Slidell reached Washington. He reported that in all probability he would not be received by the Mexican government. Polk thereupon ordered Taylor to move from Corpus Christi to the Rio Grande.

Buchanan now instructed Slidell to press his credentials upon Paredes. On February 17, 1846, Polk informed his Cabinet that if Slidell's representations to Paredes were fruitless, he proposed to ask Congress for authority to use "aggressive measures" against Mexico.

Only the day before he made this statement to his Cabinet, Polk had had an extended conversation with Colonel A. J. Atocha, a friend and confidant of the former Mexican dictator, Santa Anna, who was then in exile at Havana. Santa Anna, so Atocha reported, favored a treaty between Mexico and the United States that would cede to the latter, for the sum of $30 million, all the country east of the Rio Grande and north of the Colorado. Santa Anna further advised the use of military and naval pressure on the Mexican government as a means of obtaining its acceptance of these terms. Santa Anna himself, Atocha declared, was ready to return to Mexico and help enforce such a treaty.

Polk heard Atocha without comment. The President confided to his diary that he had no confidence in the Colonel, but the plan for "aggressive measures" that he outlined to his Cabinet the next day was developed along the lines suggested by his Mexican visitor.[20]

[19] Richardson, *Messages and Papers,* III, 2238–2242.
[20] Polk, *Diary,* I, 227–234.

Taylor had been ordered to move to the Rio Grande on January 13, 1846. He delayed some two months, believing that torrential rains had made the march impossible. At last, March 8, 1846, he struck his leaky tents (one of the failures of the quartermaster's department) and began his fateful advance. Sixteen days later, he was opposite Matamoros on the Rio Grande, thirty-three miles from the coastal harbor of Point Isabel. He assured the Mexicans across the river that his mood was pacific; that his only purpose was to protect American property.[21]

Taylor's assurances were received by the Mexicans with a noticeable lack of enthusiasm. General Francisco Mejía and his successor, General Pedro de Ampudia, declared that Taylor's presence on what they considered Mexican soil automatically created a state of war. They demanded that he retreat to the Nueces. In response, the American general built a fort, trained his batteries on Matamoros, and then blockaded the Rio Grande so that he might prevent Mexican supplies from reaching the opposing forces.

While these events were transpiring on the Rio Grande, America's discomfited envoy extraordinary and minister plenipotentiary was returning to Washington. He reached the capital on May 8, and was at once closeted with Polk. Slidell declared that force, and force alone, was left to the United States. He urged prompt and energetic action. With this Polk agreed, remarking that he meant to act, and act soon.

The following day, Polk brought up the Mexican question in Cabinet meeting. He stated that in his opinion the United States had ample reason to fight, even though there had been no open act of aggression by the Mexicans. He declared that he would not be doing his duty if he did not, three days hence, ask Congress for a declaration of war. The Cabinet was then polled and all save one agreed with the President, although Buchanan said that he would be "better satisfied" if the Mexicans had committed some act of aggression. Secretary of the Navy Bancroft alone wanted to wait for such an act, but all agreed that Polk should prepare his war message and present it to the Cabinet on May 12. That same evening, the desired news of aggression arrived.[22]

Almost as soon as Taylor reached the Rio Grande, Mexican guerrillas began hovering about his camp, and two American officers were killed.

[21] Holman Hamilton, *Zachary Taylor, Soldier of the Republic* (Indianapolis, 1941), pp. 167, 171, 174.

[22] Polk, *Diary*, I, 382, 384–385.

This, of course, was not official action. But late in April an organized force of 1,600 Mexicans crossed the Rio Grande. A detachment of sixty-three American dragoons, sent out to spy on this troop movement, rode into a trap. Some of the Americans were killed; the others were compelled to surrender. Taylor at once sent word to Washington that hostilities had commenced. It was this news which reached the capital on Saturday, May 9.

Promptly on receipt of these momentous tidings, Polk summoned his Cabinet. All agreed that a war message should be sent to Congress the following Monday. The Cabinet adjourned at 10 P.M. and Polk, with the assistance of Bancroft and Buchanan, began preparing his war message. He finished it the next day, though its completion was somewhat delayed by his insistence upon attending church, for Polk was a religious man.[23]

Polk's message to Congress stated that war existed by act of Mexico, and this despite "every effort at reconciliation" on the part of the United States. Mexico, said the President, "has passed the boundary of the United States, has invaded our territory, and shed American blood upon the American soil." He asked Congress for recognition of the existence of war, for money with which to prosecute the struggle, and for authority to call up volunteers.[24]

Polk feared that a group of dissident Democrats might join with the Whigs to defeat congressional action on his war message. Such fears were groundless. The House, in half an hour's time, passed a bill stating that war existed and authorizing the President to call up 50,000 volunteers and use $10 million in carrying on the struggle. The vote was 174 to 14. The measure was passed by the Senate on the following day, with some minor amendments, by a vote of 40 to 2.[25]

Polk signed the bill on May 13, 1846, and on that same day issued a proclamation of war. He told Buchanan that the United States had not entered the war for purposes of conquest, but that we would take California and such other portions of Mexican territory as would be necessary to satisfy American claims against Mexico and defray the costs of the struggle.[26]

A year later, however, when peace terms were under discussion in

[23] Polk, *Diary,* I, 386–388; Hamilton, *Taylor, Soldier of the Republic,* p. 178.
[24] Richardson, *Messages and Papers,* III, 2292–2293.
[25] *Congressional Globe,* 29th Cong., first sess., 791–804.
[26] Richardson, *Messages and Papers,* IV, 2320; Polk, *Diary,* I, 395–399.

the Cabinet, Polk indirectly admitted that he had entered the war for the purpose of acquiring territory. The Cabinet was discussing how much should be paid for New Mexico and California. Secretary Walker, who wanted all of Mexico, insisted that free passage across the Isthmus of Tehuantepec should be made a *sine qua non* of peace. To this Polk demurred. Such passage, he observed, had "constituted no part of the object for which we had engaged in the war." By inference, the acquisition of territory had been such an object.[27]

The Mexican War had its origins partly in the unsatisfied claims of Americans against the Mexican government, but chiefly in the expansionism of the eighteen-forties. Polk's determination to insist upon the Rio Grande boundary and his zeal for the acquisition of additional territory had led him into a course of action that embittered Mexico, excited American public opinion, and led both nations to the brink of conflict. Polk was determined upon war, once it became apparent that Slidell's mission would fail. He probably would have had difficulty in carrying a declaration of war through Congress without a Mexican attack, just as Roosevelt would have had difficulty in getting a declaration of war against Japan without Pearl Harbor. In both cases, attack made a declaration of war inevitable.

Even as it was, not every American leader believed in the war. John Quincy Adams voted against it in the House, calling it "a most unrighteous war." Calhoun feared lest it damage the Slave Power by tying it to a war of aggression, and sat silent on the final roll call in the Senate. Benton opposed the march to the Rio Grande, and strove to prevent what he, too, felt to be a war of aggression. Some of the Whigs feared that a war, once started, might spread. "In this connected condition of the world," said Crittenden of Kentucky, "war was felt everywhere." A Whig effort in the Senate to limit the scope of the struggle by defining it as a war to repel invasion was voted down, twenty-six to twenty, but it suggested the repugnance to territorial acquisition that was to become a prominent feature of Whig criticism in the months to come.

Democratic Senator John A. Dix of New York, although he voted against the Whig effort to limit the war, did so in bitterness of spirit. Much of the Barnburner reaction to Polk's Mexican policy and to the war itself was in a letter that the New York senator wrote to Azariah

[27] Polk, *Diary,* II, 473–474; McCormac, *Polk,* p. 491.

Flagg, two days after war was proclaimed. He had not written since the declaration of war, Dix said, "because I am too sick of the miserable concern here to say anything about it. . . . The whole thing is the work of speculators and bankrupts. It was begun in fraud last winter, and I think will end in disgrace. . . . I shall not be surprised if the next accounts should show that there is no Mexican invasion of our soil. But I desist."[28]

The war clouds over America were lightened by the dazzling prospect of an easy victory and splendid territorial gains. But the political clouds hovering over the nation's capital were dark indeed.

[28] *Congressional Globe,* 29th Cong., first sess., 802–804; Flagg Papers, Dix to Flagg, May 15, 1846; Wiltse, *Calhoun,* III, 282–286; William M. Meigs, *The Life of John Caldwell Calhoun* (2 vols., New York, 1917), II, 382–388; William N. Chambers, *Old Bullion Benton, Senator from the New West* (Boston, 1956), pp. 306–308; Samuel F. Bemis, *John Quincy Adams and the Union* (New York, 1956), pp. 496–498.

CHAPTER 12

The Dose of Arsenic

THE MEXICAN WAR was American expansionism in action. Plagued by political bickerings, but under determined leadership, the nation plunged into the struggle. The stakes were high—magnificent territories, strategic advantages on the western and southwestern borders, great additions to the national income. Much was won along these lines, but the winnings brought grave and terrible problems in their train.

The opening salvos of the war set the Southwest in motion. There events occurred that meant conquest on an imperial scale. Brigadier General Stephen Watts Kearny, put in command of the Army of the West in May, 1846, marched from Fort Leavenworth to Santa Fe, which he entered on August 18 of that year. He set out a month later for the Pacific coast. There he helped complete the conquest of California which had already been begun by Frémont, Commodore Robert Field Stockton, the aging and lethargic Commodore John Drake Sloat, and the "Bear Flag" battalion of American settlers. San Francisco was occupied July 9, 1846. Los Angeles fell to Frémont and the Californians January 13, 1847. In eight months the American forces had established control over an empire.[1]

The glory of these conquests in the Southwest and on the Pacific coast was marred by a bitter quarrel between Stockton and Kearny over who was in command of the California operation. Frémont rallied to

[1] For the West in the Mexican War, see Ray Billington, *The Far Western Frontier* (New York, 1956), pp. 168–192.

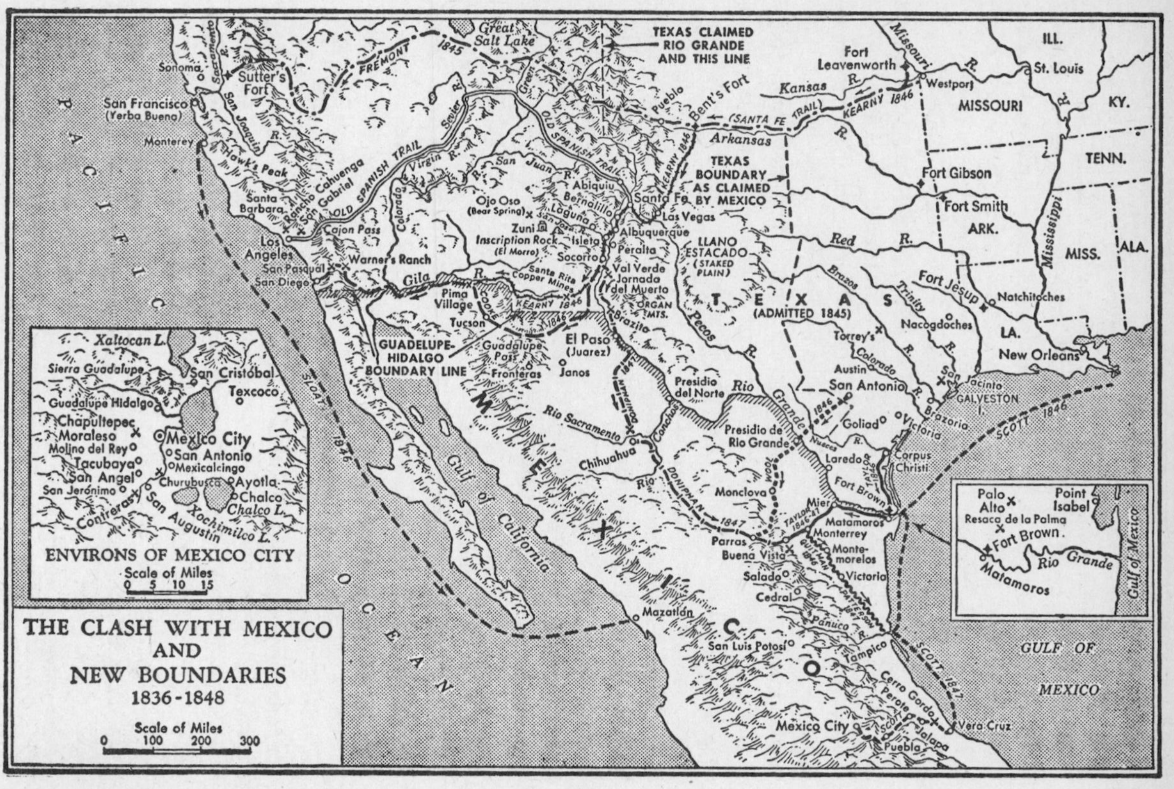
THE CLASH WITH MEXICO
AND
NEW BOUNDARIES
1836-1848
Scale of Miles
0 100 200 300
ENVIRONS OF MEXICO CITY
Scale of Miles
0 5 10 15
Xaltocan L.
Sierra Guadalupe
San Cristóbal
Texcoco
Guadalupe Hidalgo
Chapultepec
Moraleso
Molino del Rey
Tacubaya
San Angel
San Jerónimo
Mexico City
San Antonio
Mexicalcingo
Churubusco
Ayotla
Chalco
Chalco L.
Contreras
San Augustin
Xochimilco L.
TEXAS CLAIMED
RIO GRANDE
AND THIS LINE
TEXAS
BOUNDARY
AS CLAIMED
BY MEXICO
GUADELUPE-
HIDALGO
BOUNDARY LINE
LLANO
ESTACADO
(STAKED
PLAIN)
TEXAS
(ADMITTED 1845)
MEXICO
PACIFIC OCEAN
GULF OF MEXICO
Gulf of California
Gulf of Mexico
Sonoma
Sacramento
Sutter's Fort
San Francisco
(Yerba Bueno)
San Joaquin
Monterey
Hawk's Peak
Santa Barbara
Rancho Cahuenga
San Gabriel
Los Angeles
Cajon Pass
Warner's Ranch
San Pasqual
San Diego
FREMONT
1845
Great Salt Lake
OLD SPANISH TRAIL
Sevier R.
Virgin R.
Colorado
Green R.
San Juan R.
Ojo Oso
(Bear Spring)
Zuni
Inscription Rock
(El Morro)
Gila R.
Pima Village
Tucson
COOKE
KEARNY 1846
Santa Rita
Copper Mines
Guadalupe Pass
Fronteras
Abiquiu
Bernalillo
Laguna
Isleta
Albuquerque
Socorro
Peralta
Val Verde
Jornada del Muerto
ORGAN MTS.
Brazito
El Paso
(Juarez)
Janos
Santa Fe
Las Vegas
Pueblo
Bent's Fort
(SANTA FE TRAIL)
Arkansas
KEARNY 1846
Kansas R.
Fort Leavenworth
Missouri R.
Westport
MISSOURI
St. Louis
ILL.
KY.
TENN.
ALA.
MISS.
ARK.
LA.
Mississippi
Fort Gibson
Fort Smith
Red R.
Fort Jesup
Natchitoches
Nacogdoches
New Orleans
Brazos
Trinity
Torrey's
Colorado
Austin
San Antonio
San Jacinto
GALVESTON I.
Brazoria
Goliad
Victoria
Corpus Christi
Pecos R.
Rio Grande
Presidio del Norte
Presidio de Rio Grande
Nueces R.
Laredo
TAYLOR 1846
Fort Brown
SCOTT 1846
Rio Sacramento
Chihuahua
Conchos
DONIPHAN 1847
WOOL
Rio
Monclova
Mier
Matamoros
Monterrey
Monte-morelos
Victoria
Parras
Buena Vista
TAYLOR 1846-47
QUITMAN 1846
PATTERSON 1847
Salado
Cedral
Mazatlán
San Luis Potosí
Panuco R.
Tampico
SCOTT 1847
Cerro Gordo
Perote
Jalapa
Vera Cruz
Mexico City
Puebla
SLOAT 1846
Palo Alto
Point Isabel
Resaca de la Palma
Fort Brown
Rio Grande
Matamoros

Stockton, but the government at Washington supported Kearny. The War Department haled Frémont back to the nation's capital in August, 1847, for a court-martial on charges of insubordination and mutiny. Senator Benton rallied furiously in his son-in-law's support, but the latter was found guilty and sentenced to dismissal from the Army.

Polk reviewed Frémont's sentence and announced that he found the Pathmarker guilty, but only of insubordination. The President canceled the punishment, but Frémont resigned from the Army in disgust. Benton, deeply resentful of the President's attitude in the case, broke off relations with the White House and began to act in closer conjunction than theretofore with the Van Buren wing of the party.[2]

Meanwhile, the war with Mexico proper was rolling on from victory to victory. At first the Mexicans had crossed the Rio Grande in force, hoping to cut Taylor's little army to pieces, but at Palo Alto (May 6, 1846) and the following day at Resaca de la Palma, though greatly outnumbering the Americans, they were badly defeated and forced back across the river. Taylor followed them slowly, handicapped by lack of boats and of a pontoon bridge.

The victories at Palo Alto and Resaca were at least partially responsible for a change of plan at Washington in regard to the conduct of the war. The original idea had been to give General Winfield Scott command of the military operations in the Rio Grande area. The appointment was actually made, but instead of hurrying to the front Scott stayed on week after week in Washington. This was perfectly logical, for he was immersed in the problem of creating an Army where none worthy of the name had previously existed, but unfortunately he also became involved in politics. Convinced that Polk was appointing new generals who were only of the Democratic persuasion, Scott began quarreling with Secretary of War Marcy and making dark references to being caught between the fire of the Mexicans and a fire from his rear at Washington. Polk, on the other hand, became convinced that Scott was a Whig so "recklessly vindictive" and partisan in his attitude toward the administration that he could not be trusted with command of the Army in Mexico. The Cabinet being of the same conviction, and Taylor obviously doing well enough with the Army command, Scott

[2] Russell B. Nye, *George Bancroft* (New York, 1944), pp. 155–158; Allan Nevins, *Frémont, Pathmarker of the West* (3rd ed., New York, 1955), pp. 251–286; William N. Chambers, *Old Bullion Benton, Senator from the New West* (Boston, 1956), pp. 321–324.

was relieved of the post that had been given him in the field but was retained at the capital as an administrator of military affairs.

Scott's reply to the letter of dismissal was a good-tempered apology in which he declared that he had not meant to impugn the motives of the President and his immediate advisers. He was more than willing, he said, to stay on in Washington and work hard for victory. This was "Old Fuss and Feathers" at his best, which was very good indeed. But in another communication, dashed off to Marcy after discovering that the Secretary of War had visited his headquarters in his absence, Scott coined another of those phrases which rendered him peculiarly subject to ridicule. He had stepped out, he told Marcy, only for "a hasty plate of soup." This was "leaked" to the papers and there was considerable ribald comment. A member of the diplomatic corps promptly gave Scott a new title. He was now "Marshal Tureen."[3]

Politics complicated the business of warmaking at Washington while the soldiers at the front were carrying the heat and burden of the day. Taylor, having at length provided himself with boats, crossed the Rio Grande and attacked Monterrey. This was the key to northern Mexico, a strongly fortified city some 125 miles to the south of the river that now, in the eyes of practically all Americans, marked the boundary between the United States and Mexico.[4]

In a five-day operation (September 20–24, 1846), though outnumbered three to two and with almost no siege artillery, Old Zack took Monterrey. He allowed the Mexicans to march out of the city unmolested, but its capture was still a considerable feat. The United States could now boast that it was in control of something like one-third of Mexico proper.

Taylor's fame spread. More and more he was talked of as a presidential candidate for 1848. "Old Rough and Ready," as his troops called him, was not much of a tactician and he was uncomfortable in a uniform, but, simple and unpretentious though he might be, he was a fighter. Always calm in the face of danger, he had become a hero to his troops and was by way of becoming something of a legend with the

[3] Milo M. Quaife (ed.), *The Diary of James K. Polk* (4 vols., Chicago, 1910), I, 413–428; Brainard Dyer, *Zachary Taylor* (Baton Rouge, 1946), p. 182; Alfred H. Bill, *Rehearsal for Conflict* (New York, 1947), pp. 113–116; Arthur D. Howden Smith, *Old Fuss and Feathers* (New York, 1937), pp. 255–258.

[4] Justin H. Smith, *The War with Mexico* (2 vols., New York, 1919), I, 228–229.

American people. He had never voted in his life, but the Whig politicians and some Democrats too began seeing visions of "Old Whitey," as Taylor's favorite steed was called, pasturing on the White House lawn.

As politicians began dreaming dreams of Taylor's availability, the head politician of them all became increasingly cool to his victorious general. This was partly because of Taylor's mistakes (his slowness, certain errors of judgment on the battle line, the too-generous terms of the armistice which he granted to the Mexican General Ampudia at Monterrey), reports of which kept drifting back from the front. It was also because, despite Taylor's early assertions to the contrary, victory was decidedly unlikely by invasion from the north, and Polk was revolving plans for a seaborne expedition that would land at Vera Cruz. Finally, Polk's attitude was partly shaped by his rising concern over Taylor's popularity and the mounting evidence that he might become the Whig presidential candidate in 1848.

The President was quick to censure Taylor for allowing Ampudia to march out of Monterrey with the honors of war. This was to ignore the practical impossibility of holding the Mexican army prisoner, or of paroling it when the parole would almost certainly have been broken. Polk's attitude toward Taylor, in this and in other matters as well, was a combination of reason, sound judgment, and partisan rancor. But out of this complex of motives the President had determined, by November, 1846, to reduce Taylor to a minor role in the war. Scott should go to the front, after all. He should effect the landing at Vera Cruz, and perhaps strike for Mexico City itself.

Polk was not altogether happy about this change of plan. He had little confidence in Scott, and his hackles rose whenever he thought of Scott's political machinations. A good Democratic general would have been decidedly preferable to Old Fuss and Feathers, but the melancholy truth was that no good Democratic general could be found.[5]

Polk was undertaking the hard task of stemming the tide of popularity that was carrying Whig generals toward the White House while at the same time he prosecuted the war with efficiency. He was also seeking to open peace negotiations with the Mexicans. Shortly after Taylor's victory at Resaca de la Palma, Polk had Buchanan write to

[5] Polk, *Diary,* II, 353–359; Smith, *War With Mexico,* I, 259–263, 351, 353, 355–356, 507; Holman Hamilton, *Zachary Taylor, Soldier of the Republic* (Indianapolis, 1941), pp. 219–221; Bill, *Rehearsal,* pp. 112–113.

President Paredes of Mexico proposing negotiations, the letter being forwarded under a flag of truce. This gesture produced no results, but before this became apparent Polk was fostering another venture, one which was designed to promote peace but which undoubtedly prolonged the war.

Polk had kept in mind his conversation, early in 1846, with Colonel Atocha about the exiled Santa Anna. On the very day that the President signed the proclamation of war, he issued an order to Commodore Connor, who commanded the squadron blockading the Mexican gulf ports, permitting Santa Anna to enter Mexico. Then, early in June, Lieutenant Alexander Slidell Mackenzie was sent to Havana, instructed to interview the erstwhile Mexican dictator. Mackenzie was to inform Santa Anna that he could pass through the American blockade, and urge him to return to power in his native land. If Santa Anna would do so and then would negotiate a settlement of the war, Polk would suspend hostilities on land, make no claims for indemnity, and pay liberally for any territory that might be taken by the United States.

Mackenzie reported that Santa Anna wanted a friendly arrangement with the United States, and on August 8, 1846, Polk asked Congress for a $2 million appropriation to be used in negotiating a peace settlement. Eight days later, Santa Anna landed at Vera Cruz, to find the Paredes administration collapsed and conditions ripe for his resumption of power. Once installed at Mexico City, however, he showed small evidence of any desire to negotiate.

Polk later told Congress that he had fostered Santa Anna's return to Mexico in order to stimulate internal division there. There was plenty of such division after the exile's return, but it is obvious that the President had taken at face value the wily Mexican's protestations of his desire for peace.[6]

Santa Anna may have intended to start negotiations upon his return to power. If so, he was speedily disabused of the notion by the Mexican internal situation, where suspicion was rife that he intended to double-cross his countrymen. Convinced that the best way to re-establish himself firmly in control of the Mexican government would be by a victorious campaign, his distaste for the olive branch became more and

[6] James D. Richardson, *A Compilation of the Messages and Papers of the Presidents* (11 vols., New York, 1910), IV, 2309–2310, 2341–2342; Wilfrid H. Callcott, *Santa Anna* (Norman, Okla., 1936), pp. 236–241, 243; Bill, *Rehearsal*, pp. 106–107; Hamilton, *Taylor, Soldier of the Republic*, I, 222–224.

more apparent. By October 8, 1846, he was at San Luis Potosí in central Mexico, busily engaged in building up an army for operations against Taylor.[7]

Old Zack, meanwhile, had become increasingly unhappy about his situation. Polk and Marcy had gone over his head in ordering certain military movements in the Mexican province of Tamaulipas, just south of the lower Rio Grande. They had criticized him for the armistice at Monterrey and for occupying Saltillo, some seventy miles southwest of Monterrey, which he had seized in November, 1846. Now, to his disgust, another blow fell, one that made him rage and mutter in his tent.

Scott distrusted the volunteers in the American Army and with some reason. They were on the whole an unruly lot, so difficult to discipline that sometimes their officers stood in fear of them, and altogether too prone to rape, murder, and pillage.[8] In consequence, Scott drafted most of Taylor's regulars for the Vera Cruz campaign.

It did not matter that earlier Taylor himself had seen the advisability of using regulars from his Army for the Vera Cruz expedition. He was now convinced that Scott had obtained his present position by promising to deprive him, Taylor, of a major part of his forces, thus reducing him to insignificance and killing him off as a presidential prospect. Old Zack stormed and sulked, and relations between the two Whig generals descended to a new low, undoubtedly to the delight of the Democratic politicians in Washington.[9]

It is probable that the written order which depleted Taylor's forces for the benefit of the Vera Cruz expedition had other consequences than that of embittering the relations of the two American generals. The officer bearing this dispatch was ambushed and killed (it was a duplicate that finally reached Taylor), and the order itself thus became the possession of the enemy. Almost certainly it reached Santa Anna's headquarters at San Luis Potosí. At any rate, whether he knew of the order or because of domestic political exigencies, or both, Santa Anna decided upon a winter campaign against Taylor. On January 28, 1847, with an army of over 18,000 men, the Mexican left San Luis

[7] *Ibid.*, 223–224; Callcott, *Santa Anna*, pp. 242–243; Bill, *Rehearsal*, pp. 118–119.

[8] D. H. Smith, *Old Fuss and Feathers*, p. 247; Walter P. Webb, *The Texas Rangers* (Boston, 1935), pp. 99, 110, 113, 119–121; Hamilton, *Taylor, Soldier of the Republic*, pp. 200–202; Bill, *Rehearsal*, pp. 122–123, 129, 188.

[9] J. H. Smith, *War with Mexico*, I, 262–263, 363; Hamilton, *Taylor, Soldier of the Republic*, pp. 226–227; A. D. H. Smith, *Old Fuss and Feathers*, pp. 263–264; Bill, *Rehearsal*, pp. 188–191.

Potosí, heading north toward Taylor's Army, which lay south of Monterrey, at Buena Vista.

The Mexicans who attacked the American forces at Buena Vista on February 22–23, 1847, outnumbered their adversaries four to one. The battle was hotly contested. Neither side succeeded in gaining ground in any permanent fashion. The great majority of the troops on both sides were in retreat at one stage or another of the conflict. At its close the Mexicans still outnumbered their adversaries, but their morale was low. They had suffered heavy casualties, some 1,800 compared to an American casualty list of 673. The Americans stubbornly held to their main position, and Santa Anna now deemed that position impregnable. Fearing wholesale desertions, he struck camp and, with two American flags and three American cannon as evidence of a "victory," moved back to the south.[10]

Buena Vista was not a Mexican victory and it could scarcely be described as an overwhelming American triumph, but it had some definite results. It disgruntled Polk, who held that it should never have been fought. He deplored the loss of men, and forbade the Army to honor it with salutes. Taylor, furious because he believed that his lack of regulars had prevented a Mexican Waterloo, was more convinced than ever that he was the victim of political partisanship. Reluctantly, he gave up a half-formed plan for advancing on San Luis Potosí, thus surrendering all hope of a further offensive from the North.

Since his usefulness in the war was now largely at an end, Taylor applied for leave to come home. It was finally granted and on December 3, 1847, he reached New Orleans. There he was lionized at a tremendous reception. Old Whitey, the equine veteran of his campaigns in Mexico, was with the General, and suffered the indignity of having hairs pulled out of his tail by souvenir hunters. Odes, flowers, and a crescendo of huzzas greeted Old Whitey's master wherever he went. It was not so much a general of the Army as a presidential candidate who had returned to his native soil.[11]

As Taylor passed from the center of the Mexican stage, the military spotlight began to center upon the expedition of General Winfield Scott. To counterbalance Old Fuss and Feathers' Whiggism, Polk

[10] J. H. Smith, *War With Mexico,* I, 397–399.

[11] Polk, *Diary,* II, 451–453, 462; Hamilton, *Taylor, Soldier of the Republic,* pp. 228–244, 248–252; Bill, *Rehearsal,* pp. 199–204, 233.

surrounded him with a galaxy of Democratic generals in command of volunteers. There were nine of these worthies, good, bad, and indifferent leaders. Safeguarded by this entourage, Scott set sail from New York City November 30, 1846, bound for Mexican waters via New Orleans, just as Santa Anna was gathering his strength for the campaign against Taylor that ended at Buena Vista.

It was Polk's desire to send an olive branch along with the sword on the Vera Cruz expedition. The President wished to have three peace commissioners keep Scott company on his march to the enemy's capital. He was, therefore, inclined to look with favor upon a plan that emerged from the fertile brain of Senator Benton. Old Bullion, never one to keep himself in the background, was friendly with the New York Barnburners. He was also still on cordial terms with Polk, the Frémont court-martial being as yet below the horizon. Benton now proposed that he be made a lieutenant general, therefore superior in rank to both Taylor and Scott, and that he be sent with the Army as one of the peace commissioners.

Polk was delighted with Benton's plan. To give the Missouri senator such a post would be an effective political counter to the Whig generals, and would also tend to conciliate the New York State followers of Van Buren. At the President's instigation a bill to make Benton a lieutenant general was introduced in Congress by Barnburner John A. Dix of New York. It passed the House but was lost in the Senate, due to the combined efforts of the Whigs and the followers of John C. Calhoun.[12]

Scott's campaign was not devoid of risks, but it was efficiently handled. A beachhead was established, virtually without opposition, on March 9, 1847, and was rapidly extended to within about a mile of Vera Cruz. The city was reduced by bombardment and was occupied on March 29. By that time Scott had demonstrated that he had some grasp of military science, that he was desirous of conserving human life, and that his personal bravery was beyond question. The Army viewed his leadership with increasing confidence.

The advance toward Mexico City began some ten days after the occupation of Vera Cruz. After another ten days, the stronghold of Cerro Gordo was captured. Jalapa was occupied thereafter within twenty-four hours. Puebla, which was entered May 15 and which was

[12] Polk, *Diary,* II, 227–228, 261, 262, 268, 270, 277, 286; Chambers, *Benton,* p. 311; Bill, *Rehearsal,* pp. 182–185.

seventy miles from Mexico City, represented a coverage of well over half the distance from Vera Cruz to the capital.

Scott waited at Puebla until he was reinforced. Sickness, the expiration of enlistments, and battle casualties had reduced his effectives to less than 6,000 men. This array was nearly doubled during the summer, and on August 7, 1847, abandoning his line of communications with the coast, he moved out from Puebla toward Mexico City. His aim was to capture a walled city guarded by forts and defended by an army of 30,000 men led by a brave and resourceful commander.

The old Duke of Wellington, who took a great interest in the campaign, now concluded that Scott was lost; that he could neither achieve his objective nor fall back on his bases. The American situation was not an easy one, but events were to prove that Scott, on the field of action, was a better judge of the situation than was the hero of Waterloo comfortably ensconced in an easy chair in his London club.

The battles of Contreras and Churubusco, which cost the United States a thousand casualties and Santa Anna one-third of his army in killed, wounded, and missing, opened the way to the Mexican capital. On the following day, Santa Anna proposed a truce for burying the dead and for opening peace negotiations. As a result of this proposal, an armistice was signed and an uneasy cessation of hostilities ensued. The peace negotiations broke down, however, before the Mexican leader's stubborn resistance to the cession of Mexican territory. Santa Anna had deluded himself into believing that the American Army was in desperate straits.

Fighting was resumed on September 8. Six days later the capital was occupied by Scott's troops and Santa Anna's government had begun to disintegrate. The Mexican tried desperately to continue the struggle with the remnants of an army that, Scott estimated, had suffered 7,000 casualties from Puebla to the capture of Mexico City; but after his defeat at Huamantla on October 9, all organized resistance ceased. At last peace was near.

Polk's interest in ending the war had been manifested by continued but fruitless attempts to open negotiations with the Mexican government. Late in 1846, Moses Y. Beach, editor of the New York *Sun,* had appeared in Mexico armed with a British passport and authority to act as the President's secret agent in furthering the cause of peace. He was not authorized to make a treaty, but Polk confided to his diary that if

Beach brought "a good one" back, it would be submitted to the Senate.[13]

Beach brought back to the United States considerable information about the situation in Mexico, but no treaty. The United States' next emissary was the ubiquitous Colonel Atocha, who was sent to Mexico in January, 1847, to urge peace negotiations. But the Colonel's efforts failed because of Mexican demands for a raising of the blockade and the evacuation of Mexican territory. It was about this time that Benton's vision of himself as a peace commissioner collapsed before the bubble-pricking activities of the senatorial opposition.

When the news of Buena Vista and Vera Cruz arrived in Washington, Polk felt that the time had come for still another effort to bring the war to an end. Expansionist sentiment in the United States was increasing and a movement for the acquisition of all Mexico was gaining force, but the country was also being riven by an increasingly bitter dispute over the status of slavery in any territories that might be acquired as a result of the struggle. Polk may well have thought that the domestic politics of the United States would be needlessly complicated if the nation became committed to swallowing up Mexico. Polk was himself an expansionist, but his interest lay in territory which helped to round out America's natural frontiers and gave access to the Pacific trade, rather than in the conquest of a foreign nation.

What the President now had in mind as a peace move was the appointment of a commissioner with plenipotentiary powers who should accompany the Army on its march to the Mexican capital and seize any opportunity that might arise for negotiation. Buchanan would have been personally satisfactory as such a commissioner, but Polk told the Cabinet that the Secretary of State could not well be sent on a mission of such indefinite duration. Buchanan agreed with this point of view and suggested sending the chief clerk of the State Department. To this the President and Cabinet agreed. The mission was thereupon entrusted to Nicholas P. Trist.[14]

It is interesting that Scott's name as a possible peace negotiator was not mentioned by any member of the Cabinet. Old Fuss and Feathers had shown real talent in diplomacy when he had been plowing through the snows on the Canadian border. Negotiation of peace by victorious generals is a practice not unknown in the annals of diplo-

[13] Polk, *Diary,* II, 476–477; J. H. Smith, *War with Mexico,* II, 11–13.
[14] Polk, *Diary,* II, 465–467.

macy. Polk's advisers, however, do not seem to have taken such considerations into account. This was perhaps due in part to the conviction that it would be difficult for one man to fight a war and make a peace at the same time, but the main consideration was undoubtedly political.

Nicholas Philip Trist, the President's chosen emissary, was a Virginian and a devoted Democrat. He had married a granddaughter of Thomas Jefferson. Friendly by nature, honest by disposition and conviction, modest and unambitious, his chief fault seems to have been prolixity. His zest for writing long and wearisome letters amounted almost to a passion. When he left for Mexico it was with a prejudice against Scott, whom he regarded as the very model of a Whig political general.[15]

The instructions which Trist bore with him to Mexico provided for different sets of possibilities, but all involved the acquisition of large amounts of territory. For New Mexico, Upper and Lower California, and the right of transit across the isthmus of Tehuantepec, Trist was authorized to pay up to $30 million. Without Lower California, the maximum consideration would be $25 million. For New Mexico and Upper California alone, Trist was authorized to pay up to $20 million. In all cases, the claims of American citizens against Mexico would be assumed by the United States government.

Trist landed at Vera Cruz May 6, 1847, and at once became involved in a violent controversy with Scott. The President's envoy sent to Scott a sealed copy of a treaty that presumably represented the maximum American demands, with the request that it be handed over to the Mexican government. Obviously, the General was to have no knowledge of its contents, and this he deeply resented. Nor was Scott only cast in the role of Trist's errand boy on this particular occasion. The fiery general was also informed by Trist that the latter had authority to negotiate a treaty and to conclude hostilities when this had been done.

Scott, always sensitive to what appeared to be deliberate slights, had wanted to negotiate the treaty himself. He also resented bitterly the implication that Trist had any control over the Army. "I see that the Secretary of War proposes to degrade me," he remarked, and tartly informed Trist that he should keep his hands off the direction of the military forces. Trist replied at a length that would have been tiresome

15 Louis M. Sears, "Nicholas P. Trist, A Diplomat with Ideals," *Mississippi Valley Historical Review,* XI (June, 1924), 85–95.

save for its bitterness, and a violent quarrel ensued. Scott, who had ticketed Trist as an administration spy, complained bitterly to Marcy. Trist told Buchanan that Scott was "decidedly the greatest imbecile that I have ever had anything to do with." This situation was only a trifle eased when Trist was laid low by a two months' illness.

Trist, from his sickbed, made the first gesture of conciliation by sending to Scott the official documents which explained the nature of the government's mission. Scott, who for all his temper was a warm-hearted person, and who sensed the futility of the quarrel, responded amicably and soon thereafter sent a box of guava marmalade to the invalid. Within a few days, meetings were arranged. These convinced Trist that politics had obscured the administration's view of Scott, and the two men soon became fast friends.[16]

Negotiations were opened with the Mexican government through the British legation on June 6, 1847. This was while Scott was still at Puebla, before the final advance on Mexico City had begun. The American commissioner found the Mexicans obdurate, but successive defeats altered their determination to cede only a portion of Upper California and to insist on the Nueces as a boundary line.

As the Mexicans became more amenable, Polk made up his mind to increase his demands. By October, 1847, he determined to ask for more territory and give less money for it. Mexico, he felt, should pay for her obstinacy in continuing the war. Trist's instructions were now deemed insufficient in Washington, and on October 6 Buchanan sent him his recall. Trist was told that if he was in the midst of negotiations, they should be broken off; if he had concluded a treaty, he should bring it to Washington with him.

Trist now took matters into his own hands. Encouraged by Scott and by the British chargé, Edward Thornton, he decided to ignore the latest directions of his own government. He felt that if the peace efforts were terminated, the war party might again get control of the Mexican government, and that then further Mexican defeats would result in a political collapse so complete that negotiations might become next to impossible. Through Thornton, he informed the Mexicans that he would negotiate on the basis of his instructions; that if they re-

16 Robert A. Brent, "Nicholas P. Trist and the Treaty of Guadalupe Hidalgo," *Southwestern Historical Quarterly,* LVII (Apr., 1954), 456–459; J. H. Smith, *War with Mexico,* II, 128–130; St. George L. Sioussat, "Buchanan," in Samuel F. Bemis (ed.), *The American Secretaries of State and Their Diplomacy* (10 vols., New York, 1927–29), V, 282–285.

fused, the next conditions laid down by the United States would undoubtedly be more severe than those which would now be the basis of discussion. On December 6, he wrote to Buchanan that he was trying to conclude a treaty.

Faced by a hard alternative, the Mexicans reluctantly decided to negotiate and, December 28, 1847, their commissioners met with Trist at the town of Guadalupe Hidalgo, three miles north of Mexico City.

Trist's action, flying as it did in the face of his government's instructions, was insubordinate but courageous. It was also important. The demand for the acquisition of all Mexico had reached significant proportions. It was strongest in the East and West, rather than in the South, and was coming to its peak in the winter of 1847–48. Expansionist fervor and belief in the supposed industrial and commercial advantages of absorption were factors in the development of this sentiment. There was also a growing belief that slavery would not flourish in Mexico, a belief that cleared the way for free-soil expansionist convictions. Such developments, coupled with irritation at continued Mexican resistance and exultation at the news of the capture of Mexico City, helped to foster a formidable demand that the United States take over all of Mexico and rule it for the sake of the Mexicans, for the benefit of the United States, and for the advancement of world civilization. It is possible, even probable, that Trist's refusal to obey his final instructions prevented the absorption of Mexico by the United States.[17]

A month of disputes and arguments followed the beginning of the negotiations between Trist and the Mexican commissioners, but at last the treaty was drawn. It provided for recognition of the Rio Grande boundary, the cession to the United States of Upper California to just south of the port of San Diego, the cession of New Mexico, the payment to Mexico of $15 million (Trist lopped $5 million off the sum originally contemplated, due to the prolongation of the war), and the assumption by the United States of claims against Mexico amounting to $3,250,000. On February 2, 1848, the treaty was signed.

Trist could not carry the treaty to Washington. He was delayed in Mexico by a court of inquiry which had been ordered by Polk to examine the conduct of the war. The peace treaty was borne to the

[17] John D. P. Fuller, "The Movement for the Acquisition of All Mexico, 1846–1848," *Johns Hopkins University Studies in Historical and Political Science*, Series 54, No. 1, pp. 31–48, 54–56, 60–76, 79–93.

American capital by a newspaperman, James L. Freaner of the New Orleans *Delta.* There it met a cool reception indeed.

Four members of the Cabinet advised acceptance of the treaty, but both Buchanan and Walker opposed sending it to the Senate. All the Cabinet agreed with Polk that Trist had acted "very badly" in disregarding the order to break off negotiations and return home. But angered as the President was by Trist's conduct, he was not ready to throw the treaty in the waste basket. His reasons for this attitude stemmed directly from political developments that had taken place during the war.[18]

Once the war was a fact, it had been accepted as such by the great majority of both Whigs and Democrats, and no significant opposition to it had appeared in Congress during the early summer of 1846. But by the time the first session of the Twenty-ninth Congress adjourned (August 10, 1846), the mood of the people and of the politicians had begun to change. This change was due to a variety of causes.

The Whigs had never been enthusiastic about the war. Powerful religious organizations, such as the Friends, the Unitarians, and the Congregationalists, were always in opposition to the shedding of blood on Mexican soil. Unitarian William Henry Channing went far beyond most pastors when he declared that if he enlisted in this "damnable war," it would be under the Mexican banner, but his stand reflected widespread repugnance to a struggle that many felt, with Lowell, was meant "jest to lug more slave states in." This repugnance was fortified by reports coming back from the war theaters of low moral conditions there, and of the dust, heat, insects, and yellow fever that plagued the march of America's gallant warriors on the halls of the Montezumas.[19]

From the popular point of view, Polk was not a great war leader. Hard, dour, lacking in imagination, he was not the man to inspire or exalt the masses. He lacked the magnetism, the sense of the dramatic, that enabled a Pitt, a Churchill, or a Roosevelt to sustain popular enthusiasm at a high pitch.

Lacking dynamic leadership and plagued by faction, the second session of the Twenty-ninth Congress met on December 7, 1846, in scarcely a warlike mood. The Whigs had had a marked resurgence in

[18] Polk, *Diary,* III, 345–347.

[19] Clayton S. Ellsworth, "The American Churches and the Mexican War," *American Historical Review,* XLV (Jan., 1940), 316–319; Hamilton, *Taylor, Soldier of the Republic,* p. 202; Bill, *Rehearsal,* pp. 129, 245–247; J. H. Smith, *War with Mexico,* II, 268–274.

the November elections, and the Democrats had lost the House of Representatives. The opposition, in consequence, was set to criticize and complain. It was now obvious that while the conflict might be glorious, it was not going to be brief. It was also obvious, as Greeley told the Whigs in the columns of the *Tribune,* that, support the war as much as they liked, such glory as there was would go to the Democrats.

The Whigs, therefore, became more and more critical. Webster declared that the war was one of insufficient pretexts; that it was based on such feeble grounds as monetary claims, the nonreception of Slidell, and the so-called invasion of American soil. Senator Tom Corwin of Ohio waxed wroth about the war's iniquity and declared that if he were a Mexican, he would bid the American soldiers welcome to hospitable graves. The *National Intelligencer* praised the Mexicans for their courage and fortitude in the face of disaster. Greeley denounced the war in unmeasured terms and painted its hardships in lurid colors. His *Tribune* emphasized the awful price in blood that must be paid for victory. It painted dismal pictures of the hardships and moral degeneration attendant upon campaigning in Mexico. It declared that American victories were merely luring the soldiers of the United States further and further into a land from which there was no escape, just as Napoleon's victories had lured him on into Spain. The United States, said Greeley, should take warning from Napoleon's fate, and make peace before it was too late. The Whigs sedulously spread the story that Polk was taking his ease on $68 a day, while the soldiers toiled and sweated for pittances in the field. They accused the President of plotting the conquest of all Mexico.[20]

If the Whigs were being difficult about the war, the Democrats themselves were often refractory. The close contest over the Walker tariff highlighted the fact that even when the Democrats had clear majorities in both houses of Congress, that body could not be counted on for steady support of presidential policies. This was all the more evident as the solons became involved in war legislation. Barnburners feuded with Hunkers and were steadily hostile to Polk and cool to his war measures. The friends of Calhoun chafed because of his exclusion from the Cabinet. Such matters—together with the factional strife

[20] Polk, *Diary,* III, 348; J. H. Smith, *War with Mexico,* II, 275–280, 285–286; Glyndon G. Van Deusen, *Horace Greeley, Nineteenth Century Crusader* (Philadelphia, 1953), pp. 109–110. Smith believes that the Whig strategy was to make the war odious and thus delay the passage of war measures until Polk was forced to restore the protective tariff levels of 1842.

between Buchananites and Dallasites in Pennsylvania, the rage of disappointed office seekers, and the never-ending struggle for leadership that was going on between Benton, Cass, and Calhoun—made it difficult for the Democratic majority to rally behind the President. In January, 1847, Polk confided ruefully to his diary that he was "practically in a minority" at the congressional end of Pennsylvania Avenue.[21]

One great source of difficulty for the administration was the Wilmot Proviso. When in the summer of 1846 Polk asked Congress for $2 million to "facilitate negotiations" with Mexico, the House of Representatives tacked on an amendment, offered by Democrat David Wilmot of Pennsylvania, prohibiting slavery in any territory that might be acquired from Mexico. The House passed the appropriation with the Proviso attached. The Senate adjourned without action. In the second session of the Twenty-ninth Congress, the Proviso reappeared again and again, backed by the votes of those who opposed the extension of slavery on moral grounds, by the Barnburners, by Democrats from the Northwest who felt that the South had betrayed them by tamely accepting the Oregon boundary compromise instead of standing up for fifty-four forty, by western Whigs and Democrats who resented the South's lack of interest in internal improvements and protection. This was a formidable, if somewhat disjointed, array of forces. In opposition to it, Calhoun offered a series of resolutions to the effect that Congress could not exclude slavery from any of the territories of the United States. These heightened northern suspicions that the South wanted Mexican territory for the purpose of spreading and strengthening slavery. By the end of January, 1847, passions in Congress had been deeply roused by the prospect of slavery extension, and the old Jacksonian, Frank Blair, was beginning to long for Clay's reappearance in the Senate as the man best suited to combat Calhoun.

The result of all this contention over the Proviso was that the Democratic majorities in both houses of the Twenty-ninth Congress became unstable, and measures such as the ten-regiment bill that Polk deemed essential for the prosecution of the war were unconscionably delayed.

The ten-regiment bill finally made its way through Congress in February, 1847, and at about the same time Congress gave Polk $3 million for purposes of negotiation with Mexico. But from the point of view of the administration, such triumphs were sullied by the action

[21] Polk, *Diary*, II, 319, 328, 329.

of the House in again passing the Proviso, tacked on to the $3 million bill by a vote of 115 to 106. The Proviso was once more blocked by the Senate, and the $3 million bill received the President's signature, but it was clear that the 1848 election was looming over the congressional proceedings. The war appeared to be in danger of becoming a football of politics.[22]

The Thirtieth Congress had met on December 6, 1847, with the Whigs in a majority in the House and more than ever in a mood to blast the war. They had devoted much time and effort to criticizing the return of Santa Anna to Mexico and the administration's treatment of both Taylor and Scott. Much of this was sheer partisan spleen. But they also had continued to oppose the acquisition of territory, an attitude that was chiefly due to a sincere fear lest territorial enlargement, by exciting sectional strife over slavery, endanger both the Whig party and the Union.

Such fear on the part of the Whigs was justifiable. When Webster told the Senate that he foresaw only a troubled future of "contention, strife, and agitation," he spoke as one of the prophets. But in their attitude toward territorial gains the Whigs were also, in a measure, partisan. They knew, as Greeley had told them, that the glory of the war would go to the Democrats, and, in their partisan rancor at the prospect, they ignored the danger to the United States that inevitably would be involved in permitting the establishment of a rival republic, or of a foreign power, on the Pacific coast.

Whig opposition and Democratic factionalism had a harder road to travel as 1848 came on than had been the case a year earlier. Buena Vista and Scott's victories on the way to Mexico City had revived popular interest in the war. Mexico's stubbornness about ending hostilities had generated considerable resentment toward that unhappy country. The House voted down by 137 to 41 a motion for withdrawing American troops to the east bank of the Rio Grande and ending the war by a settlement of the Texas boundary at that river and the payment of American claims against Mexico. It did, nevertheless,

[22] Polk, *Diary,* II, 328; Rives Papers, J. J. Crittenden to Rives, Feb. 28, 1847; Flagg Papers, A. H. Gillet to Flagg, Jan. 15, 18, 20, 1847, Preston King to Flagg, Jan. 18, 1847; *Congressional Globe,* 29th Cong., second sess., 105, 425, 453–455; J. H. Smith, *War with Mexico,* II, 286–287; Richard R. Stenberg, "The Motivation of the Wilmot Proviso," *Mississippi Valley Historical Review,* XVIII (Mar., 1932), 535–551; William E. Smith, *The Francis Preston Blair Family in Politics* (2 vols., New York, 1933), I, 224.

pass by a vote of 85 to 81 a resolution branding the war as "unnecessary and unconstitutional." These moves reflected the fact that the campaign of 1848 was now close at hand.[23]

Such was the political background and the existing political situation that confronted Polk, who was now faced with the problem of whether or not to submit to the Senate the treaty which Trist had brought back from Mexico. A few weeks before the treaty appeared in Washington, Polk had decided to demand more than New Mexico and California.[24] This, plus the fact that Trist had broken his instructions, impelled the President to withhold the treaty. On the other hand, powerful considerations argued for sending it to the Senate. It conformed, in the main, with the instructions that had been given to Trist the preceding April. It was doubtful that additional territory could be obtained from Mexico by further negotiation; such territory would have to be wrested from the enemy by force of arms, and this would mean a resumption of the war and redoubled criticism of the government's policy. There was still another dire possibility. The Whigs had accused Polk of beginning and continuing the war with a view to seizing all of Mexico. If he now rejected a treaty which he and his Cabinet had previously approved, Congress might refuse the grants necessary for carrying on the war on the ground that it had become a war of outright conquest. Then the struggle would degenerate into a stalemate; New Mexico and California might well be lost; and the Democrats might lose the election of 1848.

So ran the thoughts of the President of the United States. The consequence of this reasoning was his determination to submit the treaty to the Senate. The document had been negotiated by "an impudent and unqualified scoundrel," so the President confided to his diary, but cold logic forbade its repudiation.[25]

The debate over the ratification of the treaty showed that the Whigs preferred to acquire no territory from Mexico, and that from eight to twelve Democratic senators wanted more territory than Trist had ob-

[23] *Congressional Globe,* 30th Cong., first sess., 93–95; Fuller, "Movement for Acquisition of All Mexico," p. 54; J. H. Smith, *War with Mexico,* II, 287–288, 290, 291; George T. Curtis, *Life of Daniel Webster* (2 vols., New York, 1870), II, 301–307; Albert J. Beveridge, *Abraham Lincoln, 1809–1858* (2 vols., Boston and New York, 1928), II, 414–437; Glyndon G. Van Deusen, *The Life of Henry Clay* (Boston, 1937), pp. 382–383, 387–388.

[24] Fuller, "Movement for Acquisition of All Mexico," p. 126.

[25] Polk, *Diary,* III, 346–358; Brent, "Trist," pp. 466–469.

tained. The vote on ratification, which was approved, thirty-eight to fourteen, was neither partisan nor sectional. Most of the Whigs, and the Calhoun Democrats also, voted for the treaty, obviously fearing that rejection would mean the annexation of all Mexico.[26]

Nicholas P. Trist, the "scoundrel" who had negotiated the peace, was put under arrest by Polk until he sailed from Vera Cruz. The purpose of this was to ensure Trist's prompt departure from Mexico after the court of inquiry had adjourned. The hapless diplomat reached Washington on May 17, 1848. There he was deprived of his post in the State Department. He was given no opportunity to explain or defend his action in Mexico. The pay for his services there, which was to come from funds controlled by the Chief Executive, was withheld by the President. He did not receive the compensation due him until some twenty-five years later, when, shortly before his death, the Forty-second Congress awarded him $14,599.20.[27] Never was a reward for services to a man's country more unjustly withheld or more richly deserved.

The treaty was accepted by the Mexican Congress in May, 1848. It was proclaimed by President Polk on July 4 of that same year.

The war with Mexico was over. The United States emerged from it with 529,000 square miles of additional territory, a magnificent outlet to the trade of the Pacific, and hundreds of millions in California gold, a bonanza the news of which was just beginning to spread as the treaty reached the final stages of ratification.

The war had cost the United States some 13,000 dead, with six and one-half times as many dying by disease as in battle. Its monetary cost was $97,705,860. It is possible to argue that these costs were more than balanced by the advantages achieved, but there was still more on the debit side. The war had opened a Pandora's box of evils for the United States. Out of it rose the specter of slavery extension, and out of this came bitter sectional strife, the disruption of parties, the beginning of a series of strains and crises that were to culminate in civil war. Ralph Waldo Emerson was a true prophet. "The United States will conquer Mexico," he said, "but it will be as the man who swallows the arsenic which brings him down in turn. Mexico will poison us." Thirteen years later, the guns of Sumter echoed Emerson's prophecy.[28]

[26] Polk, *Diary,* III, 365–366; Brent, "Trist," pp. 469–473; Fuller, "Movement for Acquisition of All Mexico," pp. 152–156.

[27] Brent, "Trist," pp. 473–474.

[28] Bernard De Voto, *The Year of Decision* (Boston, 1943), p. 492.

CHAPTER 13

The Deterioration of Parties

WITH the close of the Mexican War, the feuds and bitterness that had been building up in the Democratic party became more pronounced than ever. Similar disruptive forces were at work among the Whigs. The major parties were facing a situation in which old issues were dying or dead and new ones were riving the parties asunder. The Wilmot Proviso symbolized a sectional conflict, partly moral and partly economic in character, that threatened nothing short of party disintegration.

That the campaign of 1848 had begun almost with the beginning of the war was abundantly demonstrated by the two leading generals, and by President Polk himself. Lesser politicos had also caught the fever. The year 1846 was not half over before newspaper editors and state leaders in both camps were busily engaged in calculating the political significance of military victories, in constructing the potentiality charts of candidates, and in seeking to foster or to thwart the ambitions of these candidates for nomination to the highest office in the land.

The left wing of the Democracy, of which the Barnburners were the central core, wanted the Democratic nomination to go either to Van Buren or to "Cato," as affection (and sometimes derision) termed Silas Wright. They would also have been fairly content with the nomination of that stalwart proponent of hard money and Jacksonism, Thomas Hart Benton. The Calhoun men, and the coterie that surrounded Polk, had very different aspirations and intrigued busily to prevent any of these candidates from acquiring strength. This situation at the national level had its counterpart in the state organizations of the North. In state after state, in New England, in Pennsylvania, in Ohio, in New York itself, feuding between conservative and radical (that is to say, antislavery) Democrats had gone to lengths that bade fair to rip the party asunder. In New York, the Democratic party had ceased to exist by the close of 1846, so deep was the chasm separating Hunkers and Barnburners.[1]

Of the three left-wing Democratic candidates, Wright had by far the greatest potential strength, although it is doubtful that he could have been persuaded to make the race. He had accepted the nomination for governor of New York State in 1844 in order to save the Democratic ticket, and had been elected. The next two years had been unhappy ones for him, his administration having been hampered by the constant feuding between Hunkers and Barnburners, by his own inexplicable unwillingness to act as an aggressive leader, and by the coolness of the administration at Washington to his closest associates. Running again in 1846, much against his will, he had been knifed by the Hunkers and badly beaten at the polls. He died of a heart attack less than a year later, and Frank Blair, among others, laid his demise to the Hunkers and to Polk.[2]

"I see no hope of rallying the northern Democracy, unless it be on Mr. Van Buren," wrote John A. Dix to Flagg, three days after Wright's death. These New York politicians, like Van Buren and Frank Blair himself, were agreed that the northern wing of the Democracy must stand firm against the desire of southern Democrats to expand the area of slavery. They all knew that, as early as March, 1847, the legislatures of eight northern states had passed resolutions deprecating its spread. They knew the inroads that antislavery was making in the Democratic ranks. But there was little hope of Van Buren, or any other radical Democrat, receiving the regular Democratic nomination. The logic of circumstance, in the thinking of the majority of Democratic leaders throughout the nation, pointed inexorably to a middle-of-the-road candidate, and certainly to one who had had no connection with the Wilmot Proviso.[3]

[1] Flagg Papers, A. H. Gillet to Flagg, Jan. 18, 1847; John A. Garraty, *Silas Wright* (New York, 1949), pp. 379–399; Allan Nevins, *Ordeal of the Union* (2 vols., New York, 1947), I, 189–190.

[2] Garraty, *Wright,* pp. 336–356, 365–386; William E. Smith, *The Francis Preston Blair Family in Politics* (2 vols., New York, 1933), I, 216, 225.

[3] Flagg Papers, Dix to Flagg, Aug. 30, 1847, Preston King to Flagg, Sept. 14,

James Buchanan hoped that the presidential mantle would fall upon his shoulders, and Polk was sure that his Secretary of State was using his Cabinet position to improve his chances of the nomination. But there was powerful opposition to "Old Buck" in his own state of Pennsylvania, and it soon became apparent that his time had not yet come. Rather, men's eyes began to turn to a Middle Westerner who, in December, 1847, had thrust himself very much into the public eye on the question of slavery extension.

Lewis Cass was at this time sixty-five years of age. Of New England stock, he had made his home in Ohio, and then in Michigan territory. Serving with distinction in the War of 1812, he had then for eighteen years been a very creditable governor of Michigan Territory. Secretary of War in Jackson's Cabinet for six years, he was next appointed America's representative at the French court. He was now United States senator from Michigan.

Cass was of large frame, with a cold and severe face which on occasion could take on an appearance of benignity. Simple in his tastes and of unassuming manners, he had some claim to being considered a man of culture. But he was past his prime and the aggressive vigor that had carried him to high station had now subsided into a rather dull inertia. He was a Jacksonian of the eighteen-forties' vintage. He had always been opposed to the United States Bank, to distribution of the proceeds of public land sales, and to a comprehensive program of internal improvements at federal expense. He was still opposed to these things. But he was now definitely an imperialist, one who demanded all of Oregon, was ardent for Texan annexation, and had a vision of territorial acquisition that ranged as far as Yucatán.

There were many aspects of Cass's public life that made him suitable presidential timber for a party that shrank from the issue of slavery extension. Of his probity there was no question. He had had a distinguished career of public service. He was a temperance man, and the temperance movement, for years a growing force in American life, was now beginning to assume the aspects of a national crusade with distinct political implications.[4] He was an Anglophobe, in a period when Americans were smarting under British criticism and were suspicious of British designs in the New World. He was a moderate and a na-

Oct. 8, 1847; Andrew C. McLaughlin, *Lewis Cass* (Boston and New York, 1891), p. 229; William N. Chambers, *Old Bullion Benton, Senator from the New West* (Boston, 1956), p. 331.

[4] Alice F. Tyler, *Freedom's Ferment* (Minneapolis, 1944), pp. 308–345.

tionalist by disposition. And he was an outspoken opponent of the Wilmot Proviso.[5]

Cass had opposed the Proviso in the Senate as early as March 1, 1847. In December of that year he published the so-called Nicholson letter in which he came out for letting the inhabitants of the territories decide for themselves whether or not they would have slavery. This was the first full exposition of what later came to be known as the Douglas doctrine, and it at once drew the fire of the antislavery forces of the North. It made him utterly unacceptable to the Barnburners and their allies. It stamped him, in Greeley's opinion, as "the servile pimp of Slavery for the expected hire of its Presidential favor, and the deadly enemy of Impartial Justice and Universal Freedom." But it was a middle-of-the-road course that had a strong appeal for that great mass of public opinion which had no burning convictions, pro or con, on the subject of slavery extension.[6]

The Democratic national convention met at Baltimore on May 27, 1848. A great and fundamental problem underlay its deliberations. Were the new lands of the West, with their glittering opportunities, to be open to free labor alone, or were they to be open on equal terms to a slaveholding hierarchy against whose servile labor force free labor could not hope to compete? The nub of the problem was not whether slavery would be profitable in these areas. That no one could surely tell, save for territory as far north as Oregon. The crux of the matter lay in deciding whether or not slavery should have an *opportunity* to gain new footholds at the expense of freedom.

The only serious competitors Cass had to fear for the Democratic nomination were James Buchanan of Pennsylvania and Levi Woodbury of New Hampshire. All three were against the Wilmot Proviso, so that on this crucial point they stood on substantially the same ground. Cass had from the start more than twice the number of delegates that could be rallied by either of his competitors. He had great strength in both the West and South. Woodbury had no such hold on public opinion as that which Cass enjoyed. Neither had Buchanan, and the additional fact that the Pennsylvania Democracy's state convention, after nominating Buchanan, had signified that Cass was its second choice made the latter's triumph almost a foregone conclusion.

[5] McLaughlin, *Cass,* pp. 210, 229, 254–255.

[6] New York *Tribune,* Jan. 3, Feb. 16, 1848; Nevins, *Ordeal,* I, 192–193; Chambers, *Benton,* p. 331; McLaughlin, *Cass,* pp. 231–232.

Cass received the necessary two-thirds' majority on the fourth ballot, a result which the convention hailed with enthusiasm. The vice-presidential nominee was General William O. Butler of Kentucky. The Democrats had put the military on both ends of the ticket.

The proceedings of the Democratic convention showed that the leaders of the party, in a desperate effort to keep the party organization from splintering into fragments, were doing everything possible to keep to the middle. Both the Barnburners and the Hunkers had sent delegations to Baltimore. The convention had proposed to split the New York delegation between them. The Barnburners had thereupon withdrawn, and in the end neither delegation was seated. The nomination of Cass was, indeed, highly offensive to the Barnburners and their associates, but Butler's nomination was a sop to them and to their northern associates, since he was a protégé of Frank Blair. The platform frowned the usual Democratic frowns upon internal improvements at national expense, distribution, a national bank, and the assumption of state debts, but it weaseled on the question of slavery extension. The party had taken no stand on the one great issue of the day.

Cass's acceptance speech pledged him to stand for the Constitution and brotherly love. He defined the difference between Whiggism and Democracy as that which had separated the Hamiltonians from the Jeffersonians. This, to say the least, was oversimplification. Later, when the campaign was over, he wrote, "My day has gone by. I think I have sense enough to see that." But in the spring of 1848 such clarity of perception was denied him. Anxious for the highest honors in the land, he resigned his seat and started to campaign.[7]

The Whig nomination was a subject of much greater rivalry than was that of the Democrats. Shortly after Taylor's victories at Palo Alto and Resaca de la Palma, Thurlow Weed in the Albany *Evening Journal* had suggested Old Zack as a presidential possibility, and Major Mordecai Noah in the New York *Sunday Messenger* had prophesied that Taylor would be a "good enough Morgan" for the Whigs in 1848. Greeley's *Tribune* had promptly labeled this a silly comment. Taylor, declared the *Tribune,* though "an old-fashioned

[7] *Niles' Register,* LXXIII (Feb. 19, 1848), 393; Robert W. Johannsen, *Frontier Politics and the Sectional Conflict* (Seattle, 1955), pp. 16–18; Chambers, *Benton,* pp. 332–335; W. E. Smith, *Blair Family,* I, 232–237; McLaughlin, *Cass,* pp. 236, 240, 241.

Kentucky Whig," was without political ambition. The *Tribune* was wrong on all counts. Taylor could scarcely be called a "Kentucky Whig," since he had spent almost no time in that state after achieving manhood, and had moved from Kentucky to Louisiana as early as 1823; events were to show that he had plenty of political ambition; and the comments of Weed and Noah were clearly indicative of the fact that Taylorism was abroad in the land.[8]

The *Tribune's* ignorance of Taylor's geographical locale was a true indication of only one thing—the General's lack of political stature. Old Rough and Ready had never taken any interest in politics. He had never voted. When his attention was brought to the rumors connecting his name with the White House, his first open reaction was that he did not want any presidential nomination; that he was for Scott as the next Whig candidate. But more victories brought more reports of acclaim by populace and politicians alike. He was criticized by the administration in Washington for his conduct of the Army, criticized in ways that made his blood boil. Scott deprived him of his regulars after Monterrey. Under the circumstances, it was only natural that he should begin to cherish a desire to throw "the rascals" out of office and, whenever possible, keep any rascal from getting into high station. By December, 1846, it was clear that Taylor liked the idea of being a candidate, and by the summer of 1847 he was ready to "undergo political martyrdom rather than see Scott or Cass elected."

The year 1847 was not half over before Taylor was well launched upon the race for the Presidency. He claimed, however, and stuck to his claim with dogged pertinacity, that his candidacy was not of his own making and was not in any sense partisan. It was, he said, born solely of popular demand. Since he was then, in very truth, the people's candidate, he was ready to accept nomination from all parties and groups. The one qualification that he imposed was that he be asked to make no pledges.

Taylor's idea of running for the Presidency *in vacuo,* this "Rough-and-ready, or, rather, rough-and-tumble" way of getting nominated (as Greeley termed it), troubled the Whig leaders. Caleb Smith of

[8] New York *Tribune,* June 15, 1846; Holman Hamilton, *Zachary Taylor, Soldier of the Republic* (Indianapolis, 1941), p. 72; Glyndon G. Van Deusen, *Thurlow Weed: Wizard of the Lobby* (Boston, 1947), p. 157. "Good enough Morgan" was a term supposedly used by Thurlow Weed in the eighteen-twenties in regard to a corpse that he identified as that of the betrayer of Masonic secrets.

Indiana declared that "the man is certainly demented." The old General, however, could not be budged from his position. Against his stubborn insistence the politicians had to weigh his great popularity and the fact that, having no political principles, he had made no political enemies. These were indeed weighty considerations.

There were other difficulties with Taylor as a candidate. His avowal to correspondents that he could not declare his views on a national bank, the tariff, distribution, or internal improvements, because he had not had time to investigate these subjects, was not likely to convince the thinking part of the electorate that he was ready for the highest office in the land. Another problem was his penchant for epistolary correspondence, some of it most ineptly phrased. "It is melancholy," a New York political leader wrote to Weed, "to see how the General's *English* is suffering down there in that Spanish country. At the rate he goes on he will lose the use of his native dialect." Neither could it be overlooked that he was a southern slaveholder, and therefore not likely to draw the support of the antislavery voters, Whig or Democrat, of the North. The Ohio Whigs, among whom antislavery was strong, were decidedly cool to him. Tom Corwin, who had presidential aspirations of his own, echoed their sentiments when he remarked that Taylor's qualifications for the Presidency consisted of "sleeping forty years in the woods and cultivating moss on the calves of his legs."

But despite such obstacles, the General's candidacy became more and more formidable. He was a hero, a persecuted hero. His record, there for all to see, was that of a plain, honest man, devoted to the service of his country. The southern Whigs were rallying to this fellow slaveholder with great enthusiasm. Northern Whig conservatives saw him as a candidate under whose aegis the problem of slavery in the territories could be handled without danger of alienating the South. A group of "Young Indians" in Congress, Abraham Lincoln, Robert Toombs, Alexander H. Stephens, and others, worked constantly for him. Weed continued his support. Daily the General became more "available," and availability was a mighty word in 1848.[9]

No one was more disgusted by the Taylor boom than Horace

[9] Zachary Taylor Papers, Taylor to J. P. Taylor, June 24, 1847; Weed Papers, Washington Hunt to Weed, Dec. 26, 1847, Seward to Weed, Jan. 20, 1848; New York *Tribune,* Dec. 20, 1847, Jan. 18–22, 1848; Holman Hamilton, *Zachary Taylor, Soldier in the White House* (Indianapolis, 1951), pp. 66–67, 74; Brainerd Dyer, "Zachary Taylor and the Election of 1848"; *Pacific Historical Review,* IX (1940), 174–175; Nevins, *Ordeal,* I, 189.

Greeley. He felt that the political situation was in a state of flux; that both of the old parties were disintegrating as the old issues died and new ones arose to take their places. This being the case, a first-rate leader was a necessity. Greeley's ideal candidate for the Whigs, he told a correspondent, would be a temperance man who would advocate protection, internal improvements, unalienable homesteads for the western settlers, and more consideration for the rights of labor. In other words, his goal was a Whig party that would serve the interests and aspirations of the masses as well as the classes in northern society, and he wanted as its candidate a man devoted to such ends. But who knew what Taylor really stood for? "Old Rough," Greeley told Schuyler Colfax, "would get along tolerably well with good advisers, but it is all a lottery about that. I want to see *some* element of 'Progress' on the ticket." As events were to prove, this was a vain desire.[10]

At this time, Greeley was still close to Weed and Seward. They formed a working "team," very powerful in New York State and now actively seeking a high place in national politics. They would have liked Seward for President on the Whig ticket, but realized that this was an impossible goal. They would have been glad to see Seward in second place on the ticket, provided an outstanding man was the presidential candidate. At various times they, especially Greeley, became openly critical of candidates for the nomination, especially when those candidates' chances appeared to be bright. Greeley would "prefer" now one candidate, now another. Some believed he was for Clay. Others were sure that he was for Corwin, or John McLean, or Seward. It is distinctly possible that the "team" was hoping for a deadlocked convention which would then do for Seward what the 1844 Democratic convention had done for Polk.[11]

Another Whig who viewed the Taylor boom with a cold eye was Henry Clay. He was seventy years old in 1847, but he still dreamed of the Presidency. As the Taylor movement showed marked signs of developing, Clay is reported to have said, "I wish I could kill a

[10] New York *Tribune,* July 21, 1846; Beman Brockway, *Fifty Years in Journalism* (Watertown, 1891), p. 116; Greeley Papers (New York Public Library), Greeley to Colfax, May 1, 1847.

[11] Greeley Papers (New York Historical Society), Greeley to Weed, Jan. 13, 1847 (New York Public Library), Greeley to O. A. Bowe, July 26, 1847, Greeley to Colfax, Apr. 3, 1848; Frederic Bancroft, *The Life of William H. Seward* (2 vols., New York, 1900), I, 158, 164; George R. Poage, *Henry Clay and the Whig Party* (Chapel Hill, 1936), p. 163; Albany *Evening Journal,* June 13, 1848, Aug. 12, 1853.

Mexican." The Old Prince wanted to fight the campaign on the old issues, the tariff, internal improvements, the veto power, with the conduct of the war thrown in for good measure. By the late summer of 1847 he was definitely a candidate, and his candidacy was making strides in the North, especially in New York (where he had strong supporters in spite of Weed and Seward) and in the Western Reserve.

On November 13, 1847, at Lexington, Kentucky, Clay made what he and his supporters regarded as a very important speech. In it he attacked the administration for having precipitated the war. He maintained that Congress should define the purposes and objects of the war. He asserted further that there should be an emphatic disavowal of any wish or desire "to acquire any foreign territory whatever, for the purpose of propagating slavery, or of introducing slaves from the United States into such foreign territory."

Clay's Lexington speech was received with enthusiasm throughout the nation. Only two Whig papers failed to give it warm applause. Clay himself thought that it identified him as "a western man with northern principles." He had approached without actually assuming the Wilmot Proviso stand—approached it because he knew what its outright espousal would do to him in the South. "Sufficient for the day is the evil thereof," he told Greeley.

As it turned out, this temporizing position did not give Clay the nomination. No one knows what would have happened had he come out unequivocably for the Proviso; but had he done so, this slaveholding "western man with northern principles" might then have found himself at the head of a Whig party centered in the North and West and definitely opposed to slavery extension. Such a party, antedating Republicanism by half a dozen years, might well have changed the course of history.[12]

It looked, in the spring of 1848, as though Clay had stopped the Taylor boom. To this Taylor himself had contributed by calmly accepting all nominations and recommendations (including that of a nativist group known as the American Republicans); by continuing to assert that he must not be considered a strictly party candidate; and by throwing in, for good measure, the announcement that he would run

[12] Porter Collection (Buffalo Historical Society), Clay to Greeley, Nov. 22, 1847; Poage, *Clay,* pp. 164, 166; William C. Binkley, *The Expansionist Movement in Texas* (Berkeley, 1925), p. 178; Carl Schurz, *Life of Henry Clay* (2 vols., Boston and New York, 1887), II, 289, 299.

whether or not he was nominated by the Whigs. Then the Kentuckian himself suffered a grievous setback. His own state failed to nominate him. John J. Crittenden, a power in the Whig party in Kentucky and Clay's long-time friend, had deserted him for Taylor on the ground that Clay could not and Taylor could be elected. The report spread that if the Old Chief could not carry his own state, there was little chance of victory under his banner, and Taylor's prospects immediately improved.

Old Zack gained further ground by his so-called Allison letter of April 22, 1848, in which he declared himself a Whig, even though "not an ultra Whig"; announced his determination to accept the will of Congress regarding the tariff, the currency, and internal improvements; and asserted that he loved peace. This gave him a platform of sorts, and the waverers, who thought he could win but had found him difficult to take, now rallied to him in droves.[13]

The Whig convention that gathered on June 7, 1848, at Chinese Hall in Philadelphia was a politicians' convention. The approximately 300 delegates were primarily, basically, and fundamentally interested in one thing—victory. En route, they had been beset by Taylor advocates, among whom were included most of the Whig members of Congress. The delegates had heard over and over again that Clay could not be elected; that seven of Kentucky's twelve delegates were hostile to him; that he had only a negligible following in the cotton South. Delegates committed against Taylor were steered toward Scott, for whom a late boom had developed, and who had the Ohio delegation save for one vote. If they were from New England, they were urged to consider the merits of Daniel Webster, who had no chance whatsoever of the nomination.

The balloting showed that Clay's strongholds lay in Whig states and Whig districts of Democratic states, areas that were fairly safe under any circumstances, whereas 75 per cent of Taylor's strength came from Democratic states and Democratic districts in Whig states. The Ohio delegates kept repeating that Clay could not carry their state. Toombs of Georgia and other Southerners declared that the South would not vote for Clay, and that if he was nominated they would run Taylor as a "stump candidate." Under this withering barrage, Clay's strength steadily declined. His steadfast friends watched the balloting with

[13] Hamilton, *Taylor, Soldier in the White House,* pp. 74–81; Poage, *Clay,* pp. 175–176.

increasing anger, and by the fourth ballot, which gave Taylor the victory, they were charging treachery and deceit.[14]

The choice of Taylor's running mate presented another problem, rendered urgent by the need for conciliating Clay's friends. Abbott Lawrence, the New England textile manufacturer, was a strong contender for this post, but Clay's friends opposed Lawrence and, besides, it would not do to have cotton at both ends of the ticket. Some urged Webster's name, a suggestion for which the Clay men had no enthusiasm, but the "Godlike" refused to be considered. Truman Smith of Connecticut, a prominent and powerful Taylor man, then obtained Weed's reluctant consent to the nomination of Millard Fillmore, a Buffalo politician and friend of Clay, but distinctly not a good Weed and Seward man. Fillmore was put in nomination as Clay's friend, Smith switched from Lawrence to the New Yorker, and the deed was done. Taylor and Fillmore were the ticket. There was no platform.[15]

The Whig convention was over, but the ranks still seethed with bitterness. Greeley branded the Philadelphia meeting a "slaughter-house of Whig principles," and Taylor's nomination, "though perfectly true, nevertheless impossible." Webster pronounced the nomination one "not fit to be made." Seward, fearful of its effect upon the antislavery people of the North, and heartily disliking Fillmore, had only distaste for the result. Clay retired to Ashland, resentful at his own rejection and alarmed at an abandonment of old issues that would surely bring slavery into the forefront of politics. Antislavery Whigs generally greeted the ticket coolly. Even with the Democrats split by faction in state after state, a Whig victory was by no means a certain thing.[16]

But if a Whig victory was uncertain, one thing about the party was crystal clear. It had cast off its old leaders. It was no longer willing to take its stand on the old issues. Where its new course lay remained to be determined.

While the Whigs and Democrats had been wrestling with presidential politics, a third political movement had been taking form. The entire Northwest was politically uneasy, being distrustful of both the

[14] New York *Tribune,* June 12, Nov. 24, 1848, Nov. 17, 1851; Allan Nevins (ed.), *The Diary of Philip Hone, 1828–1851* (2 vols., New York, 1927), II, 850–851; Hamilton, *Taylor, Soldier in the White House,* pp. 57–60, 87–94; Poage, *Clay,* pp. 179–180.

[15] Weed Papers, Truman Smith to Weed, Aug. 28, 1853; New York *Tribune,* June 10, 1848; Albany *Evening Journal,* Apr. 4, 1851.

[16] Weed Papers, Seward to Weed, June 10, 1848; New York *Tribune,* June 10, 14, 1848; Albany *Evening Journal,* Apr. 22, 1850.

old parties on the slavery question. Many New Englanders shared this same distrust. Ohio, a western state with a heavy infusion of New England settlers, was especially full of political unrest, and there a convention of those devoted to free soil had been summoned to meet at Columbus in June of 1848.

News of this projected Columbus convention had been brought to the Whig convention at Baltimore by the Ohio delegates. This, coupled with Taylor's nomination, stirred a number of the antislavery Whigs at Baltimore to vigorous action. Charles Allen and Henry Wilson of Massachusetts, bitterly dissatisfied with the outcome of the proceedings, had left the Whig convention, declaring themselves to be no longer Whigs. Wilson had summoned a meeting of other rebellious delegates, and on the evening of the day Taylor was nominated, fifteen of these insurgents had met to consider future plans. They decided to urge the Columbus meeting to call a national free-soil convention in Buffalo and in the very near future. They, themselves, would take a leading part in such a convention.

Meantime, a movement similar to that of the fifteen had begun in the opposing political camp. Van Buren had advised the Barnburner delegates at the Baltimore Democratic convention to announce their nonsupport of the ticket if Cass was nominated. Once Cass had been chosen, the younger Barnburners, men like Preston King and John Van Buren ("Prince John," the son of the ex-President), together with kindred spirits such as David Wilmot of Pennsylvania and Gideon Welles of Connecticut, pressed for action. Older Democrats, Benton, Bryant, Blair, and Flagg among them, opposed an independent nomination, but they were overborne.

A mixture of motives—antislavery conviction, hatred of Cass (who was held responsible by many for Van Buren's loss of the nomination in 1844), a determination to rule or ruin the Democratic party—all played a part in the split that now developed from the Democracy. The Barnburners called a state convention at Utica in late June, 1848. There they nominated a reluctant Martin Van Buren for the Presidency, and issued a call for a national convention of antislavery men to meet at Buffalo on August 9, 1848.[17]

[17] Arthur M. Schlesinger, Jr., *The Age of Jackson* (Boston, 1945), pp. 463–465; Stewart Mitchell, *Horatio Seymour* (Cambridge, 1938), pp. 109–111; Chambers, *Benton,* p. 335; Herbert A. Donovan, *The Barnburners* (New York, 1925), pp. 89, 100–101; McLaughlin, *Cass,* pp. 246–247.

While the Barnburners were meeting at Utica, the free-soil gathering of a thousand delegates, known as the People's Convention, held its sessions at Columbus, Ohio. This convention heeded the call of the fifteen Whigs and, like the Barnburners, issued a summons for the meeting at Buffalo.

Now all eyes turned on the Liberty party, that political organization of militant antislavery men which had run national tickets in 1840 and 1844. What would the Liberty men do? The Liberty party had been in the doldrums since 1844, its demand for the complete destruction of slavery being too extreme for the great majority of antislavery men. Liberty leaders such as Salmon P. Chase and Edward M. Stanton had realized the party's weakness, and had begun casting about for a means of broadening its position. The Liberty men had themselves held a convention in Buffalo in October, 1847, and had there nominated John P. Hale of New Hampshire, a flaming spirit, Democrat, lawyer, and politician, who had broken with his party in 1845 on the Texas question but had not joined the Liberty party.

Hale's nomination was a sign of broadening on the part of the Liberty men, but Chase felt that it was not enough. The ambitious Ohioan had urged Hale to withdraw from the presidential race as early as the spring of 1848. Chase had also been one of the moving spirits back of the People's Convention at Columbus and its call for the Buffalo convention of 1848. He had little confidence in Whig antislavery pretensions, but he believed that a stand along Wilmot Proviso lines would attract many antislavery Democrats to a new and powerful party organization. A new party was all the more feasible because many Democrats had been outraged by Polk's vetoes of internal improvements bills, and by the refusal of Cass to attend the Chicago Rivers and Harbors Convention of 1847.[18] If the new party coupled with the Wilmot Proviso a firm stand for internal improvements, its prospects at the polls would be bright indeed. Chase and a number of other Liberty party leaders made up their minds to go to Buffalo.

The Buffalo free-soil convention met on August 9, 1848. There gathered together in that windy city a heterogeneous group of some ten thousand men, free-soilers from Ohio, Liberty party men, Barnburners, Conscience Whigs, disappointed Clay Whigs, Land Reformers

[18] Theodore C. Smith, *The Liberty and Free Soil Parties in the Northwest* (New York, 1897), pp. 85–116; Albert B. Hart, *Salmon Portland Chase* (Boston and New York, 1899), pp. 95–98.

demanding free land, internal improvements advocates, "Working Men of New York," and advocates of cheap postage. These milled around the streets, while a body of 465 delegates conducted the business of the convention. A spirit of idealism clearly manifested itself in the meetings of the convention, but this did not prevent deals behind the scenes.

There was a deal whereby the Barnburners were given the support of Liberty men for the ticket, in return for a promise that the platform should declare for the abolishment of slavery by the national government wherever such action was constitutional. The Conscience and Clay Whigs supported the nomination of Van Buren and in return were given a voice in platform making and a vice-presidential candidate in the person of craggy Charles Francis Adams, son of John Quincy Adams. The platform itself, written by Benjamin F. Butler of New York and Salmon P. Chase, was an agglomeration of viewpoints. It advocated cheap postage, internal improvements, a homestead law (this plank Van Buren refused to accept), a tariff for revenue, paying off the public debt, and a ringing promise to "fight on and fight ever" for "free soil, free speech, free labor, and free men."

After the nominations and the adoption of the platform, the convention broke up in a spirit of high moral enthusiasm. Hale shortly withdrew as a candidate for the Presidency on the Liberty party ticket. His withdrawal marked the amalgamation of the Liberty party in the new Free Soil movement, the leaders of which looked forward to a formidable role in the coming campaign.[19]

The campaign gathered speed in the summer of 1848, but, so far as the major parties were concerned, it never achieved much meaning. On a basis of principle, it was now difficult to distinguish Whigs from Democrats. The London *Times* had considerable reason for dismissing the contest as one of "fictitious partisanship." The politicians were busy, however, and many voters doubtless felt that they confronted a great decision in choosing between Taylor and Cass.

There was the usual vituperation and the usual effort to seize every opportunity for political advantage. Cass was denounced in the North as a Michigan Doughface, a reckless demagogue and land speculator,

[19] T. C. Smith, *Liberty and Free Soil Parties,* pp. 139–143; Schlesinger, *Age of Jackson,* pp. 465–466; McLaughlin, *Cass,* pp. 247–249; Donovan, *Barnburners,* pp. 103–105; Chambers, *Benton,* p. 336; Charles F. Adams, *Charles Francis Adams* (Boston, 1900), p. 91.

a wearer of the black cockade of slavery. Taylor was pilloried as a trafficker in human flesh. Van Buren was abused as an apostate who put personal ambition above his country's welfare. Both the major parties attempted to turn the bill organizing Oregon Territory in the summer of 1848 to their own advantage. During the debate on this measure, Douglas' proposal to extend the Missouri Compromise 36°30′ line to the Pacific gained much support from the northern followers of Cass. This was used with effect against the Democratic candidate where antislavery votes were to be gathered. On the other hand, the passage of the Oregon bill with specific prohibition of slavery angered the South and gained votes in that region for the slaveholding Taylor.[20]

As the campaign drew toward its close, there was some tightening of party lines. Webster reluctantly came out for Taylor. Greeley did the same for a variety of reasons, one of which was his intense dislike of "that fat-bellied, mutton-headed, cucumber-soled Cass." Benton, after an inner struggle, came out for Cass, as did George Bancroft and Levi Woodbury. The Free Soil men worked more and more feverishly in the North, despite the certainty of Van Buren's defeat. But on the whole it was a campaign in which Cass and Taylor were cast in the roles of Tweedledum and Tweedledee, a fact that the Whigs sought to cover up by a deluge of war and battle narratives and what Greeley described as "near-grape" ditties glorifying Taylor.

The whole nation voted for the first time on the same day in 1848. It was November 7. The vote was light, 2,878,023 ballots being cast out of a population of nearly 23 million.[21] Taylor carried eight slave and seven free states, the important northern states of New York, Pennsylvania, and Massachusetts ranging themselves under his banner. As compared with 1844, the Whigs lost ground in the East North Central states, and in the whole area lying north and west of the Ohio Taylor did not obtain a single electoral vote. This was due in part to the popularity of Cass in that region, and in part to the fact that the defection to Free Soil there was largely from the Whig ranks. The Whigs were strong in the Middle Atlantic states, due chiefly to resentment among laborers and businessmen alike over the Walker tariff. The Whigs were also strong in the South, where Taylor, the South's own

[20] Nevins, *Ordeal,* I, 208–215.

[21] Fred J. Guetter and Albert E. McKinley, *Statistical Tables Relating to the Economic Growth of the United States* (Philadelphia, 1924), p. 5. The population in 1850 was 23,191,876.

candidate, lost only Virginia, Alabama, and Mississippi, the latter two by very narrow margins.

The Democratic party emerged from the election of 1848 beaten but still strong in numbers. While the Whigs carried five of the seven geographical sections of the country,[22] they had an absolute majority only in the South Atlantic and East South Central sections. The Democrats carried the other five sections. They also carried a total of 747 counties to only 671 for the Whigs. They polled only 138,625 fewer votes than the Whigs. The Democratic strength actually increased north and west of the Ohio, where Cass was the native son. They had 127 electoral votes as against 163 for the Whigs, but had they carried New York (that is, had the Barnburners not defected there), while the votes in other states remained the same, the vote in the electoral college would have been exactly reversed.

The vote of New York was important, a fact which points to the significance of the Free Soil movement in 1848. Van Buren received about 10 per cent of the total vote cast in the country at large. This vote was centered, save for a most minute fraction, in the free states. The Free Soilers carried three New England counties, seven in the Middle Atlantic states, and twenty-one in the East North Central states. In New England, New York, and Pennsylvania, they drew their strength chiefly from the Democrats. Almost half the regular Democratic vote in New York went to the Red Fox. Elsewhere, especially in the East North Central area, the Free Soil votes came chiefly from the Whigs.

Many Whigs of antislavery sympathies were undoubtedly kept regular by the argument that a vote for Van Buren was a vote for Cass. The same argument held true, in reverse, with antislavery Democrats. Many Liberty men and antislavery Whigs refused to vote for Van Buren, either because of partisan rancor or his dubious record as President on slavery issues. When these factors are considered, together with the Free Soil vote, it becomes apparent that the years from 1844 to 1848 had witnessed a striking growth in northern antislavery sentiment.[23]

[22] These sections are New England, Middle Atlantic (New Jersey, New York, Pennsylvania), East North Central (Illinois, Indiana, Michigan, Ohio, Wisconsin), West North Central (Iowa and Missouri only in 1848), South Atlantic (Delaware, Maryland, Virginia, the Carolinas, Georgia, and Florida), East South Central (Alabama, Mississippi, Kentucky, Tennessee), West South Central (Arkansas, Louisiana, and Texas).

[23] New York *Tribune*, Nov. 25, 1864; W. Dean Burnham, *Presidential*

The election of 1848 was significant for other things than its indication of the growth of free-soil sentiment. It demonstrated the hold that the military tradition had already acquired in American politics. The Democrats had tried to capitalize on this tradition by nominating two generals who had gained their laurels in the War of 1812. The Whigs had needed only one general on their ticket, Taylor's laurels being recent and very bright. The chairman of the Democratic state central committee in Pennsylvania explained Old Zack's vote in that state as being due solely to Taylorism, which was "Jacksonism and Harrisonism over again."[24] The same explanation could have been used with even greater accuracy in other parts of the country as well.

The election also showed that the hold of the major parties on the voters was weakening; that Whigs and Democrats would leave their parties and join hands in a crusade if they judged that an important issue was at stake. In another sense, this was a demonstration that the old issues over which the parties had fought were no longer national issues. Where they still existed, they tended to subdivide rather than to separate the parties.

The distinction between Whig and Democrat had, indeed, become merely nominal, for the parties were in a state of flux. Van Buren believed that the chances were bright for Benton to reorganize the whole northern Democracy on a free-soil basis in 1852. Another New York Democrat, Jabez D. Hammond, a most shrewd and objective observer, believed that the Whigs could do the same thing with their party. In each case, the supposition was that much strength would be drawn from the opposing ranks. Salmon P. Chase felt that the defeat of Cass had "severed the last link that bound a large number of Democrats . . . to the Slave Power." Fillmore believed that the election had put the Whig party upon a strong middle ground of nationalism and that, in achieving that eminence, it had cast off both southern fire-eaters and northern abolitionist fanatics. Greeley believed that a new party was imminent. Everywhere such talk was heard.[25]

Ballots, 1836–1892 (Baltimore, 1955), pp. 37–42; T. C. Smith, *Liberty and Free Soil Parties,* pp. 144, 154–155, 158–159; Donovan, *Barnburners,* pp. 107–108; Schlesinger, *Age of Jackson,* pp. 466–468.

[24] Henry R. Mueller, *The Whig Party in Pennsylvania* (New York, 1922), p. 158.

[25] Greeley Papers (Library of Congress), Greeley to Brockway, Nov. 19, 1847; Nevins, *Ordeal,* I, 214–216; Van Deusen, *Weed,* pp. 187–188; W. E. Smith, *Blair Family,* I, 243; William O. Lynch, "Antislavery Tendencies of

The new party had not yet arrived in 1848, significant as was the part played by the Free Soilers in that election. Party loyalty and party organizations have always been stubborn facts in American political history. The Free Soil party withered as the spirit of compromise prevailed in 1850. Many of its leaders went back into the ranks of the Democracy. But it remained a portent, a foreshadowing of what was to come in 1854 when the Kansas-Nebraska Bill finally taught the opponents of slavery extension that they could sleep no more in the vain hope of compromise adjustments. Then, and not until then, was the new party born.

The period from 1828 to 1848 was one of intense political strife. During those twenty years, the heat and burden of the political day had been carried by two major parties—the Democrats on the one hand, on the other the National Republicans, soon merging into the Whigs. Splinter parties—born out of the Antimasonic excitement, the unrest of labor, slavery, resentment of foreign immigration, sometimes out of mere political machination—had appeared from time to time, but each of these wild roses in the political garden had faded. The two-party system had remained the outstanding feature of political organization.

The power of the Whig and Democratic organizations had indeed waxed and waned during the years. These ups and downs in party strength had corresponded with the appearance and disappearance of popular leaders, and with the shifting of sectional economic and social interests. But never, after the Whig party was organized, did either one of these two parties gain a position of overwhelming or even of decided superiority over its opponent. Very evenly balanced in popular strength, both centering around middle-class norms and catering to middle-class ideals, they were the natural representatives, politically speaking, of what was preeminently then, as it is now, a land of middle-class people.

Of the two parties, the Whigs were the more conservative. The nucleus of strength in the Whig party lay in the merchants, the industrialists, the bankers and businessmen—that is to say, in that shifting, mobile, ever-changing business class, constantly renewed and revitalized by accessions from the ranks of the farmers and the laborers, which was already exerting such a marked influence upon the nation's development. National in its outlook, despite the heterogeneity of the

the Democratic Party in the Northwest, 1848–50," *Mississippi Valley Historical Review,* XI (Dec., 1924), 324.

groups that rallied to its flag, the Whig party had an outstanding leader in nationalist Henry Clay. Its great and unifying objectives were the development of national wealth and power and an increasing harmony of interest, these to be obtained under the aegis of Clay's American system. The party viewed the national government as a means to be used in achieving these objectives. It fought for legislation that would establish a national bank and a sound and adequate national currency; it fought for protection of American industry, for the distribution of land-sale proceeds to the states, for internal improvements at federal expense. It shrank from slavery as an issue, because the slavery question in all its aspects was divisive and disruptive. Like the Hamiltonian Federalists, the Whig party showed a tendency to reverence the business class and to feel that, in this great land of opportunity, the masses would prosper by enjoying the benefits that would come trickling down upon them from the prosperity of their economic superiors. These benefits would derive from business activity, which in turn would be partly the product of the wisdom and initiative of America's businessmen, partly the result of benevolent governmental policies.

The Democratic party was more liberal than the Whig party. The Democratic leaders, in part from principle and conviction, in part from a keen appreciation of the political importance of the newly enfranchised masses, showed from the beginning a desire to cater to the wishes and aspirations of the common man. Early in the decade of the eighteen-thirties, the party adopted a more liberal land policy than that of the Whigs, and as the years went by the Democracy became distinguished as the champion of lower land prices and a relatively easy granting of pre-emption rights. The Democrats, too, were less zealous than were the Whigs in protecting the rising industrialists from foreign competition and, by their emphasis on a lower tariff, became the champions of the vast mass of consumers.

Democracy feared a powerful central government. Its aim was liberty and equality for all, with governmental favoritism for none. Its objective here was admirable. It failed to achieve it largely because of three limitations. Like the French philosophes of the preceding century, these American Democrats were apt to confuse liberty with equality, believing that the latter could be attained by a simple destruction of privileges which would leave all men free. Willing enough to use the state governments as agencies for promoting social and economic welfare, they had little conception of the part that the central government could play in promoting the ends of justice and in servicing the national well-being. They were also hampered by a defective monetary theory—the "hard money" myth.

Economically speaking, Democratic policy at the national level was largely negative in character. In the name of equality, the Jacksonians destroyed the national bank. They limited the scope and development of internal improvements at national expense. They inclined more and more, during the eighteen-thirties, to a hard-money policy, that is, to the establishment of a specie currency in an era when specie was insufficient to meet the currency needs of the nation's dynamic economy. They looked with misgivings upon the development of the corporate form of business activity. Leaders as closely identified with Democratic thought as Silas Wright and William Cullen Bryant were even in favor of unlimited liability for shareholders in corporations.

The high-level policy of the Democratic party changed in emphasis during the decade of the eighteen-forties. This was in part because of revolt within its own ranks against defective economic ideas, in part because the panic and depression that came on in 1837 brought political disaster in its wake, in part because of the growth of the concept of Manifest Destiny. The radical economic policies that were generally attacked by the Whigs as Locofocoism were de-emphasized and, to a considerable extent, abandoned. Cheap land became the cry of the Free Soilers, rather than of the party headed by Polk and Cass. Expansion became the Democratic watchword of the day. And southern leadership began assuming a greater and greater importance in the councils of the Democracy.

By the close of the eighteen-forties, many of the issues that had divided Whigs from Democrats had ceased being national issues. The United States Bank had disappeared, destroyed beyond hope of resurrection. Distribution of the proceeds of land sales was a vanished dream. The tariff had become more than ever a local issue, rather than one that divided the parties on a national scale. By 1848, it was difficult indeed to distinguish between the national principles of Whiggery and Democracy. Their differences over the use of the veto power were chiefly theoretical in character. Both parties contained protectionists and tariff-for-revenue men. Both had their Conscience and Cotton elements. Both quailed before the rising contention over slavery.

That contention loomed large by 1848, and the major parties were proving themselves inadequate for the task of coping with it. A new sectionalism was coming to the fore. It was rooted in moral conviction and in the rivalry between two economic systems, the one based on free, the other on slave labor. The election of Taylor and Fillmore afforded no answer, either to moral conviction or to economic rivalry, and the great political parties of the United States faced a troubled future.

The state of the nation in 1848 gave dire significance to an admonition from one of the wisest of the Founding Fathers, his parting counsel to his countrymen. "The advice nearest to my heart and deepest in my convictions [James Madison had written in 1836] is that the Union of the States be cherished and perpetuated. Let the open enemy to it be regarded as a Pandora with her box opened; and the disguised one, as a serpent creeping with his wiles into Paradise."[26]

It would be easy to be contemptuous of the political leadership of the Jacksonian period. It would be easy to dwell upon the prejudices, the narrow vision, the truckling to selfish interests, the backing away from the ideal that again and again marked the actions of both of the great parties in this era. But before assuming such a critical attitude, the historian must consider that right and wrong are relative rather than absolute terms; that man is a fallible and sometimes an irrational creature; that political democracy, if it is to be a viable system, must be a process of continual compromise and adjustment between contending forces; and that the virtue of the democratic process lies, not in the achievement of absolute objectives, but in the opportunity it affords for the improvement of society through the expression of the will of the people. Viewed in this light, the political history of these twenty years presents a hopeful rather than a gloomy picture of American democracy.

During the period from Jackson to Taylor, many mistakes had been made. From time to time, the sordid aspects of the democratic process, like so many hydras, had raised their ugly heads. But despite such handicaps, democracy in America was a living, working concern. It would have been easy to find men in the South, and in the North as well, who were unwilling to practice the democracy which they accepted in principle. But it would have been difficult to find any significant sentiment for the abandonment of the democratic process, either as a political system or as a way of life.

[26] Gaillard Hunt (ed.), *The Writings of James Madison* (9 vols., New York, 1900–10), IX, facing p. 610.

Bibliographical Essay

Bibliographical Guides

Most useful of the general bibliographies of the period is the *Harvard Guide to American History,* compiled by Oscar Handlin, Arthur M. Schlesinger, Samuel Eliot Morison, Frederick Merk, Arthur M. Schlesinger, Jr., and Paul H. Buck (Cambridge, 1954). The standard bibliographical work in the field of diplomatic history is Samuel F. Bemis and Grace Gardiner Griffin, *Guide to the Diplomatic History of the United States, 1775–1921* (Washington, 1935). There are also extensive bibliographical aids in Thomas A. Bailey, *A Diplomatic History of the American People* (rev. ed., N.Y., 1950). Many of the general histories listed below contain important bibliographical aids, and the student should consult the lists of articles on historical subjects that appear in the *American Historical Review* and the *Mississippi Valley Historical Review.*

Manuscript Collections

Some of the most important collections for the Jacksonian period are:

Adams Family Papers. Massachusetts Historical Society.

Nicholas Biddle Papers. Library of Congress.

Blair Family Papers. Library of Congress.

Blair-Lee Papers. Princeton University.

James Buchanan Papers. Historical Society of Pennsylvania and Library of Congress.

Benjamin F. Butler Papers. Princeton University.

John C. Calhoun Papers. Clemson College, Duke University, and Library of Congress.

Salmon P. Chase Papers. Historical Society of Pennsylvania, University of Pennsylvania, and Library of Congress.

Henry Clay Papers. Library of Congress.
John J. Crittenden Papers. Library of Congress.
Millard Fillmore Papers. Buffalo Historical Society.
Azariah Flagg Papers. New York Public Library.
Joshua R. Giddings Papers. Ohio State Historical and Archeological Society.
Horace Greeley Papers. New York Public Library and Library of Congress.
James H. Hammond Papers. Library of Congress.
William Henry Harrison Papers. Library of Congress.
Andrew Jackson Papers. Library of Congress.
George McDuffie Papers. Duke University and South Caroliniana Library.
John McLean Papers. Library of Congress.
Willie P. Mangum Papers. Library of Congress.
William L. Marcy Papers. Library of Congress.
James K. Polk Papers. Library of Congress.
William C. Rives Papers. Library of Congress.
William Henry Seward Papers. University of Rochester.
Zachary Taylor Papers. Library of Congress.
John Tyler Papers. Library of Congress.
Martin Van Buren Papers. Library of Congress.
Daniel Webster Papers. Library of Congress.
Thurlow Weed Papers. University of Rochester.
Gideon Welles Papers. Library of Congress.
Levi Woodbury Papers. Library of Congress.
Silas Wright Papers. St. Lawrence University, New York State Library, and Collection of Harry F. Landon, Watertown, N.Y.
Wright-Butler Letters. New York Public Library.

Newspapers and Periodicals

Among the important newspapers and periodicals published during this period are:

Albany *Argus*
Albany *Evening Journal*
American Review
National Intelligencer
New Hampshire Patriot and State Gazette
New York *Evening Post*
New York *Herald*
New York *Tribune*
Niles' Weekly Register
North American Review
Richmond *Enquirer*
Springfield *Republican*

United States Magazine and Democratic Review
United States Telegraph
Washington *Globe*
Washington *Union*

Published Correspondence, Diaries, and Memoirs

Indispensable for any serious study of the period are John Spencer Bassett (ed.), *Correspondence of Andrew Jackson* (7 vols., Washington, 1926–35); John Bassett Moore (ed.), *The Works of James Buchanan* (12 vols., Philadelphia, 1908–11); Calvin Colton (ed.), *The Private Correspondence of Henry Clay* (Boston, 1856), and *The Works of Henry Clay* (10 vols., New York, 1904); Worthington C. Ford (ed.), *The Writings of John Quincy Adams* (7 vols., New York, 1913–17); J. Franklin Jameson (ed.), "Correspondence of John C. Calhoun," American Historical Association, *Annual Report,* 1899 (Washington, 1900), II; Reginald C. McGrane (ed.), *The Correspondence of Nicholas Biddle . . . 1807–1844* (Boston, 1919); Gaillard Hunt (ed.), *The Writings of James Madison* (9 vols., New York, 1900–10); Luther Hamilton (ed.), *Memoirs, Speeches, and Writings of Robert Rantoul, Jr.* (Boston, 1854); Daniel Webster, *Writings and Speeches* (18 vols., Boston, 1903); James D. Richardson, *A Compilation of the Messages and Papers of the Presidents* (11 vols., New York, 1910); Richard K. Crallé (ed.), *The Works of John C. Calhoun* (6 vols., Charleston and New York, 1851–56).

Among the memoirs, diaries, and autobiographies of the period, the following were useful: Charles Francis Adams (ed.), *Memoirs of John Quincy Adams* (12 vols., Philadelphia, 1874–77), is full of acidulous criticism and useful information. It is indispensable for a study of the period. Thomas Hart Benton's *Thirty Years View* (2 vols., New York, 1854), cannot be overlooked, although it is sometimes inaccurate and prejudiced. William A. Butler's *A Retrospect of Forty Years* (New York, 1911) is sprightly. James A. Hamilton, *Reminiscences* (New York, 1869), is helpful, especially on the political side, while Ben: Perley Poore's *Reminiscences* (2 vols., Philadelphia, 1886), and Margaret E. Smith, *The First Forty Years of Washington Society,* ed. Gaillard Hunt (New York, 1906), give important information about the society of the nation's capital. Nathan Sargent's *Public Men and Events* (2 vols., Philadelphia, 1875) is Whiggish in tone, but perceptive. Winfield Scott, *Memoirs of Lieutenant-General Scott, LL. D.* (2 vols., New York, 1864), reveals both the strength and the weaknesses of this rather extraordinary man. Henry B. Stanton's *Random Recollections* (New York, 1886) must not be overlooked, and of course the same is true of Martin Van Buren's *Autobiography,* ed. John C. Fitzpatrick, American Historical Association, *Annual Report,* 1918 (Washington, 1920), an analysis which portrays the ex-President's point of view on the political struggles of the period.

General Works

Edward Channing, *A History of the United States* (6 vols., New York, 1912–25), is judicious in tone and valuable on the political and social side. The constitutional aspects of the period are satisfactorily covered in Andrew C. McLaughlin, *A Constitutional History of the United States* (New York, 1935); Charles Warren, *Congress, the Constitution and the Supreme Court* (Boston, 1930); and Charles G. Haines, *The American Doctrine of Judicial Supremacy* (Berkeley, 1932), also *The Role of the Supreme Court in American Government and Politics* (2 vols., Berkeley, 1944–57. The second volume is by Charles G. Haines and Foster H. Sherwood). See also Carl B. Swisher, *American Constitutional Development* (Cambridge, 1954). John Bach McMaster's *A History of the People of the United States* (8 vols., New York, 1883–1914) treats political and social developments. Its attempt to give both sides of every question sometimes leaves the reader floundering between two stools. James Schouler, *The History of the United States* (7 vols., New York, 1891–1913), written by a lawyer, contains viewpoints that ought not to be ignored.

The best history of political parties is James A. Woodburn, *Political Parties and Party Problems in the United States* (3rd ed., New York, 1924). Useful also are Edgar E. Robinson, *The Evolution of American Political Parties* (New York, 1924), and Charles E. Merriam, *A History of American Political Theories* (New York, 1928). Wilfred E. Binkley's *American Political Parties, Their Natural History* (New York, 1943) is a suggestive treatment. W. Dean Burnham, *Presidential Ballots, 1836–1892* (Baltimore, 1955), gives a valuable analysis of presidential elections, buttressed by copious statistics.

Various ideological aspects of the Jacksonian era are to be found in the following: Joseph Dorfman, *The Economic Mind in American Civilization* (3 vols., New York, 1946), is a compendious treatment of economic thought. It should be used in conjunction with Louis Hartz, *Economic Policy and Democratic Thought: Pennsylvania, 1776–1860* (Cambridge, 1948), a most suggestive treatise; the same author's *The Liberal Tradition in America: an Interpretation of American Political Thought since the Revolution* (New York, 1955); and Oscar Handlin, *Commonwealth: a Study of the Role of Government in the American Economy, Massachusetts, 1774–1861* (New York, 1947), an illuminating analysis. Arthur M. Schlesinger, Jr., *The Age of Jackson* (Boston, 1945), is a brilliant interpretation of the political, social, and economic aspects of the period, but one that needs revision based on more recent scholarship. Frederick Jackson Turner, *The United States, 1830–1850* (New York, 1935), is a study of sectional influences at work upon political history. Arthur A. Ekirch, *The Idea of Progress in America,* is stimulating. Alice Felt Tyler, *Freedom's Ferment* (Minneapolis, 1944), is a spirited and interesting account of the Utopian and reform movements of the middle period. Leonard D. White, *The Jacksonians: A Study in Administrative History, 1829–1861* (New York, 1954), traces the development of theory and practice in the field of political administration.

The following economic studies are useful: Thomas S. Berry, *Western Prices Before 1861* (Cambridge, 1943); Fred J. Guetter and Albert E. McKinley, *Statistical Tables Relating to the Economic Growth of the United States* (Philadelphia, 1924); and Walter B. Smith and Arthur H. Cole, *Fluctuations in American Business, 1790–1860* (Cambridge, 1935). These are all helpful in the analysis of political trends. Similar values are to be found in Esther R. Taus, *Central Banking Functions of the United States Treasury, 1789–1941* (New York, 1943), and in George R. Taylor, *The Transportation Revolution, 1815–1860* (New York, 1951), a most valuable work. Frank W. Taussig, *The Tariff History of the United States* (rev. ed., 1931), and Davis R. Dewey, *Financial History of the United States* (rev. ed., 1934), are standard works. Edward Stanwood, *Tariff Controversies in the Nineteenth Century* (2 vols., Boston, 1903), is old but valuable.

On the diplomatic side, Hubert H. Bancroft, *History of Mexico* (New York, 1914), is useful for the general Mexican background. George L. Rives, *The United States and Mexico, 1821–1848* (2 vols., New York, 1913), is scholarly and exhaustive. Vito Alessio Robles, *Coahuila y Texas* (2 vols., Mexico, 1945, 1946), presents the Mexican interpretation of diplomatic relations. Hugh Ll. Keenleyside and Gerald S. Brown, *Canada and the United States* (New York, 1952), is an objective study, written with judgment and discrimination. Much valuable material is to be found in Samuel F. Bemis (ed.), *The American Secretaries of State and Their Diplomacy* (10 vols., New York, 1927–29), especially Vols. IV–V.

Biographies

Four prominent New Yorkers of this period have been the subjects of biographies. Denis T. Lynch, *An Epoch and a Man, Martin Van Buren and His Times* (New York, 1929), is popular and partial to its subject. Holmes Alexander, *The American Talleyrand* (New York, 1935), is highly critical of the Red Fox. Edward M. Shepard, *Martin Van Buren* (Boston and New York, 1889), is perhaps the best of the Van Buren biographies. It is a sympathetic treatment. Frederic Bancroft, *The Life of William H. Seward* (2 vols., New York, 1900), is judicious, but exclusively political. There is no really good life of Seward. The other members of the famous Whig partnership are studied in Glyndon G. Van Deusen, *Thurlow Weed: Wizard of the Lobby* (Boston, 1947), and *Horace Greeley, Nineteenth Century Crusader* (Philadelphia, 1953).

Andrew Jackson has been the subject of many biographies. John Spencer Bassett, *The Life of Andrew Jackson* (2 vols., New York, 1911), scholarly and balanced in its judgments, remains, on the whole, the best life of the Old Hero. Marquis James, *Andrew Jackson, Portrait of a President* (Indianapolis, 1937), is better written and based on extensive research. It is highly favorable to the General. Useful for an understanding of Jackson, though highly critical, is Thomas P. Abernethy, *From Frontier to Plantation in Tennessee: a Study in Frontier Democracy* (Chapel Hill, 1932). John W. Ward, *Andrew Jackson, Symbol of an Age* (Oxford University Press, 1955), is valuable as an analysis of the Jackson myth.

Jackson's great contemporaries, Calhoun, Webster, John Quincy Adams, and Clay, have all been the subjects of twentieth-century biographies. William M. Meigs, *The Life of John Caldwell Calhoun* (2 vols., New York, 1917), is a scholarly treatment. Charles M. Wiltse, *John C. Calhoun* (3 vols., Indianapolis, 1944–51) is well written and based on solid research, but biased in Calhoun's favor. Claude M. Fuess, *Daniel Webster* (2 vols., Boston, 1930), is adequate, but George T. Curtis, *Life of Daniel Webster* (2 vols., New York, 1870), is still indispensable for a study of the Godlike's career. For Adams, see Samuel F. Bemis, *John Quincy Adams and the Foundations of American Foreign Policy* (New York, 1949), and *John Quincy Adams and the Union* (New York, 1956), the latest and the best biography of a great statesman. Bernard Mayo, *Henry Clay* (Boston, 1937), is authoritative and brilliantly written, but carries only to the outbreak of the War of 1812. Glyndon G. Van Deusen, *The Life of Henry Clay* (Boston, 1937), covers Clay's entire career. Clement Eaton, *Henry Clay and the Art of American Politics* (Boston, 1957), is a brief treatment by a sound scholar.

Other outstanding figures of the eighteen-thirties and forties have been analyzed by recent biographers. Charles Grier Sellers, Jr., *James K. Polk, Jacksonian. 1795–1843* (New York, 1957), is the first volume of what bids fair to be the definitive life of this dour President. Eugene I. McCormac, *James K. Polk* (Berkeley, 1922), is a scholarly performance. Brainard Dyer, *Zachary Taylor* (Baton Rouge, 1946), is a good one-volume life. Holman Hamilton, *Zachary Taylor, Soldier of the Republic,* and *Zachary Taylor, Soldier in the White House* (Indianapolis, 1941–51), is the definitive life of Old Zack. Arthur D. H. Smith, *Old Fuss and Feathers* (New York, 1937), is a good treatment of Winfield Scott. Charles W. Elliott, *Winfield Scott, the Soldier and the Man* (New York, 1937), is a sympathetic biography. William N. Chambers, *Old Bullion Benton, Senator from the New West* (Boston, 1956), both scholarly and well written, is a fine study of Benton. Allan Nevins, *Frémont, Pathmarker of the West* (3rd ed., New York, 1955), is the best treatment of the dashing explorer. Oliver P. Chitwood, *John Tyler* (New York, 1939), is a much more judicious treatment of His Accidency than is the older Lyon G. Tyler, *The Letters and Times of the Tylers* (3 vols., Richmond, 1884–96). Dorothy B. Goebel, *William Henry Harrison* (Indianapolis,

1926), is good biography. Llerena Friend, *Sam Houston, the Great Designer* (Austin, 1954), is later than and to some extent supersedes Marquis James' brilliant *The Raven* (Indianapolis, 1929). William E. Smith, *The Francis Preston Blair Family in Politics* (2 vols., New York, 1933), is indispensable for a study of the Jacksonian era.

A host of lesser figures in this period have been the subjects of biographies. M. A. De Wolfe Howe, *The Life and Letters of George Bancroft* (2 vols., New York, 1908), contains samples of correspondence, but has been superseded by Russell B. Nye, *George Bancroft* (New York, 1944), a judicious appreciation of the New England historian-liberal. Carl B. Swisher, *Roger B. Taney* (New York, 1936), is excellent, and the same may be said of John A Garraty, *Silas Wright* (New York, 1949). David B. Going, *David Wilmot, Free-Soiler* (New York, 1924), is useful for the Free Soil movement, and particularly for copious reprints of correspondence. Louis M. Sears, *John Slidell* (Durham, N.C., 1925), is pedestrian but covers the ground. Stewart Mitchell, *Horatio Seymour* (Cambridge, 1938), is first-rate biography, critical in tone and unusually well written. Queena Pollack, *Peggy Eaton, Democracy's Mistress* (New York, 1931), is a popular treatment of a colorful subject. Herbert P. Gambrell, *Anson Jones, the Last President of Texas,* is useful for a study of the last days of the Texan Republic. Of the two more recent biographies of Santa Anna in English, that of Wilfrid H. Callcott, *Santa Anna* (Norman, Okla., 1936), is the more scholarly, and that of Frank C. Hanighen, *Santa Anna* (New York, 1934), while based to a considerable extent on sources, is more popular in style.

A People in Motion

Indispensable to a study of life in the age of Jackson are the shrewd observations of the conservative French philosopher Alexis de Tocqueville, *Democracy in America* (2 vols., New York, 1945). Much material on the general characteristics of life in the Jacksonian era is to be found in my biographies of Henry Clay, Thurlow Weed, and Horace Greeley. Alice Felt Tyler, *Freedom's Ferment,* is a most useful study of the reform movements of this period. George R. Taylor, *The Transportation Revolution, 1815–1860,* is essential for an understanding of the impact of transportation developments upon the life of the times. The frontier hypothesis is best studied in Frederick Jackson Turner, *The Frontier in American History* (New York, 1948), though the scholar must also consult such essays as those of Richard Hofstadter, "Turner and the Frontier Myth," *The American Scholar,* XVIII (fall, 1949), 433–443, and Murray Kane, "Some Considerations on the Frontier Concept of Frederick Jackson Turner," *Mississippi Valley Historical Review,* XXVII (1940–41), 379–400. John R. Commons *et al, History of Labour in the United States* (4 vols., New York, 1918–35) is indispensable for a study of labor in this period; and Norman Ware, *The Industrial Worker, 1840–1860* (Boston and New York, 1924), and Philip Foner, *History of the Labor Movement in the United States* (New York, 1947), are also very useful. Kirk H. Porter, *A History of Suffrage in the United States* (Chicago, 1918), is standard on its subject.

On business and banking, the inquiring reader should consult Victor S. Clark, *History of Manufactures in the United States, 1607–1928;* Walter B. Smith and Arthur H. Cole, *Fluctuations in American Business, 1790–1860* (Cambridge, 1935); and Bray Hammond, *Banks and Politics in America* (Princeton, 1957). Immigration is well treated in Marcus L. Hansen, *The Atlantic Migration, 1607–1860* (Cambridge, 1940). New viewpoints on migration are to be found in Oscar Handlin, *The Uprooted* (Boston, 1951). The nativist movement is studied in such works as Ray Billington, *The Protestant Crusade, 1800–1860* (New York, 1938), and W. Darrel Overdyke, *The Know-Nothing Party in the South* (Baton Rouge, 1950). The economic thought of the period is best examined in Joseph Dorfman, *The Economic Mind in American Civilization, 1606–1918* (3 vols., New York, 1946–49); Kenneth W. Rowe, *Mathew Carey, A Study in American Economic Development* (Baltimore, 1933); Henry Charles Carey, *The Harmony of Interests* (New York, 1852); Francis Wayland, *Elements of Political Economy* (Boston, 1837); Eugene T. Mudge, *The Social Philosophy of John Taylor of Caroline* (New York, 1939); and William Gouge, *A Short History of Paper Money and Banking in the United States* (Philadelphia, 1833).

Launching the Jacksonian Ship of State

Florence Weston, *The Presidential Election of 1828* (Washington, 1938), is the best secondary account of that spirited campaign. Binkley, *Political Parties,* and Bassett, *Andrew Jackson,* are useful on the composition of the Democratic and National Republican parties, as is Margaret Smith (in the work already cited) on Jackson's inauguration. Claude G. Bowers, *The Party Battles of the Jackson Period* (Boston and New York, 1929), is colorful and readable, but prejudiced and unreliable. Bassett's *Jackson* gives a good appreciation of Jackson's presidential potential. There is an excellent analysis of Jackson in Richard Hofstadter, *The American Political Tradition* (New York, 1948). On the administrative side, see Richard P. Longaker, "Was Jackson's Kitchen Cabinet a Cabinet?" *Mississippi Valley Historical Review,* XLIV (June, 1957), 94–108; Albert Somit, "New Papers: Some Sidelights Upon Jacksonian Administration," *ibid.,* XXXV (June, 1948), 91–98; and William MacDonald, *Jacksonian Democracy* (New York, 1906).

On the spoils system, see the works by L. D. White and Schlesinger already cited, and also Carl R. Fish, *The Civil Service and the Patronage* (New York, 1905). The Eaton scandal is portrayed in the works cited by Pollack and Poore, and by the leading female character in the drama, Peggy Eaton, *Autobiography* (New York, 1932). The story of the breach between Jackson and Calhoun is well developed in Wiltse's life of the latter figure. The influence of the public lands on politics during this period is authoritatively analyzed by Raynor G. Wellington, *The Political and Sectional Influence of the Public Lands, 1828–1842* (Cambridge, 1914).

The Party Battles of the First Term

To catch the *spirit* of the contention that raged between the parties, read Bowers, *Party Battles of the Jackson Period.* Wellington, already cited, is best on public land policy. On Indian removal, see Grant Foreman, *Indian Removal* (Norman, Okla., 1932); Annie H. Abel, "The History of Events Resulting in Indian Consolidation West of the Mississippi," American Historical Association, *Reports,* I (Washington, 1908); and Wilson Lumpkin, *The Removal of the Cherokee Indians from Georgia* (2 vols. in one, New York, 1907), a source. Important Supreme Court decisions on Indian removal are *Cherokee Nation* v. *State of Georgia,* 5 Peters 17, and *Worcester* v. *Georgia,* 6 Peters 521–579.

The standard work on Antimasonry is Charles McCarthy, "The Antimasonic Party," American Historical Association, *Reports,* I (1902). See also Glyndon G. Van Deusen, *Thurlow Weed: Wizard of the Lobby* (Boston, 1947). For the tariff of 1832, see Stanwood, *Tariff Controversies;* Bemis, *John Quincy Adams and the Union;* and Malcolm R. Eiselen, *The Rise of Pennsylvania Protectionism* (Philadelphia, 1932).

The literature on the Second Bank of the United States is extensive. Ralph C. H. Catterall, *The Second Bank of the United States* (Chicago, 1903), though old, is scholarly and very useful. Walter B. Smith, *Economic Aspects of the Second Bank of the United States* (Cambridge, 1953), is an excellent analysis of the strengths and weaknesses of that institution and of Biddle's policy in regard to it. Bray Hammond, *Banks and Politics in America* (Princeton, 1957), is indispensable, a brilliant analysis; and no student of the period should overlook his "Jackson, Biddle, and the Bank of the United States," *The Journal of Economic History,* VII (May, 1947), 1–23, and "Banking in the Early West," *The Journal of Economic History,* VIII (May, 1948), 1–25. Sister M. Grace Madeleine, *Monetary and Banking Theories of Jacksonian Democracy* (Philadelphia, 1943), is a careful study. Schlesinger, *The Age of Jackson,* presents the arguments against the Bank. Harry E. Miller, *Banking Theories in the United States before 1860* (Cambridge, 1927), and O. M. W. Sprague, "Branch Banking in the United States," *Quarterly Journal of Economics,* XVII (1902–3), 242–260, are useful for background. A book very influential with the Jacksonians was William M. Gouge, *A Short History of*

Paper Money and Banking in the United States (Philadelphia, 1833). There is a sober criticism of the Bank veto in the *North American Review,* XXXV (Oct., 1832), 485–517.

Samuel R. Gammon, Jr., "The Presidential Campaign of 1832," *Johns Hopkins University Studies in Historical and Political Science,* XL (Baltimore, 1932), 11–162, is the standard work on this particular election.

Politics, a Tariff, and a Bank

The best monographs on nullification are David F. Houston, *A Critical Study of Nullification in South Carolina* (Cambridge, 1896), and Chauncey S. Boucher, *The Nullification Controversy in South Carolina* (Chicago, 1916). William E. Dodd, *Statesmen of the Old South* (New York, 1919) is useful, as is John G. Van Deusen, *The Economic Bases of Disunion in South Carolina* (New York, 1928).

On the compromise tariff of 1833, the student should consult Frederick L. Nussbaum, "The Compromise Tariff of 1833—A Study in Practical Politics," *South Atlantic Quarterly,* XI (Oct. 1912), 337–349, and my own life of Henry Clay. There is a useful collection of source materials on this and other tariff matters in Frank W. Taussig (ed.), *State Papers and Speeches on the Tariff* (Cambridge, 1892).

On the removal of the deposits, see the works already cited by Catterall and Walter B. Smith, and Swisher's biography of Taney.

The Close of a Reign

On the Democratic party of the middle eighteen-thirties, the works by Schlesinger and Binkley already cited should be used. See also Arthur B. Darling, "The Workingmen's Party in Massachusetts," and "Jacksonian Democracy in Massachusetts," *American Historical Review,* XXIX (Oct., 1923, and Jan., 1924), 81–86, 271–287. In analyzing the party's attitude toward the economic problems of the day, the following books and articles were useful: *House Document No. 308,* first session, 22nd Congress (2 vols., Washington, 1833), pp. 222, 223 (the McLane Report on the status of American manufactures); J. D. B. DeBow, *Statistical View of the United States* (Washington, 1854); Charles Dunscombe, *Dunscombe's Free Banking* (Cleveland, 1841); Clive Day, *The Rise of Manufacturing in Connecticut, 1820–1850* (New Haven, n.d.); Isaac Lippincott, *A History of Manufactures in the Ohio Valley* (New York, 1914); Jarvis M. Morse, *A Neglected Period of Connecticut's History, 1818–1850* (New Haven, 1933); H. L. Purdy, M. L. Lindall, and W. A. Carter, *Corporate Concentration and Public Policy* (New York, 1950); Alfred Russell, *The Police Power of the State* (Chicago, 1900). William A. Sullivan, *The Industrial Worker in Pennsylvania, 1800–1840* (Harrisburg,

1955), and Chambers, *Benton,* contain pertinent information, as do the following articles: George S. Callender, "The Early Transportation and Banking Enterprises of the States in Relation to the Growth of Corporations," *Quarterly Journal of Economics,* XVII (1902–3), 110–162; Clive Day, "The Early Development of American Cotton Manufactures," *Quarterly Journal of Economics,* XXXIX (1924–25), 450–468; Bray Hammond, "Long and Short Term Credit in Early American Banking," *Quarterly Journal of Economics,* XLIX (1934–35), 79–102; Oscar and M. F. Handlin, "Origins of the American Business Corporation," *Journal of Economic History,* V (May, 1945), 1–23.

On the rise of the Whig party, see E. Malcolm Carroll, *Origins of the Whig Party* (Durham, 1925); Arthur C. Cole, *The Whig Party in the South* (Washington, 1913); Henry R. Mueller, *The Whig Party in Pennsylvania* (New York, 1922); Paul Murray, *The Whig Party in Georgia, 1825–1853* (Chapel Hill, 1948); and Charles M. Thompson, *The Illinois Whigs Before 1848* (Urbana, 1915). Light is thrown on contrasting Whig and Democratic attitudes toward government's role in an expanding economy in Samuel B. Ruggles, *Report upon the Finances and Internal Improvements of the State of New York* (New York, 1838), and Azariah Flagg's rejoinder in New York State Assembly, *Documents,* 60th and 62nd sessions (Albany, 1837, 1839).

Details in regard to Jackson's foreign policy are given in Frank L. Benns, *The American Struggle for the British West India Carrying Trade, 1815–1830* (Bloomington, 1923); Richard A. McLemore, *Franco-American Diplomatic Relations, 1816–1836* (University, La., 1941); James A. Callahan, *American Foreign Policy in Mexican Relations* (New York, 1932); and in the works of Samuel F. Bemis already cited.

Among the books which deal with the slavery controversies of the middle eighteen-thirties, three deserve special mention. Russell B. Nye, *Fettered Freedom* (East Lansing, 1949), is an important study of popular reaction, then and later, to slavery's assault on civil liberties. Dwight L. Dumond, *Antislavery Origins of the Civil War in the United States* (Ann Arbor, 1939), is an analysis of the various ways in which the abolitionist indictment of slavery and the southern defense of it were instrumental in bringing on the Civil War. Gilbert Hobbs Barnes, *The Antislavery Impulse, 1830–1844* (New York, 1933), emphasizes the moral character of the antislavery movement, and Wilbur H. Siebert, *The Underground Railroad* (New York, 1898), is also useful in its study.

Edward G. Bourne, *The History of the Surplus Revenue of 1837* (New York, 1885), is still the standard work on that subject.

On the election of 1836, see the works by Burnham, Carroll, Cole, Goebel, Lynch, Schlesinger, Bowers, and Shepard already cited.

The Little Magician Takes the Reins

On Van Buren and the general aspects of his administration, see the biographies already cited by Alexander, Lynch, and Shepard.

The panic and depression of 1837 and the years following are dealt with in Reginald C. McGrane, *The Panic of 1837* (Chicago, 1924), and Samuel Rezneck, "The Social History of an American Depression, 1837–1843," *American Historical Review,* XL (Oct., 1934), 662–687. John Macgregor, *Commercial Statistics* (4 vols., London, 1847), is also useful in a study of the depression.

Party attitudes in the middle and latter eighteen-thirties in regard to social and economic problems, and the role of government in society, are dealt with in Louis Hartz, *Economic Policy and Democratic Thought: Pennsylvania, 1776–1860* (Cambridge, 1948), and, by the same author, *The Liberal Tradition in America* (New York, 1955); Oscar Handlin, *Commonwealth: A Study of the Role of Government in the American Economy, Massachusetts, 1774–1861* (New York, 1947); Glyndon G. Van Deusen, "Some Aspects of Whig Thought and Theory in the Jacksonian Period," *American Historical Review,* LXIII (Jan., 1958), 305–322.

David Kinley, *The Independent Treasury of the United States and Its Relations to the Banks of the Country* (Washington, 1910), and, by the same author, "The Influence on Business of the Independent Treasury," *Annals of the American Academy of Political and Social Science,* III (Sept., 1892), 52–82, are the best analyses of the "Subtreasury" act and its effects. Esther R. Taus, *Central Banking Functions of the United States Treasury, 1789–1941* (New York, 1943), is also useful.

The continued battle over land policy may be followed in the pages of Wellington, Chambers, and Wiltse, works already cited.

Slavery, Patriotism, Ballyhoo

The relation of the Van Buren administration to the rising slavery controversy is treated in Julian P. Bretz, "The Economic Background of the Liberty Party," *American Historical Review,* XXXIV (Jan., 1929), 250–264; Theodore C. Smith, *The Liberty and Free Soil Parties in the Northwest* (New York, 1897); W. E. Burghardt DuBois, *The Suppression of the African Slave Trade* (New York, 1904); Hugh G. Soulsby, "The Right of Search and the Slave Trade in Anglo-American Relations, 1814–1862," *Johns Hopkins University Studies in Historical and Political Science,* series LI, No. 2.

Canadian-American relations during these four years have been dealt with in Albert B. Corey, *The Crisis of 1830–1842 in Canadian-American Relations* (New Haven, 1941), an excellent survey, and in Henry S. Burrage, *Maine in the Northeast Boundary Controversy* (Portland, 1919). A number of excellent articles treat of various phases of the subject. Among these are

Thomas Le Duc, "The Maine Frontier and the Northeastern Boundary Controversy," *American Historical Review,* LIII (Oct., 1947), 30–41; Orrin E. Tiffany, "Relations of the United States to the Canadian Rebellion of 1837–1838," Buffalo Historical Society, *Publications,* VIII (Buffalo, 1905), 7–147; Wilson P. Shortridge, "The Canadian-American Frontier During the Rebellion of 1837–1838," *Canadian Historical Review,* VII (Toronto, 1926), 13–26; Alastair Watt, "The Case of Alexander McLeod," *Canadian Historical Review,* XII (Toronto, 1931), 145–167.

The election of 1840 has been a favorite subject with historians and biographers for many years. For recent accounts, see Goebel, *Harrison;* Lynch, *Van Buren;* Van Deusen, *Clay, Weed,* and *Greeley.*

The Advent of "His Accidency"

The Tyler side of the Tyler-Clay imbroglio is given in Lyon G. Tyler's *The Letters and Times of the Tylers,* already cited. There is a more dispassionate analysis in Oliver Chitwood, *John Tyler,* and in George R. Poage's *Henry Clay and the Whig Party* (Chapel Hill, 1936). The reader might also consult my *Life of Henry Clay.*

The bankruptcy law is treated in Charles Warren, *Bankruptcy in United States History* (Cambridge, 1935).

The political impact of pre-emption is dealt with in Wellington, *Public Lands,* and in Roy Robbins, "Preemption—A Frontier Triumph," *Mississippi Valley Historical Review,* XVIII (Dec., 1932), 331–349.

The tariff of 1842 is analyzed in the works of Stanwood and Taussig already cited. Poage examines its political significance. Useful in connection with tariff legislation in this period is Walter B. Smith and Arthur H. Cole, *Fluctuations in American Business, 1790–1860* (Cambridge, 1935).

Expansion and Election

The expansionist movement that characterized the eighteen-forties is best studied in Albert K. Weinberg, *Manifest Destiny: A Study of Nationalist Expansionism in American History* (Baltimore, 1935). Of particular importance for this period is Norman A. Graebner, *Empire on the Pacific* (New York, 1955). Walker H. Donaldson, "A Politician of Expansion: Robert J. Walker," *Mississippi Valley Historical Review,* XIX (Dec., 1932), is also helpful.

Jesse S. Rives, *American Diplomacy Under Tyler and Polk* (Baltimore, 1907), is old but still useful in dealing with Anglo-American relations under Tyler. The student should also consult Richard N. Current, "Webster's Propaganda and the Ashburton Treaty," *Mississippi Valley Historical Review,* XXXIV (Oct., 1947), 187–200; Albert B. Corey's monograph on Canadian-American relations; and the biographies of Webster and Tyler already cited.

The standard work on the acquisition of Texas is Justin H. Smith, *The*

Annexation of Texas (New York, 1941), but the interested reader should also consult the following: Ephraim D. Adams, *British Interests and Activities in Texas, 1838–1846* (Baltimore, 1910); Elgin Williams, *The Animating Pursuits of Speculation* (New York, 1949); Eugene C. Barker, "The Annexation of Texas," *Southwestern Historical Quarterly,* L (July, 1946), 49–74; Richard R. Stenberg, "Intrigue for Annexation," *Southwest Review,* XXV (Oct., 1939), 58–69.

The campaign of 1844 is examined in detail in McCormac's life of Polk and my own life of Clay. See also James C. N. Paul, *Rift in the Democracy* (Philadelphia, 1951), an unusually well-written monograph, and Clark E. Persinger, "The 'Bargain of 1844' as the Origin of the Wilmot Proviso," American Historical Association, *Annual Report,* 1911 (Washington, 1913), I, 189–195.

The rise of nativism, together with its political impact, may be found in Ray A. Billington, *The Protestant Crusade, 1800–1860* (New York, 1938), and the older but standard Louis D. Scisco, *Political Nativism in New York State* (New York, 1901). Thurlow Weed's role in the development of political nativism is treated in my biography of this skillful politician.

The New Jacksonians

Any account of the Polk administration would be inadequate without careful study of Milo M. Quaife (ed.), *The Diary of James K. Polk* (4 vols., Chicago, 1910).

The growing breach between Polk and the followers of Van Buren is examined in James Paul, *Rift in the Democracy;* in the biographies of Calhoun, Polk, Benton, and Wright already mentioned, and in Herbert A. Donovan, *The Barnburners* (New York, 1925). See also Joseph G. Rayback, "Martin Van Buren's Break with James K. Polk," *New York History,* XXXIV (Jan., 1955), 51–62.

The tariff of 1846 and its effects are analyzed in the works by Stanwood, Taussig, Dewey, and Eiselen already cited. See also Frank W. Taussig, "The Iron Industry in the United States," *Quarterly Journal of Economics,* XIV (Feb., 1900).

For the final establishment of the Independent Treasury and its historical significance, see the works cited on that subject for Chapter 5, and also Esther R. Taus, *Central Banking Functions;* Henry P. Willis, *The Theory and Practice of Central Banking* (New York, 1936); John J. Knox, *United States Notes* (New York, 1884); and William G. Sumner, *A History of American Currency* (New York, 1874).

Dangerous Diplomacy

The negotiation of the Oregon treaty of 1846 is best studied in Polk's

Diary, in the lives of Polk and Buchanan already cited, and in the following articles: Frederick Merk, "The British Corn Crisis of 1845–46 and the Oregon Treaty," *Agricultural History,* VIII (July, 1934), and also "The Oregon Pioneers and the Boundary," "British Party Politics and the Oregon Treaty," "British Government Propaganda and the Oregon Treaty," these to be found, respectively, in *American Historical Review,* XXIX (July, 1924), XXXVII (July, 1932), XL (Oct., 1934); Julius W. Pratt, "James K. Polk and John Bull," *Canadian Historical Review,* XXIV (Dec., 1943); Henry S. Commager, "England and Oregon Treaty of 1846," *Oregon Historical Quarterly,* XXVII (Mar., 1927); Robert L. Schuyler, "Polk and the Oregon Compromise of 1846," *Political Science Quarterly,* XXVI (Sept., 1911).

Analyses of the events leading up to the Mexican War are to be found in the *Diary* and biographies mentioned above; in Justin H. Smith, *The War with Mexico* (2 vols., New York, 1919), opinionated, but based on prodigious research; in William C. Binkley, *The Expansionist Movement in Texas* (Berkeley, 1925); and in the following articles: Ephraim D. Adams, "English Interest in California," *American Historical Review,* XIV (July, 1909); Richard R. Stenberg, "President Polk and the Annexation of Texas," *Southwestern Social Science Quarterly,* XIV (Mar., 1934), and "The Failure of Polk's Mexican War Intrigue of 1845," *Pacific Historical Review,* IV (1935); LeRoy P. Graf, "Colonizing Projects in Texas South of the Nueces, 1820–1845," *Southwestern Historical Quarterly,* L (Apr., 1947).

Polk's re-enunciation of the Monroe Doctrine is best analyzed in Dexter Perkins, *The Monroe Doctrine, 1826–1867* (Baltimore, 1933).

The Dose of Arsenic

The most exhaustive treatment of the Mexican War, viewed from the military and diplomatic angles, is that of Justin H. Smith, *The War with Mexico* (2 vols., New York, 1919). Alfred H. Bill, *Rehearsal for Conflict* (New York, 1947), is good for color, and is a stirring account. It is not the usual learned treatise, but the author obviously uses source material and the book is unusually well written. The campaigns of the war may also be followed in Holman Hamilton's spirited and authentic *Zachary Taylor, Soldier of the Republic* (Indianapolis, 1941), in Brainard Dyer, *Zachary Taylor* (Baton Rouge, 1946); in Arthur D. H. Smith, *Old Fuss and Feathers* (New York, 1937); and in Charles W. Elliott, *Winfield Scott* (New York, 1937). Walter P. Webb, *The Texas Rangers* (Boston and New York, 1935), is a sympathetic account of a brave but often lawless and undisciplined band that took part in the war.

The following letters, diaries, and memoirs give much valuable information about the various aspects of the war: Justin H. Smith (ed.), "Letters of General Antonio Lopez de Santa Anna Relating to the War Between the

United States and Mexico, 1846–1848," American Historical Association, *Report,* 1917 (Washington, 1920), pp. 355–428; William S. Meyers (ed.), *The Mexican War Diary of George B. McClellan* (Princeton, 1917); Zachary Taylor, *Letters of Zachary Taylor from the Battlefields of the Mexican War* (Rochester, N.Y., 1908); Robert Anderson, *An Artillery Officer in the Mexican War, 1846–7* (New York, 1911); Ulysses S. Grant, *Personal Memoirs of U. S. Grant* (2 vols., New York, 1885–86); Ephraim K. Smith, *To Mexico with Scott* (Cambridge, 1917); Winfield Scott, *Memoirs of Lieutenant-General Scott, LL. D.* (2 vols., New York, 1864); J. T. Hughes, "Doniphan's Expedition," 63rd Congress, second session, *Senate Document No. 608;* John Sedgwick, *Correspondence of John Sedgwick, Major-General* (2 vols., New York, 1902–3); William T. Sherman, *Memoirs* (2 vols., New York, 1891); F. A. Golder *et al.* (eds.), *The March of the Mormon Battalion from Council Bluffs to California* (New York, 1928); George G. Meade (ed.), *The Life and Letters of George Gordon Meade* (2 vols., New York, 1913); and Mrs. Chapman Coleman (ed.), *The Life of John J. Crittenden* (2 vols., Philadelphia, 1871). Samuel E. Chamberlain, *My Confession* (New York, 1956), is colorful, if not wholly reliable.

Smith's *War with Mexico* gives the best secondary account of the political side of the war. The origins of the Wilmot Proviso are examined in Charles B. Going, *David Wilmot, Free Soiler* (New York, 1924); Richard R. Stenberg, "The Motivation of the Wilmot Proviso," *Mississippi Valley Historical Review* (Mar., 1932); and Clark E. Persinger, "The 'Bargain of 1844' as the Origin of the Wilmot Proviso," all cited in Chapter 8.

In regard to the movement to acquire all Mexico, consult John D. P. Fuller, "The Slavery Question and the Movement to Acquire Mexico, 1846–1848," *Mississippi Valley Historical Review,* XXI (June, 1934), and "The Movement for the Acquisition of All Mexico, 1846–1848," *Johns Hopkins University Studies in Historical and Political Science,* Series 54, No. 1. See also Chauncey S. Boucher, "In Re That Aggressive Slavocracy," *Mississippi Valley Historical Review,* VIII (June, 1921), 13–79.

The Deterioration of Parties

Among the valuable studies which deal with the campaign of 1848 are the following: the biographies of Cass, Calhoun, Clay, and Taylor previously cited, and Poage's *Henry Clay and the Whig Party,* especially good for the story of the Whig nomination. Allan Nevins, *Ordeal of the Union* (2 vols., New York, 1947), also gives a balanced and thoughtful analysis. Schlesinger's *Age of Jackson* is useful. Beman Brockway, *Fifty Years in Journalism* (Watertown, 1891), though old, gives some interesting sidelights. Donovan's *Barnburners* remains a standard treatment, but its analysis of that movement should be balanced by the critical appreciation in Stewart Mitchell, *Horatio*

Seymour (Cambridge, 1938). A scholarly study of the Free Soil movement, based on the source materials now available, will be a genuine contribution to the history of this period. Useful articles are Brainerd Dyer, "Zachary Taylor and the Election of 1848," *Pacific Historical Review,* IX (1940), 173–182; Joseph G. Rayback, "The American Workingman and the Antislavery Crusade," *Journal of Economic History,* III (Nov., 1943), 152–163, valuable for insight regarding the attitude of the laboring class in the election of 1848. William O. Lynch, "Antislavery Tendencies of the Democratic Party in the Northwest, 1848–50," *Mississippi Valley Historical Review,* XI (Dec., 1924), 319–331, is a perceptive analysis.

Index